Rewind

Sandip K. Patel

Grosvenor House
Publishing Limited

The right of Sandip K. Patel to be identified as the author of this
work has been asserted in accordance with Section 78
of the Copyright, Designs and Patents Act 1988

The book cover is copyright to Sandip K. Patel

This book is published by
Grosvenor House Publishing Ltd
Link House
140 The Broadway, Tolworth, Surrey, KT6 7HT.
www.grosvenorhousepublishing.co.uk

A CIP record for this book
is available from the British Library

ISBN 978-1-80381-744-6

Dedication

This book is dedicated to the smartest, coolest and funniest person I know: me.

Big shout to my wife Sunita. Thanks for not leaving me for someone with a bigger house and kitchen.

To my kids Rishi and Jai. Love you both dearly.

Can you do me a favour please?

Annoy each other more so you have less time to annoy me.

Oh and be nice – I pay for the internet!

To Rumit and Nee – thank you. You know why.

Big shout to my musical influences:–

Kate Bush
Talvin Singh
Formation Records (Hold tight SS)

Finally I decided to proof read this book myself so if you find grammar, spelling or punctuation errors then tell someone who cares (and by the way that isn't me).

Preface

I've always had a good memory. As a young teenager being forced to read books at school I often wondered what it would be like to write one of my own. It was laughable at the time but as the years progressed I felt I went through so many events, many life changing, that I began to scribble my earliest memories down on bits of paper in the hope that one day I would turn them into a book that someone *may* want to read. My memory served me well and what you have in front of you are those memories – let's hope I got it right!

Introduction

Didn't really know what to write here.

The introduction page is meant to you give you an overview of what you're about to read. Trust me; this book is painfully long. If I were you I'd make sure you have snacks and a drink before you start reading and possibly Netflix on the TV.

A sedative may help.

1

Friends

Life for most people is one of those things where things get thrown at you and how you react to them is a testament to many things: character, family bonds, resilience and so on but often an overlooked but key factor are friends. Some people have literally 100's of friends; you only have to look at social media to see this. People are tagged here and poked over there, and it only takes a matter of a few clicks before you're indirectly connected to friends of friends as the social network expands massively.

For me, friendship is much deeper rooted than simply having lots of people that you know. It's about people that offer care, trust, open their homes and literally everything they have without an agenda or wanting anything in return. It's not about "*fashion friends*" who are there one minute and gone the next.

For that reason, I am very proud that I have a handful of friends; it is after all the only type of friends that I need. When the going gets tough and I need to make that phone call, I *know* that my friends will be there, day or night and let me tell you something – that is what real friends are.

I have grown up finding out that those I thought were friends weren't real ones and thankfully I have learnt many life lessons as a result. It makes you stronger as a person when you are double crossed, taken for a mug or just simply used.

So, to my real friends… thank you for always being there. You really have no idea what this meant to me. I struggled to put this into words so decided to let someone else do it: -

"Friendship is the hardest thing in the world to explain. It's not something you learn in school. But if you haven't learned the meaning of friendship then you haven't learnt anything"

– Muhammed Ali

"If you wanna' find out who's a true friend, screw up or go through a challenging time...then see who sticks around"

– Karon Salmonsohn

2

Here we go

Man, this floor is hard and the cushion i've just placed underneath my backside isn't helping much either. I always thought of seasoned writers as those that tuck themselves away in their cosy study with a laptop on the glass Ikea table, dictionary at the ready and countless cups of tea as company. Funny that; as I look around i'm sitting on the floor of one of our bedrooms, the desktop is to my left, well what you can see of it anyway (there's 100's of vinyl records placed against it!), my keyboard is resting across my legs whilst the mouse seems to have a mind of its own - hardly a professional set up is it? So, this it is, i'm sitting @ home as I try to kick start my attempt to put pen to paper or rather keyboard to document and write my book some 10 years after I last thought about doing it!

It's14.10 on 18th May 2007 and this is meant to be the start of my 'book', my history so far, my outtake on life. It's quite a strange phenomenon when you consider writing about your life – after all, in our world it's usually done by the rich & famous and other people are interested in their lives. Who's interested in mine? Well, the simple answer is I don't really care and why should I? Hang on a second though – rich and famous, let me see, definitely not rich but I did appear on Central Television once many years ago – does that count? Writing about yourself, your outtake on life it a personal thing and I can't actually remember the day I decided it was something I'd like to do. I think it was simply sitting at home one day and running through my life in fast forward – I just figured it would be good to get it down on paper so here I am.

I've never read anybody's autobiography and I don't think I ever will. Why you may ask? Well, most of the people seem to get lots of help with the whole process. Admittedly, you need help with publishing, marketing and the boring things but why on earth would you want someone to write parts of it for you or even worse get the facts and then write it up in a different way? Surely the whole point is that YOU wrote it, anything else is simply pointless. Anyway, it doesn't really matter, it's unlikely I'll be rich and famous and to be frank (not literally of course!) I'm quite happy the way I am.

I'm 53 years old now and I was 44 when I started to write this and optimistically thought I would have finished by the time I hit 50. I cannot actually believe how old I am. I don't feel 53 but the speed at which the years are flying past it does frighten me. When I was younger, the thought of being 30+ years was 'old' let alone being over 50.

So, what am I up to? What have I been doing? Don't you find that these are the *same* questions you hear time and time again when meeting old friends. Well, at present I'm happily married to Sunita and have 2 great kids: Rishi who's 8 and Jai who's close to turning 1. Well actually, there is the problem - that *was* the age of the kids when I started to write this! The kids are now older; Rishi is 22 and Jai is 14. I've been with Sunita (unofficially for 32 years) and married for 25, I can honestly say I feel the same way towards Sunita as I did the day we got married - a rare thing nowadays where most relationships last marginally longer than the honeymoon!

It must be an 'Indian' thing, Indian parents don't tend to let go of their kids and you'll find that most 'kids' tend to run things past their parents first. I thought it would be a lot easier to get started with this than it actually is. Over the years and throughout the time I've been thinking about writing this, I've been desperately writing my life long memories and things of big significance on scraps of paper. In fact, some of these scraps are 12 years old so you can see I've been thinking about this for a very long time. However, I think my take on writing this book will simply to be @ the start and begin with my earliest memories & basically see what happens.

3

The early years

"I didn't do it" - I think this is what I said anyway. I must have been about 3 years old, perhaps older, and all I remember is a girl crying her eyes out. As it turned out I didn't realise that the little car I had hurled across the room hit the girl right in the face and as blood started to pour from her nose, I knew I was in trouble. The girl, Ravinder Kaur, who incidentally I became good friends with a few years later, was being looked after (as I was) by an Indian couple living in a house in St.Saviours Road in Leicester. In case you're wondering, yes, I do have a pretty good memory. Some of my friends struggle to remember what they did the previous week let alone almost 37 years ago!

In those days I don't think there any kind of official child care – if you had a house and a few toys I think anyone could look after kids. This is a far cry from today's world where saying a simple 'hello' to a kid could get you into deep trouble or accusations of being a pervert could come flying your way. Anyway, I can't actually remember why I threw the car at her. I do remember the crying continued for a very long time but don't actually remember getting into trouble for it – phew! What I do remember very clearly is that the house I was left in was very, very warm and had cream carpet with a strange collection of patterns in it. Yes, I know, sounds very strange, how on earth could I remember such irrelevant detail? Anyway, by today' standards, that carpet was definitely 'pimped'!

I have extremely fond memories of living in a house in Parry Street which is just off the Green Lane Road in Leicester. In fact, we shared a house with another family. I think we had just arrived

in Leicester and with little or no money, sharing was the best choice. The family we shared the house with had 3 sons, I know for a fact that one of them was called Chetan. He was a very dark skinned person and although I did bump into him during my early teen years hasn't seen him since. There was an older brother who now reminds me of Joe 90, a very clever person, he was the brains of the family! I can't actually remember the names of brains or the youngest, but I have nothing but happy memories there. Their father was a happy go lucky chap who always seemed to have a smile and was always friendly. The house, a typically 2 up and 2 down was the last house and overlooked my nursery / infant school.

Endless days were spent outside running around and although most kids nowadays may not like to be so close to the school, it was fantastic. I have a vague recollection of eating lots of walker's crisps at this house. I really remember whether this was actually true or not, but the memory has stuck so I'm convinced there's some truth in it. Bath times (or lack of them!) were fun too – you see there was *no* bath or shower at all. I remember getting all cleaned up in the kitchen sink. My mum used to take everything out of the sink that was in there and basically just shove me in – no worries – everyone just got on with it. I'm sure there was some kind of rota system, as each kid was basically just plonked in and out of the bath with a refill in between.

After the car throwing incident my most vivid recollections seem to be with my nursery and infant days. I went to Green Lane Nursery school where I met Ranjan, Bindy, Nila and Nalini; very close friends who i'm still with contact and meet up with to this day. Nursery was great but infants were more enjoyable. I remember the classrooms were completely open plan – no doors like you have nowadays. We could see all the classes, here what was being said and walk in and out of them with no trouble at all. I remember always having 'my own' hanger and if anyone dared to put their coats on mine, I would promptly move theirs out of the way!

The jingle of the little milk bottles being brought into the class was a great time of the day – our daily milk ration had arrived. Remember, these were *glass* bottles, no worries about health and safety then and as far as I can remember nobody ever got hurt. As the milk was handled out to the kids (complete with silver tops), the straws went straight in and the race began. As each kid sucked on the milk, the race was over in a matter of seconds. Not to worry, the biscuits will be here soon. Not sure if anyone else remembers this but we even had a biscuit round! Unless mistaken, the biscuits were the 'malt' type – quite similar (in looks anyway) to the 'sports' biscuits you get today!

Watching 'play school' was a daily thing too – I'm sure all kids loved this classic program, and could any kid avoid shouting which window they wanted to go through that day? I remember being mesmerized by the whole experience. For a 15 minute period you were taken into a different world, I wasn't sitting in the classroom anymore but instead transformed into whatever world the BBC were broadcasting at the time! It was a true adventure, something I feel our kids don't really get nowadays. No computers, no fancy toys, just simple down to earth learning in its simplest form. I just feel the fun out of school in general has leaked out over the years.

The playground we had in those days would be bulldozed and closed by today's standards. We had solid concrete play shapes that the little children would climb all over. These weren't tiny concrete structures either – at least 2 foot high – imagine falling off that? The playground was on 2 levels with a fair number of steps in between. As soon as we came out of the classrooms, we would throw ourselves from the top step and hopefully land on our feet. I remember Mrs Parker, my teacher at the time, embarrassing me in front of the entire class. My hair had grown so much that she was trying to put a pin in my hair to stop it covering my face - much to the amusement of the other children. I'm not actually sure why my hair was so long but I guess it was basically that we simply couldn't afford to have it cut more frequently. With all the children pointing and laughing at me, I felt like crying but thankfully Mrs. Parker stepped in, laid down 'Parker's law' and with that all the kids stopped their jeering and all was quiet!

I don't care what anyone says, school dinners were the best thing ever. At dinner times, the kids would try to queue up sensibly whilst the 'dinner monitors' (tasked with helping to set up the dinner tables) went into the main hall which, incidentally, was also used for assemblies, school plays, PE (or physical education) and anything else that was too big for the classes. I remember pulling out each of the tiny tables and setting the chairs around them for all the children. The food was great, except 'Swede', some kind of carrot thing. To this day I still don't really know what they are. All I know is that they were the worst tasting thing ever and 'remember to eat up all your food' used to frighten the life out of me. I remember just swallowing them whole and drinking lots of water to dampen the taste. It's quite ironic therefore that as a parent myself, i'm telling Rishi to 'finish all his food' – why is it we do this?

The chocolate pudding dessert was my favourite part of school dinners and when it came to 'seconds' there was no contest. As soon as the words left the dinner ladies mouth, I was at the front of the queue. There was no doubt 'smiler' was back for more. Err, in case you're wondering who 'smiler' was well it was me! The name was given to me by one of the 'nice' dinner ladies, presumably because I smiled a lot! Mind you all dinner ladies were nice then and treated like you as if they were your mum. This particular lady had dark hair and used to say 'here's smiler'. I'm, sure she gave me a slightly bigger piece than the rest of the kids. Whether she did or not was irrelevant, I had my second piece and life couldn't be better....

You may have noticed I put the word 'nice' inside speech marks. Well, the reason I did this was that my secondary school teacher (Mrs Blunt) gave me a lecture once about the word 'nice'. She used to say 'cakes are nice' but nice is a very general word – use something more 'descriptive'. Hmmm, descriptive, what does that mean then? I *was* only 11; did all the kids know what this word meant? Was I the only one who thought that food was 'nice' and didn't realise I had to be more descriptive? I'm not sure how or why that has stuck with me; it just goes to show that things people tell you *can* stick with you so watch what you say!

When it came to PE, the dinner hall was transformed yet again. We used to get changed into our 'PE gear' which consisted of shorts of some kind, white vests (regardless of the weather or how cold it was) and black plimsolls. The sides of the hall had climbing frames which, after being freed, would swing into action and in a matter of minutes we had our own ropes, climbing frames, mats and beams for the PE session. I remember the mats being very hard and had a distinctive rubbery smell that you never forget.

Does anyone remember the 'horse' or whatever it was? It looked like a chest of drawers that was wider at the bottom than the top and we used to have to run at this thing and either jump on it or as we got older handstand on it. The pain as you hit your legs hard on the horse due to a badly timed jump was unbearable, but you simply got to the back of the queue and tried again. I did, however, enjoy many more memories in this street as I grew older, and we used to hang around that area during that time.

Our time at the house in Parry Street was quite short lived. I have been told (I had to check with my sister on this), that after Parry Street, we ended up living in some more shared accommodation on St.Saviours Road, found in the 'Highfields' area of Leicester. I remember the house; it was blue, very big and occupied a corner plot. I cannot remember who we shared the house with and to be honest cannot remember much at this place. One thing I do remember is that just around the corner from this house was an old Austin car – it was blue in colour, and it was simply abandoned. I loved that car; I spent what must have been many hours each day sitting in the driver's seat. I used to pretend I was driving and desperately tried to press the pedals at the same time I was trying to change gears and look out the window!

Unfortunately, I remember all my adventures being solo ones, not sure if that was because I had no friends or none of the other kids could be bothered but at the time I didn't care – why should I? This was *my* car and I think it was the time I spent in this car that hooked me onto cars in general...

Opposite this house was Spinney Hill Park – an infamous park during my childhood for all my family and in fact most kids from my generation who lived around the area. The park itself had something quite unique at that time – an adventure playground and it was exactly that. The 'adventure' bit was at the top of the park, and I remember there used to be a muddy area and a solid brick building at one end. If you accessed the adventure playground from the park itself, I would squeeze myself through a broken part of the fencing and be confronted with a huge muddy section.

I say 'huge' because when you're young most things are quite big aren't they? Once you clambered over the first obstacle all you could see what lots of rope hanging from trees – trust me, these weren't ordinary ropes but really long things. I remember watching the kids grabbing hold of them not realising they were about to be catapulted for the ride of their lives! When it came to my turn, I was a little afraid at the start but once you were on, it was the best thing. Gliding through the air several feet off the ground was awesome and I lost count of how many times I went on there. I don't recall being with anyone else at this time, perhaps I was or perhaps I've simply forgotten (& maybe my memory isn't that good after all!!). After what seemed like a lifetime swinging around, I would walk up to the building. I forgot to mention that this adventure playground had animals in it.

Inside the building itself I'm pretty certain there were spiders, various insects and even snakes. I remember hearing a story when I was a few years older that a snake had escaped from the adventure playground and for the next few weeks I was petrified of coming face to face with it. On my travels I remember seeing the snake several times – well I thought I saw it, it was in fact either a long piece of discarded rope or a long stick! Another exciting part to this building was getting to the top. There was, you see, lots of metal 'steps' on one side of the building which you could use to climb up. Remember, this was many, many years ago and this would never be allowed in today's world – donkeys roaming around, snakes on the loose and tiny kids climbing up the side of a building.

It was a real effort climbing to the top, lots of kids were real naturals and would scale the building in a matter of seconds whilst I took my time and tried to avoid slipping off (when it had been raining it was even more of a challenge). The feeling at the top was immense, you had a great view of the whole park and I had climbed it! I lost count of how many times I climbed up and down this over the years, but it was great fun. When it was time to go home, there was no need to squeeze through the fence again or walk 'the long way around' - no, no. I could, after all, squeeze my way through yet another opening that backed out onto St Saviours Road and I could see the blue house right in front of me so it was easy really. Unfortunately, this is all I can recall about this house and i'm not really sure how long we stayed there although by the time I finish this book I may have all the answers...

During my early childhood years, we moved around a lot and our next abode (or house!) was in Mere Road – number 79 to be exact. I've never really spoken to my brothers and sister about this house and what *they* can remember because I wanted to recall my own experiences. However, they may remember something of significance that I did or got up to so you never know I might just ask them!

The house we lived in had 3 floors to it so even by today's standards it was big. I remember the house being very 'clean'. It had large rooms and if I remember correctly there was a front room, a lounge straight after it which then led into the kitchen. I can't recall much about the upstairs at all. I do recall closing the little gate that was at the front of the house and then walking up the 5-6 small steps that led up to the front door. The little brick wall outside the house was often used as a mini climbing frame and just a place to sit and watch everyone else go about their daily chores.

I would then take the little key that was hanging around my neck and let myself in. In fact, I don't actually remember ever going into the house with anybody else – just myself. This *is* bizarre – I must only have been 4 or 5 years old but here I was with my own key letting myself into the house. The actual door lock must have been very low down, or I've imagined the whole thing! I don't know anybody who today would let their child have a key to their house let alone having it dangling around their neck! The house, positioned in the middle of a row of terraced houses, was directly opposite the Imperial Pub. The pub took central stage around that area mainly due to its sheer size. It occupied a massive area, very tall and still looks the same today as it did all those years ago...

Around the corner was the good old Hartington Road, filled with countless shops selling everything you'd ever want. I figured my mum shopped from here given that in those days there were none of the mega supermarkets we have nowadays. If you wanted to do your weekly shop you'd have to trek in and out of many shops and carry all the shopping home the hard way - by foot! I remember the house being very clean indeed and quite big. One thing that does stick in my mind was the downstairs toilet. It was one of those that you had to crouch down to use – literally a hole in the ground although it wasn't one of those extremely dirty ones – it was pretty clean. At that age it seemed pretty normal, even fun in a bizarre sort of way.

As a child playing around this house used to be great fun. My parents bought me one of those red tricycles which were almost standard issue for small kids at that time. I used to play on it all the time in the back garden and outside on the pavement. My brother, Kiran, took me for 'rides' 'around the block'. This involved me sitting on the seat and holding on tight – very tight in fact whilst he had one foot on the rear 'step' whilst the other was used to propel us along. I'm pretty certain that he did the steering to. Our route would take us towards St.Saviours Road and past the white building on the corner which has remained a doctor's surgery for as long as I can remember. Provided we hadn't fallen off, he would then speed up as we raced down the hill. Trust me; we really did hit some top speeds down this hill. The next road wasn't far away and as we hit top speed it was time to slow down or at least try to slowdown. This was *fun, real fun* and I lost count of how many times we did this. Being the youngest (and not able to push!), meant I didn't have to do anything, all I did was sit & hold on!

Our fun, however, came to a halt one evening as we raced around the corner of the street just behind Mere Road. As we screeched around the corner and headed into the straight, Kiran decided to do a sharp left turn into a mound of mud – it looked like mud anyway but regardless of what it was, we hit it hard – real hard. As we came to a sudden stop, it was a miracle that we were both still on the tricycle – the force at which we stopped would usually send you hurling into mid-air but all we heard was the twisting of metal – my beloved red tricycle was dead. The front forks or whatever you call then bent up like a banana due to the sheer force of the impact and the front wheel was almost detached from the tricycle altogether. That was the last time we went out on that bike – I'm sure Kiran got into trouble for that – thanks bro for the good times we had there!

The Imperial pub opposite played a huge part of our lives whilst we lived at the Mere Road house. The owner was a Singh, I was never sure of his name and to be honest still don't know his name now. What I do know is that everyone called him 'cha, cha' which means "uncle" in Punjabi; I simply knew him as cha cha Singh. Married to an English woman, he had 3 kids and we got on really well with the youngest: Jason Singh. Most people have their "local" pub, and this was about as local as you could get; it was literally 20 seconds from our house! My dad took me there all the time and I never saw any other kids there! In those days i'm pretty certain it wasn't even legal to take under 18's into pubs let alone a 5 year old! The main bar area seemed to span the entire width of the whole building and a few floors up was where the family lived (I managed to get up there too!).

In those days few people had cars so the chance to go into one (a real one that is) was very exciting to an excitable kid. My dad would regularly take me out in silver Ford Cortina 1600E. I can almost picture the car even today – it was a limited edition sports version of the legendary car and it had the black section at the back that gave it the 'E' badge. To this day I have no idea whose car it was – mind you, I sometimes wonder whether my dad knew either! This was some of the best times I had, it was my dad taking me for a cruise in the car – could it get better than this? We'd go out for a cruise, park the car outside our house and then head straight back over to the pub.

My dad was probably drink driving at the time and who knows what he was up to (if anything…) but once back in the pub, it was coke and cheese + onion crisps. One thing to note was that this was the *original* coke bottle, not the flimsy cans we have nowadays. There was always something about those bottles that made the coke taste much better – ask most people and they would agree to this somewhat sweeping statement. To this day, I may not drink coke that often but the combination of coke & cheese + onion crisps have to be one of the best combinations for taste.

When younger it's not often you hear your mum screaming, well in our house it rarely happened during the early years anyway. However, there was one incident which sent my mum crazy and it was a small kid – namely me where the curiosity definitely got the better of me. I must have been bored, very bored in fact otherwise I wouldn't have wondered around this big house looking for things to do. I have no idea where my brothers or sisters were. They may have been hiding from this crazy young kid who just wanted to play all the time. Anyway, as I was nosing around, I came across something which looked like a series of light switches all together. Even as a small child you start to understand how things work in a house and that pushing or pulling something generally does *something*. Being extremely curious I grabbed hold of a switch and tugged on it and when I finally gave up all hope of it moving at all I tried to move it in any direction when suddenly it moved and the whole house went dark.

It was night time you see and the lights were on. What happened? Who switched the lights off? Scared isn't the word – I was petrified, all alone in the dark when suddenly the screaming voice rang out all over the house – "*&!$%" – I cannot remember exactly what my mum said but I knew I was in trouble. I had, you see, taken out all the lights in the house with the flick of a switch – well I know it was a switch now. After being yelled at for what seemed an eternity, the lights came back on, and everything went back to normal. Well, I say normal because since that day I have learnt a very big lesson indeed – *never* mess with electricity. Dinner times were great in this house and for a very strange reason. Although the house was big – I don't think we ever sat at a table to eat whether it was breakfast or evening dinner. The only thing we sat on during dinner was empty grain sacks. Trust me, these sacks were great and there was just something about them – they had a distinctive smell – a grainy smell! (ok, ok, no pun intended!!) but I loved sitting on them. We'd all sit around and there was no better moment when potatoes and onions were served up – a favourite dish of mine to this day.

We had great neighbours (well, they were great on one side – I don't' think ever saw the other neighbours at all). They had quite a big family – there were definitely several brothers, but I don't know if there were any sisters at all. The youngest kid had a yellow toy with wheels. Yes, I know, not much of a description but it was literally that although it did have a seat on it. We used to drag it up & down the stairs that led to the house and they used to let me play on it all the time. Bizarrely, although we left Mere Road, I have bumped into the kids over the last 30 or so years and I believe they still live in Leicester. In fact, it was only a few months ago that I bumped into the youngest kid at my local BP some 30 years after I had first met them. You may be thinking 'so what', 'what's the big deal' – well at that moment, it took me back to the early days and that was a good place to be. The reality of how fast the years have passed by really hit home – we're talking 30 years – can you believe it? I struggled to believe it but as I got home, I remember telling Sunita I bumped into my neighbour – anyway, he instantly recognised me and as always, it was great to see him.

Before my red tricycle was ceremoniously trashed by my brother Kiran 'Schumacher' Patel, I would take it into the rear garden & just cycle anywhere I could over and over again. I'm not sure if I just got extremely bored again (yes, another of those 'bored' days!) or just fancied something different but I decided to pick at the wall – well at the cement in particular and err, started to eat it. Yes, you read this correctly – I was eating cement/sand/mortar or whatever you want to call it. Nowadays people eat strange things, but I have still to meet anyone who ate cement. You'd think it would cause some kind of discomfort at the very least – stomach ache. Bizarre as this is, it never seemed to cause me any problems at all, no stomach ache, no vomiting, no nothing. Mind you, I say it hasn't done any damage – some might say otherwise but a true story, nevertheless.

One thing that I remember vividly was my cool, purple 't' shirt that some kind of logo on it. It's the only item of clothing I remember when I was that young. I guess it's nothing most people talk about or even remember but I do, I used to love wearing it even though I do look distressed in the picture – I think it tells a story already...I think we went to get some photos done for my passport or something but I remember going along to a photo studio not far from our house. The fun times @ this house, the tricycle days and playing in my cool t shirt was soon to be a thing of the past & this was to be my last memory at this wonderful Mere Road house...

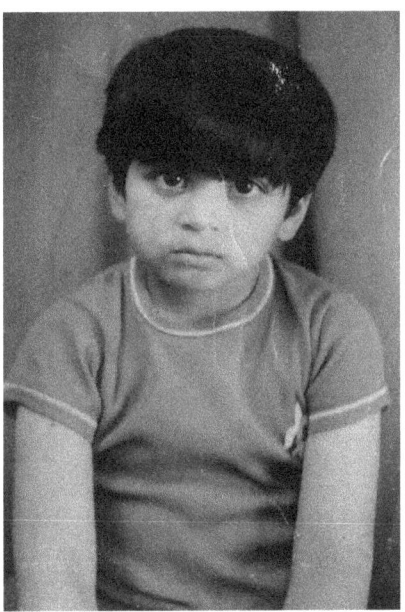

It was typical day for me, went to school, played, and ran around and at the end of the day I slowly marched up Mere Road towards our house. Having kicked various stones along the way, balancing at the edge of the pavement (health & safety!) and trying to avoid stepping on the 'lines' in the pavement (was it just me that did this?), I ended up back outside 79 Mere Road. As I opened the small gate at the front and climbed the 5 or 6 little steps that led to the front door, I grabbed the key that was dangling around my neck. As I fiddled with the key and finally worked out which way it should be inserted into the door, I could not get it open at all. At first there was nothing unusual about this, so I took it out and probably put it back in the same way and found it still didn't turn.

After a few further failed attempts, panic started to creep in, and I was soon turning the key in all directions just to get it to open the door but it just would not open. So, I was now in an unfamiliar situation. The key usually opened the door, I couldn't have the wrong key and I *was* standing outside the right house so what could it be? I knew my sister would be back soon, so I gave up and watched the cars go buy. Eventually my sister came home and wondered what I was doing outside – strange really because I was wondering what I was doing outside too. Anyhow, she couldn't open the door either so I was relieved it wasn't something to do with me. In the end there were 2 of us now sitting outside the house but it wasn't long before Kiran joined us. He then tried his key, and this failed too so by now things weren't looking too good.

Despite that & when you are so young, you don't really think anything of it - I certainly didn't. All I was wondering was what my mum will say when she got home. It never, ever occurred to me that we'd never set foot in that house ever again. After all, as a very young child, your mind isn't filled with complicated and unnecessary information. It was *our* house but why couldn't we get in? Once mum or dad got home, they would open the doors and we'd be inside and that would be that. As time ticked on and 3 out of the 4 kids sat outside (where was Vipul?), I was getting pretty bored, and my sister was probably getting quite fed up with playing the 'name the car' game whilst Vipul was nowhere to be seen. Finally, both my mum and VIP had arrived home and there were now 5 of us sitting outside and things were not looking good.

I could see the look in my mum's face – it was almost a look of expectation – that she knew this was going to happen, but the question was 'what was going to happen?

Whenever I think of the events that led up to this, it really does hurt. In fact, it hurt so much at the time that I truly believe it altered my outlook on life even though I didn't realise it at the time. The truth of the whole matter was simple. My dad, the person who I had so much fun with, the person who took me for rides in the car (still don't know whose car it was!), the person who made coke and cheese 'n' onion crisps a legendary combination had let the entire family down. In simple terms, he had not kept up the payments on the house which had resulted in the house being taken away from us or was repossessed to be exact. It was all a waste of time trying to get into the house – it's quite difficult when you have the key but lock itself has been changed! During the day the bank must have authorised someone to get inside and then change the locks so there we were - all 6 of us standing outside our house, well the bank's house.

There didn't seem to be any drama at all whilst we stood there, and I don't even remember any arguing between my parents. Up until this time I don't recall them ever arguing or perhaps they did, and I was protected from it all but nevertheless I just could not understand it. What did they mean we couldn't go inside, why couldn't my dad open the door – after all it was our house wasn't it?

So, when I left this great house of ours in the morning to head off for school, little did I know it would be the last time I would see it from the inside. No more eating cement, no more playing with light switches and no more eating on grain sacks.

As a kid I don't think the scale of what had just happened was understood but then again why should it? I have never talked about this with either my brothers or sister – I guess it was something that nobody really wanted to talk about. Mind you I think people just tend to forget and we were quite young. I could never quite remember what we did that night – what I mean is where did we stay? Were there any arguments that night? Did my mum know what had happened? I suppose I could ask around and I'd get the answer but I'm not that bothered to be honest. The damage had been done and we no longer lived there so that was that.

My brain seems to have lost memory of how we ended up in Halstead Street – a street that was literally 10 minutes' walk from our old Mere Road house. Mind you, it was also just around the corner from the big blue house on St.Saviours Road – where was our saviour that day? I wonder if the wrecked car was still there... The long hot summer of 1976 was the year that we started to live here. It was the typical 2 up & 2 down house (or mid terrace), and this was to be our new home, resting place, lodgings or whatever you want to call it for the next 3 years. It *was* very different to Mere Road, smaller rooms, tiny garden, no pub opposite (he he!) but what it lacked in appearance was made up by the characters that lived on that street.

47 Halstead Street was a rented property; probably not by choice but the fact that my parents had no money to even consider buying another place of our own – not for a few years anyway. It was owned by our neighbours who lived @ 49 Halstead Street so 'big brother' was next door. The owners were a strange bunch although the same could have been said about the Patel clan @ 47! If I remember correctly there were 3 brothers and one sister. One of the brothers, Atul, was tall – very tall and we used to call him monkey or some other name. He had long arms that used to swing unnaturally high so that's where the money resemblance probably came from! I don't think we ever said this to his face – we weren't that brave because it he didn't beat us to a pulp then his brother (a shorter, fat guy) would only have to look at us and it would scare the living daylights out of us.

How on earth can the 'living daylights' be scared out of you? Why is it that we seem to use such phrases that don't seem to make much sense when looked into further? We say "it's chilly outside" to mean it's cold yet "that was chilly" when we eat spicy food. Another favourite seems to be "it's a small world..." Really, the earth's 25,000 miles' circumference is small, is it? Another one is "that will happen once in a blue moon"; most people say this without realising that a "blue moon" does actually exist. A 'blue moon' is actually a full moon but one that doesn't occur during the regular monthly pattern. Each year has approximately 12 full moons, one per month but there are about 11 extra days per year. These 'extra' days build up and every 2-3 years the days build up and lead to an extra full moon, aka a blue moon.

Enough of that for now – I'm sure they'll be more of that later. The third brother was called Badresh or something like that. He was noticeably dark skinned, come to think of it they all were but he seemed like the calm one out of the whole lot. Finally, there was the little sister – Gita I think her name was. There wasn't much conversation between the 2 families – well, none that I could remember anyway. So, here we were, all 6 of us living in a tiny house with strange neighbours. We used to gather in the 'front room' of the house in the evenings because it would have probably been the warmest. The one thing that stuck in my mind about this front room was the red & black settees. As you walked into the house there was a 3 seater to the right with thick red cushions which I'm certain had black stripes down them. I don't actually remember there being anything else in this house – well, there was a TV, but I don't recall any other furniture...

The 'middle' room was rarely used; it was scary, cold and dark. The settees were old and very tacky, and I used to run as fast as I could through the room as I headed straight on into the kitchen or veered to the right to go upstairs. One of the bizarre things I used to do was try to play the drums. I don't quite understand what got me started on this, but I did. In case you're wondering there was no drum kit or anything that resembled drums. Instead, I got the whelen's/ velens's that were used to give the chapatti their shape and banged them on the nasty settees in the middle room. Why I chose to play them in the room I hated is a mystery to me, but I did it anyway and I loved it. I'm certain I used to make the drum noises with my mouth too – who knows - perhaps I was the original beat boxer!!

The kitchen was also a horrible place and I remember it being cold too. There was a horrible sink and a small work top from which my mum (and probably my sister) used to make the food on. Interestingly we didn't have a fridge and I cannot believe how we survived without one. However, when you don't have the money to go out and buy something you simply get on with it and make use of what you have got. Well, we certainly did that – we may not have had a fridge but in the winter, we made full use of the weather conditions! When it was time to make jelly (a rare treat for the kids), the pan itself was placed outside in the garden and covered with a plate to let it cool down. At the height of the winter, temperatures would often fall well below zero degrees and in a matter of hours out jelly was done – magic!

One of the worst things however was the shower. The house didn't have a bath at all, there was no room for one but there was a unique feature about the shower – it was outside. Oh yes – having a shower was a true experience, especially in the dark cold days of winter. Trust me, in the early years, the British winter was very, very cold and nothing like the mild climatic conditions we have today. The shower room, if you could call it that, was a few steps outside and into what was called the garden. There were copper pipes mounted on a cement wall and the water that came out of the pipes was hot and I mean hot. Once the shower was finished, it was a towel wrapped around the body and then back into the house as soon as possible.

Upstairs there were 3 rooms, the 'front' room overlooked Halstead Street itself and was where my parents slept. As you walked along the little corridor-like passage the next room to the right was where I slept along with my brothers & sister. Our room overlooked the back garden (the tiny one that is!) and as far as I could remember the room was very light and airy. The last of the 3rd upstairs room was the legendary 'box' room. Now let me see… the 'box' room – why was it called this? Was it an Indian thing? To this day the only people i've heard it call this are Indians! The name, funnily enough, is quite apt because all I remember being in this room was indeed boxes. I could never understand where all the boxes came from – after all, it's not as though we packed up all our things in Mere Road was it?

At the time that we moved to Halstead Street I must have been 7 years old or very close to that and in a strange kind of way I had some of my best times as a kid in this place. I don't mean in this house but in the area because the place was just fun, the kids around there were fun, there was lots to do, and it felt good. From Halstead Street, the journey to school would be quick if you walked straight there and back but I couldn't do that. As I closed the door to number 47 behind me, I would make sure that the door knocker (you don't get many of these now – we didn't have a bell in those days), was still attached to the door. I say this because one of my dad's friends was a big man and I mean big. When he arrived at the house you knew it and when he left you heard it because as he shut the door, the sheer strength in his hands would send part of the door knocker flying to the ground. Whoever was closer would then have the job of picking the bits off the floor and attaching them back!

Back to my journey to school – i'd head off in the direction completely opposite to Spinney Hill Park and head right passed the 20 or so houses to the left. When I got to the end of Halstead Street there was a series of steps to climb before you would reach Wood Hill. The journey up (& down for that matter) was easy when it was dry but in the winter, I had to take extra care. One slip and I'd be hurling down those steps with one outcome – lots of pain and a likely trip to the hospital. I would always look at the sweet shop to the right of me but we never had money so I would just think about it for a few seconds and then continue on my way. Once across the road, the Milap Club (an Indian pub where all the dads would drink whilst the mums were at home) was on the left hand side. There was a black metal fence that sort of separated the building from the pavement. I'd climb on the wall adjacent to the fence and follow it up to the highest point (sounds scary doesn't it – it was only about 2 metres!) Once I had successfully navigated down the other side it was a quick jump high as I could, and I'd be back on the pavement.

I'd cross the road again and in a matter of seconds i'd be turning right onto Mere Road – yes, I just couldn't get away from this place. Thankfully, I couldn't see our house (our ex house that is) from here – that would be too much especially since I still had no idea of what had really happened. At some point I would get across the road and Bridge County Junior School was just on the left. Junior school was great fun and the 4 years I spent there (whilst I was at school that is) were some of the most enjoyable of my life. Bridge school (shortened for now!) was a typical type of school in those days. It had a 'main' block to it but due to expansion had a few 'mobiles' too. These were not the mobiles of today (ha ha) but mini classrooms where real lessons were taught. The strange thing about these mobile classrooms was that they had a unique smell about them – I'm sure anyone who has ever been taught in a mobile would agree.

Films – we all like them but as a 7/8 year old I remember making our own films whilst in this school! It may not have been technically challenging but Mr. Pryne (our well liked teacher) used to get all the kids involved and we'd all started doing daft things like loosening our shoes and kicking them off whilst he recorded it. This may not be exciting when played back but when played back in reverse the effect was truly awesome (remember we are 7/8 year olds here). The tears of laughter would drip down the sides of our faces whilst the air filled with the unforgettable sound of children having fun. All of my friends - white, black & brown – all together, not questioning why we were different colour all having a great time. Just like infant school, good old PE (physical education) was a right laugh too – our main hall/dinner hall/ assembly hall etc. would once again be transformed into a gymnasium and out came the climbing ropes and climbing frames that only moments earlier had been securely attached to the side wall.

When the weather was warm it was a real treat as we'd be playing outside and that meant one thing – cricket. Mind you it wasn't the traditional type of cricket – this was far too complicated. Instead, we had small, soft balls, a couple of posts and a small round bat (similar to a tennis table bat). There was *no* denying it – I was clearly the best out of them all. When it came to table tennis type batting game thingy, I was the ultimate player and nobody, (not even Jennifer James – she was a tough girl) came close. I could hit the ball like no one else and each time we played it was a matter of time before the other kids could mutter "is it my turn yet". Actually, no – it wasn't your turn as I was still batting. Only a genius stroke of bowling (or getting extremely tired!) would lead to my down fall and someone else would take over. Sometimes we'd actually have a PE lesson out of school completely and would head to the playing fields on Davenport Road. Most school kids of that era would have heard about this place – lots of school children came here. Mind you, it was really only those schools that didn't have their own grass field who you would see there. Nowadays this is virtually un-heard of and schools tend to have most of their main facilities on site.

Davenport road was way too far to walk to so we had a bus, a special bus with '99 school special' as the destination that would arrive to take us there & bring us back. The bus was one of those famous cream coloured ones that ferried people all over Leicester many years ago before they decided to change the colours and before private firms started taking control of certain routes. The old Leicester buses were great fun – it was great just to be able to jump on & off a bus whilst the conductor held on at the rear. In those days we had *proper* buses where the conductor asked where you wanted to go and told you how much it would cost. He would then click a few buttons on the portable ticket machine that would be dangling around the neck and finally turn the handle 360 degrees and out popped the ticket. The tickets were tiny & typically blue (adult) or orange/red) (kids). The conductor would wait until passengers were off the bus or had taken their seats safely before pressing the bell to let the driver know he could continue.

I remember the insides of these buses well, there was no buttons to press –instead there was a single line in the roof of the bus so no matter where you sat (or stood) you were always within reach. The driver could look above his head and see what was going on in the top floor as there was a huge mirror in the top deck roof that panned out to show the entire top floor. As kids we used to sit upstairs and look down at the driver and giggle away whenever they looked up towards us. Things have changed drastically now; the legendary conductors have all but vanished, drivers now ask you where you want to go, take the money, don't worry about whether you're safely on/off the bus and simply try to complete the route as quickly as possible.

You don't even have to speak with the driver nowadays due to the credit card type pre-pay cards that are available. You simply swipe the card and that's it. The bus that took us to Davenport Road always seemed to arrive on time & the excitement on seeing the bus make its way down Mere Road and stop outside the school was fantastic. I remember looking at all the other kids, most of who were my friends and thinking "that seat is mine". The thing was I *had* to get my special seat and no other kid would ever get it as long as I had something to do with it.

As the teacher summoned us all to 'make a line children' I would always get to the front or as close to the front as possible. We'd start walking along the playground and back up towards the classrooms. Once we had passed the mobile on the right hand side and walked past Miss Manner's Saab 99 (blue & brand spanking new) we were out the gate and heading close to the bus. (Miss Manners was the head teacher...). As we were 15 seconds from the bus the walking pace turned dramatically into a slight jog and before long all the kids were running towards the front. There was no need to worry though – I was there, on the bus and got my place yet again.

I always sat on one of the side seats right at the front of the bus so that I could see the driver and the road ahead. I loved sitting here and as the bus started & stopped amongst the traffic and meandered through Green Lane Road all the kids started to change into their football kit. I lost count of the number of times I held on as the driver swung around corners whilst I was holding on with one hand whilst trying to get my shorts on with the other! Once at the ground there would be another mad rush as we all tried to get off the bus as quick as possible and race towards the playing fields. In comparison to our school playground, the grounds @ Davenport Road were huge and as kids tend to do, we all used to race around the pitch playing 'tick' whilst Mr. Gamble; our sports teacher; got the footballs out and decided activities we were going to do that day.

Others may disagree but as with table tennis cricket thingy (you remember – the batting game in the playground...), I was good at football and sometimes wondered how far I would have progressed if I had taken more of an interest as I grew older. I'd tend to be one of the first picked when the captains were picking their sides. Once on the pitch, I used to devastate the left hand side and scored several memorable goals. I was also a dab hand at the old defence too – so good that Mr. Gamble himself called me into the office several weeks later.

I was in class and remember a kid coming into our lesson and heading straight for our teacher. Within seconds I could hear my name being called and thought I was in trouble. In fact, all the kids thought I was in trouble – there they were all sitting looking at me wondering what i'd been up to. I too was petrified and wondered why I was called up. As I made my way (albeit slowly) to our teacher, I was told to see Mr. Gamble and so I made my way to his classroom. Within 3 seconds I was there and within 3 minutes I was back in my class. The kids looked at me again trying to figure out what happened, what had I done? Would I be sent to Miss Manners the head teacher?). No, I wouldn't – you see what had happened was that I was told that they wanted me to play for Bridge Junior School football team.

This was exciting – a chance to play football for the school. You see not everybody got this chance, so I had to take it. The downside was it meant Saturday mornings were spent back at Davenport Road because the inter school football matches were held there. In a 3 month period I played 4 games because the teacher liked to rotate the team quite a bit. I actually think that I was a crap player and not the budding football start after all!! The best game by far was when we played Sacred Hearts. This was a real local derby – I don't think you could get any closer because their school was next to ours – literally! In football terms, I didn't have a great game and neither did my team as a whole. By the time the half time whistle blew we were losing 4-1. I'm not quite sure what the kids at Sacred Heart had for dinner but we needed some of that. They were huge, big players compared to us and when one of their players came running full speed to get the ball off me, I literally jumped out of his way. It may be football but trust me; I wasn't going to stand in the way of him... Mr. Gamble wasn't too impressed; I wasn't impressed either, but I was still alive – for now.

A mistake by the other team meant we scored another goal so the score was now 4-2 to the other team but oh no, they had a corner cross, and I had the opportunity to show my defensive skills. As the opposition towered over me, I made my way towards the back goal post and waited for their team to take the corner. The ball came flying in and headed straight towards me. This was my chance, my moment, my defining point to ensure they didn't score and trust me I was fantastic. The ball got closer & closer and there was no way I was going to head that ball away (it would hurt you know!). Instead, I had to swap position slightly and as the ball glided down towards me I kicked it away with all the energy I had. 'Take that' I was thinking to myself, I had saved our team from the misery of another goal – Mr. Gamble would be pleased with me and soon my team mates would be congratulating me.

Unfortunately, something had gone wrong – why were the other team celebrating and why were my team mates looking as if I'd scored a goal or something? Er, I had in fact scored a goal. You see I did indeed kick the ball very hard but it went the wrong way and straight into our net. The score was 5-2 to them and I had scored arguably the greatest goal that Bridge Junior had ever seen but unfortunately, I had scored it for the other team. I never played for the school team again as I wasn't asked to after that performance. When some of the kids used to take the piss for scoring an own goal I used to say "well at least I scored a goal" – this often led to quite a few bemused looks from the kids...

In my 3rd year at junior school a group of children, including me, were put into a 4th year class which I guess was to spread the number of kids per class evenly or something. Our teacher, Mr. Wildman, was a typical know it all but great fun at the same time. I can't recall the work being any harder but definitely remember it being quite cool that we were in an older year. The teacher often liked to start the day with random general knowledge questions and offered hard cash to those who could answer. To this day I vividly recall one of his questions for which he was offering the staggering amount of £1.00 to the person who got it right. The question was "On the UK bank notes, there is a sentence that starts "I promise..." – what does the sentence actually say in full?

I didn't get this right, but this was ok because nobody else got it right too. This meant that no money ever parted the teachers' hands! When I think about it now, it's a pretty hard question and probably one that most people even today wouldn't be able to answer let alone a 9/10 years old. You may be thinking well what's the answer then? Well, the answer is *"I promise to pay the bear on demand the sum of XX pounds"*. Go on – don't take my word for it, pull out a note and see for yourself! General knowledge aside, Mr. Wildman was renowned for his discipline. If you ever did anything wrong in class such as not listening or generally being a nuisance, you were in for a real lesson.

Mr. Wildman you see was a big advocate in giving kids a quick 'knuckle' to the head. He would come up to you, clench his hand and give you a swift knock to the head and take my word for it that it hurt really bad! Just think about it for a moment – a teacher inflicting this kind of pain on a kid with his knuckle... Nowadays an accidental tap on the back of the head could see a teacher in trouble but no one in Wildman's class was safe and the knuckle busting antics ensured that most kids behaved themselves!

My junior school used to hold open days or 'summer days' where relatives of the kids including brothers & sisters could come along and take part in a fun filled afternoon (usually close to the end of term). On one such occasion there was a competition to see who could light the most candles with a single match. Stepping up to the challenge was my brother Kiran who managed to win the contest by a huge margin. I remember seeing him lighting each one quickly and soon lost count of how many candles were now alight. As the champion stepped up to claim his prize a spider plant was handed to him, and this plant was in our household for many years. Spider plants were synonymous with Indians – almost all Indian household had these plants;

probably because they were almost indestructible. As for Kiran I can't remember if he was excited about his prize or not; I think he was just happy at winning something!

At the end of the school day, I would rush out and head back towards the gate. After walking up Mere Road I would wait for a gap in the road and run as fast as my legs would take me until I was safely on the other side. I'd turn left into Wood Hill, cross over the road again and walk up the side of the wall outside the Milap Club. A quick jump over the metal fence and I was back on the pavement where I would see the corner shop on the left once again. A final dash over Prospect Road and I would be heading down hill until I'd make my final right turn and head down the steps that led to Halstead Street. At this point I'd cross the road and then start knocking on the door once I had reached home – our rented home that is. If you speak to most people and ask them about their lives, they'll probably be able to tell you several life changing or significant defining moments that they haven't & probably never will forget. I was to get one of those moments and it was one that changed my outlook on life forever...

4

Life changing

Arguments in the Patel household were very rare, so rare in fact that when one happened, I didn't realise what had happened. The first I knew if it were the raised voices. Had it been someone else I would never have given it a second thought but hang on a second, here I was with my brothers and sisters, mum & dad sitting in our front room at Halstead Street and it happened – one of the defining moments in my life that would change everything was happening right in front of me - my dad was *hitting* my mother. As I sit here (now September 2nd, 2007) writing this it still hurts me to this day on the events that I saw that day. One minute there was silence and the next I vividly recall my dad, his face full of extreme anger & hatred punching my mum and clenching her hair.

My dad, the person who I loved going to the pub with, the person who took me for cruises in the Ford Cortina, had turned into a crazed person repeatedly hitting the kindest & loving person in my world – my mum. As the blows seemed to get faster and stronger, the cries of pain filled our front room. It all seemed to be in extreme slow motion. I remember all the kids; my 2 brothers and sister, using all the strength we had to try to pull my dad off my mum. Being so small it was a huge struggle, there were screams from my sister begging my dad to stop, my 2 brothers were using all their energy whilst I was almost in shock – perhaps I was just too young and naïve to digest what was happening around me. The whole incident lasted about 10-15 minutes and by the time my dad had calmed down, my mother had been left bruised and crying.

This was the first of many violent outbursts from my dad for many years to come. I've often heard that a mother's love is endless and will never stop – I witnessed this on this terrible day. Whilst we were trying to wrestle my dad away from my mum, I think one of his hands hit one of us and on seeing this my mum forgot about herself and tried in vain to throw her arm around us and protect us. Here was a person suffering a terrible beating yet amidst all this she was still doing what a mother does best... I don't think anyone who has ever experienced violent outbursts such as this forgets it in a hurry. As I grew up and started to learn about life as such, you often hear and read about terrible family issues such as this but here I was; we were one of those terrible statistics and it was happening – this was real and I from that day I hated my dad...

The word 'hate' is a terrible word; just saying it makes it sound so crude but there was no other word that described how I felt at the time. I now know that the argument was caused by *money*. Money – it's a strange thing & to this day I hate every part of this word. I know this sounds daft and perhaps those of you reading this may not fully understand why but this word, this 5 letter thing called *money* was the single root cause of the years of beatings that my mother had to suffer from our so called dad. Fuelled by an alcohol addiction, the cause of the arguments was simply that my dad spent virtually all of the money he'd earnt on drink. He wasn't a casual drinker; that would have probably been ok but whenever he came back from a drinking session, he was hammered to the point that he could barely walk. Out of his weekly wages he'd give my mum a small amount of money from which she was meant to feed us and pay the bills but there was never enough money.

My mum pleaded with him to stop but it was no good, all he cared about was alcohol, everything else just didn't matter. As the days, weeks & months flew by the arguments and alcohol fuelled beatings continued whilst us kids, too small to do anything about it, stood and watched my mum endure this heinous crime. My dad spent less time at work and would get home late on Fridays because it was pay day which meant he would stop off at the pub before deciding to come home. Overtime stopped and was replaced with 'pub time'; I know for a fact that my mum struggled to pay the rent and that the neighbours who owned the house repeatedly came round asking for money. I have no idea how my mum kept the household going and I really wished there was something I could have done to stop the hurting.

The amount of money he gave my mum for shopping and whatever else soon dwindled to such a degree that it hit our family hard – real hard. As my poor mother desperately tried to work even harder to support the family, she had 4 kids to bring up and fought a daily battle with a drunk, violent man who had virtually given up on his family and the responsibility that goes along with it. The winters in those days were particularly harsh and not as mild as the ones we have today. On one particular winter season I often wished I could be taken away from all this. The violence seemed to go on and on – whenever my dad got home in a drunken stupor my mum would always try to reason with him and try to make him understand what he was doing to us all.

Unfortunately, this was the ultimate trigger, when a person is intoxicated the behavioural patterns generally go 2 ways. The first is to remain calm whilst the other (the one my dad fell into) was to turn angry and unleash his anger on the weakest point. Sadly, the weakest point in his eyes was my mother; this loving soul endured the most awful psychological & physical punishment that I have ever seen & I would not want to see that ever again. So, there we were 4 young kids and a helpless mother struggling to survive with a man who we called our dad. It makes me sick to my stomach thinking about what this cruel person did to us all yet despite the cruelty, despite having to work hard to keep us fed & despite having to stand up and accept the awful verbal abuse this person looked after & protected us throughout from being little kids to the moment my dad died. It is for this reason that there is no other person in my world whom I respect more so that my dear mother. I sometimes look at my lifestyle now, have a comfortable home, cars and a good income but compared to what my mother had at that time she worked miracles & continues to do so. Sadly, the violence didn't stop here, it continued for many years but this is how it all started...

One particular event I recall vividly is that of my father getting out of a car in Halstead Street. I clearly remember he was wearing a suit and as he stepped out the car, he looked at me and gave me a huge smile. There was the person that I had loved so much – it was hard to believe that he could turn into a violent man – all I could think of was 'here's my dad'. Ironically, the smile he had on his face hid the shame of what he had done. The thing is you see, he had just returned from India. Nothing wrong with that I hear you say... Well, when most people go away from home you usually know about it & discuss it as families do. We didn't discuss anything; I grew up thinking our family was very dysfunctional.

My dad had decided to book a flight to India and one day simply disappeared only to return several weeks later as if nothing had happened. Behind that smile was a trail of lies and deceit. Whilst in India he decided to sell anything of value he could get his hands on. I don't really know what he sold but I'm pretty certain he cleared out several bank accounts and probably sold some gold that my mum was saving in a bank. He had the holiday of a lifetime at the expense of my mum – the ironic thing is my mum had probably been saving up gold for my sister's wedding. As well as being an alcoholic, this violent man was now a thief...

Life at Halstead Street was an endless cycle of good & bad days. I used to hate coming home from school as I dreaded the endless arguments that would kick off at any time. Mind you, along with my brothers, I spent many days away from school and sitting at home. With my father spending virtually all the income on alcohol and my mum struggling to pay for food and rent something had to give and it did. With no money to pay for our school dinners, I remember spending a few days here and there at home as my mum simply did not have the money to send the kids to school. Interestingly, it was the brothers that seemed to be at home; I don't recall my sister being forced to keep away from school at all! Unfortunately, the days off school turned into weeks and before we knew it the school was on our case. As young kids we thought it was quite good fun to start off with. We'd sit in our front room and make 'dens' and houses out of the red & black cushions off the settee and play games. In those days a truant officer used to patrol the streets and actually visit homes where the children living there spent more time at home than at school.

When somebody knocked at the door, we'd all freeze and it scared the life out of us – trust me, this happened on a regular occurrence. We'd all sit under our dens; all 3 of us, making sure we didn't say a word. The 'truant' officer stood there for ages – mind you when you're sitting in one place trying to keep still, time really goes slowly. We were off school lots in those days and unbeknown to me, the principal @ Green lane juniors wasn't happy about it. It was just another ordinary day – for once I was actually going to school, so I headed off as usual. Once in class none of the other children ever wondered where I'd been but half way through the lesson I was called for. My teacher at the time shouted out "Sandip – go to Miss Manner's office". Kids being kids, they all started to stare at me with that open mouthed wonder that only kids can do...

I was quite shocked too – why do I need to see her I kept asking myself. Once I got into her office, she closed the door and asked me why I was away from school so much. I don't think she was too happy with my answer – I simply didn't know why I was away. If my mum told me to stay at home then I did, it was quite simple really. I cannot remember what else she said to me but one thing I clearly remember is her telling me to "put my hands out". I did this and before I knew it, she pulled out a huge ruler, this thing was very long and after being told to keep still she raised it up high and hit my hands very hard with it at least 5 times.

The pain was unbearable, especially when you're young and the tears started. Looking back at this now it's amazing to think yet again that they could get away with doing such things. It never achieved anything at all anyway, it didn't stop my mum from telling me to stay at home but the one thing that did stick was the memory of it all. Yet again, that damn thing called money had yet again caused pain & anger in our lives. Anyway, it suddenly dawned on me that i've mentioned all my family but haven't really said much about them so here goes!

I may as well start with my dad - as the book described, I had lots of fun times with my dad but only until he hit my mum for the first time. My dad was always one of those quiet people, he never said much to any of us or to anyone who came around to visit. He always kept himself to himself and during the early years was always smiling and a bit of a joker. He was always neat & tidy, if there was something slightly out of place, he'd make sure it was put back properly and if he saw some dirt or anything on the floor/carpet, he's spot it and pick it up. My dad lost his mum & dad when he was quite young so it must have been hard for him growing up at that time. I sometimes wonder if this contributed to the way he turned out but all I know is that he rarely wanted to see his closest relations either.

His sister moved to Coventry after getting married and still lives there. When they used to get together, you'd think they weren't even friends, let alone brother & sister. All you would hear is a gentle hello from one to the other and that's it. When my parents got married, they moved to East Africa where they had farmland and presumably were farmers. Yes, I know, I should know all this I guess but does anyone know exactly what our parents did when they were married – I suspect not! When the political climate turned nasty in the early 1970's we were one of those families that were thrown out of the country and headed for the UK having lost everything we owned...

Since arriving in the UK, my dad has always, as far as I'm aware, been into engineering of some sort. He worked for many years at *Gimson's* which was an engineering firm on Vulcan road in the Highfields area of Leicester. He was a welder or something and on Saturday mornings (when working overtime), we (the kids that is) used to walk there and just say hello. It was very hot inside and the red hot glow from the steel would warm us up & light up our small faces. He was quite a short person, and this affected me too. Whilst growing up I was very conscious of how short I was too. I was so short that my sister (well I think it was my sister anyway) that started to call me "tich" which stuck through my life, and she still calls me that to this day – thanks sis! The good news for me is that I grew much taller than my dad so that's a relief!

My dad ate very little too, in the mornings he would have one cup of tea and that was it, no breakfast at all. When it was lunch time, he may have another cup of tea but again would probably not eat anything. This was why he was so slim – the only time he would eat was in the evening. Mind you, he wasn't too keen on vegetables and arguments would often kick off simply because my mum had cooked a vegetarian dish which my dad didn't like. It actually got to a stage where my dad started to cook his own food. Intoxicated to the maximum, he would come home after spending all the money in the local pub and start to cook sausages and added so much chilli powder to it that your mouth would burn for several hours after – I should know, I tried it...

Mum

It's quite hard trying to write about my mum, I have so many things I want to express and write down that it's one of those situations where you just don't know where to start. Inspirational – there you go, that's a good start, and this is the word that I would use to describe my mum. My mum is probably typical of most mums around the world – always happy to see you, always making sure you're ok, always asking if you're hungry and would always fuss over you. This is special, really special and in your mums' eyes you're always their little babies (no matter how old you are!). In our house hold my mum was much stricter than my dad by far. She tended to lay down the rules and I was scared of her at times but only because I knew I'd done something wrong and would be in trouble.

Mum visiting her parents (Surat, India).

She was a very sensible lady, always drilling into us that you need to study and do well and I could often sense that she felt she was letting us down during the early years – mum, you never let us down EVER, quite the contrary actually. The way she handled what we had been through so far, the way she protected us, the way she just got on with it was truly remarkable and has made me a much stronger person as a result. Star signs are a funny thing & something I've never taken seriously but the characteristics of star signs are quite interesting and my mum fits in with being a Virgo. With Virgo's you see, it's all about exaggeration and she used to exaggerate lots. In true Virgo style she was always neat and tidy (yes – something I've inherited!!) but my mum was always strict about one thing – *money*. Yes, here it is again that special word – money.

Her rule was simple, *"don't borrow money if you don't have to & don't buy something if you can't afford to pay it back"*. These simple rules have become permanently fixed in my brain and would change my financial status in my adult life – we'll return to this later. I mentioned she was neat and tidy, but I almost forgot one thing. She didn't like clutter at all, and anything left around too long would soon vanish. In my later years there was one occasion where I had a small pool table. I had wanted a pool table for many years and was terribly excited about getting one and when it finally arrived, I would be on it for hours. One day after getting home I noticed something was different in the room – the pool table was missing. Very strange but the mystery was soon solved – my mum decided on the spur of the moment to give it away to the son of one of her good friends. It wasn't his birthday or anything like that – he just saw it, liked it and my mum said "have it". Thanks mum.

Bena (my sister)

My sister, "Bena" to me, "Nalini" to her friends is the oldest of the kids. "Bena" is case you're wondering is Indian for 'sister'. To this day I've never called my sister by her real name, and I don't think she's ever called me by my real name. In fact, no-one in my family called me by my real name (it's a miracle that I still know my name!!). I'm closer to my sister than I am with either of my 2 brothers. I'm not sure why this is but I guess I'm always the 'little kid', the little brother. If she needs something done or needs to go anywhere, she'll always ring me up because she knows I'll do whatever I can to help her. Mind you, if I ever need to talk, I know I can speak to her so it just works between us...

Always happy to see you, my sister hasn't changed one bit and she's still the cheery person I've always known. Always up for a party my sister knows how to have a good time and loves it when everybody goes around there. Over the years she's had many parties at their house, and they've run well into the night and into the early hours. Many times, I've had to call it a day but she's partied on and I doubt if that will ever change. One thing that is super special about her is that she has freckles – nothing special about that I hear you say. Well, maybe if she was English or another nationality then I would agree but I've yet to see another Indian person that has freckles. You simply don't see them on other Indians.

She's worked very hard to get where she has; it's a just a shame she still can't park cars! (Sorry sis!!!). I still remember the day she started to work at Motor Ross which, many years ago, was a chain of motorway service stations. She'd go to work in the nasty, dark brown uniform and we'd often go to pick her up at the bus stop once the MotorRoss transport bus had dropped the employees off. She went to Moat girl's school which was off East Park Road, close to Spinney Hill Park. At college she studied A levels but didn't get the results she was expecting. Sorry to drag this up sister but in a funny kind of way I actually think this changed things for the better. After getting over the disappointment of this she decided she wanted a career in nursing and was accepted by Charles Frears nursing school (they used to accept anyone in those days… - only joking sis!!). She hasn't really looked back since then and went on to get diplomas in many skilled positions and needless to say she has worked had to get where she is so well done.

Vipul

Vipul or "VIP" to his friends is the second oldest of us kids. Over the years i've been quite close to him but to be honest perhaps not as close as I would have liked to have been. In the early years we used to mess about as most brothers do and we had plenty of time together – making 'dens' at home was a brotherly affair! He went to Moat boy's school and like Kiran, wasn't too interested in school and never went onto higher education. After working in my uncle's shop (London) for a while, he came back to Leicester and worked in various places including a shoe factory (where my mum also worked), a shoe distribution company and at one point moved to Wakefield for several years where he worked for Sainsbury's.

During the time he was in Wakefield there was a period where I never saw him for over 2 years. This was a troublesome time for him, he had major ups and downs and a nasty relationship break up hit him hard. I just think he needed to get away from it all and he certainly did that. I remember going to my sister's house where I saw him for the first time after 2 years as I said and it was quite surreal – it was almost like seeing an old school friend but this was my brother and apart from a few words and smiles the relationship was definitely not as close as it once was. Anyway, time moves on, and the main thing now is he is happy so good for you brother...

One thing about vip is that he is sci-fi mad. Give him a science fiction film and you could keep him quiet for hours – he absolutely loved them. Star Trek, Dr. Who, Battle of the planets (er, a cartoon!!) and the list goes on and on and on. In general though he *loves* watching films which is still true today – go round to his house and he has downloaded copies of loads of films. As a youngster I could always count on vip to give me a few pence here and there and he was extremely generous. When he used to give me pound coins my eyes lit up – a pound was big money in those days. A lot has happened over the years but we're still here and closer than we've ever been so it's all good. He has now focussed his efforts on a career in nursing so hope it goes well.

Kiran

In most families there is always at least one joker and in our family, it was Kiran. Always ready to unleash a witty line you're always guaranteed a laugh when he's around. Even to this day whenever you see him, he always has to say something that is guaranteed to make you smile - provided he's awake that is. The thing is Kiran loves his sleep; he could sleep for 12 hours, get up, have something to eat and then simply go back to bed as if he hadn't slept!! Whilst I went to Bridge Junior School, he went to Crown Hills Secondary. Following on from vip's footsteps, he wasn't that too bothered about education at all and did just enough to see him through each of the 5 years at this school. One thing he was very good at was making cakes. Many a times he would come home to Halstead Street with his brown cooking basket with a delicious cake – chocolate log was the best. His cooking habits didn't leave him either – to this day he's quite a chef in the kitchen (although his chicken still isn't as good as my sisters!).

Hang on a second; I forgot to mention that Vip is also a bit of a cook, so I guess that makes me the odd one out in the family. My cooking skills never quite took off, but I can make gravy & custard without lumps – does that count? Throughout the years he has worked in loads of different places and one of them, his YTS scheme is pottery making is still one that I use to this day to take the piss out of him. You see in the Thatcher prime ministerial days (Kiran was a strong conservative voter); he decided to embark on a **Y**outh **T**raining **S**cheme which was to help youngsters get some qualifications. Each day he would make his way near Narborough Road where the training centre was & get stuck into clay and baking clay casts and all the other stuff you do in a pottery centre.

It would only be a matter of time before he'd get fed up with all this and it wasn't long before his pottery days were behind him. Other ventures since then included working in a general store shop in Syston, selling 'Kirby' hoovers – you know the ones that cost about £1000, and nobody ever buys! He had various spells fitting double glazed windows as well as working in a shoe distribution company for several years. Whilst I was growing up, I remember Kiran being quite good at art stuff and drawings. So much so that one day when I got some homework which required drawing a coal miner and his tools (it was geography homework...), Kiran helped me out and drew a fantastic picture and I went back to school thinking my teacher would be well impressed. Amazingly, when the homework was marked, I got the lowest mark with a comment "could do better". Thanks mate – "could do better" – the teacher didn't have a clue. I never told Kiran about this as I didn't want to hurt his feelings.

Apart from the violent outbursts from my dad, life at Halstead Street was fun at times & it was the kids that made it so. Between Halstead Street and Ashfordby Street there was an alley way that ran between the gardens of the houses. This was quite typical of houses in those days, and you don't often hear of 'alley ways' anymore. If any of you reading this have seen the film 'East Is East' then you'll probably remember the street scene where the kids are playing outside – this was *very* similar to Halstead Street. This gap between the houses was always a hive of activity. The kids would run around in the evenings and weekends playing 'tick' and riding their bikes/trikes and anything else they could get their hands on.

One family there had several 'mini' racing cars, and they would let me play on it for hours on end. It was purple and when you got inside your feet would rest on the pedals which were used to propel the racing car forward. I used to drive like mad along the alley and often had mock crashes. Another family who lived further up Halstead Street used to have a huge truck parked outside their house. Sharon, the girl who lived there, had a father who worked for 'Frisby Shoes' so each evening this truck would come down the road and almost take up the entire road. Nothing special in this I hear you say but we loved this truck. We'd play for hours on end running around it, climbing underneath it. The stereotypical smell of old trucks was very clear and it's one of those smells that never leaves you. Just thinking about it now puts a huge smile on my face.

Sharon's dad actually took us out in the truck once too. We had to be lifted up (we were so tiny, our little legs wouldn't even reach the first step & us kids could hardly contain our excitement. With a turn of the key and a big growl from the engine we were soon kings of the road. We'd wave at the other kids with a "we're in the truck and you're not" style which always upset them. Sharon had several sisters and for some bizarre reason she loved eating salt. She would get the salt and pour it into her hands and lick it like it was a sweet or something. As kids do, I tried it; only to be violently sick *in her house* which didn't go down well with her parents. Since that day I have never added salt to my food at all and often wonder whether it was this incident that put me off!

Nowadays it can be difficult to find a safe place for kids to play but in those days, it was unbelievably safe – it's just a shame things are so much different now. Close to where we lived there was a kind of walkway that joined up many of the streets. In fact, this walk way started out from London Street, ran through Baggrave Street, crossed over Ashfordby Street, onto Halstead Street and then up the steep hill to Prospect Road. If you kept on walking, you'd end up back on Mere Road. The kids could safely and easily navigate the roads and streets without fear from anyone or anything and we all definitely made the most of it. The steep hill had a little shop at the bottom of it which became known as the 'downhill shop'; it was a shop, and it was down the hill so the name was accurate! In winter time, when the heavy snow would fall, we used to try desperately to walk up the hill and would have lots of fun sliding around. As you walk up this hill, there were little alley ways that led to the back gardens of adjoining houses and lots of various nook & crannies along the way which we'd use when playing hide 'n' seek.

Right at the top of Halstead Street was another shop but this one sold everything including alcohol. My dad, never one for paying for anything, used to scribble some notes on a sheet of paper and would send me off to this shop. Once I was in there, I handed over the note to the shop keeper. The man, an Indian, had very dark skin and I'm certain that whenever he saw me, he always gave just a hint of a smile even though he was probably annoyed at handing over stuff without getting paid for it!

The shop keeper, who incidentally, looked like someone from thunderbirds, handed over the beer, which usually consisted of 4 cans of Skol together with a packet of cigarettes. He would then take out a small notepad and presumably scribble down what my dad owed him. I have no idea when my dad used to clear his debts, but this was my dad – never pay for anything unless you have to.

The one bonus on going to this shop was that my dad would ask me what I wanted. The answer was simply – I *always* asked for a packet of 'Poppets'. These poppets were small pieces of chocolate in a rectangular shaped red packet, and I loved eating them. Once outside the shop with my beer, cigarettes and chocolate I'd race down the road as fast as possible so that I could get home and tuck into my sweets. Can you imagine a 7/8 year old going into an off-licence today and buying alcohol and cigarettes?

One of my closest friends I had in that street was 'Ketan Kava'. He lived half way up Halstead Street, just past the 'downhill' shop where the houses were much bigger. In fact, they had a basement and 3 stories so they were much bigger. The basement was accessed via a winding staircase where from the pavement; you could see food being cooked. I spent many days at this house and knew Ketan, his sisters, cousins and the rest of the family quite well. His mum was very kind and I spent many hours playing & eating there too. I'd see Ketan at Bridge Junior School too as most of the kids that played around that area went to the same school. Sadly, after leaving junior school his family moved to a different part of Leicester and my close friend had gone. We didn't have a car, I didn't have a bike and I guess more importantly I didn't even have his address I had no chance of finding him but amazingly after almost 29 years I spotted him whilst out shopping.

At first, I didn't know whether he'd recognise me but as we got closer and closer, his look said it all - he *knew* who I was. As I lifted my right arm to offer a handshake all I could say was "Ketan..." hoping that he'd remember my name. It was clear he had a pretty good memory too as he said "How are you Sandip?" We both stood there forgetting about the sub-zero wind chill factor - it was winter and freezing. We talked about the old times and laughed out loud as we remembered some of the things we got up to. We shared our life stories, were we married? Did we have kids? Where do we live? Along with other quick fire questions as we tried to cram 29 lost years into 15 minutes. It was a chance meeting but a great one at that but my determination not to let 29 years pass by before meeting up again took a nasty turn because later that day I realised that his mobile number that I hurriedly punched into my phone were entered wrong and each time I tried to SMS him or call, I got "message sending failed" or a dead tone.

Thankfully i'm still in contact with many of my friends, most of which i've known all my life. For me anyway, it's been incredible watching us all grow up as we ventured up the school hierarchy including nursery, infants, junior, secondary and sixth form schools/

colleges - quite a feat i'd say! We've been through the good and bad times together, consoled when things are bad and laughed when things were good but above all; the sheer fact that we still meet up and keep in touch is a phenomenal achievement even though to others it may seem like nothing special. One evening whilst we played as usual, the whole area turned into a scene of flashing lights and blaring of police sirens could be heard.

Close to the downhill shop lived another family whose kids also went to bridge junior school – I knew the kids well. It turned out that one of the younger brothers decided to jump out the window, but this was no ordinary window – it happened to be the one right at the top of their house and they had one of the bigger houses. Luckily, although he was injured quite badly, he made a full recovery. Ironically, almost 30 years later I bumped into one of the brothers at Rishi's school and we both instantly recognised each other. Moments like that are very surreal, it's like seeing your life in fast forward, one minute we were little kids and here both of us were – picking up our children from school...

A few houses up the road lived another kid – a kid called 'Kevin' who had a younger brother. I never quite worked out what nationality he was, he looked English but with a tan if that makes sense. They actually moved into their house after we did so they were the 'new' family and at the start no-one played with the kids. Being the kid, I was (& the adult I am now – isn't that right Sunita?), I made the effort and got speaking to them. He had a bike, something that not many kids had in those days, and after playing together for a while he would take me for 'kroggies' or 'croggy'. I don't actually think this is a word – well it can't be, as I sit here and type this, good old Microsoft Word is underlining these words in red as they are not recognised. You don't hear this word often; perhaps it's just a Leicester thing?

A 'croggy' is when 2 of you get onto a bicycle – one pedals and steers whilst the other sits of the seats – almost like being chauffeured. It's not bad for the person being croggied but it can get quite tiring for the person pedalling. One particular day we went for a real adventure. As we headed out of Halstead Street and onto Green Lane Road, I was already out of my usual territory but decided to rebel on this day. Before I knew it cars were hurtling past us at great speed. Buses would roar past, and we'd get strange looks from passengers standing at the back of the buses. Little did I know that we were now on Uppingham Road – a very busy road in Leicester. Kevin was getting quite tired and soon we were in Humberstone Park.

As we continued to cycle into the park, Kevin got to a woody area and then stopped. We then climbed through the trees and undergrowth and appeared on top of an embankment which had a railway track. This was very strange, you usually associate train tracks with train stations but here were in the middle of a park with a track running through it. It may not sound that exciting now but as a youngster it was *truly* great and it's the little things like this that have remained lodged in my mind since I was a youngster. Nobody ever asked where I'd been that day, so it remained one of those great little secret's kids love to keep to themselves. After we moved out of Halstead Street, I never saw Kevin or his little brother ever again; I often wonder what he's up to now. In the late 70's there were many excellent records that were released but I clearly remember my sister singing away to one particular track. It was "yes sir, I can boogie" by a group called Baccara - she used to sing away at this for ages. It's quite strange how music can influence your life or relate to a particular part in your life, but this was definitely one of them...

For many years I watched as other kids cycled around on their bikes thoroughly enjoying themselves and I really wished I had one of my own. I used to have a tricycle but that was destroyed by my brother, and I really wanted a new one so I could tear around the streets with the other kids. About 10 minutes' walk from where we lived was a bicycle shop called 'Bones' – it was one of those original, and now rare, cycle shops that was kitted out in full Raleigh advertising all over the glass and windows. On the frequent trips to the shops with my mum & dad we used to walk past this shop where you'd see all the shiny new bikes glittering in the sun. Often, we'd go inside and the first thing to hit you would be the smell of new bikes, and in particular, the smell of new rubber. In those days we had the Raleigh Budgie, Tomahawk, Grifter and the infamous Chopper. One of the kids on the street had a chopper; a fantastic bike. It was very comfortable and had a gear lever just in front of the seat and nowadays you'll be lucky to even find one and if you did, you'd have to part with several thousand pounds to get your hand on it!

For weeks and probably months I asked if I could get a new bike and when I was almost at the point of giving up my dad said 'ok', and we headed off to the bike shop. As soon as we entered the shop my eyes were fixed onto a green bike & I knew that this was the one, it had my name on it and no-one else could have it. My dad left a £15.00 deposit and I clearly remember the shop assistant telling us it would be delivered on Tuesday. The feeling of knowing I was to get my own bike cannot be expressed in words. I was so happy that it made me forget about the violent outbursts for just a short period of time. When we got home, I remember talking about it non-stop and probably boring everyone to death; including the kids in the street. From that point onwards, I willed the days to pass quickly, each day seem to drag on and I was forever asking what day it was. On the morning the bike was meant to be delivered I remember asking my dad about it. He said it would be here after school and I was so happy that day and when school ended, I raced home as fast as my little legs could take me.

Once I was inside the house, I was fixed to the front room window. It was Christmas time, it was cold & frosty outside, a real winter's day and I sat on the pile of red & black cushions so that I could see out of the window. It was very quiet and as I saw the lights vehicles turning into our street my eyes lit up expecting it to be the delivery van. Cars came and went, vans came and went but they all drove straight past our house. Despite that I continued to look and listen eagerly for the delivery van but still nothing. I ate my dinner as fast as I could knowing full well that i'd have to get into bed soon. I desperately looked out of the window, hoping the next van would stop outside our house.

Where was the delivery? Perhaps they were lost? These were just some of the questions I was asking myself and my dad for that matter. My dad, incidentally, just sat there looking quite concerned that the bike had not arrived. In those days we had no house phone so we couldn't call anyone, so it was just a case of sit and wait. After several reassurances from my dad that it would arrive, it was just too late, and I had to go to bed.

Well, the bike *never* arrived, and I learnt a lesson that has remained with me all my life and that is to *never* promise anything unless you intend to keep it. What happened with my bike? My dad, despite knowing how much I wanted the bike, despite seeing my eyes light up, despite watching me sit there for hours waiting for it to arrive, despite lying to me and telling me it would arrive, broke his promise. The day after we left the deposit for the bike, my dad went back to the shop, cancelled the order and took back the £15.00 he left as the deposit. He then went out drinking, knowing full well, that he was using money that was for my bike. No doubt he came home drunk that day, but the scars of that day have stuck with me throughout my life.

So much so in fact that to this day I would never, ever promise anyone anything unless I could keep it. If there was a slight chance, I could not keep it then I would simply not promise it in the first place. I know full well the consequences of not seeing a promise through and to this day I have stuck to this commitment, and it has made me a better person for it. Whilst at this house I never did get a bike; the enthusiasm I had for wanting one soon dwindled away anyway and things just returned to 'normal' whatever that means.

One of the things we did as kids was to go 'brook walking' – probably something most people wouldn't understand. Brook walking was basically following a stream as it meandered through the city and the stream that ran through Spinney Hill Park actually worked its way through many roads close to where we lived. On one particular day, Kiran decided to go on his own adventure but dragged me along too. As we approached the green, metal fence that spanned the stream in London Street, I looked down in horror. How on earth was I meant to get down there? As the water rushed past, it must have been a good 9' drop to get to the bottom and the only way to get there was to climb over precariously, hang on, jump onto the side retaining wall and then jump down a distance of about 5 foot.

Kiran, being taller than me, was soon hanging over like an experienced professional and before I knew it was waiting for me to do the same. As I climbed over, everything was going well and by the time I was on the *inside* of the fence it seemed pretty easy. As I turned however, my foot slipped on the moss, and as I fell towards the ground, I knew this would hurt. I hit the concrete floor and my chin took most of the impact, split open and the blood gushed out. Before I knew it there was blood everywhere and Kiran was panicking; how would he explain this to my mum? As I fought back the tears, we somehow managed to get back up onto the road and slowly made our way home. All I could think of was how angry my mum would be, and she was furious. As soon as we stepped into the house it all kicked off. Kiran was told off with the usual 'should have known better routine' whilst I'm pretty certain I was given harsh words too – hang on a second, wasn't I the victim here?

To this day I have 2 scars that provide a timely reminder of our adventure that day. I have a scar on my chin where the skin has kind of fixed itself but where nothing ever grows, and I have a scar on my left eye brow which actually looks as if it's been shaved or something. Despite this accident, brook walking was fantastic fun. When we eventually jumped down into the brook, we could go in 2 directions. The first was quite boring and would take you underneath St. Saviours Road and back into Spinney Hill Park.

If you actually followed the stream, it would pass through several roads & streets and finally, after running past several scary dogs, would change from being a stream to a wide expanse of water where you could go no further.

If, however, you walked the other way, you would walk past the rear gardens of many houses as well as the rear of many businesses. One of the tunnels was extremely dark, very long and slippery too. As we ducked down and entered into the bridge, the excitement was immense; we'd look behind us and slowly watch the light dwindle away until all we could see was a glimmer of light at the other side of the tunnel. We'd have to carefully avoid the slimy growth of plants that were fuelled by the discharge of waste water from these factories. If we managed to avoid slipping, falling in and bumping our heads into the metal structure above us, we had survived. If you were brave and continued along the path, you would walk up to the bridge that crossed Green Lane Road and after that the streams would kind of merge together and create a mini pool of water. At that point there was a concrete slope and if you'd walked up it you'd end up near Rossa's ice cream factory which is on Cottesmore Road. On the many occasions where we just kept going, we'd be walking parallel to the rear gardens on Harewood Street and eventually after about an hour's walk you'd end up underneath Catherine Street and towards the Melton Road area of Leicester.

Brook walking, in the rain, was a totally different experience. Following heavy rain, the brook walking turned dangerous – the gentle pace of the stream turned into a vicious torrent of water that engulfed all the walking area & you'd be mad to go down there and luckily for me, we never did. Oh well, as you can see life in & around Halstead Street was a daily adventure. A few doors away from our rented house lived a girl called Bernadette. Hearing that name quite now is quite strange – it is, after all, quite a rare name hardly heard of these days. I guess you could associate that name with a girl who owes you money (get it – burn a debt?) – Oh well, never mind! This girl had a big dog who terrorised all the kids; it ran after anything; kids, adults and even cars. Whenever we saw the dog in the distance, we'd used to tease it which would make it made. It soon started racing towards us and we used to see who could wait the longest before legging it into their house!

As the dog stood outside our house, we'd make faces at it from the safety of our home but thinking about it now I wonder if this crazy dog was made crazy by us kids! By the way 'legging it' means run quickly (just in case there are some of you reading this wondering what on earth that meant!). After many weeks & months of teasing and chasing, it became a normal thing to do for the kids – not sure that Bernadette liked this. After a few days of not seeing the dog, we began to wonder what had happened to it; for some reason I'm certain the dog had been killed – with an iron! Whether this is true or not I couldn't say but all I know is that without that dog, things just weren't the same...

I never played in our garden at this house & come to think of it neither did my brothers or sisters. It was a horrible place, weeds everywhere and huge snails crawled around the place. In the mornings when I used to look out the 'middle room' window, I used to see the slimy trail that snails leave behind – they actually look quite neat & I often picked a trail and followed it until I found the snail.

The garden was tiny but the one strange thing about it was that it didn't have a wall at the end of the garden – it has a massive rock or what appeared to be a rock. It was like a huge cliff edge & the reason for this is that the houses that backed onto the rear of Halstead Street were built on ground about 50 feet higher than those below (ok, ok it may not *actually* be 50 feet but it looked that high to a small kid!). In the summer months, huge plants used to grow downwards and swing around – they had blackberries on them which we used to pull off & eat.

I think they were blackberries anyway but you don't really see much of these plants anymore, do you? Initially the berries would start off green and slowly change to red. If you were brave, you'd eat them but they'd be pretty sour. The best ones were black – these were the really tasty ones...In our house it was rare that us kids fought with each other; sadly, it was my dad that did all the fighting. On one rare occasion my sister and Vipul were arguing about something upstairs. I remember it getting quite heated and at the end of it my sister poured milk over VIPs' head. I'm certain it was milk – I have a clear memory of seeing the white stuff dripping down his head. He wasn't pleased about that, but he didn't do anything – it *was* my sister after all but it was well funny!

Most Indian families have lots of cousins; in fact, even if you met someone for the first time, they tend to become your cousins, aunties & uncles. Some of these cousins lived in London and at various times of the year they came to Leicester to visit – we couldn't visit them as we had no car. When I say cousins I mean Paresh, Jay, Chetan, Chandresh, Divya & Daksha as well as their parents. Once they were in Leicester, the fun began – the parents would sit downstairs to catch up on what was happening whilst the kids – lots of kids now, would run upstairs and do what all kids do – cause chaos! We used to all go outside into the street and start to mingle with our other friends and before long all the kids knew our 'cousins' and we were all playing together as if everyone had known each other for years. No-one cared who you were, we just loved playing and playing we did.

Remember the downhill shop? We got to know them pretty well too and one lasting memory I have of this shop is sherbet. The shop had so many varieties of sherbet it was unreal. Daksha loved sherbet and we used to take our pennies into the shop and stock up on the stuff. For a few pence the shopkeeper would hand over a white bag full of it and we'd all gobble it down quickly. Every time someone mentions sherbet it makes me think of Daksha straight away. After a hard day playing outside, we'd all come in and start the dinner process – the kids would get fed first and would head upstairs to the bedrooms where after several further hours of playing, we'd crash out. I could never remember who slept where but it didn't matter; there was room for everyone – just!

As we all lay down in our beds, we used to talk for ages but as time went on and we got more & more tired and slowly, one by one, each of us nodded off. Mind you I sometimes wonder how we managed to sleep at all. The parents, downstairs, made enough noise and would stay up late into the night and into the early hours. Often, one of us would wake up and once a kid is up you often look around you in case anyone else was awake too. Once this happened, it started a 'Chinese whisper' type of effect – one of us would nudge another kid who in turn would nudge someone else. Within a few minutes, we'd all be awake all staring at each other, half-awake with none of us really knowing what we were doing. During times like these, there was only one thing we could do – eat!

One by one we'd creep downstairs (if we couldn't hear any voices downstairs then we didn't want to wake the adults!) & then make our way to the kitchen. Before long we'd grab anything we liked the look of and start munching it down. It wasn't *exactly* curry munching per say, but you get the idea & this cycle of creeping downstairs for a midnight feast happened each time our cousins came to visit. Another big part of our lives at the time was the good old fairground. When our cousins came down, the fair always seemed to be in town & for us it was great because the fair was in Spinney Hill Park – a short walk away. We'd watch eagerly as they set everything up and be amazed (well I was amazed anyway) at how these trucks would pull up and transform into a fairground ride in a matter of hours...

When the fair opened, we were in our element, we had a small amount of money in our pockets and to this day the Waltzer *has* to be one of the most exciting, yet simplest fairground rides of all time. We'd get into several waltzers and pull the guard rail towards us. As the Waltzer controller slowly started to spin us around, he would speak into the mic and pick out any empty seats which was a rare thing. Whilst this was happening, the other fairground staff would come around and collect the money and before long we were all set. As the tempo increased you'd hear 'hold on tight' booming out of the speakers and before long we'd be spinning round & round & around. Often, the Waltzer wouldn't do much and they'd hardly been any spinning happening but the staff would soon see this and with a flick of their hand the Waltzer would enter Mach 1 – we span so fast that everything was just a blur.

The force was immense and if anyone reading this has been on a Waltzer you'd agree – it was virtually impossible to move your neck forwards. Sometimes the staff would stop you spinning and then leave you there not knowing what to expect next. They never said anything – just smiled at the kids and with that special flick of their hand would send us hurtling in the opposite direction. As the waltzers started to slow down, the 'wait for the ride to stop' would be heard over and over again and when it finally came to a complete halt, you'd have to try to get out of your seat whilst your head was still spinning around and round. Finally, we'd get out and stagger down the stairs passing the other kids desperate to get onto the rides.

Fairgrounds in those days were special; they had a special 'feel' to them and it was like having your own mini city right on your door step. If you stopped for a minute to look around you'd see happy faces, flashing lights, screams of kids (& adults) enjoying themselves, the smoke from the trucks as their generators worked harder & harder & the smell of burgers and candy floss would fill the air. This was a happy place to be and some of fondest memories of my childhood were spent here. When my cousins came to stay it was generally for a weekend so we'd make the most of it and if the fair was on, we'd come as often as we could. Sometimes my cousins would arrive and the fair would be packing up the next day. This was a *good* day; not because the fair was leaving, but because if the fair was packing up then we'd be able to scrounge round and pick up all the loose change that people had dropped whilst walking around or whilst on rides. Trust me, we used to get lots of money on some days and it was straight to the downhill shop after that to spend our (or somebody else's) hard earned money!

One day we (mainly the boys), were getting quite bored so we all headed off to Abbey Park which is one of the main parks towards the city centre of Leicester. It's a huge place with the river running through it, a mini golf area, boating lake, band stand, pavilion and a tea / cake shop. We used to walk there and get up to lots of mischief along the way. Just before we walked through the main gates we'd walk past the bus garage which was directly opposite the park. As the youngest of all the kids, I'd stare in amazement at the cream coloured buses. They would all be parked neatly row by row and the smell of diesel would drift past you. Abbey Park actually had a greenhouse; this was pretty special in those days and it was a massive place. Inside it had all kinds of tropical plants that stretched as high as the greenhouse roof itself & it was extremely warm inside. I guess this is why the bananas grew so well inside!

In the middle of the green house was a huge pond with all kinds of fish. To this day I have no idea what made us do it but all I know is we went home that day with a huge fish kicking and splashing around in a bucket that we somehow found somewhere. I can remember it clearly - it must have been close to 12" long but why on earth did we steal it? I say 'we' but I shouldn't. I had no part in this theft at all and when we got the fish home we headed straight for the nasty outside shower where it flapped around for a bit and I have no recollection of what happened after that. It was a cruel, inevitable end for a fish that should never have been stolen in the first place. I often think about this and still cannot remember who or why we (they I mean!) decided to steal it. Several years after that, the greenhouse closed down which was quite sad – nothing to do with us – honest!

My 2 brothers decided that they needed to earn some money and got themselves a paper round. They would walk up the newsagent on Green Lane Road (a few doors away from 'Bones' cycles – you know, the one where my virtual bike was ordered from) & pick up the bag of newspapers. The bag looked huge and i'm sure it weighed lots too. I can't remember if they had a paper round each or they shared one but when it was close to Christmas I loved it. We'd breathe out and watch our breath evaporate into the chilly night sky whilst the traffic hurried past the very busy road. At Christmas time and with the weather very cold, households became very generous and we had a neat trick up our sleeves. Rather than posting the newspaper through the door as we'd usually do, we would *knock* on the door and then wait and wait and wait. Often nobody would arrive for several minutes but we stood fast.

As long as we could see any sign of someone being in, we would stand there until someone opened the door – this was business after all. As the door opened, they'd see a small young boy who was cold, carrying a huge bag of newspapers and they fell for it. As I handed over the newspaper (I was more financially viable than my 2 brothers you see), the person would say 'just a minute' and then head inside). Before long they would come back to the front door with some money in their hands and would then hand it over to us. After delivering about 50-60 newspapers in this way our pockets were soon bulging and we were in the money! In those days you were meant to take all the money back to the newsagent where it would be split equally between the other paper boys & girls – it was fair after all. When the last paper was delivered we headed back to the shop and handed over a fraction of the money we received & the shop keeper would then share this between us again. The shop keeper never knew that most of the money was still hidden in our pockets; we'd done all the hard work after all...The money we earnt lasted for weeks and weeks and during that period I'd never seen that much money in change ever before.

Since we didn't have a car, it was rare for us to go anywhere further than a few miles. I mean when you have to walk or catch the bus you're quite limited (in those days at least) on where you can go. One day our cousins, fortunate enough to have a car, drove up to Leicester and asked us to go back with them. Ordinarily this would be fine but there were 3 families and 1 car; a blue Hillman Hunter estate if my memory serves me right. How we managed it I have no idea but somehow we got to London. I remember all the kids squashing in – there was no consideration for seat belts & being Indian it gave us the go ahead to squeeze as many people as possible we could in the car - there must have been at least 10-12 inside! Both sets of cousins used to live in Wembley at this time, I think it was a place called First Avenue. It was a Cul De Sac; Paresh's house was in the middle of the street whilst Chetan's was right at the top. It was a small, narrow street & just like in Halstead Street, the kids in all the houses would all come out to play. I remember Paresh's house, their garden in fact, quite well. They had a large pond with many frogs and Clams as well as a swing and a cherry tree. A short walk away was a park and around the corner there was a mirror factory and we would sometimes head there and come back loaded with small mirrors simply because we got them free!

I also recall travelling on a train via a station at the top of the road, I can't remember where we went but I certainly remember it being there. Several years after this time, both our cousins bought shops - another stereo typical thing for Indians to do. The shops were both in Buckinghamshire; one was in a place called Iver Heath whilst the other was in Denham. Paresh, Divya & Jay lived in Iver Heath which was close to Pinewood Studios – a famous film studio in the UK. They would often tell us that they'd see famous people walking by & one day, despite being very young, I witnessed this myself. As I stood outside their shop one summer, Michael Fish, the UK weatherman, casually walked by – he obviously lived close by.

Close to the shop there was a big park (Black Park) where part of the Superman set of films was made – it was the scene where he freezes a lake or something. Chetan, Chandresh (Chunk) & Daksha, lived at their shop in Denham and on one occasion, one of the old Dr. Who's popped into the shop to buy a newspaper. During the summer we'd often walk down the side roads behind the shop.

As the road twisted & turned, it would eventually end up close to a small stream that ran through the village. We'd see little trout swimming around & would often walk around in our bare feet until we realised that there were Crayfish in there too which gave a painful pinch!

Although very young, all the boys loved fishing and all of them except us (my brothers & I that is) had fishing gear. Our uncles would make us work in the shop and only let us go fishing if the work had been done. Frantically, we'd get the stock out the back and fill the shelves with anything that looked as if it was running low. This wasn't the end of it either; often we'd have to do the paper rounds which, in the summer, would leave us hot & very bothered! However as soon as the work was done, we'd grab the food we'd packed together, grab the fishing rods, bait, chairs and all the rest of the bits you need to have a good fishing day & off we went. Around Denham & Iver Heath there were lots of great places to fish and some of the lakes had the biggest fish I'd ever seen – predominantly 'Carp'. These fish can grow to an amazing size and as we walked down towards the fishing lakes you'd see them as big black objects coming to the top for a breath of air.

Jay, being the eldest one out of the boys, would order us around and all the little kids would end up carrying most of the heavy stuff. Once we were there it was great fun, in the summer it was warm, we had lots of food & drink and we just lazed around catching the occasional fish and watching in amazement as others caught huge fish. In the early 80s', the BMX craze started and the Raleigh Burner was one of the most common BMX bikes you'd see around. This wasn't the case in Iver Heath though. Paresh had just returned back from living in America and shortly after they bought the Iver shop he got his own BMX – a Redline. It was one of the best bikes around and had pedal back brakes – yes, to slow down you simply pedalled back. I think it was red but it was extremely cool. It was so cool that someone decided they'd like one too and promptly stole Paresh's bike but if I remember correctly it wasn't long before the word spread and he got it back.

When we weren't fishing we would just hang around as kids do and often wander into the small lanes that encircled Iver.

Bizarrely the others (i'd just like to make it clear it wasn't me!), had a sudden interest in cat's eyes and I don't mean the feline type; it was the cat's eyes that you find in the road. Armed with screw drivers we would wait until the cars had gone and would prise out the cat's eyes as quickly as we could. Often it would take several minutes before we could them out as cars would approach and we'd have to run back to the pavement and act as if nothing was going on. You can just imagine those drivers at night time – wandering where the cat's eyes had disappeared to! We did this for many weeks and ended up with a huge collection of small round objects which didn't seem that exciting once they had been forced out of the road. As we shone small torches on them we could see what colour they would light up but most of them were white anyway so it was hard to tell if they worked since the torch gave off a white light too! When we thought about this a little more, we figured out the roads approaching other roads often had different coloured cats' eyes so we went for those too – these were the real prized ones!

Cousins with a shop? For a very young child this was like a dream come true and trust me that summer I made sure I made the most of it. My aunties, generous as ever, always gave me sweets and chocolates after a hard day's work! Some of the sweets you could get in those days were awesome; Spangles, Space Dust - small pieces of rock that you put in your mouth which then fizz uncontrollably! We'd rush to open the packet, tilt our heads back and shove a whole load of them into our mouth and then wait.... in a few moments, the fizzing and loud popping started - wicked!! Then there were "Spangles" - the name of a sweet that i've never forgotten about. Small square sweets wrapped in a small tube which had a truly unique flavour.

Despite hours of searching, I still cannot find anywhere that makes these fabulous retro sweets. Finally, before I move on (I could go on about these sweets forever...), does anyone remember the famous fish and chips crisps? If I remember correctly, they were savoury snacks that had plenty of vinegar in them in a black and white bag. I'm certain most shops sold them and they were a favourite in the swimming pool vending machines. Finally (I mean it this time), remember Salt and Vinegar flavour puffs? I think they were a blue coloured bag with strips of potato crisps in them, with lots of vinegar too!

When we wanted to go fishing, we'd usually have to walk there and back but sometimes, when we got lucky, we'd get a lift. My uncle had just bought himself a brand new Datsun 180B; it was an orange coloured estate and was yet another thing that Indians do – buy Datsun cars! To this day I maintain that if uncle had set foot on a race track he could have made it big. The thing was you see he *loved* driving fast and I mean so fast that the kids, and probably the adults, were petrified at the thought of getting into the car with him. As we got inside the car, it had that great 'new car' scent and I remember the black interior and the seats being extremely comfortable.

No sooner had we shut the doors, we were on our way and hanging on for the ride of our lives. At traffic lights, we always seemed to be next to some boy racer who gave us that 'paki's in the Datsun' look and you just knew he would try to beat us off the line. This smugness was short lived because as the lights changed from red to amber, uncle was on a mission. With the eagerness of a racing driver the 1.8 litre Datsun engine growled and the boy racer was left standing at the lights. I would often look behind and see their faces of astonishment as the Datsun left them behind. The best rides we had were when we actually sat in the back end of the car so we were looking out the back as we drove on. Throughout the summer we had many of these occasions and I cannot remember *anyone* ever beating my uncle either from standstill or on the motorway. The Datsun was in those days a super car but only my uncle could drive it like that and the best thing about it is that he loved it too – he never said it but you knew he got great satisfaction from racing around.

One summer's day it was decided that we'd head off to Woburn Zoo for the day. This time I was in my other uncle's car (Chetan & Chunk's dad) whilst 'racer' uncle was following behind us. Everything was normal until we hit some traffic and we were at a standstill. Whilst I sat in the BMW, hardly able to see out of the window, my uncle suddenly shouted to us to 'hold on'. He then said that we about to have a crash which I found quite bizarre as we weren't even moving. Just as he stopped speaking there was a huge jolt forward and the sound of glass smashing. In a matter of seconds, it all went quiet and one by one we started to get out of the car. Suddenly it became clear what had happened. My uncle, in a bid to catch up with us had really put his foot down and was racing behind us in the Datsun.

Unfortunately for him (& the car) he didn't notice that the traffic had come to a halt until the last minute at which point he had slammed on the brakes. Without the aid of ABS braking systems, the car slid around and the inevitable happened – he had crashed into the back of us. Thankfully, nobody was injured and Divya (sitting in the Datsun) had quickly put on her seat belt moments before it crashed which probably saved her from major injuries. Sadly, the Datsun was a wreck, there were huge skid marks along the road, the radiator was smashed and water was leaking out. Ironically, it was the BMW that towed the Datsun back to Iver Heath that day so we never made it to Woburn Abbey. It was the end of the road for the Datsun; there was too much damage for it to be repaired but the BMW was repaired several weeks later...

Back in Leicester & back in school after the summer holidays, why is it that teachers always ask what we did during the summer? Whilst the other kids in my class @ Bridge Junior were writing about playing outside, I had to be careful. If I had written about stealing fish from green houses, stealing cat's eyes from country lanes and enjoying myself as my uncle had continuous road rage, this probably wouldn't have gone down too well! Luckily for me, I could spell my name. One of my friends regularly spelt his name as 'Brain'. A simple typo with the 'a' & 'I' would transform his *real* name from Brian to a part of the body and we used to be in hysterics whenever he did this. Brian lived so close to the school that if you walked out using the rear entrance he would be in his house within 10 seconds of leaving the school gate.

On one particular day, I was walking along St. Saviours Road with my sister and about to turn right into Ashfordby Street. As we did my sister told me to 'wait here a minute'. By this time we were a little way into Ashfordby Street and I was standing by an entrance to a factory set between 2 houses. Being the younger kid, I did what my sister asked but after a few minutes of kicking stones around was getting quite bored. My sister seemed to head in the direction of the factory and being curious I looked inside the factory drive way but couldn't see anything. Not seeing her made me panic a little; I was only young and felt very alone so I started to walk inside the drive.

I had only walked a few steps and around the corner was my sister kissing someone. I froze, not knowing what was going on or what to do. Should I walk back? Should I say something? What were they actually doing? In the end it was clear my sister had seen me so I hurried back to the road and waited there. A few minutes later she came back with a worried look on her face and promptly to me "not to say anything to mum". The fact that she asked me *not* to tell mum told me that she had done something wrong so this was my turn to call the shots. After asking for various things from the shop, I agreed to keep quiet but only if I got 5p and 2 bubbly gums in return!

The deal was done, 5p was a huge amount of money; I could buy 4 'mojo' sweets for 1p – I was rich! I never did tell my mum what I saw that day and the bizarre thing is her boyfriend took me for rides in his car after that. He had a new Ford Cortina – not many people had cars in those days so going for a cruise was a real treat. A few doors away from where my sister bribed me lived a friend of mine called Melvin McCool. He was great fun to be with and lived in a big, terraced house with 3 floors to it. He had an older sister, a dad that never smiled and a mum who looked so old that I thought it was his grandmother – that didn't go down too well...

There were times when I seemed to spend all my time there. I think this was because his dad had a huge railway set with real steam and everything – something I'd never seen before. Every time i'd be round there, his mum used to give me a plate of chocolate biscuits which I'd finish each time – quite rude by today's standards but they were nice! His dad also had a green Reliant Robin car and he used to take us for rides in that too – I remember it being very quick for such a small car. I'm not actually sure what happened to him after that. Once we left Halstead Street I never saw him again...

Apart from the 'poppet' chocolates I would get in return for going to the shop for my dad, we never really ate chocolates. It wasn't something my parents would buy from the shop which looking back now I fully understand. My dad simply wanted to get drunk whilst my mum was trying to (understandably) save money and watch every penny. One of my dad's friends, however, used to always give me a packet of Opal fruits whenever he would see me playing outside. He was kind, gentle man but spoke very little. He was quite dark skinned and was always smoking, wore one of those blue jackets that had diamond shapes on it – it reminds me of a duvet we used to have! In a bizarre kind of way I really wish I could meet him now just to say thank you for giving me these little gifts. It may only have been a packet of sweets but the fact I'm writing about this now is testament to the fact that kids do remember lots of things when young – adults should remember this!

When I wasn't eating poppets or getting packets of opal fruits, we (my brothers, cousins and my school friends) would often walk to the top of Prospect Road, turn right and then right again into Sylvan Avenue. At the bottom of this Cul de sac was a tip top factory. Many people nowadays won't understand what 'tip-tops' are – I think they're called Mr. Freeze or something like that. We'd stand outside and simply wait kicking stones around as kids do. If we were lucky, one of the workers would notice us and before long, freshly made tip tops would come hurling over the fence. There were loads of them; all in liquid form and still warm! Hurriedly we would grab as many as our little hands would allow and then excited would walk back home with a multitude of tip-tops in various flavours waiting to be frozen. Unfortunately for us, we had a slight problem as we had no fridge but in winter it was no problem – we simply left them outside (just like the jelly!) and in the morning they were done. The only problem was we didn't feel like eating them first thing in the morning.

One of my lasting memories whilst living at Halstead Street was the famous *old* Spence Street swimming baths. Spence Street was about 20 minutes' walk from our house and I clearly remember going there not to swim, but simply have a shower. My most vivid memory there is of the old steam baths. The building itself was old, dirty and had green swing doors in the changing rooms. The doors themselves swung inside and outside just like a door in a Western film bar! The steam room was extremely hot and I often sat there with my brothers thinking I was about to melt. On one particular day, the receptionist had the radio on and the song playing that day has stuck with me through the years – so much so that whenever someone mentions Spence street or I think of it myself, it reminds me of the song called *"We're only making plans for Nigel"*, sung by a group called XTC in 1979. The Spence street baths were knocked down and rebuilt a few years after that and now doesn't look anything like the original one which is a good thing…

It was now 1979 and my parents were busy trying to find us a new place to live. We saw many houses and the closest one we looked at was on Ashfordby Street which was the next street along but it was no good – I think the orange door put them off!! Deciding to *buy* another house really scared me because we were moving away from the fantastic friends in Halstead Street and the surrounding areas. Furthermore, what guarantee was there that nothing bad would happen to us in the new house? After several weeks of house hunting our new house was found; 119 Lancaster Street, situated off the Green Lane Road was our new home and was about 20 minutes' walk from Halstead Street. I was very apprehensive about moving as I didn't know what lied ahead...

Looking back at it now, the move from Halstead to Lancaster Street is a bit of a blur – I simply don't remember much about it. Usually people remember boxes of packed stuff, a big van and constant coming & goings between the 2 houses but surprisingly for me I recall little of it. In fact my first memory of living in our new house was seeing the large wooden front door. It was another terraced house in a row of 6 houses. As you turned right into the street from Green Lane Road it was the 2nd house on the left. First appearances were great; it was clean and brilliant white in colour & was rendered everywhere (that means covered in stones!). Compared to our previous home (if you could call it home), this place was 5 star in comparison. Inside the rooms were all clean & no sign of snails anywhere!

As you walked in there was the 'front room' followed by the 'living room'. I never did understand this. Why is it the 'living room'? Surely each room is a living room. As you walked past the living room you would get into the kitchen which was tiny. Up to that point I had never seen such a small kitchen, with 3 people in there it would be quite packed. The kitchen had a door which led to the garden. As with most terraced houses the garden, although divided by a small wall, felt more like a communal one. As you walked further into the garden, it seemed to merge seamlessly with the neighbour's garden to the left of us. In fact, the only high dividing wall was to separate our garden from the neighbours to the right.

To get upstairs you had to walk through the living room which then led onto the landing where there was 2 bedrooms and finally a bathroom/toilet. The house itself was actually fractionally bigger than our previous house. Since we were so close to Green Lane Road, the surrounding area was noticeably busier. There was a pub, the *Lancaster Arms* literally across the road, a large shoe factory opposite, a newsagent, butchers, take away shops and even a fish 'n' chip shop. It may be hard to believe but until we moved into this house, I'd never seen a fish 'n' chip shop let alone been in one. The shop itself was iconic in that area and to this day when you go there on a Friday evening, the queue would form a circle inside the shop and then lead out onto the wide pavement.

Fridays generally was one of those days where people just fancied fish & chips and at the time Paul's chip shop was simply the best (yes ok, no pun intended). Inside the shop there were 'fish' tiles, a fruit machine so you could lose all your money whilst you waited and staff that spoke so fast I never had a clue what they were going on about. They also had one of them very old cash registers – the ones that didn't actually calculate how much customers owed them – they simply pushed the huge lever type buttons and the total would appear. What was the point of those you tell me? Paul, the 'chippy' owner never served the customers but instead you'd see him out the back with huge white buckets of cut potatoes ready for the fryer. He would often give you a wry smile and then head off into the back again. Having bought the chips, I would cross over Jellicoe Road, looked at the objects in 'Bouldins' (still there)' which was the hardware store and then slowly walk past all other shops before I'd turn left into Lancaster Street again trying not to drop the chips as the heat went through the thin bags and started to melt my tiny hands...

I think it was around February time (1979) that we moved to our new house. I was only 9 and still going to Bridge Junior School. My junior school seemed such a long way from home and I couldn't believe that I would never be walking up those steps in Halstead Street on my way to school. The journey to Bridge was much simpler; get out of my house, head right towards green lane road, turn left and then keep walking. The first few walks to school were quite scary because the traffic along Green Lane Road was relentless and with only a few feet separating me from the road, the huge buses used to whiz past on their way into town. As I walked down green lane road I would first cross over Roseberry Street and look into the car dealer / petrol station that was on the corner.

There were never many cars in there and I'm pretty certain they were Leyland cars and were full with Allegro, Morris Marina and Austin Princess cars; something of a rarity nowadays and probably only found in Museums. As you walked past the car dealer you'd often hear the 'ding ding' sound and at first I had no idea where this noise was coming from. In the end I worked it out – as cars drove into the dealer ship to get petrol, they would have no choice but to drive over black circular pipes lying on the concrete – the pressure of something squashing them (i.e. the tyres) used to trigger the 'ding' noise. The workers inside would then hear the noise and come outside to help.

In the late 70's you didn't get the big supermarkets like we have today but further up on green lane road was a huge place called 'Belco'. This place sold everything and really was a 'one-shop' stop for all your grocery needs. Inside, as a little kid, you'd be overwhelmed by the rows and rows of freezers and aisles that were packed to the top with packets & cans of food. At the back of the shop was the meat section where the 2-3 staff would sell you everything from a few sausages to a whole lamb! Dressed in their customary blue & white outfits, I remember standing there whilst they cut the meat into pieces. The chocolate section was impressive too; so impressive in fact that they had the biggest chocolate bars I'd ever seen. One day, after being in there several times and simply looking at the chocolate I decided enough was enough. With no money to buy chocolate (we just had enough money to eat) I decided that I was going to have that chocolate. After stalking out the area for what seemed ages I took my chance and grabbed the biggest bar of chocolate I could find and promptly stuffed it down my jacket. My jacket was very cool; it has fur inside which made it super warm and on the outside has red squares with black lines running through it – I've seen them today – I was a trendsetter in those days!!

The chocolate section was quite close to the tills and the exit so as I started to make my way for the door I could feel my heart beating faster & faster. It was huge relief when I got out but I wouldn't go home – that would be dangerous. Instead I'd quickly walk up East Park Road and quickly eat all the chocolate. The taste was awesome and i'm surprised I wasn't sick with the amount I'd eaten. As I sit here writing this, it's quite embarrassing that as a 9/10 year old I had resorted to stealing from the shops – something I regret greatly. Unfortunately, I had the taste for it now and it wasn't long before I was helping myself to different chocolates on a regular basis; one day, however, it all came to an end. It was a normal day – by that I mean I had no money in my pockets so I strolled into Belco and grabbed a chocolate bar. As I walked towards the door with my unpaid chocolate stuffed down my jacket, this huge person stopped me in my tracks. As it turned out, the manager must have been watching me over many days and although he didn't call the police *or* ask where I lived, he gave me a polite warning that if I had stolen something then he would call the police the next time.

As the manager uttered 'Do you understand' I remember shaking and slowly nodded my head and swiftly left as fast as I could. That was the last time I went into Belco alone and was extremely lucky that I was not in trouble. So, getting back to my journey to school… Belco was at the junction of Green Lane road and East Park Road. To get to school I'd press the button on the pedestrian crossing and wait until the green man lit up. Once across the road, the first shop you'd see was an old cycle shop. It was a dingy shop on the corner and whenever I went inside there it took several minutes before the owner would make their way downstairs and come to speak to you. The bikes looked old & it was a horrible place to be but in those days bike shops were a rarity which is the only reason I went in.

Further along the road there was a video shop that is still there today. When the video and VHS age boomed in the last 70's /

early 80's this shop was packed with videos to hire but all that has now changed to DVD's. After passing an electrical repair shop and a few other grocer shops I'd cross over the walk way where the brook ran underneath. A few minutes later I'd pass the 2nd hand shop on the left, Barlow blinds on the right hand side and the infamous Green Lane Social was just ahead on the left hand side. The social club was really a place where all Asian men hung out and my dad was no exception. There were many times when my dad took me with him to this pub where, just like earlier in Mere Road, he would buy me crisps and coke and I'd sit in the corner minding my own business. The image I have of this social club hasn't changed one bit and ironically the club is still there, still called the same and physically it hasn't changed one bit.

After passing this social club you'd walk past 'Gordon's' hair dressers and a few shops after that was 'Aradna' supermarket where all the Indians would go to get their groceries. Inside Aradna's all the Indian (female) women would be working the till whilst their male co-workers would be carrying out huge bags of flower and oil drums into their Mercedes vans ready for delivery. With few people having cars, there was no way you'd be able to carry 25 kilos of flour on your back! Opposite the supermarket was the launderette which was always a great place to go to - it was very warm inside and the aroma of washing powder filled the air. Once I'd crossed over Ashfordby & Harewood Street I wasn't far from school and one final dash over Prospect Road and I'd soon be walking past Green Lane Nursery / Infants to the right with Bridge junior right across Mere Road.

It may sound strange but I *loved,* really *loved* the journey to & from school. Each day was different and although nothing really exciting happened it was just seeing the people; the *real* people from school kids to adults going about their daily chores and just getting on with it. Walking down the road you'd meet friendly people who always had time for you. Everyone seemed to be equal and everybody just got on – I mean really got on regardless of colour, religious beliefs or where you came from. I often wish I could be transported back to those days; back to the days where life was so simple.

During the winter it would start to get dark on my way home and at Christmas my journey home would take even longer as I looked into each shop and stare at the Christmas lights that lit up the window displays. On my way back home, just as I was at the junction of Green Lane & East Park Road, I'd often see my dad walking home himself. In the first few months after we moved into Lancaster Street he was still working but on the odd occasion he'd go into the 'bookies' (i.e. betting shop). The Ladbrokes shop was hidden from the outside world by advertising plastered over the glass. I tried to glance inside and the fact that I couldn't see what was going on made me even more curious. The only image I have of this shop is the bespoke red colour and the 100's of mini Ladbroke pens we had at home. Each time my dad went into the shop he made sure he came home with 100's of betting slips and pens too. On Saturday afternoons when the BBC 'World of Sport' was aired, my dad would sit fixated to the TV watching the horse racing and scribble out his 'virtual' bets. He would then urge the horses on and watched each race to see if he would have won!

In terms of neighbours we had a strange bunch of people living around us. Number 121 had a Sikh family that lived there with 3 lads. We got to know the lads quite well for many years after that and we used to hang out and do the things that kids do. Their father was a great character; he couldn't speak English (he came straight from the Punjab region several years earlier to make a better life for them all here in the UK). Each time he saw me he would speak in Punjabi and I would speak in English. I never knew what he said to me & he had no idea what I said to him but I just responded in an "I've understood" manner and that was that. The house to the left of us, number 117, was totally different. Over the years there must have been 4-5 different families living there. There was an Asian lady with a young girl who got on really well with my mum and when they went another family moved in. Unfortunately, their father was an alcoholic too and I could hear the shouting, violence and screams from the little kids that were too young to do anything about it.

So, the story continues, here we were in another house and another family was suffering at the hands of a father too tied up with drink to care. When you see & hear this day in day out it makes you wonder (as a young kid) whether this is simply 'normal'. Luckily for me it didn't seem right then and it's definitely not right now. The violent outbursts from my own father didn't stop either. Though he was still working, the violence became progressively worse as his drinking habits increased.

Many nights an argument would flare up because he hadn't given my mum any money for food or utility bills and my mum would continually try to make him understand that she wasn't asking for money so she could go out and enjoy herself. She would often point to the kids and say "who's going to feed them". Sadly, this would be my dad's excuse to hit out and he did many times. As he had done many times before, my dad vented out all his anger on my mum who yet again endured a series of beatings and was left crying afterwards whilst all the kids were forced to look on and not be able to do anything about it.

Often my dad would get violent simply because he didn't like the look of the dinner my mum had prepared. She would stand there and ask him what he wanted and would always be prepared to make something else. He would stand there swearing at her, calling her crude names that should never come out of anyone's mouth. Yet despite the beatings, despite working all the hours she could, she stood by his side and just got on with it. On many days I would often just leave the house and walk aimlessly; it was better than staying at home anyway. Just further up the road was a factory with a huge set of green doors that opened up to accept deliveries. During the evenings & weekends, however, we'd play football there. Somebody had sprayed "Sam Spade" in huge writing over these doors and for many years I had no idea what this meant. Was it the name of a local kid? Someone famous or what? It didn't matter anyway – the real focus was football and it was great to enjoy something at last. We'd use the green gates as one goal and the shoe factory opposite as the other one.

During the summer, when the evenings seemed to go on forever, we'd be outside playing for hours and would reluctantly go inside when we were summoned to – often it was getting so dark that we could hardly see the ball! As we were new to the area I would often just walk around and a few streets away I came across 'Bromleys' wine shop. Many years ago these types of shops flourished as people came in to buy their beers & wines. Nowadays, with the ever expansion of large scale supermarkets, these shops have died out; unable to compete with the huge buying power of the supermarkets who can afford to undercut the rest. Although the stop itself was small, the area occupied by Bromleys as a whole was very big. To the back of the shop was a warehouse where all the stock was kept and we actually used their car park as a football ground! One particular day, whilst I was running to get the ball back, I got very close to the storage area that was protected by large gates. The actual stock was at the back, well out of reach, but close to the gate were crates & crates of empty coke bottles.

To say I'd struck lucky would be an understatement – in front of me was money, real money and it was there for the taking. Common sense went out the window, the fact that it was wrong didn't register and the incident with the chocolates @ Belco supermarket was forgotten about. You may be wondering how on earth I would make money out of coke bottles. Well during the late 70's, early 80's the coke bottles were *all* glass and you didn't have the plastic bottles we're accustomed to nowadays. When you'd finished with your coke bottle you would take it back to the shop you bought it from and they would give you the 'deposit' back which was either 5 or 10p. So, the raid was planned, I slipped my tiny hands through the gaps in the metal gates and slowly pulled out several empty coke bottles. I only took 2 at a time because I couldn't carry more than that and would then head out to the shop on the corner of Green Lane Road. As I walked into the shop, the owner would look at me in disbelief because they were thinking "I've never seen this kid before – he didn't buy them coke bottles from me".

It didn't matter, there were no 'rules' on where you could return your bottles so I'd hand them over and in return I'd get money. To make it look real I never bought sweets from this shop – I'd used another one and then enjoyed myself as I scoffed out on whatever the money would buy. This was a real niche in the market; none of the other kids thought of it. See - I had the makings of a real entrepreneur / apprentice even in those days! Yes I know it was wrong and I did stop doing it after a few months but there is no way you could do this now; mainly due to CCTV watching & recording everything you do. On the subject of coke, I've always been a big fan of the original glass bottles. You can actually still get the smaller versions of these glass bottles in some pubs & bars but i'm adamant that coke always tastes better from bottles than the plastic bottles and cans we have now. Several of my friends agree too so there's either something in it or it's a psychological thing – either way I'm convinced it's true! When I got bored of playing football or simply wanted a change of scenery I used to head back towards my junior school and join my friends who lived close to the school. Several of them lived in Prospect Road whilst others lived in Mornington Street, just a short distance away.

During the weekends we'd all play 'tick' or hide 'n' seek and the hours would fly past as we just 'hung' out. A favourite game in those days was '7 stones' where you'd build up a tower of stones and would then have to knock them down with another stone. I think that's how it worked anyway and once the stone was thrown all the kids would be running all over the place trying to get you out.

Ranjan, one of my friends who lived on Prospect Road, never had kids playing close to his house as they were simply scared to death. The thing is you see, he had a vicious dog called 'Roomie'- pronounced 'room e'. Trust me, this dog was crazy & I think he was like this because he was hardly let outside so when he was he was too excited and would try to eat anything; including kids! As soon as you knocked on his door, the dog would start barking and we'd run as we had no idea if the dog was in the house or not.

Around the corner from Ranjan's house was Mount Avenue. One of my best friends at the time, Manish Thanki, lived here with his young brother and 2 sisters. At the time, he was a true friend and we were always together and at times there were days where I spent more time in his house than I did at my own. His dad had a grey Morris Minor which we'd sit in and play our own driving games. When it was time for lunch his mum would call us in and all I ever recall eating there was jam sandwiches.

One day when I went round there to play, there was whole load of dust coming out of their front door and it seemed pretty chaotic. After a few minutes Manish surfaced, covered head to toe in so much dust that you could just about recognise him. It turned out that the bathroom had literally fallen into the kitchen / dining room below it. At the time I was just interested in seeing inside without thought whether anyone was hurt or not. Luckily, no-one was taking a bath or were standing in the kitchen at the time otherwise it would have been a different story.

The kids from my school never came to my house because they were told it was too far to go which is why I always had to go round there. A few weeks after the bathroom fell through the ceiling I went back there and the place was all cleaned up − no traces of dust anywhere. It was now lunchtime so as usual his mum called us back inside and we headed back the kitchen where I looked up and could see the ceiling had been repaired. When I say repaired I mean it was repaired by his dad and it didn't look safe at all. It has uneven cement and plaster all over it and a small bulge on one side.

This time I decided to eat my lunch standing up & made sure I wasn't underneath it – just in case... (Sunita - safety first!!). After that incident I rarely went into their house as I had visions of the bath falling through again as I tucked into my jam sandwiches! I lost contact with Manish a few years after this as his family moved out of Leicester although I have heard rumours that they are back now.

5

It's good to talk...

As a youngster I would walk loads – when I was out with my brothers, sisters or mum/dad we'd go by foot – there was no car to jump into and it was the normal thing to do. Telephones were a rarity too and it was only after we moved into Lancaster Street that we actually had a phone. The day we moved in I remember seeing it clearly; it was a green 'trim' phone and was sitting on the window sill in the 'middle' room. When I first lifted the receiver up I could hear nothing but as I'd never used a phone before I had no idea what to expect anyway. I never did understand why they called it a 'trim' phone but what I do know is that when the phone line was actually connected it had a strange ringing sound and had push buttons to dial the numbers. Having a phone was a novelty and ringing the speaking clock was exciting. Ok, thinking back on this it wasn't a clever thing to do at all. I may have known the exact GMT time but more destructively was the fact that I was single handily running up a phone bill unnecessarily. When the phone bill came my mum hit the roof – there was little money to go round in the first place without having to deal with high telephone bills too.

After that & without me knowing the phone was changed. Out went the green trim phone and in came a cream coloured phone with one of those circular dialling mechanisms. It didn't bother me, it was good fun turning the wheel and hearing it spin back! The only thing it did was slow down the time it took to make a phone call. In frustration my mum went a step further and put a lock on the phone. It was one of those circular ended locks that actually fit into the hole on the phone where your fingers sits whilst dialling. The lock made a huge difference to the phone bills as the only one really using the phone was my mum and to be honest most people would ring us anyway.

One day, after being particularly curious, things changed – I somehow managed to work out that the 2 black spring loaded buttons that are pushed down when you replace the handset can be used to make calls! Strange but very true – all you do is push the buttons down. So, if you want to ring 234456 you would: -

Press the buttons 2 times (this would be read as number '2')
Press the buttons 3 times (this would be read as number '3')
Press the buttons 4 times
Press the buttons 4 times
Press the buttons 5 times
Press the buttons 6 times

… and bingo – the number would start to dial. I never told anyone about this and when I wanted to know the time I wouldn't bother looking at the clocks in our house – I'd ring speaking clock again. The end result was inevitable; the next phone bill came and my mum was furious. She couldn't understand how the bill was so high, especially with a lock on it. My mum then took things further – the phone service was changed to be incoming only so there was no way whatsoever to make calls (I did try pushing the buttons but it didn't work!). So there you go, I was responsible for probably having the only phone in Leicester that could only accept incoming calls & adding to my mum's financial issues – sorry mum!

Most kids play lots of games including board games. As a family, we hardly did anything together. I was the annoying little brother, Kiran wanted to sleep all day, Vipul wanted to watch films all day, my dad wanted to drink all day, my mum was trying to cope all day whilst my sister… well, to be honest I don't really know what my sister got up to! In the evenings it was a rarity that we'd all sit together & watch television. This was a major achievement in itself because there were 6 of us in a small room that we were sprawled all over the place. One day, completely out of character, my mum bought one of those cheap scratch cards and as we scratched frantically it looked as if we'd won something. After staring at the card for ages it was true – we were winners! Racing to the newsagents, we were thinking several thousand pounds was coming our way, perhaps a car, perhaps a holiday or perhaps all of that!

The chap behind the counter told my mum that the prize was £5.00 which was a real let down. I could almost see the frustration in my mum's eyes on hearing this. However, she quickly put this aside and decided we could spend the money on a game so we bought our first ever board game – Monopoly from this shop and headed home. I think if you ask anyone about 'Monopoly' they'll tell you it's a great game which seems to have made a remarkable recovery recently. There are so many versions available nowadays and you can even make your own board and customise it however you want. With little money to go around we have never had 'spending money'- whilst my other friends talked about getting a few pence here and there to buy sweets I just kept my mouth shut hoping they wouldn't ask me about it. One of the shops around the corner from our house was a lady's clothes shop. I think it was actually called 'Gwen's Clothing' or some other derivative. It was quite a strange shop, never seemed to be busy and it was really hard to see inside because the shop window had a sort of green tint to it and it wasn't the standard clear glass shop front at all. The owner, presumably 'Gwen' must have been in her late forties and was always friendly.

She drove a huge Vauxhall car, it was white and always seemed pretty clean. One day whilst I was outside messing around she started to speak to me and asked if i'd clean her car. At the time I thought this would be great fun - we never had a car to clean, I liked cars so I was a winner all round. Within a few minutes she'd opened up the gates, gave me a bucket with soapy water in it and I started to clean the car. It was great fun, I could actually sit in the driving seat and pretend to drive a car again, just like I had done many times before in the abandoned Austin. I'm sure I cleaned the car for ages and as I wiped the last drop of water off the car she gave me a huge smile and handed over something. As I looked into my hands it was a five pound note and I couldn't believe it. Five pounds was a lot of money and extremely generous. I'd never been given so much money and was standing there in shock. As 'thank you' came out of my mouth I think Gwen knew I was shocked and just said 'don't spend it all at once'. I don't think you'll ever get that sort of generosity now - mind you I doubt very much if kids would be prepared to wash cars for free now either.

With some money in my back pocket I really didn't know what to do, I mean in the past I was restricted as I didn't have money but here I was a small kid with *real* money & real spending power. I never expected to get paid for cleaning the car at all - I think this is the difference between kids then and now. I only ever cleaned her car once and she was only at that shop for a little while afterwards. Further up Green Lane Road was another sweet shop run by a couple. They had loads of sweets in there and the first time I went into the shop I thought something was wrong. As you walked in, the door would make a chiming sound to alert the owners. You'd expect someone to pop up from behind the counter or come into the shop from a back room or something but nothing - nothing at all. Seconds would turn into minutes and often it would take ages before the shop owners finally revealed themselves.

The bizarre thing is this happened every time and I got quite fed up with waiting so my naughty streak, which should have stopped when I got caught stealing chocolate at Belco's, should have told me 'no' but it didn't and I started to steal again. I would go into the shop knowing full well that the owners would take ages before they surfaced so I made the most of this. As soon as I stepped inside my eyes instantly focused on what I fancied that day. Many times, the chocolate of choice was Easter eggs - they were tasty, easy to find (in a jar on the counter) and most importantly small so they could fit into my pockets easily. As I shoved 2 into my little pockets, the owner would come down smiling and I would return the favour and provide a little boy smile which fooled everyone.

After spending a few pence I was out of there and as soon as I was close to our house I start enjoying the stolen eggs. This cycle continued for ages but one day when I had the customary eggs stuffed into my pockets, the owner came out quicker than usual and his eyes were fixated at the pockets of my trousers. I could sense that he knew I was up to no good, you could tell he knew I had stolen something from him and I thought I had been busted but miraculously I paid for whatever it was I bought and then left - never to return again. This was too close for comfort and I knew I didn't want to steal again!

When my cousins came to visit us from London they had a new area to play in - we were no longer in Halstead Street & things were very different. The regular visits to the fairground still happened but not as often but one thing we found by accident was a 'transfer' factory. One day whilst all the boys were out in the street just passing time we decided to wonder the streets and ended up on Kitchener Road which is only a 5 minute walk from our house. As we headed into new territory we realised we'd entered an industrial estate, there were no houses and no other kids to be seen but we also noticed a huge brick spire shooting into sky from one of the factories. Drawn by curiosity we headed towards it and could smell a distinct aroma that we'd never smelt before. As we got closer we could see huge skips and boxes lying around with white bits of paper being caught by the wind and filling the air. We picked some up and saw pictures of wombles on them. Wombles are the fictitious characters of a kid's tv programme but one of my cousin shouted out 'transfers'.

It turned out that the white bits of paper flying around were actually 'seconds' or 'reject' womble transfers that were destined for the shops but had slight defects and were hence being thrown away. For many days after that we went back there and grabbed as many transfers as we could. In the end we had piles of them; so many that even after sharing them out we had stacks of them left. We then tried to find some t shirts when we got home and began ironing the transfers onto them and were amazed when the image on a rubbish bit of paper transformed itself onto the t shirt. At this point we were hooked onto transfers and this became our playing ground for many months after that. There was a huge sign on top of this building and it read "Debonair Yarn" - I don't think the name was in any way related to the transfers but the name stuck and to this day when I talk about this with my friends we always refer to debonair yarns! The building is still there too although with once booming yarn and engineering trade suffering from cheap foreign imports, the building is probably used for something totally different.

When my cousins came to stay we have so much fun that it awful saying goodbye when it was time for them to head back home. When that time came, the house was always quiet again and my 2 brothers, who up until that point were lots of fun, suddenly seemed as if they couldn't be bothered with me. As usual I was therefore left to fend for myself so to speak - the days were long, the evenings were uneventful and inside the house nobody really wanted to know me - I think a lodger would have had more fun and interaction! Once a week though things got a little more exciting; well exciting for me anyway. You see the Corona / Alpine "truck" would come up the road with a full load of multi coloured sparkling drinks. I was always amazed at how many different flavours there were - Cherryade, Raspberryade, Cream Soda, Orange, Dandelion & Burdock and on and on. They would pull up outside the house and all the kids and their parents (well some parents anyway), would come outside. The kids would shout out all the colours they wanted whilst the mums carefully picked out a fraction of them & you'd see the disappointed looks on the kids as they trawled back inside with less than their expected quota.

The warm winters we have now are in stark contrast to those I can remember as a young boy. When the summer officially ended and the clocks reverted back to BST - British Summer Time that is, you *really* felt it. Not only did it get progressively darker but it felt like a real winter. Lancaster Street like all the other houses we seemed to live in was very cold and it wasn't until about 12 years later that we had central heating fitted. It's hard to imagine how we survived but we did. At home there was a gas fire in the 'front' and 'tv' room. With very few visitors, the heater in the front room was used rarely; well in fact only used when we had guests. It only took a few people to visit and the house would seem quite small - we'd then spill into the front room and light the heater. Upstairs it was a different story altogether - with no heating in any room, it was freezing. I remember almost running anywhere just to keep warm. Eventually we got some fan heaters and I think one of the rooms had an electric heater mounted on the wall. My mum used to always tell us to close doors to keep the heat it - mainly so we could turn down the fan heater.

During the months of November, December and into January we inevitably had snow and lots of it. The first snowflakes were always exciting and before long they'd turn into bigger & bigger flakes. In a matter of hours, we literally had a Christmas wonderland on our door steps and I knew that we were in for lots of fun that week. Whilst the snow flurried down i'd often sit on the window ledge of the front room and watch the millions of flakes come down from the sky. I'd watch as the people out on the streets started walking faster, watch as the occasional person would get could off guard and slip. After the snow stopped falling there would always seem to be an eerie silence - all was quiet, there didn't seem to be any people outside, few cars and it looked beautiful; even Lancaster Street looked great in a bizarre sort of way.

If the snow had fallen during the early part of the evening we'd go outside and start to play instantly. Snow ball fighting was a constant cycle of rolling up as many balls as you could and launching them at targets - cars, buses, cats & people in random orders. After a few minutes, especially without gloves, you'd feel your hands start stinging as the cold really set in. Within a few minutes your hands would be useless - cold, red and you'd start to wish you'd left the snow well alone. Worst still was once we were safely back inside, we'd try to dry out our hands close to the heater which was a bad mistake. The warm heat would somehow cause a bizarre reaction with our cold hands and they would ache like anything. In reality what we should have done was let our hands heat up slowly but we were kids and I for one didn't know any better! Our soaking shoes would be sat on top of piles of newspaper that my mum would leave in the front room so as to not wet the floor. Inside our shoes on the other hand would be balls of newspaper used to soak up all the wetness!

The next morning we'd all pull out the soaking newspaper from our shoes expecting them to be clean & dry but they never were so we'd sometimes put on 2 pairs of socks and off we went to school. It was common then to wear 2 pairs of socks but I cannot remember it being that cold in recent times to warrant this. I also remember seeing people wearing their socks on the *outside* of their shoes which was an eye opener the first time it was seen. Somehow this was meant to stop them slipping but I never did understand how that worked! It snowed so much that it lasted for days and often weeks. The roads would turn into ice rinks as the cars would crush the snow and turn it into compacted, extremely slippery ice blocks.

I clearly recall running up & down the middle of the road without a care in the world. I knew there wouldn't be any cars there so i'd run as fast as I could, stop running and then see how far I could slide - if it wasn't for the aching hands I could have done that all day! When the snow finally started to melt huge chunks of black ice would form and on my way to & from school i'd watch as huge bits that were clinging onto cars, trucks and buses would dislodge and turn into mini missiles as they broke free and hurtled along the road.

Worse still were the nights - as the meltdown continued and the temperature dropped, the melting snow turned into a lethal thing - ice. In the morning the outside had been transformed - no longer could you hear the slight 'crunch' as your feet crushed down on the freshly fallen snow. Instead you'd be hanging on for dear life as you struggled to walk on slippery ice. Trust me, I could hardly walk straight and it added at least 20 minutes to my journey. I was actually more concerned with others seeing me fall -there's something quite funny about this!

Well it's now 9th November 2007 and my plan to get this finished by the end of year is not looking promising. I think part of the reason for this is that I started on it so late but never mind. It's actually Diwali today -the Hindu festival of good winning over evil. I'm sure there's a deep meaning to it that goes back several hundred, if not thousands of years. If I were a true believer I guess I would celebrate it much more than I actually do. In fact, bizarrely as it sounds I prefer Christmas much better. The build-up to Christmas is long - starts as early as August in some London shops and as you get closer and closer, the shops open later & later and it just has a great atmosphere to it. I've never given anyone a Diwali gift but when it comes to Christmas i'd happily (& still do) spend ages carefully planning what to get the kids so they can happily open them on Christmas morning.

Diwali whilst at junior school was full of dance, colourful costumes and music & all the kids, regardless of faith & background would be encourage to take part and join in the festivities. At the time I loved being in plays, dramas or whatever you want to call it. During Navratri (the 9 day festival of light), all the girls would dress up in sari's and perform dances to Indian music and all the boys would sit and take the piss. It was good, humoured fun and I still talk about it to this day with Nalini, Nila & Bindy - 3 of my friends that i've remained in contact with since we were youngsters.

The year after the Diwali celebrations was my last at Bridge Junior School and it was a really tough time. With all the "issues" at home, school was a safe place to be. For 6-7 hours of the day I could literally forget about my home. I realise this is quite a harsh thing to say but this is what I was thinking as a 10 year old which I truly find very frightening indeed. As if I didn't have enough psychological scars at the time, I came home one day and mentioned to my mum that I needed some trainers as mine were ripped beyond belief. I remember the rain seeping in but I kept quiet and often shoved newspaper into them to soak it up (a trick I remembered from throwing snowballs!)

I knew there was no real point asking my mum as I was assured of the answer and I was right. There was no money for new shoes but out of nowhere my mum pulled out a pair of football boots that had plastic moulded studs in them. A few minutes later and she was frantically cutting away at them with a kitchen knife. In amazement I simply stood there, curious as to what she was up to and then it dawned on me. After cutting off all the studs she handed me a pair of "trainers"; physically changed & transformed from football boot to trainers in a matter of minutes.

Problem solved - I had a new pair of trainers which apart from being loose just about stayed on my feet. This was not the end of it - as I strolled into school trying not to make it obvious that I was wearing football boots that were too big, the noise of the studs made a loud resonating sound on the polished floor of the multipurpose assembly hall. Wondering what the noise was, Mr.Gamble summoned me over and in front of the class told me to take my hybrid trainers off. As he turned each one upside down for a closer inspection, a large chunk of newspaper fell out & it was at that moment just as the kids started to laugh and point fingers at me, that I wondered how much more of this would I be able to take? The teacher wasn't happy with me, the class continually laughed and I was ordered to "put them back on" and that I wasn't allowed to join in with football or PE until I had proper trainers. I felt alone, helpless and on the receiving end of cruel and nasty comments on "Sandips really poor..." on school kids who to be fair didn't realise the true impact of what they were doing. Deep down I was really hurt but all I could think of was that my mum did what she thought was best and I couldn't have asked anymore of here...

A few months after that incident, some teachers from my chosen secondary school came to visit & it was then I realised I was off to a "big" school. In the preceding weeks I'd already heard of new starters having their head stuck in the toilet and flushed and / or your books thrown about. To say I was scared was an understatement but luckily some of my friends were going to the same secondary school so that was ok. By the time June 1981 had arrived, my time at junior school was over and the good byes to teachers and friends had been said. The summer holidays, or "summer of school" as I nicknamed it, was a long stretch - 7 weeks to be exact and at the end of it I would be starting at "Mundella Secondary School". The summer was a long hot one and once I found out that my neighbours were already attending the school & their younger brother was about to start too, it made things a little easier.

BRIDGE COUNTY JUNIOR SCHOOL

Name Sandip Patel   Class 4. P.

197.8...

SUBJECT	REMARKS ON YEAR'S WORK
ENGLISH	Sandip expresses himself very well with much confidence. He has a wide range of vocabulary which he uses both orally and with his written work. His reading is now of a very high standard where he is fluent and reads with full comprehension. Regularly learns his spellings with good results
MATHEMATICS	Sandip has now mastered the basic rules and concepts of Maths (+, -, x, ÷). He has covered a lot of work this year and has been very accurate with results. Can concentrate well for long periods
TOPICS & GENERAL STUDIES	Very keen at all project work. Always tries very hard. Sandip can research a subject using the library well. Has done a lot of good work this year.
GENERAL	Sandip is a well behaved, polite and good-natured boy who gets on well with the other children in class. He works very hard on all tasks given him and has produced some good results this year. He has a keen and enthusiastic approach to school, wanting to be involved fully in all school activities. Sandip is a lively, friendly and fully trustworthy person who, I am quite certain, will do very well at his secondary school. Good luck Sandip.

S. Lynne
Class Teacher

B. Hawkins
Headmistress

E.1237

90

The days turned into weeks and before I knew it there was a matter of days before the new term would start. As it was a secondary school, I had to wear a school uniform but thankfully it wasn't strictly enforced. The condition was that we had to wear black trousers and a grey top – easy really. One afternoon my mum took me to "Gani's" which was a general clothes shop on Green Lane Road. It was one of those typical Indian shops where you could buy anything and about 30 minutes later we were on our way back home with our new school clothes. So I was all set for school and with only a few days of our summer holidays left, the kids (me & the neighbours that is), made the most if it. With long summer days to enjoy, we'd be out in the street and started off our next craze which was to steal car badges. With mini screw drivers in our hands (you know – the triple ones that you win at fairground rides where you've paid £2.00 to win a prize with a value of 10p), we'd start to walk the streets. Ford badges were pretty good – they just looked better than all the others. Trying not to attract too much attention, we'd lean up against the chosen car and slowly manoeuvre the screw driver into place and with lightning speed the badge would be off in seconds.

Shamefully we'd leg it home (perhaps I should explain 'leg it' – a term used to mean running away quickly!!) and throw the badge into our ever-growing stash of stolen items. I often think about this and the times we used to steal the odd Volkswagen "VW" badge which were very cool. Was it us that started the craze with the Beastie Boys? I guess we'll never know! Our collection by now was really gathering pace and we had so many bits and pieces off cars that we looked like real criminals and had we been caught, I dread to think of the consequences. We all agreed to calm things down & stopped our badge escapades. However with one thing finishing we had to do something else and it was only a matter of time before we were up to further mischief.

As you may remember, we lived close to several factories – they were all around us so one day we decided we would take a closer look. All the factories were closed during the weekends and evenings so we would wait until all the workers had gone. One of the factories had lots of black greasy paint stuff sprayed all over the roofs and on the roof ledges in an attempt to stop people getting onto it. It didn't stop us – we would give one person a 'leg up' (you'd use your hand a sort of step and they would put their foot into it & then launch you into the air) so they could get onto the ledge and one by one we'd join them. The strongest of us all would go last as there wouldn't be anyone to give them a leg up at all. The scary thing about this is that we rarely worried about the police or about our parents for that matter. I mean, we only lived a few minutes away and here we were trying to get inside a factory. If any of our family had been in our garden they could probably see us because the factory roofs were clearly visible. Back to the ledge – once we were all on it, the whole process would start again – each giving leg-ups until we were safely on the roof.

The roof itself was pretty dangerous - we had to walk along a small gap where the roof lines met and it was cluttered with years of rubbish that had been kicked or thrown up into the air and had somehow landed there. After navigating our way through old footballs, bricks, items of clothing and an old shoe (why is it you *always* find a single black shoe?), we would get to a point where we could actually see inside the factory. It wasn't that secure and once we'd plucked up the courage to jump down about 8 feet, we'd land on the factory floor. So, there we were; myself, my brothers & our neighbours walking without a care in the world completely oblivious to the fact that what we were doing was totally wrong & illegal!

After walking around for about 30 minutes it got quite boring especially as there wasn't anything interesting inside. We did pinch a few things from there, a few tools and bizarrely I took a door handle. Yes I know why on earth would you want a door handle? Most people would try to forget past memories such as this but this is one that I couldn't or still cannot forget. The thing is you see, the door handle that I was so fond of is currently fixed to a downstairs door at my mum's house so every time I move from the front to the middle room, I grasp firmly on it and the memory comes flooding back every time. Nobody ever questioned where it came to and despite being only 11 I remember thinking to myself that if anyone ever started to poke around and get suspicious I would tell them that I stole it from the factory (knowing full well that everyone else would think I had an over imaginative mind)...

6

Life @ Mundella Secondary School

It was now August 1981 and it was the night before my first day at the "big" school. I was scared, apprehensive and hardly slept that night. I tried to but just couldn't get those questions out of my head. Would I get beaten up? Would I get my head flushed down the toilet? These questions repeated themselves inside my head over and over all night so by the time morning arrived I was tired and already off to a bad start! That morning I went to school with my neighbours - 2 of them. The youngest was also starting Mundella whilst the other (his brother) was just making sure we got there! I had no choice - there was nobody else to go with. Some of my dear friends such as Ranjan had gone to a different school and I couldn't really go with Nalini, Nila etc. because they lived in the opposite direction.

The walk to school had a bit of a twist to it. As we were made our way up Kitchener Road, we'd just walked past some new houses and my neighbour stopped walking, looked around the jumped straight over a wall. I had no choice but to follow and once I was over the brick wall, we were facing out into the brook! I was amazed, I thought it was only me that went brook walking and to be honest I never thought i'd be doing this again but here I was on my first day at school going the 'alternative' way! It totally changed my mood and after meandering underneath Debonair Yarns we were soon heading towards Coleman Road and a few minutes after that we climbed over the wall again and ended up on Freeman Road North. As we walked towards Humberstone Road, the number of kids visible on the streets increased tremendously and the nerves started to kick in. By the time we got into the road leading to the school I was shitting myself and just wanted to go home.

Just like cattle, we were herded into the playground and after some organised chaos the teachers started to call out the names of the kids - in a matter of minutes we'd know who our "form tutor" would be, whatever that meant. As it turned out I ended up in 1MQ which was 1st year McQuone. How on earth did I end up with a teacher who looked 90 years old, had about 200 keys hanging off his trousers and wore sandals with no socks. Oh, I forgot to mention that his beard looked as if something had, or still was, living inside it. "Hurry up children" he would say over and over again as he ushered us towards our class room which would be our home for the next year. Once we were in his class I vividly remember looking around very worriedly at all the crazy kids. Based on the looks alone (from the children) I knew that this was a rough looking class and worst still an even rougher looking school. Amazingly I spotted Malkit Singh - one of my friends from Bridge Junior School so that made me quite happy and I clung onto him (not literally of course) for the rest of the day.

The classroom was dull, boring and scary. The desks opened up like a big book and there was a hole at the top right of the desks where many years ago they were probably used for ink holes or something like that. If i'd known what break time was like I would have never left that class room. During break we were let out into the playground where we had no choice but to mix with the masses. It was like letting foxes out in a room full of hunting dogs but unfortunately we were the foxes! I must explain something now - the late 1970's & early 1980's was an awful time for race relations and if you were from an ethnic background you were in real trouble and I was no exception. My first day at Mundella would be one i'd never forget and the fact that i'm writing about it now proves this. "Paki bashing" was a favourite phrase that I quickly learnt meant danger. No sooner were all the kids released, the "white" boys would gather around the "white" girls and try it on, giving it the smooth talk (even as 10/11 year olds!).

When they got bored they *had* to show the girls that they were the greater race by gathering in gangs and literally pace bashing. If, like me, you were unfortunate to get caught you were in line for serious beatings. I was kicked around, punched all over and spat on - all within 2 hours of arriving at this damn school. Things never changed at this horrible place - it did get marginally better in the years to come but every day was a challenge of the highest order. If I wasn't getting beaten up, I was asked for money. Since I had no money I was beaten again. Home time wasn't even safe - gangs would chase us (my friends & I) up Humberstone Road but the adrenaline was pumping around our bodies so much that we had untold energy and always managed to lose the racists. We'd usually just jump down the brook and this would confuse the life out of them.

The insults were bad; very bad in fact and one of the worst bouts of 'name calling' came from the "black" kids who repeatedly told me that I was a "black bastard" and that I had to get out of *their* country. I never did understand how that worked. On one occasion, when I felt rather cheeky, I was called "Paki" but retorted by saying that I was born in Africa so how could I be a "Paki" (on the assumption that "Paki" was short for Pakistan). The look on their face was magic - they just didn't understand what I was saying thus proving who the thick ones really were! In hindsight, however, I should have just kept my mouth shut because this outburst from me got me a good kicking to show for it. Half way through the first week, things seemed to get better and I was slowly but surely thinking maybe it wasn't that bad after all. Perhaps the "paki bashing" was for the 1st few days only? Boy I was wrong – by the time Thursday had arrived of my first full week I was so scared of being attacked yet again (I'd already been attacked twice before 11am) that I rushed home for my lunch time dinner. I wasn't even hungry – just desperate to get as far away as possible from that damn school.

To make things even worse we were forced to read out chapters from the bible. Now, before I go on, I have to make it clear that I am not religious in any way at all and the issue I have with this is that it was forced upon everybody irrespective of their religious beliefs. We would stand there, all the kids who parents came from a mixture of backgrounds and expected to learn verses. This is ok but something was morally wrong about this, I knew this as a 10 year old so why didn't the others? Like I said, I'm not interested into religious stuff – "each to their own" and all that but it just seemed wrong. In life having friends can make the difference between going off the rails and staying on the straight & narrow. Your friends, the *real* friends that is, are always watching your back & expect nothing in return – well this is my interpretation of what real friends are anyway. In my first year @ Mundella I needed real friends and I was pretty certain I had them. With all the chaos in the home life I really didn't know if I could take anymore. I mean it got to a stage where I was miserable at home and at school so what was the alternative? I felt alone, truly alone & hated being at home and school so life really couldn't get worse could it?

I made many new friends in the first few weeks at Mundella & they would often run with me whilst we were being chased around the playground trying to evade the pace bashing gangs. Unfortunately, several of these friends, if you could call them that, decided that one day they couldn't be bothered with me. One minute I'd be laughing with them and the next they'd all be laughing at me and the rare smiles I had were wiped clean from my face. The friends would slowly start to distance themselves from me and then the whispering would start, the fingers would point towards me and the sniggering would begin. This was without doubt school boy antics at their worst and no sooner had the sniggering stopped, they would walk back over to me and tell me "they weren't my friends anymore". When I first heard this it left me a little shocked and I didn't really know how to react. "They're not my friends anymore...." Hmmm, let me see, i've done nothing to them, haven't call them names, haven't been rude to them so what have I done? This wasn't the worst part - this was still to come. One of the *friends* was actually my neighbour and whilst the others made it obvious I wasn't welcome anymore he came over and said "I'm still your friend".

By now I really didn't know what was happening - I stood there in the middle of the playground and suddenly felt very alone. I just couldn't understand it, I just didn't know what I had done to deserve this. In reality and as the weeks, months & unfortunately years went on I realised that my neighbour, my loyal trusting neighbour couldn't give a damn about me really. The only reason he pretended to stick with me was because he was worried I might tell my mum who would then tell his mum. Well, he didn't have to worry; there was no way I was telling anyone about my torrid time at school. What was the point, nobody at home was interested and if I had mentioned it i'm certain that nothing would be done about it anyway. What I have learnt since then is that bullying; real bullying is one of the worst crimes you can commit. I may have used the word *crime* loosely but this is what I truly believe. Unless you have been the victim of bullying you have no idea what it feels like.

There were several weeks where I walked to & from school alone, I sat by myself during break time, ate my lunch alone and nobody wanted to sit next to me, I was the last to be picked on the football team or any other team for that matter. When you endure this so young - remember I was only 11, it takes a very long time for the wounds to heal and if i'm honest it was about 5 years after that when things started to improve. One particular day after getting home after another eventful day at school, I was just about to get the house key out of my pocket when I felt someone grab my hands. Before I realised what was going on I had a small knife shoved against my throat and before I could shout anything my mouth was covered and all I could see what a huge lad grinning at me. I should have been petrified at this moment but the speed at which it all happened left me very confused but suddenly it dawned on me that this guy meant business and I could feel the metal of the knife rubbing against my throat.

Fearing the worst I just accepted that I was in real trouble. The fact that it was daylight and in full view of everyone made me think that this guy really had lost the plot and didn't care about anyone or anything. However, my neighbours mum came to my rescue, I have no idea where she came from but thankfully she did and somehow she scared him off. It was very surreal and I dread to think what could have happened had she not intervened. A few days after that I found out that the lad had done this before and was a bit of a loose cannon; often picking on smaller kids simply because he could.

100

7

It's the holidays – get me outta here...

Whilst most kids looked forward to the holidays I dreaded them - with no friends to play with and my own brothers & sisters not knowing the scale of my problems at school, I was stuck at home alone. Often whilst I sat in the front room staring out into the street all the ex-friends would knock at my neighbour's door and i'd hear them joking around whilst they planned what they would do that day. I always made sure I hid behind the curtain net as I didn't want to give them the satisfaction of seeing me. I'm certain they raised their voices knowing full well that I was inside & would hear them; it was their way to have a little 'dig'. The bullying continued for the next 4 years and I just had to get on with it. Some days were ok, some were bad but most of all - way above everything was the fact that everyone around me was false. To your face they'd be friendly but when your back was turned they were just cruel, nasty people. From a young age I learnt a harsh lesson in life and at that moment I didn't trust anyone. I often told myself I didn't need anyone else but who was I kidding?

One of my cousins "Rick" was the one person who helped me through these terrible times. He lived close to us and we were related by our grandmothers or something (yes, I guess I should know exactly but I don't ok!). During the holidays he'll call me over and as he was into football we'd play footie in Spinney Hill Park. I always liked football but I went off it for many years but playing again was awesome. I was starting to have fun again and for the hour or so that we played all thoughts of my home life and school left my mind. One day, whilst in goal, I had just made a diving save (it was good - trust me!) and as I went to pick up the ball I could see a bunch of lads walking into the park. Yep - it was the ex-friends joking & laughing and once they saw me the laughter got louder and the jeering started. Rick just told me to ignore them and i'm pretty certain he was about to go over and have a word with them but I told him not to. If he had done I would be in for an even harder time at school the following Monday so he left it alone. I don't think I ever thanked Rick for being there for me and as we grew up we never saw each other as much as we did in the earlier years. Rick - *thank you very much* for sticking with me amid the chaos going on in my life at the time - I'll never forgot it...

That evening I was sitting at home watching tv, can't remember what was on, my dad came home drunk and the arguments started and I thought "here we go again". I just couldn't take it so I went upstairs. I put on the radio and just as I did, Radio 1 started to play "Cruel Summer" by Bananarama. At that precise moment in time, a defining thing happened. This song became firmly embedded into my long term memory. It was almost summer and to say it had been cruel was an understatement. It may sound daft but the lyrics to it "cruel summer .... leaving me here on my own..." told it how it was. Ok, so it's just a song but it has stuck with me ever since. To this day, as soon as I hear the first few bars of this track, it transports me to my school days but the pain has gone now; i'm just glad I got through it...

As there was nothing else to do, i'd often just run upstairs and stare outside the window to see what was happening. During the weekdays there was always lots of activity in our street mainly because of the shoe factory opposite. Once it was 5pm the shift was over and the hundreds of employees spilled out of the many gates that circled the building. For about 20 minutes the whole area would become packed with people starting to walk home, getting on their bikes, getting into their cars and trying to nudge their way out onto the busy Green Lane Road. During the hot summer months when virtually all the upstairs windows were left open, you'd hear the shouting and swearing as the men were slowly kicked out of the Lancaster Arms pub. In addition to that, the Railways Men's Club was a short walk in the opposite direction and between the 2 you had to ensure noisy, drunken louts who would piss in the street and kick anything they could.

At Lancaster Street, my dad would initially only drink at home. A short while after though he started going more & more to the pub – the Lancaster Arms. This pub was the "local" and he would come home from work, sometimes eat something but usually wait till about 7.30 – 8pm and then head out. My mum knew exactly what time he would go and knew his exact movements before he headed out. She always confronted him – "You've got money to go to the pub but what about food & bills?" she would ask. Depending on his mood he would either ignore her or vent out his anger via a torrent of bad language. By this stage my mum was used to it all but she never gave in and always made him hear that his behaviour was unacceptable. When he shouted she shouted back, usually out of anger and frustration and although she would often try to reason with him it just didn't work. It was obvious that when my dad came back from the pub things would get heated at home but just for a few hours my mum had some peace. She could sit down, have something to eat without being shouted at or used as a punch bag.

Often my mum would be so tired that she actually went to bed. Everyone except my dad would have been fed and the kitchen would be cleaned up. Hesitantly she'd go to bed hoping it would be a quiet night. Sadly 9/10 times this was not the case. Soon we'd hear the sound of someone trying to get into the house - it was quite funny actually. My dad would be so drunk that he'd spent several minutes outside just trying to get his key into the door lock! When he couldn't do it you'd also hear him start swearing too but he would manage to get in somehow. One of his friends, a Punjabi man who we used to refer to as "Singh" would often go with him. Singh loved a drink too and they were no more than drinking buddies but this chap was completely different to my dad. He used to get very drunk but he was one of those 'happy' drunks & was harmless. He lived in the next street and was always happy to see me, always stopping for a chat. Most of these chats were meaningless though - mainly because he was rarely sober and I didn't know what he was talking about.

Once my dad was inside it would take several minutes before he finally surfaced; it all depended on how many drinks he'd had that night. He would usually drink so much that he struggled to do anything once he was home. He fell over many times and quite badly too. One day after another heavy drinking session, he fell straight onto the hard kitchen floor head first and since he didn't move I actually thought he was dead. Not knowing what to do I started to nudge him and could hear the moans of what was probably pain and then he just got up as if nothing had happened. Once he'd finally got his bearings sorted he would then rummage around the kitchen looking for food.

Even though my mum had prepared food my dad wasn't interested and he would start swearing and keep on swearing until my mum had no choice but to get up and try and sort it out. It would often be a standoff; my dad swearing and throwing verbal abuse yet again whilst my mum would try and reason with him offering him choices of food but he just wasn't interested anymore. All he wanted to do was vent his anger out and he did just that. On most nights my dad would eventually just eat the food she had prepared and after using the toilet several times would settle down to sleep. In the morning, he'd get up and have his cup of tea as if nothing had happened the night before. When he was in a talking mood which was rare, my mum would ask if he recalled the previous night's events but he simply shook his head - he had no recollection & wasn't bothered.

When we visited our cousins or had to go somewhere we were either fortunate enough to get a lift or had to use public transport. My dad's sister who lives in Coventry would often call us over and we'd often travel there by bus which was quite exciting. We'd take the bus into town and then walk down Churchgate to St.Margaret's Bus Station where we'd have to sit in the freezing semi circled shaped bus stop that were made out of concrete. The journey took ages considering that Coventry isn't that far and once we'd arrived there, we'd then walk to my aunt's house - a far cry from today where most people think walking is some strange ritual behaviour that they didn't want to be part of.

It was 1981 and my sister was learning to drive. Her instructor (I think the driving school name was "Sharma" or something) had a tiny car and one day he actually let me come with them which was quite good fun. How she did it I have no idea (sorry sis!) but she passed her test first time and soon after that we bought our first car. At that time the car dealers were definitely for the rich so our car was sourced the Indian way - through the *Indian network*. The Indian network is my term for the way in which any kind of scandal or news travels across the city & country by simple word of mouth. Since us Indians know so many people, it's like Chinese whispers but on a truly global scale! If something has happened to a family or a marriage is on the cards, you only have to mention it to one person and in a matter of days the news would filter out across the country.

I think we had the world's fastest search engines well before Google was born!

Anyway, our first car was 'sourced' via the Indian network and for the sum of £325.00 the little 4 door Datsun 1200 was ours to keep & was now sitting proudly outside our house. At the time there were only 2 people who could drive - my dad & sister and it was great having our own car. The car looked rough and had a few little scratches here and there but my dad made sure he got the most out of the engine. Forget the bus, we now had a car so trips to Coventry meant a drive down the M69 and door to door we would be there is just over an hour. I'm not sure what it is about Datsuns. If there was ever a survey of cars owned by Indians then Datsuns would come out on top every time. It soon became a stereo type, including the gold coloured tissue box permanently fixed in the car (I must say that i've never had this tissue box!). I think part of the Datsun craze goes back to the Indian network - basically they're good reliable, cheap cars and Indians like cheap hence word spreads and before you know it, we're all driving them!

Once we were in Coventry the mums would stay @ home and cook dinner whilst the dads would head out to the pub. Since I loved cars I would tag along and as soon as we got to the pub i'd be sitting in the corner with my bag of crisps and glass of coke - just like the old days. Up until then alcoholism was largely confided to our home life but there was to be an unexpected turn of events.

As my dad & uncle sat there knocking back the pints, the effect of the alcohol was soon getting to my dad. Being such a small person didn't help either - my dad would feel the effects of drink quite quickly and this is where the problem began. Once we'd finished from the pub we had to get back by car - except this time we would be driven by someone clearly unfit to drive. The journey back to my uncle's house wasn't the best of journeys but the trip back to Leicester was something else.

In those days all the men drank and *nobody* considered the effect it had on driving. So, on the way back home it was truly a lottery; we had no idea if we'd get home in one piece or not. With my dad severely intoxicated, my mum not knowing what to do and a small boy in the back we just had to endure it. I would sit in the back and try not to look out of the window as it was way too scary - traffic lights would change to red and as we got closer and closer my dad clearly had no intention of stopping. At the last minute (after screams from my mum) he would slow down but this was stupid.

This drink driving continued for many years and the journeys were awful; my sister wasn't confident enough driving on the motorways and my dad *had* to drive so we were stuck. However, there was one occasion where all 6 of us actually went out together in the car. This was something we'd never done before. Mind you this was daft really - the car wasn't designed to sit 6 people but we crammed in somehow.

We were on our way to London to drop Vipul off as he was about to start work at my uncle's newsagent shop. I can't remember why he decided to move down there but he did and I remember getting stuck on the North Circular Road in London whilst I was forced to duck down every time we saw the police. After dropping him off we headed straight back to Leicester.

This was the first and last time we all travelled anywhere as a *family*. Whilst we were growing up one thing I will say about my dad was that he never shouted at us kids. He may have raised his voice a few times but when it came to the kids he seemed quite chilled out. Unfortunately there was always some kind of rift between my dad & Vipul and I never understood what triggered this. It was horrible and the way my dad used to treat him was really bad. It was almost as if they weren't related and this continued for many years but the fact that Vipul was now in London gave them both (Vip especially some breathing space).

In comparison to Indians, other non-Indians had an interest in other types of cars. The workers at the shoe factory opposite had some cool cars. Well I mean cool for those days anyway. Outside our house was a black Toyota Celica; it was brand new and one of the sportiest looking cars i'd ever seen anyway. You'd also see gold Ford Granada - these were big, luxurious cars which had so many gadgets inside it our car looked like a toy in comparison. Both these cars are quite rare now, so rare in fact that I think i've only seen one Celica in the last 2 years. When the car registrations changed, the first car I saw with the new "A" registration was a white Datsun estate and bizarrely an English man owned it (an Englishman in a Datsun - was he feeling ok?). I remember seeing this shiny white car; it was so clean you just didn't want to get it dirty at all and the car was always clean & shiny.

Having a car meant we were no longer stuck at home in the evenings and a weekends. We actually had the ability to go out by car which was a novelty in itself. My mum would rarely get into the car - she just seemed to be busy all the time but the kids loved it. We'd wash the car, take a look at the engine without knowing what we were really looking at and start to check things like oil & water. The car's speedo only showed a top speed of 100 mph and looking at the car you'd wonder if it would hit 50 let alone anything faster. Yet despite its looks it used to fly on the motorway. My dad never hung around and whenever we drove to Coventry we'd be in the 'fast' lane all the way. If any car blocked my dad's path he would flash the car's lights and force them out of the way whilst the little engine screamed along at a maximum speed of 100 mph!

As the time progressed, the amount of money coming into the house seemed to increase and we ended up with some cool things to play with - well, when I say 'we' I meant my 2 brothers. I think one Christmas or something they combined their money and bought an Atari console. Atari consoles were one of the greatest moments of the 80's and almost every kid in the UK wanted one. We had one, it was a black & brown console with long switches to tithe games were well expensive but our favourites were space invaders & Pac man. We spent so much time on them that we became expert players on both games and if anyone challenged us to a game they left the house defeated!

As the weeks turned into months, our home life continued in pretty much the same way. They'd be good and bad days but some of the worst days were when there was no money for utility bills. My mum would tell it as it was - she couldn't have made it any clearer. She asked my dad for more money than he usually gave (he always gave a small amount of his wages for shopping and kept the rest to fuel his alcohol addiction). Refusing to agree, there was little my mum except push on and try to clothe us, feed us and keep on top of the bills but it was a real uphill battle. Unfortunately something had to give and as the electricity reminders continued to build up, there was nothing my mum could do about it and we knew the inevitable would happen. One day, unannounced the electricity supply was totally cut off simply because we had no money to pay the bill and hence the supplier had no choice. With no lights inside the house we had to use candles which flickered and reflected the blue coloured wall paper to such a degree that when I was standing in the garden, our neighbours would often look at the room and wonder what the shadows were.

Nervously I used to tell them that my mum lit candles and switched off the lights but whether they saw through that lie I'll never know. All I do know is that this was embarrassing and to this day I hate candles. I'm not sure if it's because it reminds me of this time but regardless of that, this was a horrid time. These cycles continued for many years but luckily our gas supply was pretty much connected all the time. This was partly due to the fact that our gas meter had been changed to a coin operated one. Before the gas would work, 50p pieces would need to be added which actually worked out more expensive that paying quarterly or whatever. However, with the Patel budget in the state it was, this was by far the better choice. With little money this was how we lived; everything was on a very tight budget. I think this is why I am the way I am right now. I have no qualms about wanting this or that. I do with what I have and my 'wants' are very minimal and i'm very thankful for what I have today - I should be, it was my mum who got us through it.

One particular summer, after arriving back from spending several weeks in High Wycombe with Chetan, Chandresh & Paresh, my mum noticed I was wearing new trainers. It was true - my others were so battered, water was seeping through them and my aunt bought me a new pair. At the time I didn't want a new pair of trainers; I was so used to 'getting by' that I would have continued to wear them until we could afford to buy a new pair and I felt extremely awkward taking them as gifts from my aunt despite her generosity. I could see the look of pain in my mum's eyes. She didn't have to say anything, the look in her eyes of knowing that someone else had bought trainers for her child was choking her up and i'm sure she felt embarrassed. In my eyes there was no need for embarrassment but I can understand what she must have been feeling at that time. I'm fairly certain that the next time my cousins came down, my mum paid my aunt for the cost of the trainers which made her feel much better as it 'squared' things out.

The start of my 2nd at Mundella was just as awful as the first. The summer had come and gone & whilst the other kids all joked around telling each other what they got up to during the summer break I had nothing to say as I did sod all. As August turned to September, the weather started to change and the infamous cold winters were on their way back. During P.E. (Physical Education), there was no let-up & us kids *had* to play football or rugby whatever the weather. When it was frosty it was really bad and you had no choice but to run about the pitch just to stay warm. When playing rugby I would try & stay well out of the way. In the rare cases that I actually had the rugby ball I simply pretended it slipped out of my hands as I watched some huge kid run towards me. There was no way I was going to let someone tackle me so I just literally gave the ball away with a bit of drama added just for fun.

During football matches I once felt the full force of the ball - it hit me right in the thigh. Trust me, the pain of a wet ball hitting your leg at full pelt is a very painful one. By the time PE was over we'd all walk slowly back to the changing rooms where I would always wonder whether my clothes would still be in the bag. Usually, the other kids would play football *inside* and clothes would end up on the floor, inside the showers or anywhere else they could shove them. It was so cold sometimes that I couldn't even do up my shirt buttons and the idea was to get dressed as soon as possible and head into the main school building to warm up. During most lessons something would kick off; on one occasions, Malkit Singh literally got onto the floor and somehow managed to crawl his way to the front of the class. With a ruler in his hand he then tried to measure the width of the teacher's trousers. The thing was you see, the teacher's trousers were really flary and the whole class burst into laughter when the teacher looked down to find a kid with a ruler in his hand measuring up! It was funny but usually when things kicked off it wasn't as amusing as this.

During a Geography lesson, the teacher, Mr Molten, asked a group of girls (Shaney I think her name was) to quieten down. After asking the group several times, Shaney continued to chat away and the teacher went berserk. He grabbed hold of her and shook her violently whilst the rest of us watched in total shock. Once he stopped Shaney's hair was all over the place and the whole room went quiet. I think she was more embarrassed at her hair being all ruffled up than she was at the severe shaking she received. After that we knew this teacher meant business but it wasn't over. The next day Mr. Molten was wearing dark glasses which hid the back eye he had received from Shaney's dad. I think the teacher and the school learnt a harsh lesson that day. Mr. Molten was always quiet & reserved after that but every day something new would happen and I really couldn't wait to get out of this school.

During science lessons, all the kids would take up their place around 2 huge science desks. They were like extra-long conference room tables with several sinks and gas pipes protruding from the desks. I never did understand how health and safety didn't pick up on this. As we sat close to live gas pipes, it wasn't long before the disruptive lads in the class planned their next course of action. Paul Chapman (I remember the name well!), suddenly put his mouth straight onto the taps and twisted the on/off part of it and his mouth started to fill up with this gas. Within a few seconds of taking his mouth away, out came a lighter which he lit and then went ahead to blow the gas out causing a huge trail of flames that scared the life out of all of us. The teacher was busy writing up bits of the periodic table on the board but the noise of the flames soon got his attention and as soon as he saw what was happening he ran towards Paul. In a flash the flame went out and all went quiet. Miraculously nobody was injured but the teacher was furious as you can imagine.

As soon as I got home I would detach myself from my school as much as possible and it was now October 1982. My sister decided to have a 21st birthday party so this was quite a good distraction. In true Indian style, we were to make all the food at home by gathering as many volunteers as possible. Getting volunteers isn't that hard anyway - in our culture whenever something needs to be done people (friends, neighbours, cousins, the owner of the corner shop etc.) just seem to rally round until the job is done. The night before the party, a whole load of my sister's friends came round and it was quite a good laugh actually. Everyone was in a good mood and most of them kept asking me what I was getting my sister for her birthday. I remember being extremely shy and just keeping quiet which seemed to do the trick. I was given the task of 'buttering' the bread so I had an important job you know! There's nothing worse than a badly buttered sandwich! Our house was small and looked tiny with all the helpers crammed in. There was food everywhere, part filled sandwiches, cheese, ham, cocktail sticks and on and on.

In those days I wasn't into the latest fashions - some might say i'm the same now but I was treated to a new pair of trousers. That's one pair actually - I never did understand why we say 'trousers'. I mean, most people do need 2 legs to their trousers don't they. It's not as if you're going to say "I bought a pair of jumpers" are you? Oh well, the trousers I bought were quite radical, kind of a dark red colour although Kiran maintained they were pink - they weren't - honest! That night my sister wore a brand new white dress and looked very pretty, I had my red trousers with a grey, striped top, Kiran wore his prison t shirt (just to be clear - he *never* went to prison - he simply bought a replica t shirt) whilst Vipul seemed to be dressed normally.

The party was held in a small function room called "Reflections" which was part of a larger nightclub. There were loads of people there all dancing, singing & getting drunk. My dad was there too; not for the dancing but to enjoy himself and have a few drinks. Naturally the few drinks turned into many but that night he behaved himself and nothing untoward happened which is good. One of the lasting memories I have of this day is hearing Eddie Grant's "I don't wanna dance" track which was quite apt really. I couldn't dance and didn't want to either so i'm with you Eddie!

Kiran and Divya helping
with the food.

Kiran in his prison T shirt! VIP
in his pyjama top!

Smart boy!

Cake time.

The ability to defend yourself was almost a pre-requisite at Mundella but my defence was simply legging it. If I did get caught then there was little I could do except take the beating. The last thing I was going to do was retaliate. If I did, i'd definitely get an even bigger kicking for my troubles the next time and there was no way I wanted that. Vipul (back from working in London a few months earlier) & Rick decided that they wanted to start karate lessons and after looking around at various classes found one that took place in the Belgrave Neighbourhood Centre just off Melton Road in Leicester. It was winter when we started going and the first thing we had to do was sort out how to get there and back. Thankfully Rick's dad was quite happy to lend us his car whenever ours wasn't available. He too had a Datsun - it was an orange coloured 120Y which was common in those days and it was in immaculate condition. On the days when we couldn't have the car, it was a walk down Green Lane Road, Forest Road, under the bridge at Ulverscroft Road, past the Bostik factory, right onto Catherine Street and onto Melton Road.

It was a mixed 'bag' of people at this class and our teacher was a 5th dan or something. Not really sure what all the 'dans' mean but all we needed to know was not to mess with him - ever. The first few sessions were brilliant, we wore our customary white outfits and looked the business. Learning the karate moves was great fun but it was cold in the hall and dirty too. I often wanted to wear my socks but can you imagine me standing there with my karate suit & socks on! I was always hungry too and often longed for some chocolate. I sometimes wondered whether I was more suited to being the Milky Bar kid rather than the Karate Kid! As soon we got there it would be warm up time - running around the hall, then press ups followed by sit ups. "Give me 10 more..." - why is it that all these fitness type people use the same words?

The best part was sparring - we'd all stick our gloves on and then the teacher / the "chosen one" / my dan or whatever you want to call him would put us into pairs. We'd often get paired with girls which wasn't very productive. Whenever a blow landed on them we'd have to wait for a few minutes whilst the false cries of pain quietened down and they had finished checking that their nails weren't broken. After the lesson it was time for a quick change and then head home. If we had the car or not it didn't matter - it was always chips on the way home. So, after working out for almost an hour and turning our bodies into fighting machines, we'd then stuff our faces with chips but they *did* taste great! We stuck with karate for many months but I never told anyone at school about it. If I did they'd all want to challenge me and would probably take the piss. As it turned out the karate lessons didn't last for long. Although all 3 of us passed 2 belts and had the certificates to prove it, karate got very boring and in the end we just gave up. Hindsight is a fantastic thing and yes I know, if i'd stuck with it i'd probably be a kung foo master by now but never mind - it just wasn't to be.

After another dull day at school I was close to home and as I walked around the corner into Lancaster Street there seemed to be lots of activity close to our house and a police car was outside. As I got closer, the police were in *our* house and I was filled with curiosity. From the outside everything seemed normal but when I tried getting into the house I was stopped by one of the police officers and told to "wait here". After a few minutes I was allowed inside and my mum was there too. In the front room it just looked as if someone had been moving stuff around, the small cupboards that hid the gas meter were open and you could see that the meter itself had been smashed to pieces. As I went into the middle room this too looked normal and untouched but in the kitchen I saw something which frightened the life out of me for many years afterwards.

We'd been burgled and the thief had made his way into the house by breaking the plastic on the kitchen Louvre windows and simply pulled out 2 panes of glass. With the top glass panels removed he simply climbed in. The scariest part of this was seeing the burglars hand print on the kitchen frame. It was made easier to see by police forensics brushing over it with their special powder. In the garden you could also see huge foot prints as the person walked into & out of the garden. Upstairs the rooms were ransacked, the suitcases were strewn over the floor with the contents all over the bed. I don't think the thief got away with much that day because we never had anything that valuable in the house. I suspect he made more by collecting the 50p pieces from the coin operated gas meter that he broke.

We never knew this at the time but once we realised we'd been burgled my mum sent Vipul to my dad's work (an engineering firm called Gimson's) to tell him the bad news. When my dad came home, he searched for his briefcase (my dad hardly had any possessions but he loved his briefcase) and then realised it was stolen. The brief case had all our family photos inside it and they were gone for good now. Today we only have a handful of old photos and it feels like we've lost some of our history.

My neighbours (all 3 brothers) were heavily into science fiction and we'd often talk in our gardens for ages. Most of the time the topic was the latest sci fi toy that was available or a new poster that was due to come out. With little or no money, getting these sci fi things was impossible but somehow they talked me into an alternate way. Yes, just when you thought i'd learnt my lesson I was about to do it all again and for the next 2 months I am embarrassed to say I helped them steal like there was no tomorrow. It was easy; we'd walk into town and just go into Lewis's. In those days, the store was simply Lewis's and not John Lewis or Menzies as the stores are now called. Lewis's was a huge department store and you could almost buy anything you wanted. It has about 7 floors to it with a huge toy section. After deciding what we (or my neighbours wanted) we'd walk down, pick up the stuff and simply walk out. I have to say that 90% of all the things we stole were not for me. The only things I stole were chocolate (can't seem to resist!) and looking back at it now we really took the piss. We had a bagful of stuff and literally helped ourselves to whatever we fancied.

Once we crossed off all the items on our "steal list", it was a long, slow walk home with all our goodies stuffed in the bag. By the time we were home, my neighbours would take our all their stuff and would hand me the chocolate. People often say that those that steal never get caught the first time and how true this is. Unfortunately the inevitable *did* happen and as I write this I still feel a complete idiot for the things I did. With our bags packed yet again I remember stepping onto the 'going up' escalators in the basement at Lewis's. Once we were on the ground floor, it was a quick dash outside and across a narrow road into the rear entrance of Marks & Spencer. Something wasn't right and it was then I noticed a man following us.

He was a short man with a cap on and was wearing a checked blazer and he had that "i'll get you" look about him. I remember shouting at my neighbour and telling him about it but all he did was walk even faster. It was a case of "you're on your own" so I had no choice - I had to do whatever I could to avoid getting caught. As I walked faster and faster I was soon into Gallowtree Gate and rushed past all the shoppers and then walked into WH Smith. As I turned around I couldn't see anyone following me. Thinking I was ok, I started to slow down a bit but as soon as I rushed out the back door and into the market area I felt a firm hand grip my shoulders.

This was it, i'd been an idiot and was caught. Little did I know that my neighbour had been caught too. We were both frog marched back to Lewis's where we ended up in a security office where it became clear that we had been tracked by undercover security guards who spotted our brash methods of stealing. Since our bags were full of stolen stuff they couldn't just let us go - we'd taken too much and the police were called. So there we were, 2 young thieves sat inside the back of a Ford Transit van and on our way to Charles Street police station. At the time there was only one thing on my mind - my mum. I knew she would go ballistic and I was more scared of her than the police. A few minutes after arriving at the police station the whole process had been explained to us. The goods were on their way back to the rightful owners and we were being taken home to our parents - my worst nightmare had begun.

My luck changed that day, whilst sitting inside the back of the police car that was driving the 2 thieves' home I maintained that this would be my last run in with the law. I had been extremely stupid and I really deserved whatever came my way. As we turned into Lancaster Street there was no one to be seen which was a good thing. The last thing we needed was for the other neighbours to see the kids get out of the car as they'd know full well that something wasn't right and the gossiping would start. My heart started beating ferociously and as the police officer rang the bell I was expecting to see a furious mum open the door. She didn't - my dad opened the door and after the police explained why they were there we all went inside. A few minutes later and my dad knew the full story but hardly said a word. The police explained "what happens next" and promptly left, only leaving my dad & I sat in the front room. I felt very ashamed that day but my dad never shouted at me but did tell me that what I did was very bad.

A few minutes later my mum walked in and must have somehow worked out that the police had been here (the Indian network working wonders again!). Fearing the worse she accused me of everything and demanded to know what i'd been up to. She was furious as i'd expected but my dad lied for me. Despite the shameful deed I had done, he covered up for me and told my mum that I had damaged someone's flowers in their garden. My mum still went mad and who could blame her? She was very upset and I truly felt awful because her little boy had added to her worries - worries that she could do without. I have no idea what fate my neighbour endured but I didn't care. Our mums didn't speak to each other about it either which was a good thing otherwise the *real* truth would have come out and my mum would be even more upset. Over the next few days everything seemed to get back to normal but after about 2 weeks my dad came running upstairs with a letter in his hand from the police. In it, it said that I didn't have to go to court but I did have to visit Charles Street police station.

My dad was very upbeat by this and when the time arrived he took me to the police station where I had no idea what would happen. Once inside a huge police officer led us to a private room where he pulled out my file and promptly explained why were there. Over the next 5 minutes I received the grilling of my life. The severity of what I had done several weeks earlier was explained to me again (not that I needed it) and it hit home very hard. With the grilling over I was free to go and no further action would be taken against me as Lewis's didn't want to take it further. The condition was that I was banned from that store for good and if I ever stole again I would be in *real* trouble. My mum still doesn't know the actual truth but that's that. I learnt from that experience and have never repeated it since. It took a long while before I could go into town without thinking of the terrible thing I did that day. The only thing that made me smile was the frequent trips into Dixons where the computers would be on display. We'd walk up to them and type: -

10 PRINT "SANDIP"
20 GOTO 10

… then promptly leave as the screen filled up with my name. There's nothing clever about this but it was just something to do. My dad was always a quiet person and never really shouted at the kids at all. In fact when my sister started dating Pravin, my dad played an integral part in the relationship. Pravin used to ring our house and if my mum or dad answered would ask for Kiran. Once Kiran was on the phone, Pravin would ask Kiran to pass on a message to my sister which was basically where and when Pravin wanted to meet my sister. It was just like Chinese whispers all over again except that this time the information being passed around had to be correct! My dad never once (as far as I can remember anyway) got angry with my sister even though he knew exactly what was going on. In fact, he used to say that the "taxman" was on the phone (meaning Pravin) but never once mentioned anything to my mum.

Most of the kids around our area had bikes of some sort, large or small, new or old it really didn't matter. The fact was that they had one, were having lots of fun and I used to sit and watch them from the window. I'd just like to explain that during my earlier teens this was quite the norm. I knew our household was struggling with money and as a result I rarely asked for anything as I knew the answer would be no. As a family we never went out to eat, never went on holiday and never really seemed like a family unit at all. My brother Kiran was now working as a shop assistant in Syston, just north of Leicester. He knew I was after a bike and one day after getting dropped off by his boss he mentioned that he saw a bike that seemed to have been dumped around the corner where he worked. I did ask him why he didn't bring it home but he said he wanted to wait another day before claiming it as his! That day came & wait and I could hardly believe it when I found out he was bringing it home.

I waited anxiously that day and wondered what it would look like. I imagined myself cruising around the streets with my new 'ride' with all the kids staring at me wishing they had a bike as unique as mine. When the Kiran came home part of my daydreaming came true. The bike was definitely unique; so unique in fact that I hardly recognised like it. As Kiran took it out the back of the car and wheeled it towards the house, it looked like some hybrid contraption. When we got it into our garden we took a proper look and it wasn't good. The bike itself was actually a Raleigh Grifter which was a great bike and a popular one too. The original handle bars were missing and had been replaced with something that looked like an old gas pipe. The gears didn't work, the paintwork was terrible and the tyres were flat. At the time I remember standing there in shock more than anything. Kiran didn't say much - I wanted a bike and he got me one - simple as that.

I wasn't going to be defeated and over the next few weeks I slowly took the remainder of the bike to bits. I sanded it down, cleaned it up, greased it and polished and after fixing the tyres it was ready for the road. Ok, the handle bars were crap but it was in much better shape and I could finally ride it! Although I took it out several times, the stares from the other kids got too much for me and in the end the bike was just scrapped and from that day I really didn't want a bike unless it was a decent one. I just kept recalling past history, Kiran had broken my trike, my brand new bike never arrived as my dad took back the deposit he had left and the bike I had recently was something out of scrapheap challenge.

Kiran on the other hand had a much better bike. It was a blue racer and was immaculate. The paintwork was clean, sparkled in the sun and the wheels sparkled like they were brand new.

My mum wasn't too happy though, her outside store room was now filled with bikes, bits of bikes and all kinds of tools together with spray cans. In the garden you could see where Kiran and I had gone a little mad with the spray. All over the doors and in the alley way (used to get access to the house from the rear) were "SP 1983" and "KP 1983"- our own mini graffiti marks. To this day the marks are still there which now serve as a timely reminder of the early days at this house. When the weather was good, Kiran used to go out bike riding with his own mates but we'd often go out together. With only one bike between us, I used to heave myself onto it and balance precariously whilst Kiran peddled away like mad.

We would ride up to Stoughton Drive North, past Raj Motors and then head out until we came to a clearing where there were loads of apple trees. The apples were delicious and seem to taste better when you're scrumping! I never did tire of sitting on that bike and it was good just to get out of the house for once. Once or twice whilst we were helping ourselves to apples, the owner came out and we'd have to run (well i'd usually run whilst Kiran rode away!). Whenever I had plimsolls on I could run *really* fast and could almost out sprint anyone. Looking at this logically, there was nothing special about those plimsolls but each time I put them on it was like putting on super shoes. At the time plimsolls were, and in fact still are, a huge part of the school attire and we used to buy ours from a place called "Percival Shoes" - they weren't expensive then and even now you can get a pair for a few quid.

My mum worked for many years in shoe factories and she spent a long time working at a place called "D Henderson's" which was on St. Saviours Road about 10 minutes' walk from our house.

She had many friends at this factory and to their credit, the company used to arrange day trips around the UK. One day my mum told me we were going to the seaside and I couldn't believe it. She's paid for us to go on a day trip to Scarborough and many families would be going. On the morning of the trip, the weather looked promising. Well, it looked promising in Leicester anyway.

As a youngster I used to just look outside and assumed the weather was the same all over the world!

My mum had been up early cooking food for the journey and her friends would be doing the same. We all knew that one thing was for sure - we would *not* be going hungry that day! With our food stuffed in several bags, we started our short walk to the factory where we were all meeting up. As a youngster I always had a fascination with transport - I was the original trains, plans and automobiles junkie and as we walked around the corner and onto St. Saviours Road I could see what could only be described as a fleet of coaches. There must have been about 4 of them and if my memory serves me right, the writing on the side was "Greens".

Within a few minutes our "group" had met up and I was glad to see there were lots of other kids too. Mind you once we were on the coach I seemed to be the only one who wasn't playing. I was too busy looking at the other coaches and laughing as the coach drivers continuously overtook each other with rapturous clapping inside the coaches as we did so... It was a long way to Scarborough and the weather was getting warmer and warmer. The coach even had its own music system and we sped up the motorway with "Love Is In The Air" (sung by John Paul Young) blasting out of the speakers. After about 4 hours we were there; it was warm, sunny and we had the whole day to go. For the first few hours we headed straight for the beach. Apart from a trip to Skegness whilst in Junior school, this was my first *real* trip to a decent beach.

The water was clean and I jumped in and out of the water, tried to find crabs and anything else that would move and splashed anyone that walked by. The mums all sat away from the water and started to unload the food they'd prepared earlier. Within a few minutes a large section of the beach was taken up by plastic tubs, plastic plates, drink bottles and cutlery - let the feast begin! After eating a large meal it was time to relax so we all bought ice creams and sat there watching the world go by. Ok, this is Scarborough we're talking about but regardless of where we were, it was the company and atmosphere that made it so special...

Everyone then decided it would be better if we went for a short walk. Still very excited, I started to walk ahead of the group with another girl "Alka" who was a close family friend. As we chatted we didn't realise that we were walking much faster than the others. My mum clearly told us to stay close but as we turned around they were nowhere to be seen - we were lost! We were actually walking along the main promenade and it was early evening by now. With 1000's of people lining the streets we had no idea where we were so we just stopped walking in the hope that our group would soon catch up with us. Thankfully, about 30 minutes later they did - we never got into trouble but both of us learnt a harsh lesson that day.

Back at home, there was always something on at or around the shoe factory opposite our house. The caretaker of the factory used to live in a house 30 seconds from the factory itself (made sense I guess...) and one day, whilst I was looking out from the bedroom window I could see the caretaker and another guy fighting. It looked like a scene from a Benny Hill sketch at first but I soon realised this was no joke. The 2 guys were chasing and beating one another with brooms. I later found out that they were actually cousins but the brawl lasted for about 30 minutes. That evening when everything had calmed down I was looking out the window again (yes - I didn't have anything else to do ok!) and could see someone hiding in the evergreen bushes that surrounded the buildings. I kept a low profile and could see the person looking around as if they were waiting for the coast to clear.

I knew it was a matter of minutes before he would break into the factory so I called the police and within minutes they had arrived, caught the man and whisked him off. The would be thief was stupid - you could hear the police sirens several minutes before the police actually arrived and in that time he could have made a run for it but he decided to just stand there. I felt like i'd achieved something that day; rather than stealing i'd turned things around and actually did something positive. I still felt awful for the pain and suffering I had brought onto the family and was keen to do anything I could to make things better and this was a good start. I often wonder what happened to that guy that day. I had no real proof he was a burglar at all; he just looked suspicious so perhaps I helped to convict an innocent man?

The house to the left of us always had families coming and going. For a long period during a particularly warm summer the house was unoccupied and the plants (more like weeds) were growing so much that they were as tall as the garden's brick wall. Close to the end of that summer, there seemed to be some activity from this house and it looked like a new family were moving in. The new owner didn't waste any time and I guess it was the state of the garden that was his prime focus. Armed with a can of petrol he poured it all over the out of control weeds and lit it. The sound of the petrol burning made a huge roar and in seconds the entire garden was alight. As time ticked on, the flames grew higher and the intensity of the heat became unbearable. We were then forced to move back towards our house and I was scared to death.

In fact I was so scared that I urged someone to call the fire brigade. By this time burning pieces of weeds were landing in our garden, were hitting our roof and at this point I feared that our own house would catch fire. Nobody called the fire brigade and luckily for us all, the fire died down as quickly as it started up. After about 30 minutes I peered over the garden wall to see a garden burnt to the ground and the smell of petrol still lingered in the summer air. This 30 minute fire started an 8 year cycle of nightmares and a fire phobia that nobody knew I had. The vision of that fire, the way it started and the fear of it spreading to our house gave me untold nightmares and i'd often wake up sweating. I endured night after night of frightening nightmares where i'd be stuck in a burning house unable to get out. The nightmares were incredibly scary and there was no let up at all. It got to a stage where I was scared to go to sleep and would often wake up shouting and drenched in sweat.

How I managed to get over it I have no idea but since that day it has made me extremely cautious at home. Each week, without fail, I check all the smoke alarms in our house and double check that one triggers the other and vice versa. The smoke alarm as well as being powered directly has a battery backup and the batteries are changed every year with the best batteries money can buy. Whilst the windows in the house may be shut, they are *never* locked - the thought of being trapped in a room and unable to find a key to the window means that nobody in our house has ever used the window locks. Although many people like candles, they are banned from our house - yes it might sound too extreme but no candles drastically reduces the chance of fire so there you go. On the whole though, I think that experience has just made me a cautious person and prior to going to bed I always check that the gas is off and give the place a quick check over...

Day to day life at home had always been tough but since we were burgled things got even worse. My dad wasn't bothered about work anymore - I don't think he enjoyed what he did but he would often work overtime if he was offered to it. As the months wore on, he seemed to spend more time at home than work and the tensions rose as a result. With money already tight, it was getting even tighter and the arguments between my mum and dad continued. My dad's drinking money virtually vanished and he thought of other ways to make money. I never had him down as a salesperson but he would try and sell anything. In fact he got so desperate that he even sold my brothers jeans. He took them out of the draw (they were new at the time) and offered them at a super discount price to a shop owner on Green Lane Road. The owner couldn't resist a bargain so he bought them for his son.

When he wasn't selling his own family's clothes, he started his own unique painting and decorating service. Whilst in the pub, he'd use the Indian network to his advantage and after casually telling a few people that he was a dab hand at painting/decorating he would start to take deposits. My dad actually kept his secret painting skills from us and his secret was only revealed when lots of people started knocking on our door asking for my dad. I often wondered why the doorbell would ring and my dad would say "Tell them i'm not in..." Once we answered the front door we would often get a torrent of abuse from angry customers who had been duped by my dad. He would take a hefty deposit from them, promise them a date that he would start and then not bother to turn up. To make it worse, he'd end up in the pub spending *their* money. My mum had good reason to be furious and she was. This unfortunately caused many arguments and as before it generally ended up with swearing, physical violence and a mum fighting yet another losing battle.

One of the worst periods was when we literally had to kick my dad out of the house. The violence was a daily occurrence, my mum seemed to be crying more and more and something needed to be done. As the month and years progressed, the kids were growing up and finally after many years of just sitting back and not being able to do something, we could finally protect our mother. Enough was enough and I can't remember if we changed the lock or we simply took the key from my dad but the end result was that he couldn't get into the house. He'd go to the pub, get drunk and then come home, banging on the door for so long that the neighbours would come out and start to wonder what was happening. During this time we would tell our mum to ignore him whilst we tried to deal with it. It was hard though, he shouted and swore and we often thought we should let him in simply to quieten him down. I'm not sure where he stayed the first night but after that we saw him sitting in a car opposite our house. The car (yes another Datsun 120Y) actually belonged to an Indian shop keeper who lived just around the corner.

What was he doing in his car? What was he doing driving this car whilst drunk? These and many other questions rang through our brains and my dad tried to get his own back by revving the engine so hard that i'm surprised it didn't blow a gasket or something. Many times he would walk up to the house and try to get in but on one occasion Kiran and I had to restrain him and as my dad slipped he fell onto the pavement. I have had many defying moments in my life and this was another one. My dad, the one who is meant to look after & protect us was lying on the pavement, drunk and in a sorry state. It was then that I knew this person was not fit to be called a dad and from that day onwards he was dead in my mind. You don't need to tell me that these were harsh words - I know they are but I had endured as much as I could take and I kept thinking about my poor mum and the fact that she had endured much more. As a father or anyone else for that matter with a level of responsibility you can make mistakes. The key to this is *learning* from these mistakes and ensuring that you don't make them again. The drunken episodes were entering their 6/7th year so there had been plenty of time for my dad to take note of what he had done and sort himself out but he decided not to.

My dad's actions were not confined to our house and with the Indian network working at full speed, virtually all our family friends and relatives knew what he was like and knew what was happening in our household. Many of my uncles tried desperately to make my dad see sense but they were all defeated by my dad's ignorance in facing up to his family responsibilities and sadly nobody could make a tiny bit of difference. With this in mind, my mum made the decision that she never thought she would make in her lifetime - she considered splitting from dad. The mere thought of this would have sent shockwaves across the Indian community. The thing is you see - vip, splitting up or whatever you want to call it is virtually unheard of - it was certainly a very taboo subject during this time of our life anyway.

It got to a stage where my mum was tired, both physically and mentally, from the years of abuse at the hands of an alcoholic. She deserved better than this and was simply a weak target and it had to stop. Since I was young, i'm pretty certain that my sister played a huge role in this and was a great pillar of support to my mum. I knew something serious was happening when I was kept off school one day and we all seemed to head into town. I remember lots of office space and people busily going about their duties and my mum had to make a formal approach to start off the proceedings. I never questioned the wisdom in what she was doing - we were all worried about her and although the kids never said it, i'm certain we all worried whether my mum could continue if things didn't change. Sadly, my mum decided not to go through with the proceedings. I'm certain my dad got an idea of what was happening and got to her somehow - he probably just said things would change or something and before we knew it we were back at home. I actually think it was the 'for better or worse' equivalent of the Indian marriage vows that helped my mum make her decision.

Once we got home, I just ignored everyone; I was very angry and couldn't believe that we were so close to making all the bad things go away and here we were back to square one. Nobody in our community would have said a thing had the marriage break up taken place. So many of my aunts and uncles have over the years commented on how brave she has been and that she is one of the strongest minded people they've ever met. In the end I suspect it was maintaining the Hindu tradition that prevented my mum from separating from my dad. So there you have it, I just had to get used to continuing life in the way I had become accustomed to. At school the bullying continued and at home the drunken episodes became part of everyday life. My dad realised that the kids were no longer kids anymore and spent more time in the pub than he did at home but the nightly routine of coming home drunk and abusive continued.

At school fashions were always changing and for the fortunate, wealthier kids, their attire changed almost weekly. One of the biggest 'phases' virtually all kids went through was wearing designer jumpers with the designer's name stitched into it. The genuine, expensive jumpers had "Pierre Cardin" stitched into them and other kids who couldn't afford the real thing started to wear alternate jumpers with "Leo Gemelli" and other non-designer names that were quickly being made by the sweat shop factories to make a quick fortune. The other fashion statement was Farah trousers - these trousers came in various colours with the unique "F" orange label sticking out the side of them. The Farah's were a good quality pair of trousers and to be seen in a pair was very cool. As ever, I always stood out from the crowd - indeed I did want a pair but at 4/5 times the price of a 'normal' pair of trousers, we couldn't afford it so I just stuck with what I had.

There was also a 'conker' phase during my early years at Mundella secondary. Conkers are the seeds of the horse chestnut tree and there were competitions to see who had the best conker. I remember going to Spinney Hill Park where there were many horse chestnut trees there. We'd search around for the right stick and then look high into the trees to pick out the biggest ones. With our target in sight we'd hurl the sticks into the trees hoping to knock the conkers to the ground. After doing this over and over again we started to get pretty good at it and we could spend hours doing this. It became very competitive, so competitive in fact that some kids used to soak them in vinegar and even bake them in the oven to make them harder. Once ready, they would make a hole through it, push some string through and challenge another kid. If you ask a kid nowadays what a conker is they'd probably look at you in a strange way. Playing computer games has superseded the *traditional, real* games which is a real shame.

8

Ditch my ride

One particular winter, during the Hindu 'Navratri' festival, my brothers & I drove to Wanlip Lake which is north of the city in a small place called Syston. Inside the grounds of the lake was a hall where the celebrations were taking place and due to the popularity of this festival there was 100's of cars parked outside. This was too good to be true. My brother had a Datsun 180B and he noticed a Datsun Stanza parked close by which had some wheels that looked pretty cool. So cool in fact that before I knew what was happening (I had no idea - honest), he was pulling the car jack from out of the boot and was jacking up the doomed Stanza. There was no time to think - I was on watch duty and as I saw the light from cars getting closer or heard strange noises I shouted out and both my brothers would run back into our car until the danger was over. They would then rush back out and continued to jack up the car only stopping when they thought it was high enough. The wheel spanner came out and within minutes the first wheel was off.

I know it's not funny but at the time all I could think of was the look on the driver's face when he got back to his car. After the wheel was safely stored, the next wheel was targeted and so it continued. The whole process took about 45 minutes and we were regularly interrupted with cars passing by. Can you just imagine if the owner had come back? Finally the last wheel was wedged into the back of our car – how they all fitted I have no idea but regardless of that we had to get out of there and quickly. Somehow we pulled it off; I cannot believe I was an accomplice to such crime yet 24 hours later my brother was driving around with his new 'wheels' without a thought for the unfortunate owner of that Datsun Stanza who came back to his car with his (presumably) wife & kids and stared in amazement at his beloved car firmly stuck to the grass with no wheels!

As the years progressed from one to the other nothing much happened. Academically I fell behind but this was due pressures at school and home. It's pretty hard to study when your mind is elsewhere and my school work suffered terribly as a result. I don't recall a single parents evening and if there was one, the results wouldn't have been encouraging anyway. All I wanted to do was to get out of this rotten school but there was nothing I could do at all. The only thing I could do was to try and forget about school as soon as I got home. As with many summers in the 80's, the summer of 1984 was particularly warm too. It was my cousin Rick yet again, that helped me through the year. As the school term ended and I breathed a heavy sigh of relief, the film "Breakdance" was released. For me, this film was instrumental in my life and allowed me to put my efforts into something else - music. I always loved music but breakdancing *and* music together in one film was too good to be true.

Rick came to call for me one day and mentioned that they (Rick and a few other mates of his) were going into town to watch this new film that was causing such a stir. I couldn't see the film as I had no money but Rick insisted I go with them and that he would pay for me. By this time I couldn't stand the thought of someone having to pay for me to do something so simple as watch a film. Everything seemed to revolve around money and it seemed you couldn't do anything if you didn't have money in your pocket. I really wanted to watch the film but I didn't want to feel like I owed anybody anything. In the end Rick won and i'm glad he did - we watched the film and to this day it's one of my favourite films of all time.

The mischievous streak in me had got me into a fair amount of trouble up to this stage and I knew I had been extremely lucky so far (especially after the last time when I got caught in town).

Another boring day at Mundella had ended but rather than going straight home I decided to go to the library first. The St. Barnabas library was on East Park Road (ok, for those of you know Leicester it's actually St. Barnabas Road) and was used a sort of after school hang out place. I'd go in there and would no doubt bump into Nalini, Nila and other girls from Mundella. Libraries are a strange place, you know you have to be quiet but you always ended up making lots of noise. A joke that isn't even funny would have you laughing your head off to a point where you'd had tears streaming down the side of your face. The more you tried to hold it in, the more you'd laugh and this continued each time we met here.

That day there were 2 other boys there; they weren't from Mundella and were talking to Nalini. This was strange and at the time I felt like a big brother to Nalini and wondering who they were, delved a little deeper. It turned out that they were from Spencefield school and E2; one of the lads, lived close to the library. Nalini would walk home in the direction of E2's house and this is how they started chatting. Anyhow, I got to know E2 and Nelesh indirectly which was the start of a lifelong friendship. With the introductions over I never really gave it a second thought and after saying good byes headed home. As I turned into our street there were a few people standing outside our house and as they laid eyes on me I knew something wasn't right. No sooner had I entered my house I felt like public enemy number 1. The police were inside, my mum was looking angry, my sister looked even angrier and I could hear a description of my own BMX bike being fed into the policeman's walkie talkie.

The police were there because a BMX bike had been stolen from a house in Jellicoe Street (the next street up) and the description of the thief matched me perfectly. Immediately I mentioned that I knew nothing about it and that I was in school all afternoon but it didn't matter. I was guilty till proven innocent and not the other way round. The boy whose bike was stolen and his sisters gave me a smug look as if to say "gotcha" and my sister kept asking me if I stole it. It didn't matter what I said and my previous run in with the police didn't help either. I stood there, a 14 year old boy and listened as the policeman read out the infamous "I am arresting you on...." and in the distant I could hear the faint sounds of a police car. I remember thinking to myself that there was no need for the sirens to be on - it would simply attract more attention. The car arrived, I had been told my rights and I was shoved into the police car with my sister. A few minutes later we arrived at Humberstone Road police station where the accusation was put in writing and I gave my reply. In the end the police agreed that they would come to Mundella the next day to clarify 'my story' as they called it.

After getting back home, the accused walk into the house and my mum wasn't too happy as you'd expect and I didn't blame her at all. It did look bad but I knew that for once I didn't do it and I was in school all day. The next day the police officer came to school and checked the attendance records with the teachers who confirmed that I was at school during the theft of the bike - I was a free man (or boy!). When I got home, my family already knew that I was cleared as the police officer had already been home. Bizarrely, nobody seemed to be pleased to see me and I felt as if I was still accused. A few days later I saw the boy whose bike was stolen and gave him a smug look back. I shouldn't have done it really - after all he was just upset at someone stealing his bike.

9

Close encounters of the snow kind 1985 / 1986

The visits to the library increased over the next few months and in that time I got to know E2 & Nee (aka Nelesh) much better. I didn't go round their house or anything but we just seemed to get on pretty well. The best bit about this pseudo friendship was that it seemed to be real but it would take much more than a few meetings in the library before I trusted them. It was my experience with so called friends at Mundella that made me like this but I knew I had *real* friends a few weeks later during the winter months. We were all heading home after a trip to the library and were walking along East Park Road. It was a cold, wintry day and the snow was falling and starting to settle. So much snow had fallen that we started to make snow balls and the inevitable snowball fight started. At first we just started throwing them at each other but then both E2 & Nee shouted "leg it!!" At first I didn't know what was going on and as I stood there trying to understand why they wanted me to run I noticed they were running themselves - in opposite directions.

As I turned around a car travelling towards the library suddenly did a 180 degree turn and started coming towards us - the people inside the car were very angry and I knew something wasn't right. It turned out that my new friends decided to liven things up a little by throwing snowballs at cars. The occupants of this car took offence and decided to chase us. I was still dazed by the speed at which all this happened that I simply stood there. As the occupants raced towards me, I thought I was in for a serious beating but I simply told them that "it wasn't me". Surprisingly they got back into their car and sped off leaving me even more shocked.

My first trip home with my new friends was one that i'd never forget but both of them were just having fun *their* way and weren't phased by what had happened at all. Winter came and went and as the months flew by Nee & E2 became good friends of mine - all of us just seemed to bond really well. It made a huge difference to me - the bullies at school didn't faze me that much because I knew that outside of school I had others I could mess around with. Both of them would often come to my school because together they spent more time out of school than in it! At the time there was plenty of inter school rivalry and if they came too close to Mundella there was always the risk that they'd be spotted and could get chased home. Even if they did get chased I knew they'd be ok; they seemed to have a way of getting out of trouble and it felt safe being with them.

If I was offered a chance to get away from Mundella i'd take it and soon an opportunity came my way. My uncle - my mum's youngest brother was getting married in March 1985 and my mum suggested that Kiran and I go to the wedding. At the time neither of us had been to India and I was excited at the thought of the trip.

There was enough planning to do; getting the tickets sorted, getting our vaccinations and arranging time off school. Time off school was really easy - I don't think the school really cared if kids were in school anyway and for me it was 7 weeks of bliss. I had seen pictures of India and sat through several documentaries of the country but I was a little worried at the precautions once there. Hepatitis, polio, malaria and tablets to purify the water - did I need to worry about all this?

To be honest I was *really* only excited about the travel there as i'd finally get to fly on a plane. Money as i'm sure you're aware by now was tight so we ended up booking tickets with Syrian Arab airlines; an airline that most people had never heard of. The night before my mum & sister packed our suitcases; I have no idea what was in them but there seemed to be an awful lot more than just clothes. We had an early start the next morning as the flight was departing from Heathrow at something like 9am so we were woken up at 4am by my mum. I'm not sure how she does it but my mum manages to wake up at any time she likes. She has never had an alarm clock and has never had the need for one. With perfect timing I remember looking at the clock and somehow managed to get up and staggered out of bed. I'm sure it was the earliest i'd ever woken up and after trying to eat something (and failing), we grabbed our suitcases and were ready for the trip.

We left the UK on a cold and frosty morning and it was around -4 degrees which is pretty cold for March. The flight took off on time and I spent the first few hours in awe at the fact that I was on the plane and 1000's of feet up in the sky. Kiran wasn't too bothered about that and was just trying to sleep but I made the most of it and was awake for the entire journey! It was an indirect flight and about 6 hours after we departed Heathrow Airport we landed at Sharjah International Airport (Sharjah is part of the United Arab Emirates) where we had a wait of about 3 hours. Once back on the next leg of our flight we settled down to watch a film and before we knew it the captain was telling us all that we would soon be landing in India. Both my parents and grandparents are from India so it was quite strange that I would literally be going home to my native home land. Even though I was actually born in Africa, India has always been my ancestral home and I was getting really nervous. I'd only seen pictures of my uncle and vice versa so my mum had sent him pictures of both myself and Kiran just so he could show them to us and more importantly to ensure we didn't walk off with some stranger.

Our first meeting with our uncle was a sombre affair. As we came out of immigration you could see 1000's of people staring at everyone coming out the doors. Offers of food and taxi rides had to be brushed aside and both of us stood there and felt really small in this huge country and we hadn't even left the airport yet! Out of nowhere 2 men came forward and shoved a picture of us in our faces - we had met our uncle but apart from a quite 'hello' we were led out of the airport without any further talk. I thought my uncle would be really excited but this didn't seem to be the case at all. Once we crammed our suitcases into their tiny car we settled down for the 9 hour road trip back to my mum's town of Surat in the state of Gujarat. As we started our journey, I began looking around and poverty and filth was astounding and shocking. People of all ages were begging, there were mums carrying young children with all kinds of physical disabilities, others were trying to cross the roads with missing limbs. The culture shock really hit home and it felt like a really bad dream. In reality this was India, the *real* India where all people, regardless of their stature in life all meet together and at that particular moment in time I already wanted to go home.

A few hundred kilometres later and we stopped for a drink break. I was desperate to use the toilet and was ushered around the back of a building so I just walked around expecting to find a toilet there. There was no toilet and being very naive came back to my uncle and told him I couldn't find it. He simply took me back and pointed to the direction of a small hut which was the actual toilet. Never before had I used such a thing; it was dirty, didn't flush, didn't have a door and didn't smell too good either. That was it; I *really* wanted to go home now but my uncle just seemed to find this whole thing funny. I must admit that I was starting to wonder if this really was my uncle; he didn't seem to give a damn about it but there was nothing we could do about it.

The remainder of the journey was awful - cars, bikes, trucks and people all shared the road and there isn't a sense of priority at all. I lost track of the number of times I saw an accident in the making, there were accidents every 20/30 kilometres and evidence of the victims lay in the road for all to see. I was terrified and spent most of the journey with my eyes closed - too scared to look out into the road. By the time we got into Surat it was late in the day and both Kiran and I were tired. After getting out of the car we noticed we had an audience. We lived in a place called 'Patel Nagar Society' which basically meant that all the local residents shared the same surname as us. My grandparents and my mum's 6 brothers (including the one who picked us up from the airport) all came out to look at the nephews from England and we stood out big time!

It was also hot - 41 degrees to be exact and our bodies went through a massive temperature change. For the first few days we stayed in Surat and basically met everyone. In those days anyone arriving from the UK was the talk of the town and everything from the way we spoke to the clothes we wore was heavily scrutinised. I found it very hard to settle in and the different food and water really played havoc with my fragile body. Despite using the water purifying tablets (which made the water taste horrible) I was struck down by bug after bug and the vomiting started and then continued for days on end. During the night time, the little food I managed to get down me would soon come back up and as I headed towards the toilet, I passed many creepy crawlies along the way. One of the worst nights of my life as a youngster was when I was vomiting badly in the toilet; the heat was immense and a lizard came within inches of my face whilst cockroaches scuttered close to my feet.

In a matter of weeks I had lost over a stone in weight and a trip to the doctor made no difference except for getting an injection in my backside and some tablets to stop me being sick. Kiran on the other hand was fine and neither the food nor the heat seemed to bother him. There was no choice, I *had* to struggle on and I did. My uncles wedding would take place in another town which was a few hours' drive from their home. Whilst the rest of them went on a coach, Kiran and I got the VIP treatment and went there in the car. The journey started well but as the kilometres clocked up I could feel my stomach churning yet again and before long the inevitable happened. In the next hour we must have stopped 3-4 times so that I could be sick - it was nasty and I just willed it to stop. Thankfully it did and somehow we arrived at the wedding venue feeling quite refreshed. It was a large venue and several weddings were taking place that day - the idea was that with more simultaneous wedding the costs were driven down - kind of Indian economies of scale!

After sitting around for most of the day and not understanding a word of what the priest was saying it was time for the dreaded journey back to Surat which surprisingly went ok. Now that my uncle was married I had a new aunt and they were heading out on their honeymoon with one notable difference - we were going with them!! I was looking forward to getting out of Surat simply because up until that time I had been confined to the bed with all my sickness. We boarded the train which would take us to Mahabaleshwar which is a cool mountain retreat popular amongst Indian nationals and foreign tourists. The train itself was awesome - the Indian rail network is one of the oldest networks in the world and still runs as efficiently now as it did many years ago. We would sit on the train and watch India go by, the colours of crops in the fields would change as we passed from town to town. When we pulled into small stations we would drink tea offered to us through the windows and eat fresh fruit pulled straight off the trees. Once off the train we got onto a coach for our final leg to the mountain retreat - it was a slow journey and to this day I can still hear the moaning of the coach engine as it meandered through the unforgiving mountains.

Some of the hills we went up were incredibly steep and there were many occasions where I looked out of the window to see nothing below us - the wheels of the coach must have been inches from the edge of the dusty road and one lapse of concentration would have sent us plummeting to the bottom. After a crash involving another van I could take no more and crouched into my seat - I was too scared to look out of the window and only surfaced when we arrived. By that time I was amazed that the coach (and us for that matter) were in one piece and we headed off to our hotel. As we walked up a small road, you knew you had escaped the hustle and bustle of the city - the air was crisp and clean and it was so quiet. Our room was basic but thankfully clean so we were off to a good start. We stayed there for about 3 days and just wondered around and it really is a great place and somewhere i'd like to see again. On our way back home we had to endure the coach ride again but stopped over in Pune for a few days too after which we headed back home to Surat.

 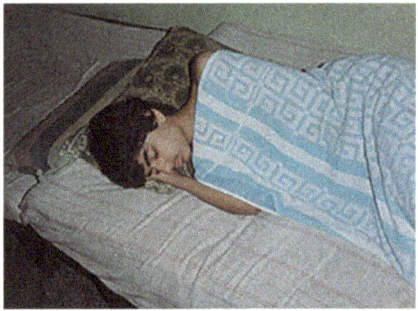

During the evenings all the locals (but typically the men) would head out and meet with their friends for a drink and a chat. It was simplistic but great to see, everyone seemed to be very chilled out and I really felt at home. As the weeks flew by it was time to sort out our return tickets to get back home. My uncle rang up the travel agent and booked us onto the Wednesday flight back home. After saying our goodbyes to all our family it was time to jump into the car for an overnight trip back to Bombay (or Mumbai) airport. Unfortunately, things didn't go to plan - once we got to the check in desk our names were not on the list and we couldn't travel. Nobody knew the real reason why our names weren't called but it didn't matter - we weren't going anywhere and since there was only 1 flight per week (the down side of buying a cheap ticket!), we either headed back to Surat or stayed in Bombay for a week. Amazingly, the decision was made for us and we were staying in Bombay. Naively I assumed my uncle would stay with us but after finding us a cheap place to stay in the 'fort' area of Bombay they left us there telling us they'd be back a week later.

As we watched our uncle disappear into the hustle and bustle of Bombay, it suddenly dawned on us that we were alone in one of the world's biggest cities with a small amount of money. We didn't know our way around, didn't know anyone else and were really left to fend for ourselves. Our hotel room was basically just a bed and was centrally located in the business quarter of the city. When we ventured out we kept it as short as possible and used the money we had sparingly. In fact we virtually survived the whole week on grapes and bananas. We willed the days to go by quicker and 5 days later we headed out to the office of the Syrian Arab Airlines to get ourselves on the next flight asap. Somehow we found it after navigating across the entire city and we were both delighted when the agent confirmed that we had seats on the flight home. We were happy now and my uncle would be meeting us the next day so we treated ourselves to a sit down meal in a chicken restaurant and boy did it taste great.

To this day the topic of my uncle dumping us in Bombay still comes up and my mum never understood why it happened. In a bizarre kind of way though, this turn of events allowed us to have our own mini adventure but although we lived to tell the tale, we should have never been left alone in the first place. Once we landed back at Heathrow (Vipul and my sister came to pick us up) the first thing my sister said was "you've lost weight and need a haircut". She was right, I looked very thin and needed some hair therapy. With that we got back into Kiran's Datsun 180B and headed home, via Burger King!

10

Failure & and the Patel bandwagon

As the months flew past it was now 1986 and I was close to sitting my final exams. E2, Nee, Nalini, Nila, Shanti and a few others all decided they were going to Wyggeston Collegiate College afterwards, so I put my name down for that college too. With time running out I tried to study as hard as I could but it just wasn't to be. I struggled big time in Maths and all the science subjects whilst all the other ex-friends came up triumphant. By the time the results came out in August of 1986, they all have 5+ O level passes to their names and were moving on to study A Levels. I barely obtained passes and I would have to re-take the O Levels at college.

The only good thing that came out of this was that all the other idiots at Mundella were going to a different college - I was free of them at last. The impact of Mundella on my academic ability was astounding; I really struggled to do well and it showed in the results I received. My mum was disappointed, and I could hardly look at her as I felt so ashamed. I think it was just expected of me to do well despite everything that was happening at home. Nobody really knew what was going through my head then and I just felt a major failure. Since that day I vowed that I would never fail another exam again and true to my word I haven't.

Many years have passed since I left Mundella and those kids who made my life a misery are still living in Leicester. From time to time I bump into them and they all look miserable.

They may have really good high powered jobs earning lots of money but if they're miserable then what's the point? The saying "what goes around comes around" definitely applies to this miserable bunch. They made my life hell and are now suffering from it. Whilst out and about I often saw them looking smug with themselves but as the years passed things changed; each time I set eyes on them I got the feeling they wanted to talk. It was as if they suddenly forgot about the school years. Well guess what; they can all go shove it - whenever they made an attempt to talk to me I ignored them, whenever they looked as if they were about to stop walking in the hope I did too so we could chat, I pretended i'd forgotten something and walked in a different direction.

Morecambe and Wise, Little and Large, Cheese 'n' onion crisps and coke - what do they all have in common? Well, they're great in pairs and guess what, the stereotypical view of Indians and their corner shops (another 'pair') was coming home to us too. For years, the financial situation at home was pretty bleak; not *really* knowing how much money would come in and for how long, my mum was always trying to think of ways that we could make ourselves financially secure. Many of our so called 'uncles' were very successful with their corner shops and each time we met, they made sure they shoved their success in our face. One of them whose name i'm glad I cannot remember, used to say "quite a small house you have...". Why do people talk down to others like that? If you're successful good on you but we're all just people man - get over yourselves... It really used to piss me off and I never hid my feelings either. Whenever they knocked on our door, I used to run upstairs and try to hide myself away.

In a matter of minutes the inevitable "get down here" echoed up the stairs as I was ushered downstairs where i'd have to hear all their shit again. The worst thing about it all though was the "what do you want to be when you grow up?" question. I used to think "well, firstly I hope i'm not a greedy twat like you." There was little point trying to answer this question because no matter what I said it would never be good enough for his massive ego. I wanted to tell him to get stuffed and mind his own business. I mean who the hell was he to come into our house and question me like that?

The questions didn't stop there, "why don't you know what you want to become?", "you're retaking your O Levels again - why?", "you're only doing 5 O Levels"...

I couldn't be arsed to reply to him and decided to sit there and not say a word. Unfortunately doing that just made things worse and if I wasn't going to say anything he certainly was. I listened to him going on and on about the fact that I had to work harder otherwise the only future I had was to stack shelves in a supermarket, become a dustbin man, sweep the roads or do some other kind of work that *he* regarded as one for the lower class. Rather than stir up more trouble I just took it and listened to his repetitive rants. At the time nobody in my house never said a word to back me up. My mum was never in the room when all this was going on; it's as if twat uncle chose his moment perfectly so as not to tarnish the perfect reputation everyone assumed he had.

Our financial situation looked to be getting a boost because my brother decided that he wanted to invest in a shop; yes it was a corner shop - the Patel's were finally joining the millions of other Patels and fellow Indians running this infamous business! With the assistance of yet another uncle, the bank had agreed to loan the money required to secure the business which was located in a large village called 'Wing' situated in Aylesbury, Buckinghamshire. It was decided that both my dad and brother would run the shop which obviously meant moving out. At home that only left my mum and I - my sister was married and Vip was living on his own so it was going to be quite strange.

As it turned out, the shop was incredibly hard work and both my brother Kiran and my dad had to work incredibly long hours but as everyone kept saying "it will be worth it in the end." This wasn't the case; the weekly takings were much less than those stated by the previous owner and hence with less takings but a fixed amount of payments going out, you don't have to be a smart ass to work out that things weren't good. Month after month, they'd get up early, stand in the shop all day, do the usual shop chores such as the banking, going to the cash and carry and get to bed late and my brother looked really tired from it all. With finances tight, there was little money to splash out on things like decent furniture.

It may sound daft but it's true - any spare money they had was shoved back into the shop which meant they just 'made do' with the basic living accommodation (no central heating, no carpets). My dad's drinking habits remained the same; at the end of the day he'd go upstairs and get pissed whilst Kiran, too tired from the day, relaxed for a short time watching TV on his 7" TV screen on his combined Radio/Cassette/TV audio system! Every fortnight they'd drive up to Leicester after closing the shop early on Sunday. Once they arrived, Kiran just chilled out, my dad went out whilst my mum cooked up a massive feast for them.

The visits were unfortunately short; I say unfortunate because I could tell from my brother's reaction that he really didn't want to go back. He was looking tired from the immense pressure of the shop and I really didn't know how long he could last there. I say "he" because not only did Kiran have the shop to contend with but he also had my dad and his drinking habit to deal with too. Sadly Patel's corner shop adventure was no more, the turnover and profit margins just weren't there. In the end, the business was sold on and we were left with just a few thousand pounds to show for all the effort they had put into the business. With all the rest of the doom and gloom surrounding our lives, this was yet another failure that didn't do much to boost confidence at all. Above all I just felt sorry for my brother who had put a heinous amount of time, effort and money into the business but still, despite all that, we were all still together - would it last?

One of the best periods in my life was the first year in college. I had new mates, a new college and for the first time in many years was actually focused and had targets to reach. When enrolling for college you could give the names of 3 other friends you wanted in your form (tutor) class so I gave E2 and Nee's name. It worked out well, as we all stood in the assembly room of our college all our names were read out and we were in Mr. Campbell's class. His class was actually a mobile and I remember thinking the last time I went in a mobile was at junior school. It didn't matter, we used to have great laughs during form time.

The rest of the kids were a mixed bag; there a kid we used to call "Spock" because of his protruding ears. Spock also drove a VW Passat that he was very proud of. He also boasted that he could change gear *without* using the clutch. Strange that - especially when you consider the car was a manual! He was one of those 'boasting' kids - the one who always has something better, more expensive or faster than you have. With e2 and nee he didn't have a chance and all year we just took the piss out of him and he knew it. There were occasions though when he *really* got on our nerves and something drastic needed to be done. One particular day he was going on and on about something he'd just bought and how good it was. We switched off ages ago but this time he was doing our heads in big time and when his babbling continued on, E2 or myself shouted "your dad!". I can't actually remember which one of us it was but the result was spectacular. One minute he was chatting and then next old Spock was silenced by those 2 words.

I can't even begin to imagine what he thought we meant. I mean if someone says "your dad" to you what are you meant to do? Clearly not an abusive statement, it knocked people for 6 every time we used it and believe me we used it loads after that. Whenever someone was chatting shit or just needed to shut up we'd be like "yeah ok, your dad..." and bang that was the end of it. After that it was our most famous punch line and it would get used everywhere. I must admit to someone reading this it does sound pretty crazy to say the least but those 2 words are legendary - I guess you just had to be there to appreciate it!

The others in our class were strange too; there were some girls who constantly laughed all the time, one who ate all the time whilst we just took the piss all the time. We all planned to re-take our O Levels and one of the funniest moments was when e2 stepped up to the teacher's desk and said "I'm here to do GCE" whilst the teacher replied "No, CPVE". CPVE for those that don't know was a type of foundation course to increase your academic knowledge so you could take GCE's the next year. Sorry E2 but you know it was funny! I opted to take 5 GCE's in Maths, English, Biology, Computer Science and Economics. I really enjoyed all the lessons and made sure that when I got home I read the notes and *really* understood them.

The key for me was all about understanding the topics and not about memorising facts. If you actually understand how something works there really isn't any need for parrot style memorising. During break time we'd meet up with Nalini, Nila, Shanti and Bindy and would have a great laugh just joking around really. We had a kid's version of a staff room where you were meant to just get together. At collegiate (short hand for our college), this was a chance for the opportunists to make a quick fortune by playing cards. A few minutes after the end of a lesson, the cards would be dealt out as quickly as possible with people shouting 10 blind and 20 seen. In the middle of it all would be "Chuddy" / "Chuds" (real name 'Sanjay') who was actually Nee's 1st cousin. He would sit in the middle with his legendary hat and cream coloured long coat and made sure everyone played the game correctly...

Chip cobs were addictive in this college and there's something about them that makes you want more and more. The canteen was downstairs so we'd often head down there and stand in the queue watching all the chaos. If i'm honest we would actually be

checking out the girls there in true teenage style and just laughing amongst ourselves. Whilst E2 seemed to know everyone in the college, Nee and myself knew few people. There used to be a huge crowd that would all sit together all laughing and joking together. We just kept away from them whilst E2 would often switch between them and us. During lunch times we had a whole hour to ourselves and on most days would walk out of the college and down London Road where we found a chip shop in one of the side streets. Chips covered in vinegar soon became our favourite lunch time food. With a daily diet consisting mainly of chips you'd think we would put on lots of weight but it never happened. The thing was we would walk to college and then walk home too. As a result whatever calories we consumed would burn off on our way back home.

On our way to college there were 2 meeting points. I would walk to the corner of East Park Road and Green Lane Road where E2 would turn up - he was always late! I can still remember seeing him from a distance with his blue jumper and cream coloured jacket. From there both of us would walk towards Spinney Hill park where Mahendra and Nee would meet us and from there we'd all walk together. Each time we met we'd all greet each other Leicester style by saying "ezee" whilst on our way back home it'd be "laterz".

Mahendra had arrived from Zambia (Africa) a few years earlier and was very advanced (academically that is...) for his age. He became one of the most intelligent kids at Spencefield school but after a few years with the 'spenny' (nickname for Spencefield school) boys (aka e2 and nee) he too became very mischievous and his school work suffered as a result. On our way to college we used to talk like real friends and life again was good. Things at home were still bad but the balance was shifting for the better.

One of my friends from Mundella was a girl called Alka whom I knew very well. Mahendra took a real shining to her but was soon head over heels to such a degree that when she knocked him back, he embarked on a downward journey of keeping to himself, listening to Luther Vandross songs and writing letters. He even let us read them and I know it was cruel but we used to sit in his room trying very hard not to laugh as we read out the lyrics from many sad love songs that he had changed slightly and turned into his own poem / letter. One of the worst acts of friendship was when we tried to speak to him about Alka. He was really cut up about her and we told him that he had to move on. "I can't help it man, I still think about her" were the words that sprung out of his mouth. I looked at E2, E2 looked at Nee and we were pissing ourselves in laughter but somehow kept it to ourselves. I know this looks bad but we genuinely tried to help but let me tell you one thing - with E2 and Nee around its virtually impossible to keep a straight face at any time. After several months where Mahendra thought life wasn't worth living without Alka, things changed and he snapped out of it. We all breathed a sigh of relief as we were seriously worried that he might do something really daft.

Our journey home from college was never straightforward either. We'd pass De Montfort Hall and then head down Evington Road. Sanjay ("chuddie") lived on Evington Road and would always tell us to come inside for a few minutes. We knew that a few minutes would actually be about 30 minutes at the least. Once inside his mum, always happy to see us, would make us all tea and if the weather was good we'd head into the garden where his brother would get out his rifle. Before I go on, this was a *safe* rifle and we weren't about to shoot anyone or do anything sinister. Instead we would line up old cans and practice shooting them from a safe distance. Sanjay, Nee and most of the others were super sharp shooters. Whilst E2, Mahendra and I struggled just to hit the can, these guys were hitting specific targets on the cans themselves and were more likes trained expert shooter (good job I was on their side...). After the shooting was over we'd say our good byes and head home. Once I was home the first thing I would is say "yes" to my mum's question of "Do you want some tea" and i'd rush upstairs and get out the books - something i'd never done whilst at Mundella.

After my homework was done and i'd read up on the day's notes i'd often get into "DJ" mode. From an early day i'd always liked the idea of DJ'ing and would spend many hours messing about with my cousins (Paresh's) legendary Technics SL1200 turntables. Sadly I didn't have these turntables but what I did have was my brothers 3-in-1 hi fi unit. Having found another tape player I then took various connecter cables and somehow joined them together. I could now play either tape or vinyl and using a 'mixer' control on the hi fi unit to switch the audio between the two - music mixing was here! I could now find 2 pieces of music and try my hardest to mix it up. Initially it all went horribly wrong and the beats didn't match and the music sounded so bad it would have probably sounded better if played in reverse. When my mum came in and saw a whole heap of wires running all over the bed she wasn't quite sure to make of it but she just left me to it. I *loved* messing around with tapes and records even though I hardly got any of the tunes to beat mix perfectly.

Both Nee and E2 had cool hi fi units in their house. Nee had a Technics system whose turntable looked the SL1200's. Technics SL1200's by the way are *the* industry standard turntables and though many would argue that they have been superseded by newer ones I whole heartedly disagree. Technics are synonymous with the original DJ Culture and always will be. When the rest of Nee's family were out he'd turn up the bass and we'd sit there nodding ours heads to the beat. At E2's house he had a Kenwood / Trio system which also punched out some serious sound. E2's dad also ran their own gift shop business where they sold 'That's tapes that became very popular and in a matter of months E2 collected a huge collection of these tapes which, when cranked up, would make everything start to shake...

Ever since we bought our first car I was fascinated with them as most young boys are. Over the years after watching and learning how to drive in my head, my brothers used to let me have a go. They'd drive close to Debonair Yarns (the good old transfer factory) and I would then get into the driving seat. Even though I say it myself, I was a good driver and always very careful on the roads. It's obvious that I shouldn't have been driving at all but I just couldn't resist it and my brothers felt safe so that was ok. Towards Christmas 1986, my cousins (Chetan & Chandresh) who were studying in Leicester would give me the keys to their yellow Datsun car. (Now do you see what I mean about Datsun's & Indians?) The first time they gave me the keys I didn't tell E2 or Nee but simply told them to follow me.

I led them to the car and they didn't know what was going on. Once they saw me open the door and get into the driver's seat their expression changed and they had smiles on their faces - we had wheels! Ok, yes I know, I know it was a very daft thing to do.

No licence, no insurance and I was a 16 year old driving around in a car. Thankfully I drove ok and although I took the car out many times afterwards I tried not to do it often - the last thing I needed was another run in with the police. On many occasions we'd take the car into college, stopping off at the petrol station along the way. After filling it up with £2.00 (yes £2.00!) of fuel, the person behind the counter always gave us one of those strange looks but trust me this small amount of money went a long way in this car!

I really enjoyed all the subjects at college and having my friends in the same class was a bonus. I shared Maths lessons with Nalini, English lessons with Shanti, Biology with Nee and Chuddy and Economics with Bindy. Our maths classes were a laugh all the way. As I was walking towards the room for the very first lesson I remember thinking I hope I know someone in there. Thankfully I saw Nalini sitting inside so I was pleased and she was too. The other students were a mixed bag - there was a Sikh guy (Inderjit I think) who sat in front of us. He looked very shy and hardly spoke but Nalini who can't stop talking started off a conversation and in a few minutes this shy guy had plenty to say! On one particular day we started talking about food for some reason and he told us that he *only* ate chicken. He would eat a 'normal' breakfast but for lunch and his evening meal it was chicken every day of the week.

After revealing his eating habits we couldn't call him "Inderjit" anymore and the nickname "Chicken man" was used. Often I would look around the class and make some passing comment about the other students (slapstick type comedy) and Nalini would crack up. It was quite hard to stop her laughing sometimes but this was just the start. Her laughing would set me off and chicken man wouldn't be able to control himself. He had one of the squeaky laughs and soon had tears of laughter running down his face. In front on chicken man were 2 other girls and they were even worse - they had a loud laugh and between Nalini, Chicken man and these 2 girls, the whole class would wonder what was going on. Our teacher, Mrs. Webster was also intrigued and would casually stroll over and say "So, what's the joke then?". She was one of those cool teachers who you could have a laugh with and didn't mind a few hysterics now and then. Unfortunately for her, she just got used to them - she had no choice, the laughing outbursts were a weekly occurrence!

Winter was drawing in now and to celebrate one of our friends' birthdays we headed off for a pub crawl (with a difference). It was only Chuddy that really drank alcohol in those days and we ended up in Evington Village. Having finished our drink, we headed out and started the long walk home but were stopped in our path by a gang of "paki bashers". I couldn't believe it; I thought i'd left all this behind at Mundella but here I was again. Fortunately I had my friends with me but we were heavily outnumbered. There must have been about 12 of them and one of them swung a baseball bat at Chuddy. Thankfully it missed and Chuddy (someone not to be messed with) put his hand in his pocket and seemed to pull out something. "Come on then" he said and as soon as the gang saw and heard this they seemed to retreat. The rest of us, not really knowing what to do, searched frantically for milk bottles. We weren't thirsty - simply looking for anything we could throw at them. This sounds horrific and let's be honest it is, but when faced with thugs like this in the middle of nowhere you have no choice but to defend yourself and that's what we did. After a long standoff period, the thugs left and we continued on our way - none of our 'weapons' had to be used.

One of the best times at this college was the Christmas of 1986 - the snow was falling quite heavily and our walk to and from college was transformed. Very few cars braved the snow and the roads were quiet, leaving us to take control of them. Whilst I tried to keep my head down, the Spencefield boys (E2, Nee and Mahendra) caused chaos by throwing snowballs at bus drivers, the postman and anyone else who caught their attention. These boys knew how to upset people - in their old school they would wait for bus drivers to pull into the bus stop, open the doors and would then throw snowballs at the driver. During break time virtually all the students would be outside throwing snowballs. Nalini, Shanti, Bindy and Nila would be our main targets. Often we'd hide outside and wait for them to surface. Once we saw them they didn't know what hit them. Snowball after snowball would land on them and in minutes they'd be transformed into wrecks and hurry off to the girl's toilet to dry off.

By now both Nee and I had started to take driving lessons. Our driving instructor was a joker. He had a clapped out car silver car and when we were out on road only did 2 things - look at the women and swear. He used to say "turn left", "turn right" when he wasn't even looking at the road - he had some kind of sensory perception about him How he became an instructor i'll never know but he did made learning to drive fun. In February 1987 I applied for my driving test and failed - not because of my driving - I never even got a chance to take the test!. The problem was with the car; before an examiner takes you out on the road he inspects the car and on this occasion decided that the broken brake light needed to be fixed. He was right of course and I was very annoyed at our instructor who should have known better. I couldn't wait to take my test so I rang up the driving test centre and explained the situation and was told that they would send out a new test if anyone cancelled.

I was lucky, within a few days of my original cancelled test I had a new test date of 10th March and I was determined that nothing would go wrong. I didn't mention this test date to anyone as I was very nervous about it already and telling others would simply make it worse. In my English class all the students had to put together a presentation on any topic they wished and we were to speak for 10 minutes. My chosen topic was driving tests and in that I would explain the whole process using my own experience as a valuable tool. Interestingly, the date of the presentation was on the same day of my driving test and before long the big day had arrived. The instructor picked me up and we headed to the test centre. The nerves crept it yet again and I had one of those straight faced, no talking examiners. After negotiating several tricky, and very busy roundabouts, I carried out my emergency brake and 3 point turn faultlessly and was very happy with myself. This meant nothing though and as the expressionless examiner told me to drive back to the centre I had no idea if I passed or failed.

Once back at the centre I was asked some questions from the highway code and then I heard the words "Well, Mr Patel i'm happy to tell you that you've passed your driving test". The relief was overwhelming; i'd done it and I was so happy. The instructor was very happy too and we drove back to my house whilst he sat there looking at all the women again. When I got home I grabbed my things and headed straight to college - I had a presentation to do! As I walked past the main entrance, the others were asking me where I was that morning so I told them I went for my driving test and passed! They were all very pleased but I couldn't chat and went to my English class. The teacher asked if anyone wanted to go first and I opted to go for it. The presentation was great and that the fact that I could tell everyone that i'd passed my test a few hours earlier made the speech even better.

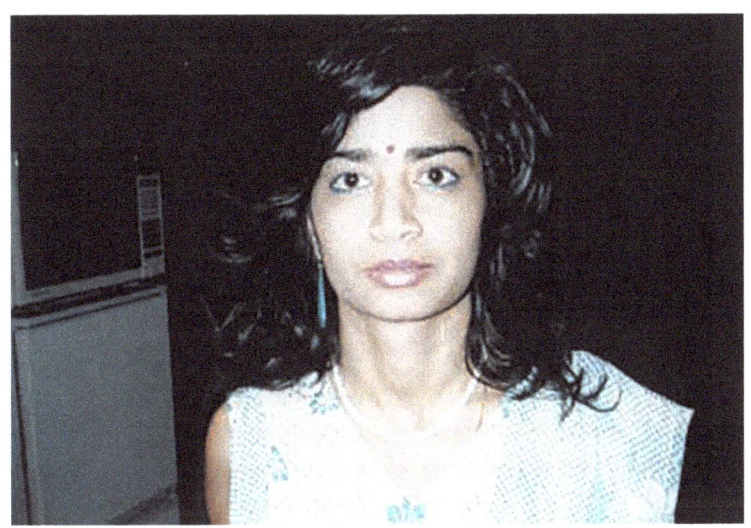

My sister, the model look, the student, still can't park though!

11

Revision, revision

As the months passed we were getting closer and closer to our exam dates. Driven by the fact that failure was not an option, I planned out my revision schedule - subjects, dates and times and I made sure I stuck to it. As I shared some subjects with Nee and Chuddy we would often head to Nee's house to revise but this wasn't a good plan. Whilst those 2 were more interested about their fish tanks and TV, I was trying to focus on the subjects in hand but before long I got them hooked into my way of thinking. I was very committed; as soon as I got home i'd have my cuppa and a bite to eat and then i'd be upstairs revising and only come down for short breaks. This strict regime worked well and helped me through many years of exams. My sister was also getting married right in the middle of my exams and I was worried about the impact of that too. In the end it wasn't that bad and I squeezed in revision around the wedding preparations that were happening at the time. Before I knew it the exams came and went and I was feeling fairly confident that I must have passed but we all had a 7 week wait until the results came out so there was nothing else to do except have fun...

Rather than do nothing all summer I applied to work on the M1 Services in Leicester Forest East - this is where my sister worked many years earlier. Once I applied, E2 and Nee applied and by the end of it there were so many of my friends working there that we literally ran an entire shift. Since it was on motorway and we had no cars (Nee had also passed his test by the way), the company laid on transport to take us there and back which was a

mission in itself. The journey to and from work took about an hour but we had great fun working there. Every day was different, one day we'd be shoving dirty cutlery into the industrial dishwashers, sometimes we'd be clearing the tables and on other days we'd be serving the general public. When it came to lunch time (or evening dinner) we would make full use of it. Our friends would be dishing out the food and would pile it on our plates to ensure we ate properly - had the supervisors seen this we would be in trouble but it never stopped us - you have to eat after all...

During this time we earnt a mammoth £52.00 for a 35 hour shift; admittedly not a huge amount of money but we were doing something that got us out of the house, we enjoyed and getting paid for it - bargain! The only real downside of this job was that we had weird days off. The rota meant that you may work 7 days in a row but then have 4 days off or have a Monday and Thursday off - not really useful for planning at all. On the rare occasions that we managed to get the same days off, we would head out on our bikes to Bradgate Park. From where we live, this park is about 15 miles away and we cycled there and back with our lunch strapped to the seats. One part of Bradgate park - Old John (a historic monument high in the hills) is very popular and if you stand at the top on a clear day you could see as far as East Midlands Airport - some 20 miles away.

The hard part was getting up to old John and the best part was getting down. After checking our path was clear off we went. The incline meant we hit some serious speeds coming down the hill; Mahendra always looked as if he was about to fall off but somehow managed to stay on. I was making full use of my BMX by jumping off small rocks whilst Nee (in his finely tuned touring cycle) flew down the hill so fast he vanished from view! The night before the exam results came out I was extremely nervous again and found it hard to sleep. We had to give self-addressed envelopes prior to sitting the exams so that the results would be posted to us. I heard the noise of the letter box which meant the results arrived. There was no point wasting time and I opened the letter as fast as I could and boy what a relief - I passed *all* my exams getting 1 A, 3 B's and a C so I now had 5 GCE O levels to my name.

My mum was happy but not as happy as I thought she'd be - in Indian households you're expected to pass anyway so it wasn't a big deal! It was for me; all the hard work had paid off and these were respectable grades. Nalini (who sat next to me in our maths lesson) didn't pass her maths exam at all and to this day I still cannot believe she could have failed. I remember telling her she could get her paper re-marked as I was certain there was a mistake but she didn't bother and it's become a long running joke now. For my A Levels I decided to take Economics, Biology and Computer Studies. I think E2 went on to start his O Levels whilst Nee & Chuddy took 2 A Levels. The transition from O to A levels was quite hard and was made even harder because of the teacher we had. Mr Harvey was a know it all, we had him for computer studies, biology, he was a professor and a qualified vet. We had no idea what he was talking about most of the time and he baffled us with his knowledge. He never explained anything and we left the lessons knowing less than when we went in.

12

Gigs, the FBI &
C C C Calibar Roadshow

Music was playing a bigger part of our lives and the 3 of us (E2, Nee and moi) decided to take things further - we were going to put on parties ourselves. My cousin Paresh and another lifelong friend "Munsha" were major players in the Asian DJ scene in and around London and they headlined most of the huge gigs. The plan was simple, rather than put on a party at night-time we'd do something different. We would start *daytime* parties in Leicester which would be something no-one had done before. It would mean all the 16/17/18 year old girls who couldn't get out at night could come to our parent friendly party! They didn't have to tell their parents; just bring a change of clothes and get changed - job done!

We looked at which clubs were available, secured a booking, got some A4 paper and drew out the posters, got them printed through E2's dad's mate who owned a printing business and drove around at night armed with a bucket of wallpaper paste and a brush. In the 2-3 hours we were out, we stuck posters all over Leicester and the stir it caused was amazing. Over the next 2-3 weeks everyone was talking about it and we knew tickets would sell fast. We printed the tickets too (with an authentic "VIP5" stamp on the back of it from E2's dad's business!) and then issued piles of tickets to our sellers. The tickets sold so quickly that in a matter of weeks they were gone. The first gig we did was at a place called Aviary's in Lee Circle and that was one of the best days ever. The party kicked off at midday and ended at 5pm and the queue was building up. Loads of people were still wondering who masterminded this party and just like a VIP guest entering a film premiere, E2, Nee and I stepped up towards the club and the crowd just parted. Once we were at the door, the bouncers let us in - everyone knew who the master minds were now.

Paresh and Munsha (known as 'FBI' on the DJ Circuit) soon had the party rocking with their fusion of soul, funk and bhangra which boomed out of the heavy soundsystem creating an electric atmosphere. It was rare to see Indian DJ's playing music but to mix it up was totally radicle. As Apna Sangeet met Erick B and Michael Jackson mixed in with Heera, the dance floor was packed and the crowd didn't know what hit them. We would stand at the side of the dance floor looking at all the happy faces and thinking "we did this". I must make it clear that many friends helped us so a big thanks to you all. Just when the crowd thought they'd seen everything, in stepped arguably the best Indian DJ in the UK - Avtar from Calibar Roadshow. I'd seen this guy before and he had the ability to transform a party within minutes. Within seconds of stepping behind the turntables he was sharpening the treble, deepening the bass and fine tuning the mic As he turned down the volume, he announced who he was and got the crowd in a frenzy. Over the next 45 minutes he played a DJ set that took the dance floor to another level and something that Leicester had never seen before and may never see again.

The music tore down the club, samples of records from Indian movies mixed in and out teasing the crowd. He was scratching records and creating an awesome effect to such a degree that a crowd started to gather around the DJ booth. That 45 minutes and in fact that gig in particular was in my opinion the best Leicester has *ever* had. When you consider that the ingredients were simple; people, DJ, music - we created an atmosphere that afternoon that people still talk about today.

Over the next year we put on many other parties at other venues which were just as successful. As soon as the posters went up they knew it would be good and the tickets, just as before, sold quickly. One day we decided to take things to the next level and hired out one of the biggest venues in Leicester - the Ritzy night club. We made an appointment, were shown around and agreed a hiring fee of £700.00 which, in those days, was a huge amount of money.

We were still teenagers but knew we could pull it off but sadly we never managed to see it through. Other people (who had to be known as 'promoters') weren't happy with us stealing their limelight and started to make it very difficult for us to promote our party. These people had organised a party for the *same* day and we weren't worried in the slightest - after all, our parties just worked. Sadly, these guys were just tossers and knew their party would be a flop so did all they could to stop us. Not wanting to get into trouble we gave in and cancelled the gig; something I regret doing to this day but we have fond memories of putting on the best shows in Leicester...

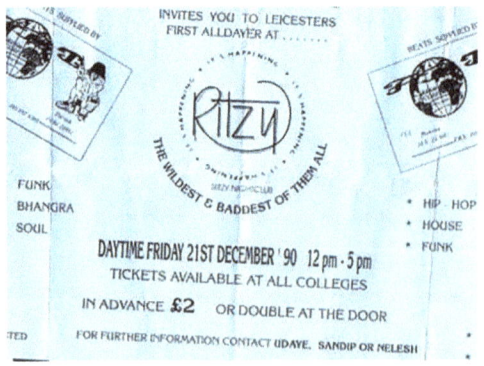

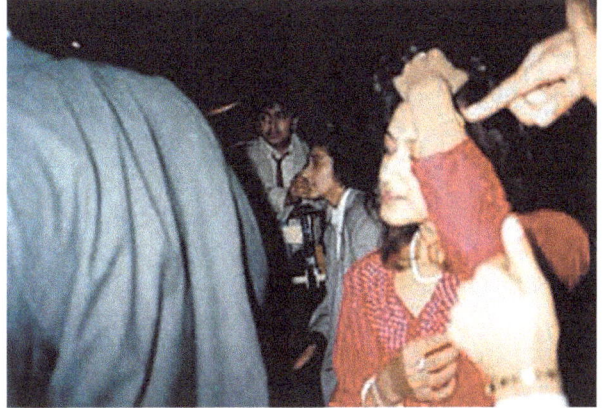

Aarti hitting the floor!

Bindy and Nila jamming!

167

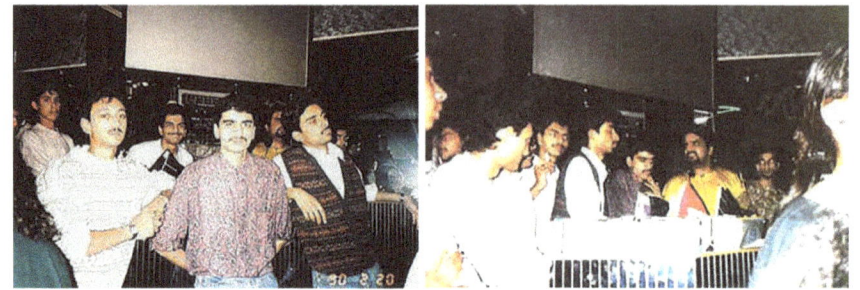

Man like Nee / Me with bad shirt!

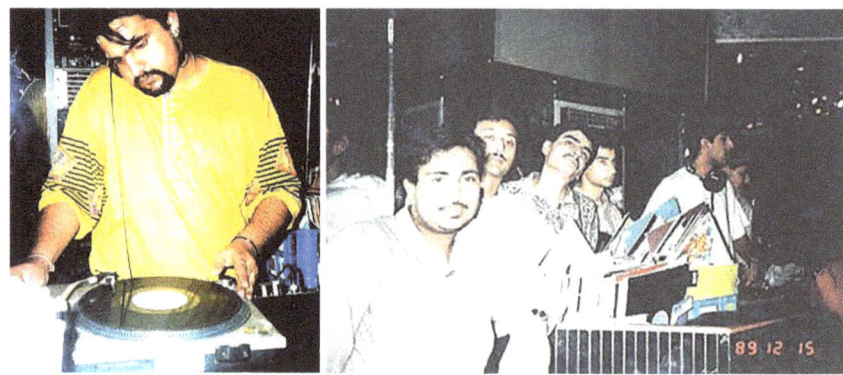

Munsha touching down.
Chuddy making sure everyone behaves!

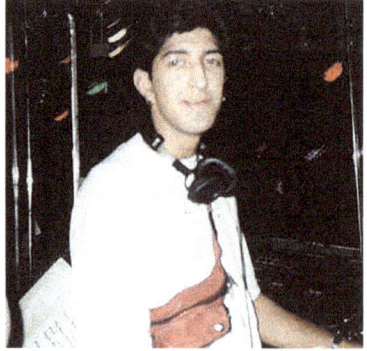

Another rammed daytime party @ Jokers, Leicester...

Yours truly on turntable duty with E2 & Nee...

The first year of A Levels really flew by and the exams were extremely tough. My results weren't brilliant but were on par with other students and I knew I had to do much better after the summer. The summer was a long drawn out affair and nothing really exciting happened. Nee jetted out to Africa for several weeks whilst Mahendra started to detach himself from us for no obvious reason. The truth is he got involved with the wrong crowd and despite his friends (i.e. us) trying to steer him in the right direction he didn't want to listen and finally he lost contact with us and didn't want to know. That left myself and E2 to occupy ourselves during the summer. E2 had now moved to the north part of the city and just to pass time we'd often agree to meet up half way between our houses. The rendezvous point was Vaughan Way and it was quite daft really; once we met up we would just sit on the wall and watch the people & traffic go by. We'd talk for what seemed ages and then would walk back to our homes...

Rather than spend the summer doing absolutely nothing, we (can't remember who exactly) decided that we should head out of Leicester with no real itinerary and end up wherever. After spreading the word amongst our friends there was about 9/10 of us ready to head off. Since none of us had our own cars we decided to hire cars and luckily for us, Hertz rented cars out to people as young as 17! So we hired 2 brand new cars - a Ford Escort and a Vauxhall Astra, grabbed some clothes and off we went. The south west seemed to be a good direction to head into and our first stop was Western Super Mare in Somerset. None of us had been there before but it was a great choice. When we arrived, it was a warm evening and we watched the sunset over a fantastic clean beach. We had nowhere to sleep except the cars - nobody even considered sleeping arrangements but it didn't matter; it was warm, we were with friends and we were enjoying ourselves. After finding a secluded area close to the beach, Nee put together a barbeque he got from somewhere.

I should mention at this point that if you're having a barbeque and Nee isn't with you then you may as well just give up; you need this man - end of story. In a matter of minutes you could the smell of sausages filled the air and things were good. Feeling a little tired, I laid down on the grass and looked up into the sky. It was a clear night and bright stars filled the night sky. Since my childhood I had a slight fascination with the stars. I think it must have been the endless hours I would star out into the street and sky since I had nothing better to do. Although we were close to the beach, there was very little light around us which allowed us to get a phenomenal view of the stars above. Then it happened - I saw something dash across the sky. Quickly I jumped out and shouted out to the others as I wanted to know if anyone else saw it. No-one did so I settled back down and before long there it was again; bright streaks of light were shooting across the sky and it was only then I realised that I was actually seeing shooting stars! I was in complete awe at what i'd seen even though the others weren't really bothered. It was an amazing experience seeing something that i'd heard so much about...

We talked and ate well into the early hours of the morning and before falling asleep we found a safe car park where we settled down for the night. We were so tired that the fact we were sleeping in cars didn't really bother anyone. From here we drove to Exmoor where the weather turned and we were caught up in horrific winds and torrential rain. Somehow, we managed to find our way out of there and then headed for Bournemouth. On our way there, we tested the cars to their limits. We would see how hard we could drive them around roundabouts, test their handling through the A roads on our way further South and check the top speed on the motorways. In the 4-5 days we were away from home we had such a good time that we really didn't want to go back home but there was no choice.

We had to get back to our routine life and get back to college and boy what a year that was. The work load increased, the assignments were tougher and mixed in with that we began the process of choosing which universities we wanted to attend.

In September of 1988 all the 2nd year A Level students went to Aberglaslyn in North Wales to take part in biological studies after which we would have to write up a dissertation style project. Though the summer was virtually over, it was a warm 29 degrees when we got there and it seemed like more of a holiday than a working week!

That evening the children were separated and then shown to their bedrooms. In with me was Nee, Chuddy and another lad called Dilip. We found it quite hard to sleep at nights so we would lie in our beds and talk. Dilip coped with this the first night but after the 2nd night he couldn't take anymore and left leaving the 3 of us! Wales is a beautiful place and before long we were measuring the number of insects in a square metre, measuring the density, locality and width of marram grass and examining bladder wrack (a type of seaweed with a high iodine content sometimes used for medical treatments). It may sound quite boring but it was pretty good fun and we stayed at this place for about 5 days. Since I was fairly young I got into a habit of listening to music whilst in bed and nowadays I find it hard to get to sleep without it. I took a very old Walkman with me to Wales and of the tracks playing was "That's where you'll find me" by "Deja". Since that day every time I hear this track it takes me back to those days and brings back fond memories.

At college the pressure was piling on; we had our mock A Level exams in early December and I did just enough to scrape a pass in all 3 subjects. This wasn't good enough; I knew it and my Economics teacher made a point of it. As she handed out the results to us, she would shout out our percentage and grade out to all the class. When I got mine she simply said "42%, E grade, you'll be lucky if you pass the real exam". I was quite shocked at this but thankfully it was only this particular teacher, Miss Nixon, who acted this way. Most of the class knew they had to improve and didn't need telling that in such a manner but we just got on with it. So, as you can imagine, having an advance warning that I was likely to fail didn't do much to boost my confidence but I just

Our room for the week.

Clean beaches of Wales.

Time to sleep.

September 1990 – Nee's 21st @ home.

shrugged it off and got on with it. My predicted results meant I couldn't apply to my 1st choice universities and I was forced to choose others instead. Nee and Chuddy were also looking to study elsewhere but deep down I think they really wanted to stay in Leicester.

Both of them wanted to check out Plymouth University and I decided to go along for the ride. We hired ourselves a car from Hertz again and were given a brand new Austin Maestro! The university was ok but we drove down on a freezing winters day and I think the weather put the other 2 off! After spending most of the day looking around the campus and then checking out their town centre we thought we would make the most of the day by driving to Lands' End. It was a fairly long drive and the one thing that sticks firmly in my mind that particular day is the record "Break for love" by Raze playing over and over. Nee had brought his own cassettes with him and I was hooked to this track and in fact became the first ever vinyl record I bought. We got to Lands' End quite late at night which was a bit of an anti-climax - it was dark and we obviously couldn't see much apart from the sign telling you that you had arrived.

The noise of sea crashing against the rocks was pretty loud and scary at the same time. So, we had arrived and with nothing else to do turned around and headed back. The journey back was more hectic - the stormy weather drew inland and almost instantly the snow began to fall and fall and fall. Within an hour, a fresh dusting of snow covered the roads and after finding a huge car park we started our hand brake turns in the car. We drove up to 20-25 MPH and then turned the steering wheel and pulled the hand brake at the same time - it would send the car hurtling round! After doing this for an hour or so we continued on our way back to Leicester. By the time we arrived back we'd been awake for almost 24 hours and the worst part of it was having to drop the car off and then having to walk back. Nee and Chuddy were talking about going home to bed but I was having none of it - this was our final year and couldn't miss lessons so I talked them into going back to college! I personally put in more hours into revision during this year than any other previous years and when it came close to the exams I felt confident I would pass but just wanted to get them over and done with. From March (1989) onwards most of my spare time was spent reading and then re-reading my college notes - I *had* to pass my A Levels; there was simply no room for failure.

Although many people have bizarre dreams, one of the dreams I used to have was dreaming that I hadn't finished my computer project that needed to be handed in the next day. They were so real

that during them I would get extremely panicky and would sweat profoundly only to wake up suddenly with the realisation that it was all just a dream. At first I thought I was the only one to have these dreams but I know many others, including Nee, who have had these too. Well, the exams came and before long they were all over. 2 years of solid work would be decided by the results of a couple of projects and several 3 hour exam papers. Nee and Chuddy decided they needed a well earnt rest and headed off to Africa for sun, sand and the Serengeti. Both of them would be away when their results came so they handed in their self-addressed envelopes with *my* address which meant that i'd be opening 3 sets of results.

The night before the results came I was more nervous that i'd ever been. I was up very early the next morning and it was a beautiful sunny day. In those days, you could rely on the postman to deliver the mail on time virtually every day and our post typically arrived between 8.30 and 9am. I opened the front door and looked to the right - at the far end of the street I could see the postman moving door to door and within 15 minutes the wait would over. Like a hawk I watched his every movement until finally he headed our way. There was no post for our neighbours and we were next. He looked into his bag, pulled out a pile of letters and then handed them over. I had mine, Chuddie and Nee's results in my hand and quickly started to open mine. I had passed *all* my A Levels and was ecstatic. I got an 'A' for Economics, 'D' for Computer Studies and an 'E' for Biology.

All those weeks of revising and ensuring I understood the work finally paid off and as I shared the results with the rest of my family we were all very happy. In all the excitement I forgot that I still had other results to open. Nee passed one of this A Levels but unfortunately Chuddy didn't pass any of them. I told them I would phone them as soon as the results were out so I did just like - Nee was sort of pleased but Chuddy wasn't. However, his character got him through this and he later decided that further academic study wasn't for him and took up full time work after that. Nee decided he would stay local and enrolled on a 2 year IT advanced course.

Later that day I went into college as I needed to sort out what I wanted to do next. I had already applied for a BSc in Computer Science but was predicted lower grades than I actually got so I had a better range of courses to choose from. In college I saw Miss Nixon (the one who told me I would be lucky to pass my A Level economics) and you could tell by the look on her face that she felt pretty daft. I didn't say much to her; there was no point - my grades said it all. The exam results and the letters associated with the grades always made us laugh. The letters are A,B,C,D,E,N and U with A-E denoting an A Level pass. Bizarrely 'N' actually means "Near Miss" - basically that the overall score achieved was only a few marks below the minimum required to achieve an A Level pass. I cannot believe any student would want to know that they 'nearly passed' - the fact that they had failed is bad enough but knowing you failed by a few marks simply makes it worse! E2 and I would often refer to 'N' as 'Never mind' or 'Not Today'. Students were given a 'U' grade to denote a very low A Level score and again we used to make up our own descriptions such as "U have failed" / "U nearly passed" / "U better try harder next time" - all of which would send us into fits of laughter.

After several days of weighing up which university I should go to, I opted for Aberystwyth University in Wales. It was a big move for me; I had never really been away from home for such a long period but figured it was something I had to do. It wasn't one of those "I need to find myself" kind of things. I never did understand that - why do people need to find themselves? Anyway before I even went to Wales I knew accommodation could be an issue - I had enrolled pretty late but i'd just have to wait and see. I packed up my stuff and Kiran took me there; it was a long journey and after about 4 hours we finally got there.

The place itself was beautiful and had a small, enclosed bay area with friendly locals. We managed to find the campus and after 'registering' my details I found that there was no accommodation left at all. The campus rooms were all taken with little chance of them becoming free. I was advised to find anywhere to live and check back with the campus after a few days. In the end I managed to find a bed and breakfast down by the sea front and after saying bye to Kiran I was left on my own. The b & b was very picturesque and I simply had to look out of the window to see a glorious panoramic view of the coastline and beach.

For the next few days I caught a local bus and headed to the main campus situated high above the town but the answer was the same - no accommodation at all and as the days passed by things were not looking good. To make matters worse I soon realised that there were 100's of other students in exactly the same predicament. The final straw came when the owner of the b & b told me that due to bookings, I had to be out of there in 2 days. So, I then spent a day trying to find somewhere else to live but it was no good. The university couldn't help and with no place to stay I rang my brother who came and picked me up - I was heading back to Leicester.

When I got back to Leicester, everyone wanted to know what happened but I had no time to waste. The next morning I went into the Leicester campus and managed to enrol myself on a different course - *BSc Software Engineering*. This was a brand new course and pretty much unique to Leicester so things started shaping up for the better. I met Raj Soni there - i'd known Raj since Mundella so it was good to see a familiar face. During the next few days I settled in pretty well and my new bunch of mates consisted of Raj Soni and Gohir Rashid (who preferred being called 'G').

Our timetable was pretty good, there were very few lectures first thing in the morning and on several days the last lectures were at 3pm. We had lots of free time and spent a huge chunk of this time playing pool in the student union. The course itself was heavily geared around programming which I really enjoyed and coming back to Leicester was definitely a good decision. Part of the course was using mathematical techniques (known as 'formal structures') to ensure correct software operation but both Raj & I struggled with the maths. All was not lost - in stepped G who showed us how to work out the equations and after that we were ok - thanks G. G, a Londoner was one of those people who knew everyone and before long I found myself on nocturnal duties - parties!

There were so many parties going on that it was impossible to keep up with them but I went to as many as I could and one thing stood out - the DJs were crap. Most of them would play the records *they* wanted to hear rather than what the crowd wanted. I hate this, as a DJ your job is to watch the dance floor and feed off the crowd's reaction and then pick the tracks accordingly. Anyone in those days with 2 records and a pair of headphones classed themselves as DJ's but this was about to change.

13

Technics, The FX Soundsystem & the circle of friends

In the winter of 1991, E2 and I put our money together and bought a brand new pair of silver Technics SL1200 turntables. These were the *best* turntables you could buy then and I still maintain are the best turntables to this day. He borrowed his dad's Sierra XR 4x4 and we parked outside 'Mays' in Churchgate and excitedly headed inside to pick up our prized possessions. Once we got back to E2's we spent the next few hours putting the head shell (cartridge & stylus) together. These decks (short hand for turntables) required precision tuning and you couldn't rush this part. We (E2, myself and Vipul/Wongy/Chong - E2's brother), looked like surgeons in an operating theatre as we passed bits of turntable to each other with precise accuracy.

Finally it was done and all the equipment was connected and ready for the big test. With the amp switched on and the vinyl sitting on the platter, the cross fader was moved to the middle and out came music - bliss! I could already 'mix' records (the art of mixing 2 different pieces of music seamlessly) and I now had to teach E2 how to do it. After several days of practicing he soon got the hand of it and the FX Soundsystem was born. Ok, it wasn't an exciting DJ name but it's the best name we could think of at the time. Over the next few months we all started bulk buying records - if we wanted to DJ we *had* to buy records and lots of them. Our record collection grew so quickly that space became an issue and moving them around was even more of a problem.

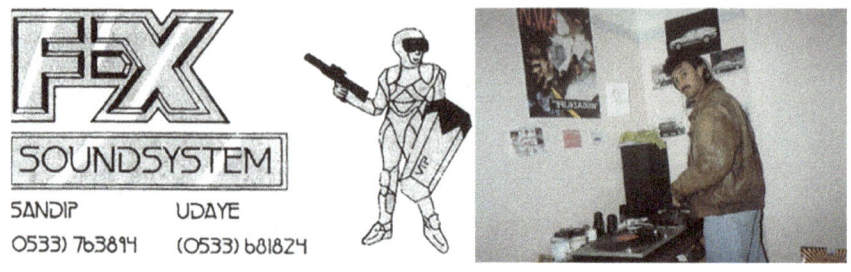

FEX
SOUNDSYSTEM

SANDIP   UDAYE
0533) 763894   (0533) 681824

Nee – the roadie!

Over the next few months university life was good and DJ'ing was getting better by the day. I used to head to London and go to lots of gigs with Paresh and Munsha from FBI who DJ'd all over the UK. One of the best gigs they had was a regular once a month booking at London's Hippodrome in Leicester Square. The DJ booth was huge and there were 4 decks, tape decks and a huge mixing console. In between DJ's there would often be live bands playing to the crowd and during this time I would sneak down and mess about with records. The promoters or club owners would look at me wondering what the hell I was doing but never said a word. With FBI I went to many parties all over the UK, in the middle of fields (during the early hard-core days) where during one gig we were standing next to this really tall guy - this tall guy was actually Tim Westwood from BBC Radio 1. It was winter and I remember standing in this freezing field with gloves on whilst the DJ's played records trying to look as if they were enjoying themselves!

Back in Leicester the word had spread and we made sure everyone knew we were on the scene. Before long we started to get DJ bookings for a variety of 'gigs' including birthday parties and wedding receptions. Our pricing strategy was simple - charge as much as you can - this was *business* after all. The records were crammed into milk bottle crates that we had previously cut to bits and removed the inside part of it. It may not look professional as people saw us carry our records in Kirby and West crates but it was the music that mattered so that was that. My mum wasn't too happy with the equipment and records that were building up. When

I set it all up at my house, my mum said to me "Why do you need 2 record players; you can't listen to 2 at the same time can you?" Well actually mum yes you can but I wasn't about to try and explain the concept of mixing to her. One of the strangest bookings we had was through my sister. One of her friends was having a party at quite a posh venue in Quorn, a little village on the outskirts of Leicester, so we didn't think anything about it and accepted the booking. When we got there, we set everything up and were offered some food.

Nee – looking suspicious.
Shifty – looking shifty.

Wongy – looking like
a China man.

We hardly recognised the food, it looked so neat and tidy that we didn't know whether to look at it or eat it. When it came to party time, the first request I had was "Have you got any Adam Ant mate?" Er, no we don't and when the next person came up and asked for Frank Sinatra we knew this gig wasn't going well! The crowd looked very upmarket and we *really* stood out as we played Soul II Soul from our battered milk crates looking like youths from a young offender's institution. In the end almost everyone was so drunk that they didn't care what music was playing so we just about got away with it. Some of the best parties we did were at my sister's house. She and her husband Pravin grew up in the great musical era of disco and all their friends knew how to have a good time. We would take our turntables down there and before long we'd be playing disco classics all night and the atmosphere was fantastic. When you get a bunch of people who love music and dancing you have all the ingredients for a great night and over the years we had many of them.

Young boys! Our tops matched the curtains!

Pravin had been on the "scene" a long time before my mum knew about him. If you recall my dad knew of Pravin early on and would pass on messages from him and never once told my mum. I liked Pravin from the start; and when I first met him he came across as one of the "lads". If there was talk of a good party then he would know about it and more than likely turn up there. During the Hindu festival of Navratri, Granby Halls was the number 1 place to. Tickets would sell out as soon as they were released and Pravin *never* bought a ticket. He would either know someone at the door, find a back way in or simply climb over the walls. If I were to sum him up in a few words it would be intelligent, witty and funny. He arrived from India when he was very young and with little education really has made something of himself and I have the utmost respect for him. I often worked with Pravin - he had a double glazing business and I would pass some of the holidays helping him out and all I can say is that every day something funny happened. He would always have time for people and I believe is one of the most genuine people I have ever met.

The man from SuperGlaze had a super shot!

Setting up all the equipment was a mammoth task and we were fortunate to have good friends that came with us. There were many of us in our 'crew'; myself, Nee, E2 as well as Chong and his mates. Chong's mates (Hemal, Rumit, Bobby and Shifty) loved the whole DJ thing too but we didn't really know them well but over the next few weeks and months we got to know all of them and i'd just like to say thanks for all your help. Over the next 2 years life was pretty much the same. The gigs flooded in and I would keep my head down at university and continued to work as hard as I could. In between this i'd hop onto the National Express 440 service from Leicester to London Victoria where I would arrange to meet up with the FBI to join them on their DJ gigs across London. During these times i'd be able to hear all the latest tunes that were devastating the dance floors and scribble the names of the tracks down using the pen and paper that i'd have with me at all times. Often I would meet Gee in Oxford Street - he would often work in Top Man during the holidays and would fill my bag with lots of free goodies including Nike Jogging bottoms, Nike badges and other things.

When it was time for revision the 3 of us - myself, Raj and Gee would meet up and help each other understand the work and it worked really well. Gee was always into his gadgets; whilst most students walked around with huge Sony Walkmans, Gee would pull out something that was about a quarter of the size and would often say "It's a London thing" with his east London accent! Raj Soni on the other hand was always on the prowl for free software. He didn't care what it was or where it came from. If it was free he'd have it and would add to his ever growing software library collection.

So far i've mentioned only a handful of names and it's a good time to name those people who I have spent the best parts of my life with. Well E2 and Nee were the first of my new friends and both of them are always up for a laugh: -

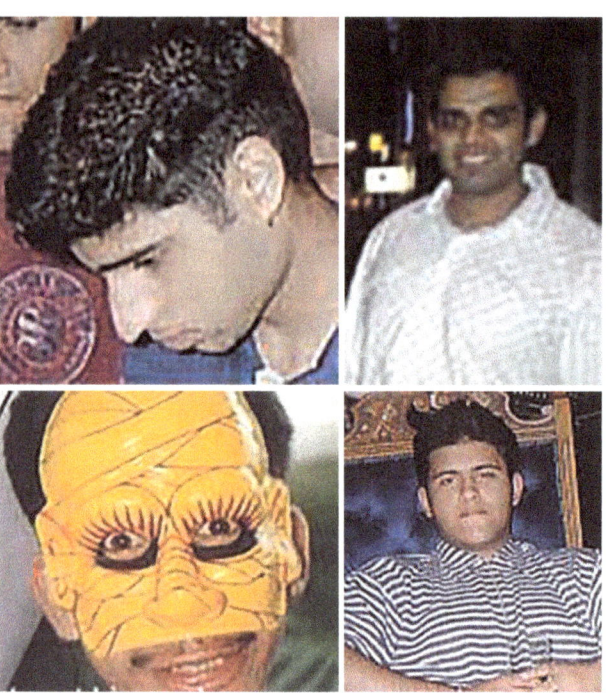

E2 - Before I carry on this isn't his real name - the real name is Udaye Rana and apparently his mum gave him the 'E2' name which sounds like something from Star Wars. E2 used to spend more time out of school than in it and was always joking around. Only a few people knew him by this name and he only liked a few people calling him that. As we grew up, we went through many traumatic times together and let's just say we've shared many life changing events and I wouldn't have had it any other way.

Sadly he turned into a 'fashion friend' and my attempts at continuing the friendship suffered. Trust me that hurt but it's his loss, not mine.

Nee (real name Nelesh Chudasama) is also from Spencefield school and caused utter chaos at that school to such an extent that the teachers were scared of them - usually it's the other way round. Nee is one of those happy go lucky kind of guys and nothing really phases him but cross him and you'll be sorry. Always happy to see you, Nee has always been there for me for which i'll always be grateful and we have a great mutual understanding and friendship - something I value greatly...

Shifty (real name Iftikhar Ahmed) used to be an adrenaline junkie who could drive faster than anyone in Leicester no matter what car they drove. He *loved* driving and would always take you wherever you wanted to go and never asked for anything in return. I think it's a shame that others around him didn't give him the backing and support when he needed it most. However - good to still have you on board mate.

Rumit is another of my friends that I really only got to know quite late in life. He is extremely chilled out and very little phases him. He's one of those people who sees people for what they are and is 100% genuine - what you see is what you get. If you need help, one phone call, day or night is all it takes and he'll be there - you can't say that about many people.

Hemal & **Bobby** are the jokers amongst the pack. From the first day I met this pair, they were always messing around and likely to get us all into trouble. Little has changed since those early days and it's been good fun having them as friends. When we get together now, the laughs we have are just the same as they were many years ago which can only be a good sign.

Chongy (aka Chong / Ping / Vipul Rana) has had many names over the years; 'Wong' and 'Rip' are just a small selection. He was always on the creative side and just like E2 was always game for a laugh. Over the years, he has slowly shunted the clubbing life for quiet evenings in - definitely a sign that he is ready to settle down now - innit? Along with E2, he also turned into a fashion friend so good riddance to him too.

Breej – aka Mr party animal... this guy is always one of the last men standing and always the one looking for the last drink and definitely on the look out for that party. I don't think I have ever seen him even look slightly drunk let alone get drunk.

Sharmil – I was at the same junior school as Sharmil and we lost touch when I left. Thinking about it now I think it was a case of him getting lost because as the years went by we have all learnt that his sense of direction is not very good. Sharmil takes short cuts and navigation to a new level and there isn't enough time to go into the detail; put it simply he is unique – let's leave it there!

For many people, birthdays are definitely something to look forward to. Once you get into your 'teens' the only birthdays that most celebrate are the significant ones such as 16th, 18th or 21st. I for one didn't want any fuss when it came to my birthday and to be honest nobody else in our family really bothered about theirs either. My 18th birthday came and went just like a normal day but when it came to my 21st things were different. I remember being in 2 minds on whether to have a party or not and after many hours of debating I decided I may as well have one so the decision was made. The party was at Asquiths which is a small club in the city centre and there would only be about 50-60 people there. My sister ordered me a cake with a turntable on the top of it which was a very cool touch; my cousins came from London and Paresh drove up too to supply the music (FBI style).

As the day grew closer the nerves kicked in and I began to wonder why on earth I decided to have a party at all - it all seemed like too much work and why on earth would I want to put on a party that simply made me nervous? I really couldn't believe I had decided to continue with it but it was done now so I just had to get on with it. On the day of the party, I was only worried about people not turning up but in the end it was ok - there was a good crowd and everyone I wanted there turned up. The only embarrassing things that night were the clothes I wore and attempting to make a speech - both were a disaster! I never did understand why we just assume that the 16th, 18th and 21st birthdays need celebrating. As with many "life" events, the majority of us never question this and simply get on with it - I guess it's just a rare few (like me?) that think that much deeper - who knows?

Ask yourself this - have any of you ever looked at the way water goes down the sink? If you live in the northern hemisphere, the water will always flow down in a clockwise direction. If you stood on the equator, the water would go straight down whilst in the southern hemisphere (Rita Rai - this one's for you!), the water flows down anti clockwise. Strange pointless fact for most of you but true, nevertheless. I find things like this fascinating - most of you are probably thinking "so what!" Mind you, there is much debate over this phenomenon and the *real* cause of the water spinning in different directions is often put down to the size of the basin that contains the water!

Anyway enough of that - although the software engineering course I was on was actually a 3 year course, the time really seemed to fly past and the second year was extremely tough and undoubtedly the third year would be even tougher. As 1990 came to an end I was watching the TV at home and as the time ticked over into 1991, the fireworks along the Thames burst into life and as one year ended, another started. Little did I know that this year would be a life changing one but thankfully this time, it was for the better...

One day whilst I was E2 he asked me "What do you think of Sunita?". This was completely 'out of the blue' and at first didn't really know how to respond. Before I carry on, there it is again - a phrase that we use but may not know the history behind it. Searching the internet via our good friend 'Google', it says that the earliest citation of 'out of the blue' was by someone called Thomas Carlyle in a book *"The French Revolution, 1837"*

"Arrestment, sudden really as a bolt out of the Blue, has hit strange victims."

I must explain - I knew of Sunita but didn't know her very well at all. In fact, I probably wouldn't even have said hi if i'd walked past her so it's probably fair to say we weren't even friends. E2, on the other hand, knew her very well and this was probably because E2's girlfriend at the time (Aarti) was good friends with Sunita too. Anyhow, back to the question in hand... I think my response was "what do you mean?". After several minutes of trying to understand why he was asking me this question, I figured out there was more to this - he was trying to match make and we (Sunita and I) were the chosen ones. At the same time, RT (aka Aarti) was also playing Cilla and asking Sunita the same question about me. I would have loved to have heard her response as i'm sure it wouldn't be good. Over the next few weeks nothing much happened but the little digs about Sunita kept creeping in. At the time, I thought they were just having a laugh but they were serious and after many weeks I agreed to meet Sunita at the university library. I couldn't believe I was going through with it and thought that once we'd met, we'd probably hate each other anyway and that would be that.

The plan was to meet at the university library and I had my own arrangements to do. I told Raj Soni and Gee that I had to meet someone at the library to help them with their Maths. Yes, this was a blatant lie but the last thing I needed was others egging me on and wanting to know the details. So, the day came and I forced myself to go to the library and as I walked through the door I really wanted to turn around and head in the opposite direction. The way I looked at it was this - how can 2 people who never expressed any kind of interest in each other and who were being encouraged to meet get on? It could never work - could it?

As I got into the library and headed upstairs I could see various people from our college and then in a small corner were the college posse- E2,RT and various others - oh and Sunita was there too. Both E2 and RT (definitely sounds like names from

Star Wars now) had cheeky grins on their faces and then Sunita and I went off to talk. At first there wasn't much to talk about and the topic was really about our friends and the lengths they went to get us to meet. The nerves soon vanished and we seemed to be getting on ok but we couldn't sustain the conversation for long so we headed back to the others. The sniggers soon started and E2 had a huge grin on his face. It was time for me to go; I didn't want to hang around any longer so after saying goodbye I was out of there pretty sharpish! Sunita no doubt got asked lots of questions and I got the inquisition later on that day when E2 phoned me.

It was quite tricky answering the question "What do you think of her?" and my answer was pretty vague - I *really* didn't know what to say because i'd never been in that position before. Yes she was a *nice* person but and that's it! As the weeks progressed we met up a few times after that and we both entered new territory - we decided to 'give it a go' / ' go out' - call it what you want but we were officially dating. Our first date was pretty much a standard affair and we had agreed to watch a film. The morning of our first date; *14th May 1991*, was a dry and fairly mild day and I remember looking in the mirror still kind of wondering what I was doing. With blue jeans and my striped 'Next' top on, I closed the front door behind me and walked a short distance to the bus stop. The bus arrived and about 30 minutes later I met up with Sunita who looked as if she didn't want to be there!

We made our way to the Odeon Cinema and decided to watch "Misery"; I can't remember why we picked this film but I can only assume that there wasn't much on and our choices were pretty limited. Either way, with Sunita not looking "too bovvered" and us watching a film with this title, the signs weren't good. The film was ok and throughout the film I was willing time to go quicker. Yes I know, I shouldn't be thinking that but I wasn't used to all this - it seemed like too much hard work.

Thankfully the film only lasted about 90 minutes and afterwards I think we just went home. I don't think you could really call this a date as such but I felt extremely uncomfortable throughout it and Sunita was the same. You'd have thought with both of us feeling like this we would never see each other again but we did - several times in fact and on one occasion we went out to Stoney Stanton, home to a scuba diving training centre. It was a hot, summers day and not having a car meant Sunita drove and she came to pick me up in her green Mini Metro. As the days and weeks progressed things changed and this whole dating thing was quite good fun - for now at least.

My 2nd year university exams were fast approaching and both Raj and Gee knew about Sunita by now. To this day Gee keeps going on about my visit to the library to help someone with their maths - they knew full well that I didn't help anyone that day but instead went on a not so secret rendezvous. Raj, Gee and I got our heads together and drew up a revision schedule and before long we were in the library or at home studying hard. Often, Raj and I would walk from our house all the way to Gee's house in Narborough Road. We (Raj and I that is) always walked into university anyway. After walking down Green Lane Road towards his house, memories always flooded back as I recalled making the same journey as a youngster many years earlier. Once there, he'd always be sipping the last of his morning (very milky) coffee and we would head off into town. After getting to Gee's, Gee would often want to talk but i'd lay down the law and in a matter of minutes we'd be working hard; testing each other and generally making sure we understood the work. As quick as the exams came, they were over and after finding out we had all passed that year, we had the long summer ahead of us. Raj headed off to India, Gee headed off to London and I headed off home.

That summer Pravin wanted an extra pair of hands so I decided to work with him fitting double glazed windows. It was something to do, it got me out and each day was different - oh and i'd got paid too! Sometimes Kiran would work too and often it would be just Kiran and I removing and installing the new windows, doors and anything else that needed fixing. It was August and the A Level results had just come out. I was having my breakfast when the phone rang - it was Sunita telling me she needed to see me. She didn't ring that often so it was a pleasant surprise to hear from her. However it was quite early in the morning and although I was looking forward to seeing her I did have a suspicion that something wasn't quite right. She arrived with immaculate timing and basically she said she had something to tell me and that it was all in 'this'. She was pointing to a letter she pulled out of nowhere. I asked what the letter was about and you could sense she wasn't comfortable with it at all. After handing it to me she said bye and drove off. I opened the letter immediately; was she about to express her feelings for me? Did she feel she couldn't openly tell me and had to write it down instead? Was she whisking me away on a whirlwind holiday?

Er, no - she was telling me to get stuffed in a diplomatic way. It wasn't a letter; it was more of a mini-essay and to sum it up she was breaking the relationship up. I didn't really think we were in a relationship but whatever we had between us was over - period. There were many reasons for this break up but it was her family and in particular her dad that helped Sunita make her mind up. She explained how it would really hurt her dad's feelings if he ever found out and that she wanted to get married to someone in her 'cast' who her dad would approve of. The last sentence she wrote was "Anyway, I got C C D" - referring to the A Level results she got. If I said it didn't bother me i'd be lying; I liked her and we seemed to get on well so it did come as a bit of a shock. Her reasons for the break up were tight and no way in this world would I want to interfere with her family and risk upsetting her or them. The truth was that I knew all too well about families and judging by the way she spoke (or wrote I should say) it was clear that she had a great one and I would rather us break up than her rock the boat at home.

Later that day I spoke to E2 and explained what happened. I'm pretty certain I told him not to try and talk to her - she had her reasons and we *all* had to respect that. Whether I liked it or not was irrelevant - the decision was made and that was that. Just before Sunita had arrived with the news I was actually going to call her as I wanted her help with E2's party. His parents wanted to throw a surprise 21st birthday party for him and the lads were in charge. As the days passed by, each of the items on the 'to do' list were slowly being crossed off. I was actually hoping Sunita could help with the food and try to use some of her creative traits to help in any way. As it turned out, I didn't ask her for help and in the back of my mind I knew our paths would cross soon - real soon.

On the evening of E2's birthday, we told him we were going out with the lads. Dressed in his black corduroy trousers and red shirt, we walked across the road outside the club only for his dad to drive by in their 4x4. Unfortunately, the surprise was no more a surprise so there was no point pretending it was. When we got inside there was a roar of cheers and i'm pretty certain he was pleased to see all his friends there. We were on turntable duties ourselves and all the lads - Nee, Bob, Hemal, Shifty, Rumit and Chongy were there to pitch in and help out. The food was great and in true Indian style, there was plenty for everyone.

After that, it was time to sing "happy birthday" and for E2 to cut the cake. Most of the cake people were giving him went into his mouth but with Bob there you knew things were about to change and they did. The cake in Bob's hand went everywhere except E2's mouth to the cheers from the birthday crowd. After the cake cutting it was speech time which was short and sweet and then it was onto the dance floor where Mantronix boomed out of the speakers. Sunita was there but seemed to be keeping in the background - it felt as if we were trying to avoid each other but to be honest the break-up didn't bother me anymore.

I remember wanting to sit down - my legs were aching and it had been a long day so I went over to Sunita and sat next to her thinking nothing of it. I think she was glad I came over and things weren't over. It was clear that she wanted to 'give it another go' and although I was still a little sceptical about it, agreed and we were apparently dating again. With the summer slowly drawing to an end, E2 and Sunita would be moving to High Wycombe to further their careers. In total there were 4 of them moving up - RT and Alpa (more friends from college) would be moving too. On the day that they were moving up, I borrowed my sister's cream coloured Datsun Estate, picked Nee up, drove to E2's loaded up the car and headed off. High Wycombe isn't a particularly 'nice' town. Most of the student houses and accommodation was in the 'old' part of Wycombe and it helped to know some of the locals. They didn't have to worry - my cousin Paresh lived there and so did Munsha and both of them were well known and well respected in this town and nobody would mess with them or anyone they knew if you know what I mean.

When we got there, most of the time was spent unloading and moving stuff between rooms. We also had to avoid the parents - some of them didn't know that the girls would be sharing the house with a boy and when we knew they'd be arriving soon, we literally had to leave the house, wait for them to go and then head back. This was just daft but there was nothing you could do about it. Once the parents had left, the rest of the evening was just spent messing around and having a laugh. The new tenants would be in Wycombe for a few years so had to get used to the surroundings. I had to get the car back to my sister the next day so i'm fairly certain that Nee and I headed back quite early.

For me, it was a tough year ahead, this was my last year of the Software Engineering degree and there was no way I was going to mess around now. As the workload increased so did my efforts and the group revision with Raj & Gee started even earlier and we planned well in advance of our exams. With our final year computer projects chosen, we then spent many hours in the university computer labs often staying very late whilst we all struggled to fix the logic in our code and iron out the many compilation errors! If my focus was just on my degree I would have been ok but Sunita was a huge distraction (in a good way of course!).

With Sunita, E2, RT & Alpa being away I would often head out to visit them at the weekends. My course timetable helped out with my visits as I had Fridays off which often meant heading to the coach station on a Thursday evening. I would book my seat on the National Express 440 service to London, Victoria and in a few hours would have to rush through Victoria Station and then either catch the Green Line coach to High Wycombe or jump onto the underground and then catch a train up to Wycombe. Either way, the journey from start to finish took about 3 1/2 hours and I had to endure the same journey back again!

Once I was there we had a great laugh; there was always some kind of party going on and on Friday / Saturday nights, Paresh & Munsha would DJ at one of the student clubs so we'd all pile in there (free entrance of course!) and party till the early hours. Once it was over, it was a trip to "uncles" Kebab van. I have no idea why it was called "uncles" but this guy made some really good food and it was all fresh. You might have to wait 10-15 minutes whilst he prepared and then cooked the food but freezing your pants off was well worth it. On one particular occasion, either E2 or myself ordered a cheeseburger. "Is that with or without cheese" asked uncle and to this day I have no idea why we found that so funny but we did and trust me we spent the next 20 minutes laughing so much they by the end of it we were both in tears.

To this day when I speak to E2 over the phone or email, this deadly one-liner from 'uncles' often comes out and it still makes us laugh to this day. Due to the hectic DJ schedule that Paresh & Munsha had, they would travel all over London and would get booked for some of the biggest and best gigs London had ever seen. Luckily for us, if they were invited then so were we (well kind of). We ended up as their extended "roadies" and somehow managed to get into most parties with them and this was superb. One day we'd be in Limelight and the next it would be Camden Palace. On other weekends it was Hammersmith Palais and the next it would be the Empire in Leicester Square.

One of my most vivid memories of FBI was when they DJ'd at the Empire. E2 hired a car from Wycombe - it was a Peugeot 406 and we piled in and drove down to London. After driving around for ages we managed to find a parking space and slowly made our way towards Leicester Square. It was a cold day in November and as we got closer there was a real buzz in the atmosphere. It was a mixture of being in London, being in Leicester Square and the fact that we would be heading into one of the biggest Asian gigs any of us had ever been to. If I remember correctly "Innocence" were one of the headline acts and for those of you that know, Innocence had released some huge tracks by then ("Natural Thing", "Remember The Day" & "Let's Push It") were just a few...

The queue to get in was massive and it was a proper winter's night - very cold indeed but it didn't matter - we were all too excited to care. As we slowly made our way towards the front of the queue you could see the door men / bouncers / door staff or whatever they're called nowadays. They had gloomy faces on and once in a while would appear to push some kind of button near their ears and then talk into their mic that was stuck to the front of their jackets. You'd think some kind of head of state was expected or something - the security did seem to be a little over kill, especially as all the people outside (well most of the people anyway) wanted to get onto the dance floor and bust their bhangra moves. The only dangerous people outside were the lads who had too many glasseees. ("Glasseees" for those that don't know is the term mainly used by Punjabis to indicate having a shot of whisky, Bacardi or anything else they fancy for that matter).

Before long we handed our tickets over and we were in - no sooner had we stepped into the club all you could hear was the deafening sound of the music and as we crept closer to the dance floor, the view was phenomenal. The dance floor was heaving and I mean heaving; there was just enough room to slowly work our way into the centre of the dance floor and I remember trying to find Paresh & Munsha. It was no use, there seemed to be 1000's of people there and as we prepared to dance the night away it happened. The bhangra music that *was* playing faded out and just as the crowd wondered what was coming next, the ground shaking bass line of "The chorus line" by Ultra magnetic MC's shook the whole place down.

Within seconds, the sound of "Check 1-2, 2-2-1-2 and the unmistakable sound of Munsha's voice echoed out of the club's speakers. FBI were on - as we looked towards the main stage, it was actually rotating 180 degrees. In a flash there they were - Paresh and Munsha from FBI facing the 1000's in the crowd and whilst Munsha was unleashing his lyrics to the crowd, Paresh was mixing Heera's "Sas Kutni" into the mix and created an awesome cross mix of bhangra and hip hop breaks that mesmerised the crowd. I'm not sure about the others but i'll *never* forget that moment - the atmosphere, the bass line and the look on the faces of the crowd together with the way FBI took to the stage was one of those defining moments people often talk about and i'm glad I was there to see it.

The FBI were on for about an hour and during that time they got the crowd *really* going. The music switched between funk and soul, hip hop to hip house and Indian lyrics and samples from Hindi movies cut into the mix every so often. Soon we were all sweating buckets from our dancing efforts and this was truly a night to be remembered. For the FBI boys it was all in a night's work and I don't think they thought they had done anything special but they had; we knew it and the crowd knew it. Innocence also took the stage and were wicked too - it was the first time I had seen a "live" band and they were excellent. The weekends seemed to whizz by and before long i'd be back on the 440 heading back to Leicester.

Once back at home, I made sure I was up to speed with all the university work - after all, there no way in this world I would let that slip. My chosen computer project was a really difficult one and I spent many hours researching and applying programming techniques as I slowly but surely got to grips with new technology and new methodologies. I lost count of the number of nights where Raj, Gee & I were still in the computer labs until 9pm working on our projects. Fuelled by huge plates of chips and cans of coke, we'd be in there typing like made trying to get our software to work!

Another flyer and another gig for
Paresh and Munsha from the FBI.

Whilst Raj and I would sit there scratching our heads when we were stuck, Gee would stare at the screen and you could hear the tsst tsst treble sound coming out of his Sony Walkman headphones. Gee was a small person and all his hi tech gadgets followed suit - all his electronic stuff was neater and smaller than any of us had ever seen. He would often say "Well, it's a London thing" and I think he was right. The "Leicester thing" consisted of a Binatone Walkman that was as large and probably weighed as much as a brick! Even his trainers looked as if it was something he'd brought back from the future. His Nike trainers looked like a fine tuned instrument; they had pockets of air that you could adjust, weighed less than a corn flake and probably cost the same as a third world countries total Gross Domestic Product.

There was a period of 2 weeks in October 1991 where I hardly spoke to Sunita but the letters would keep coming. We wrote to each other often; something that's pretty rare nowadays when you consider the internet revolution that has transformed the world. Most people send emails to stay in touch and letters are generally only sent to pay bills or something. Letters were cool and the ones Sunita wrote were quite funny and Sunita being Sunita managed to capture every single bit of detail that had happened and got it down on paper. Late into the night after i'd finished my work for the day I would start writing to her and found myself detailing everything that had happened too. In fact there were many occasions where I would write to Sunita but then write mini-letters to E2, RT & Alpa.

Alpa *loved* receiving letters - I think it was the manner in which I wrote them. I could picture the scene - she'd get the letter and in a matter of minutes would be hysterical with laughter sat in her tartan pyjamas and clutching her gold chain. Before long the letters really stacked up and I had to buy a folder just to store them! I'm not sure why I kept them but it was for the memories I guess. I'm pretty certain I still have them but as I sit here writing this I cannot remember where I put them or whether I kept them after all.

I never had a computer at home and my friends didn't really have email addresses either so communication was via letter or the phone. To avoid racking up a huge phone bill I would often use a BT Phone box to call E2 & co. There were 2 phone boxes near our house - one was on the corner of Roseberry Street and the other was by the post office near Kitchener Road. It must have been around 8.30pm and I decided I would make a call so I went round to the phone box on Roseberry Street. Bizarrely, there was a queue of people waiting to use it - i'd never seen this before and I never had to wait before. After 10 minutes of waiting the person on the phone looked as if he'd be there all night and with 7 people in front of me I wasn't going to wait in that queue. There was no choice; I had to use the other phone box.

When I got up to Kitchener Road there was no one there - no people, no queue, no nothing and I wondered if the phone was broken. It wasn't so I was even more curious as to why so many people were waiting at the other phone box. I ignored it for now and made my phone call, albeit it a cold one. You see this phone box had no door to it and the amount of time I spent on my phone call was determined by the weather and how cold it was! Over the next week or so, the pattern was the same. One phone box always had a queue of people waiting to use it whilst the other was empty but cold! I had enough of this; I didn't want to queue or get cold and I suspected something wasn't right.

I rang BT and told them about the situation; explaining that one phone box was particularly popular whilst the other wasn't. I eventually found out that a "scam" was taking place. You would put your £1.00 coin into the machine and push a metal road up into the phone box (where the change would come out from) - this caused the £1.00 to come out again but you'd stay connected on the call. I could now see what was happening; all the people were calling home (India, Africa, Barbados, USA or wherever) totally *free* which would explain why it was so busy. I suspect the same scam didn't work on the other phone or BT put a stop to it somehow. In a matter of days I had sorted them all out; there were no more queues and if there was the other phone box now had a door so I could make a phone call and close the *newly fitted door* behind me! I must have pissed off loads of people but it wasn't the money that bothered me - it was the principle - ha ha.

14

Notre long voyage d'entraîneur à Paris...

After many weeks of working on my final year project I needed a break and asked Sunita if she wanted to go to Paris for the weekend. I think she was a little anxious at first; it wasn't like going to London or something and there was lots to sort out but she agreed. I booked the trip with a company called Paris Travel Services but we would be going by coach so it was going to be a long journey. The trip was booked for around the 2nd week in November 1991 and I made my way down to Wycombe via the National Express and Green Line route. With our bags packed we headed for London, Victoria which was our meeting point. After lugging our cases around the London Underground we got there and the journey began.

Sunita being Sunita meant she made lots of sandwiches for the journey together with snacks and drinks to match. Around 2 hours later we were in Dover and shortly after that were aboard the ferry that would take us to Calais. Neither of us are particularly keen on ferries but whilst Sunita sat inside in the warmth, I spent most of the time outside looking around - watching the white cliffs of Dover and then walking to the front where you could see France in the distance.

By the time we'd arrived in Calais we were quite tired but we had many more hours to go and trust me, these hours really dragged on. The fellow passengers were a fairly friendly bunch whilst the driver and tour guide spent lots of time together - i'm sure there was something going on between them! We finally arrived in Paris in the early evening and checked into the Hotel De La Havane. It was a simple hotel, nothing fancy but more importantly was clean. With no time to spare we dumped our stuff and headed into the bustling Paris street life. As it was pretty close to Christmas, the place looked great, Christmas trees and lights adorned the shops and there was a real buzz as people shopped like mad.

On the first evening we bought loads of stuff including French chocolates and came back to the hotel with bags of shopping. In the evening we ventured out and decided to eat like the Parisians. We stumbled across a restaurant that looked pretty authentic and decided to give it a go. The menu, which was written completely in French (obviously!) was confusing to say the least. I remember working my way through all the items on the menu and trying to pick out words that may unravel what kind of food it was. It was no use; neither of us knew what we were ordering and when the food came I had aubergines and to this day we have no idea what Sunita ordered. Pretending our food was ok, we tried bits of it and smiled as the waiters looked at us.

We didn't stay there long and got out as soon as we could. We were both very hungry so opted for baguettes from a local shop and strolled along munching our way through them. It had been a very long day and time to call it a night so that was the end of that day. The next morning, the tour guide and her driver partner picked up all the passengers and took us for a 2 hour sightseeing tour of Paris. It was quite early in the morning so some of the major landmarks were hidden underneath morning mist but the first glimpse we had of the Eiffel Tower was awesome. It just seems to pop out of nowhere but the sight of it was truly spectacular. We got out of the coach and managed to take some pictures but they weren't very good - mainly because the mist still hadn't lifted by then. By the time the coach dropped us back at the hotel, we were ready to continue the sightseeing on our own so off we went...

With our map of the Paris Metro system in our hands we picked out where we wanted to go and headed underground to wait for the train. The metro system is quite easy to work out but when you arrive at the stop for the Eiffel tower and walk up the stairs the view is even more spectacular close up. The size of tower really dawns on you, especially as you stand underneath its 4 metal legs and look up. Thankfully there was very little wind that day and visitors could take the lift to the top of the tower (when it's windy there's usually a restriction on how far you can go up...). After queuing for ages, we had our tickets in our hands and then entered another queue for the lifts. I've never seen lifts as big as this - it felt as if there were about 30 people inside and it slowly started to move upwards in a diagonal direction. When we arrived at the "first viewing platform" very few people got off. No-one wanted a view from the Eiffel Tower; they wanted a *great* view which meant getting off at the highest point.

When we arrived at the top and the lift doors opened, the force of the wind gave some kind of indication at how high we really were. The force was phenomenal and as the tourists rushed around to get a view, we were some of the last people out of the lift. Once we managed to find a viewing spot, the views were truly wicked. The tower is really high up, much higher than it looks from the ground and people, cars and in fact buildings appeared as minute objects below. Trying to get a decent photo was pretty hard - Sunita's hair was blowing around everywhere but when the pictures were developed they didn't really give you a feel of how high you really are - it's definitely something you need to see for yourself. At that point, the long journey to Paris including the stomach churning ferry ride was all worth it simply to get such a view. The rest of the day was spent visiting Notre Dame, Champs Elysee whilst the last day was spent with a half day trip to Fontainebleau followed by more shopping. It was then time for the long journey back to the UK with bag full of shopping and lasting memories of Paris...

Since my time table was 'weekend friendly', I didn't have to worry about missing lessons on Fridays or Mondays. I think I only had a couple of lessons on those days and they were practicals anyway. However, this meant that I had missed crucial lab time and my computer project was a few days behind schedule. With no time to waste, the weeks following our trip to Paris was spent with my heads in my books and in the computer labs where I wanted to ensure my project was not only back on track but even ahead of schedule. The winter was well and truly here again and the days were cold and dark. By the time Christmas had arrived my project was back on track and I knew at that point that I would finish it on time. This may not sound like much but fellow students on my course were struggling big time and unbelievably were many months behind on their project. It never seemed to phase them though - they would prefer to sit in the student's union and get pissed whilst the rest of us were in the labs.

Just before we broke up for the Christmas holidays we also had a series of 'mock' exams so the lecturers could ascertain how much we knew. I was quite glad to have them and our group revision played a big part in ensuring all 3 of us (Raj, Gee and I) passed them all. The grades weren't brilliant but the main thing was we passed but we all knew these exams weren't for real and after Christmas the pressure would definitely be on. Between January and June 1992 I made many visits to Wycombe to see Sunita and the rest of the gang but as the months drew on, the weekend trips ground to a halt as I focused all my efforts on finishing my project, starting my revision and generally preparing for the final year exams. The project was due during the middle of April 1992 and I had finished it by then. Part of the project was an actual demo of the software and when it came to the day I was pretty nervous; the head of the course would be sitting in on the demo itself and this guy was a software expert so I expected to be grilled and asked impossible questions. I was right - I was asked so many questions that by the time I had started to answer one of them he stopped me in my tracks and switched to another question.

I felt like telling him to shut up; what was the point in asking me questions if he didn't let me answer them? By this time I was sweating profusely and although the software worked very well I wasn't too hopeful and all I could think of was the poor score he would give me. In the end I was quite shocked - I actually got a better than average score and my course tutor said I should be quite happy with that as most people get well below average. Anyway, the demo was over and I left the room with a sweat soaked t shirt and a huge sigh of relief. With the project over and done with I could now focus on the core subjects and revision. The revision time table came out a few days after the project demo and the exams were spread over a 2 week period and one of the exams was even on a Saturday.

In the weeks that followed, our lectures were cancelled as all the course content had been covered and all the classes were replaced with revision classes for those students that wanted to brush up on topics they didn't feel too comfortable with. I thought that these classes would have a good turnout but very few people turned up and on some days there were barely a handful of students in there. Raj, Gee and myself were *always* there, eager to go over all the topics and to help each other once again. The master plan was back in force and the 3 of us organised a revision schedule that meant a daily trip to Gee's house or the library. I would walk down to Raj's house and together we'd walk to meet Gee. This was the same journey and the same revision we had been doing for almost 3 years but this would be the last time it would happen and it felt quite weird at times.

On those occasions where we went to Gee's house, we'd knock on the door and find a sleepy Gee opening it - in true Gee style he'd only woken up minutes earlier and we'd have to tell him to freshen up whilst Raj & I got out the books and the study schedule. The revision worked really well and we'd go over the key points in the chosen subject. Every so often one of us wouldn't understand something and the other 2 would jump in to explain it. When it came to maths, Gee was the expert so we'd rely on him to help us understand complex mathematical concepts. After about 60 minutes on non-stop study, we'd take a break but I had to keep my eyes on Raj & Gee. These guys could easily lose focus and I had to ensure that a 15 minute break *was* a 15 minute break. At the end of a long day's revision we would sometimes go out for our dinner or order some take away.

On most evenings Raj and I would walk back home, passing through the city centre on our way back. In spring this was ok, the days were long and it was mild but when it rained it was terrible. By the time we got home it was late; often 8-9pm which may not sound that late at all but when you consider we'd been revising all day it was quite tiring and we were often mentally exhausted at the end of it and the day after we'd do the whole thing all over again. As the weeks flew by and the exams drew closer, nerves were replaced with anxiousness; I felt I was prepared for the exams and simply wanted to get on with it. When the day of the first exam arrived I was surprisingly calm and was actually looking forward to it. I knew I had prepared well and studied hard so there was none of that "if only i'd studied harder" thoughts going through my head. The exam (i'm pretty certain it was "Formal Structures") went reasonably well and I was glad to get that over and done with.

My Saturday exam was going very well until the fire alarm went off and we were forced to leave the building. Not wanting to lose focus I gathered together for the head count but then moved away from the other students. Whilst the rest of them decided to discuss the exam questions to the annoyance of the exam tutors, I didn't want to hear any of their conversation. I couldn't believe others wanted to cheat - what was the point of that? I wanted to pass my degree on my own and there was no need for cheating. I kept myself to myself and even shoved my fingers into my ears so I couldn't hear any of that chat going on. Finally I could see the tutors ushering all the students back into the exam room so I quickly obliged and sat back at my desk.

Due to the interruption, the exam finished about 25 minutes late and once it was over I didn't want to speak to anyone and tried to head home. I didn't see the point in going over the questions and answers. If you did discuss the questions you might have found that you answered something incorrectly and it would no doubt start to bother you - there was just no need for it and I didn't want any part of it. With only 3 more exams to go, there was no time for relaxing and once I was home I crossed out that exam and got out the books for the next one. My mum, knowing full week that I was revising would tip toe around the house trying not to make too much noise. Every hour or so she would come into the room and ask if I needed anything - that's what mums do - always looking out for you and making sure you're ok.

The exams seem to gather momentum and the days seemed a blur - revision - exam - revision - exam and that's how it continued until I only had one exam left. My exam sheet on my wall was looking good - only one exam left to cross out and out came the revision books for the last time. The morning of the last exam was a beautiful day; it was warm and I could hardly find a cloud in the sky. After breakfast I made my way to Raj's shop and then into town to sit the exam. We never talked about the exam as we walked in and instead discussed what we'd be doing over the summer. Just like all other exams i'd say, the final one went ok and as I saw the time approaching midday I knew I was almost there. I spent the last few minutes checking my work and then sat there quite happy with myself.

It was all very strange; 3 years of hard work had just finished and my work was done. In a few minutes the exam would be over and the next stage of my life would be heavily governed by the kind of degree I walked away with. As midday arrived, the exam was over and we were all asked to stop writing and put down our pens. As the exam tutors gathered up all the papers, all the students sat around smiling at one another and once the papers had been collected, slowly started to leave the building. It was over and there was nothing for us to do except wait a few weeks till the exam results were out. I wasted no time and headed home. The first thing I did was cross off the final exam and then happily tore the paper to bits - I waited a long time to do that and enjoyed it. I then grabbed some clothes, shoved them into my bag, said goodbye to my mum and headed for Wycombe. It was one of the most pleasant journeys I had - no exams, no worries, no nothing and I wanted to meet up with the others and have some fun. By the time I was in Wycombe I felt quite relaxed and in the 3-4 days that I stayed there went to many parties and just had a laugh. For Sunita and the rest of them, they had just finished their exams too so it was relief all round.

Not long after I sat my final exam, my mum went to India so it was very quiet at home. I spent more time with Nee and he was busy working on his final year project too. He had already completed his 2 year course but had enrolled on another advanced course which ran all year. This meant that his course ran throughout the summer so there was no let up for him! The date for our exam results had now been published and as I had done many times before I called for Raj and then made our way back into town. Once back inside the university building, we met up with Gee and the rest of the students who had all gathered to determine their fate. One by one we were called into room where our tutor would pass on the results. It was my turn and he started with the computer project first - I got a 55% which was a 2:2 mark and then started telling me the subject exam results. I was quite impressed; for many of the modules I was getting close to 70% scores but the overall score was 59% which meant I had done enough for a 2:2 honours degree. To be honest I was hoping for a 2:1 degree but I was so thrilled I could hardly believe it. I had *passed*, all the hard work had paid off and I had a degree to my name and I was very proud of myself.

After congratulating the others I just wanted to get home so I could tell as many people as I could and I did just that. Sadly, my mum wasn't there to share the good news but I knew she'd be proud of me. As I turned into Lancaster Street and looked at my neighbour's house, the thoughts of the days at Mundella came flooding back - despite the bullying; despite having friends from hell and the turmoil at home, I had done it on my own and I felt like shouting out aloud (but I didn't). At some universities, the degree presentation ceremony is often several months afterwards and would take place during autumn. I was glad that at Leicester, the presentation would take place in a matter of weeks. I didn't have a suit to wear so I hurriedly bought myself one and the next thing I had to sort out was who would come with me. With my mum in India, I got tickets for my sister whilst Sunita, E2 and Nee were also there. On the day itself, we all gathered at De Montfort Hall in Leicester which is grand venue in itself. It was a warm summers day in July and you could feel the excitement around you. I met up with Raj, Gee and the rest of the students on my Software Engineering course and knew this would be the last time I would see many of them.

Soon we were ushered into the main room where we all sat in our designated seats. We then had to watch 100's of other students take to the stage and applauded each time they received their scroll from some person (I never did work out who it was that handed out the scrolls). After a while the clapping was just automatic; to be honest I wasn't really bothered about anyone else receiving their degree and if everyone else was honest they'd agree too. However, we didn't have to wait that long and before we knew it we were summoned to the side corridor where we'd have to wait until we were called. The rules were simple - wait for your name to be called, walk onto the stage and try not to fall, accept the scroll from the lady handing them out, bow down, smile (this *was* meant to be fun after all) and walk off trying not to fall again. "Sandip Patel" rang out from the speakers and bounced around the vast hall echoing all over the place. This was it, my moment had arrived and as I slowly walked onto the stage I could feel 100's of people looking on pretending they cared. The walk was perfect, the bow was perfect and the walk off stage was perfect and come to think of it, even the automatic clapping was perfect. In about 30 seconds flat, it was all over and I had an A4 sized piece of paper to show for it.

As we got back into our seats we waited for the whole ceremony to finish and then went outside and threw whatever we could into the air. I don't even know why people do this - i'd seen it in films but everyone was doing it so we obliged accordingly and took pictures to capture the moment. It was a great morning and a fabulous end to the whole degree course. I bid farewell to most of my fellow students because I knew I would never seem them again or would even want to contact them. However, I said good bye to Raj and Gee as I knew I would see them again.

So there you are, I had reached another milestone in my life and with a degree under my belt (well scrolled up actually), it was time to enjoy the summer and then plan what I wanted to do next. It dawned on me that I was officially unemployed - I wasn't working and wasn't studying so I joined the unemployment statistic. To ensure I had some kind of money coming in, I had to make my way to the unemployment office and "sign on". The unemployment centre / job centre or whatever it was called was a strange place but always busy. There were all kinds of people in there; scruffy looking teenagers, old people, drunks whilst others wore smart dresses and some men wore suits. As you looked around you could see the vacancies stuck to the walls that enclosed the whole room and people would be busy reading them armed with a pad and paper to make note of any that they were interested in.

The first thing I did was have a read myself but it was no good and the jobs weren't for me. I wanted a software engineering role and most of the jobs on offer were for cleaners, HGV Class 3 truck drivers and warehouse order pickers. There were kids screaming and running all over the place whilst their parents tried but failed to control them. I didn't want to be here and the place was just depressing and I knew then that I had to find work quick. After filling in the standard forms and telling them what kind of job I was looking for the lady behind the counter gave me a bizarre look. It was almost as if she expected me to say "warehouse job" or "driver" but instead I said software engineering. To be honest I had my doubts on whether she could even spell "software engineering" but she scribbled something down and I knew that my prospects here weren't good at all.

The lady then sighed heavily and explained that she'd never heard of that profession and that I might need to look "elsewhere" such as newspapers or specialist recruitment agencies. With my signature on the form I could leave and I was glad to get out of there but unfortunately i'd have to go back every fortnight to sign on until I found work. I didn't do much over the summer but I did keep an eye out for jobs. Up until that point I didn't even have a C.V. so i'd need to sort that out pretty sharpish but i'd never written a curriculum vitae (or "course of life" - it's Latin you know!) before. Armed with some expert advice from the university and some reference books from the library, I began writing up the course of life and it was a hard slog. I never knew putting together a CV would be this hard but it had to be written well as this was the first thing that prospective employees would see of me.

15

Rolling with the lads

AUGUST 1992

One evening whilst driving around with lads, one of us thought it would be a great idea to get away from Leicester for a while. No-one gave it any real thought but I quite liked the idea so mentioned it again over the next few days. None of us had any real commitments so it wasn't as though there was anything stopping us. Mind you, money (the lack of it that is), would undoubtedly be the real obstacle but after checking with the others I found that everyone was well up for it. In the end 7 of us fancied going which was all of us except Nee. I think Nee was in Africa or something so with numbers confirmed we picked the dates, hired the cars and we were all set. The plan was to head towards the south-east coast and that's it - you couldn't really get any more than that from us lads! E2, myself, Bob, Hemal, Rumit, Shifty and Vip (aka Chong) were all up for it which meant we had to get 2 hire cars.

On the evening we planned to head out, one of us (I think it was Bob) was invited to a birthday party at Asquith's night club so we couldn't miss that - a party's a party after all! With 7 excited lads in the car and a few clothes shoved in the boot, we headed into town and to the party. Bob was in top form and drank himself silly (was it just drink?). Towards the end of the night he was in a *bad* state and we had to help him out of the club and had to catch him several times as he tried unsuccessfully to get into the car. Eventually he clambered in but things went from bad to really bad and he ended up throwing up on himself and inside the hire car. Whilst all this was going on, we took the piss and made sure we got lots of photos. Bob is a right joker so it was payback time. I'm sure a few of the lads pulled his pants down or something but it was messy and we had to get him sorted quick time - this wasn't a good start to our trip...

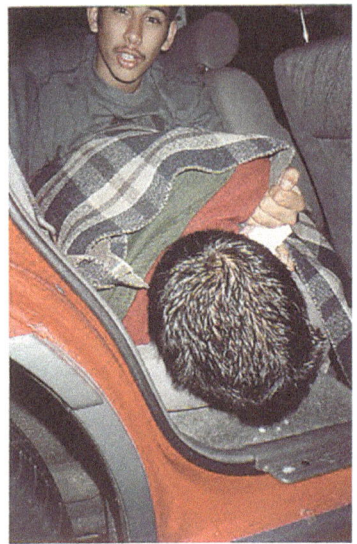 

Bobby – in need of assistance.   Bobby – still in need of assistance.

About an hour later, the vomiting stopped. Bob settled and dozed off into a deep sleep. By the time we got onto the M25, daylight had broken and we all needed some food. We pulled into a service area but left Bob in the car to sleep off his alcohol intoxication. No sooner had we left the car we heard the sound of someone running behind us - it was Bob; he'd made a miraculous recovery and was hungry too. To this day I have no idea how he made such a recovery but he did and we were quite thankful - he could finally clean up and hopefully get rid of his bad breath! After munching away on beans, sausages and toast (oh and a cuppa) we jumped back into the cars and continued on our way. In a matter of hours we had reached the south east coast and were in Margate to be exact. Trust me, I have no idea how or why we ended up here; the place was well crap but we were there, it was sunny and fairly warm so things weren't that bad.

For a while we drove around (we were good at this!) but eventually found a car park and started to change so we could get into some fresh clothes. This was chaotic; all of us were trying to get our clothes at the same time and struggling to change whilst we carefully ducked behind the back of the cars when a member of the public walked by. After all, we were in a *public* car park so we had to be careful and judging by the stares we were getting, it didn't look like we were being welcomed by the locals either. After a precarious 15 minutes in the car park, we were all raring to go so we checked out the town centre but before long we realised that there wasn't much to see. We then headed off to the beach where we had a few extra laughs and to be honest we didn't do much after that and just walked along the beach front. We had to liven things up a little bit so decided we'd check out a night club later that evening. After an evening meal of fish 'n' chips, it was back to the car to get ready yet again. One by one, we took our shirts out of our bags and laughed at each other as we put them on - they were so creased it would be a miracle if we even got into a night club.

We didn't have a clue where the clubs were so we drove around for a while - it made sense; we weren't local, didn't know the area so walking around the streets at night would almost certainly get us into trouble. It didn't take long before we found a place but it was a little out of town so with the car parked up we slowly made our way to the entrance. Something wasn't right - I could feel it and as I turned to the others I knew they felt the same. As we walked past groups of people they gave us really nasty looks. Perhaps it was the fact that we stood out - I mean there was 7 Indians walking up the road and since we arrived I never saw any other Indians so it could be a racist thing.

Bob had made a full recovery!

Time to chill!

I *really* hoped it wasn't; i'd had enough of the racist stuff when I was younger and thought all that nonsense was behind me. Eventually we arrived at the entrance to the club and the bouncers / door men or whatever they're called nowadays, looked at us in disbelief as if to say "Do they *really* want to go into the club?" They knew deep down that we would get into real trouble if we went inside and with a sudden change of facial expression, they ushered us into the club. To say we made a grand entrance was an understatement. This club and possibly this town is unlikely to have had a handful of Indians visit them yet there we were, all 7 of us, marching around as if we owned the place. Little did we know that things were about to change..

As we slowly walked deeper and deeper into the club, it took a few minutes before our eyes and ears adjusted to the dark rooms and extremely loud music but for the first 30 minutes it was ok. People seemed ok, we got served at the bar ok and nobody seemed to give us a second look. As the minutes ticked away, the place started to fill up and our free reign around the club was starting to get more and more difficult due to the sheer number of people that had suddenly arrived. It didn't stop there either, the extra crowds seem to bring in the racists too. We started to get bad looks from groups of young lads and then the jeers would start. It was the typical stuff such as "Wankers, paki's, paki's - fuck off home" and other variations. We started to get pushed around and groups of people stood in our way as we tried to get past them. The girls hanging around the racists also joined in. Feeling rather tough they'd shout things like "Curry breath & "Kick the paki's in as their male counterparts acted *real* tough.

My worst nightmare was coming true again and we all agreed to get out of there. Slowly, we made our way to the exit just as a whole load of others stopped us in our tracks and then stood there forcing us to admit that we were pakis. There were loads of them and even though we were surrounded and being asked to admit it we didn't. Why should we? The racists didn't like it but we didn't care and it was a huge relief when we managed to get out of the club in one piece. We thought that we'd be followed but no-one came after us. The door men shouted out "see ya later lads" and we knew they were just taking the piss out of us. We legged it back to the cars and knew we'd had a lucky escape but as we slowly thought about what had happened, it made us angry and rather than driving away we planned our revenge. Between us, we thought of the most embarrassing thing we could do and headed off to find a shop that was still open. Once we found one, we bought as many *eggs* as we could and drove around for a while to try and find a covered place from which we could launch them. Our luck was in and we stumbled upon a narrow road that looked down onto the road where the night club was.

I was looking forward to this and we waited for the right moment. As we crouched down behind the hedges we waited and waited for the door men to come out and after around 30 minutes their luck ran out. As the 2 guys stood at the front of the club looking like contenders to Britain's Strongest Man, we hurled egg after egg at them and watched as they lifted high into the sky and then came crashing down to earth hitting them directly and splattering in the entrance to the Ritzy night club. I know or rather we knew it would hurt but at the time we were young and didn't care. All we cared about was getting our own back and we did. The look on their face was worth all the abuse we took in the club and they were reduced to contenders for Britain's smelliest man! We then ran out of eggs and as a last insult shouted to them to let them know who the perpetrators were and then drove off knowing full well that we had sweet revenge. That night we slept in our car - something that was to become a regular thing for us over the years and we drove home a few days after that and vowed to never go back to this crappy place...

We were now into September 1992 and on the 5th of the month, Sunita would be 21 years old. Up for a party, she decided to have a 21st birthday bash at the same venue that I had mine. We were going to DJ on the night and since most of the people there were going to be our close friends it would be a good night. On the night itself, things started slowly and I think she was getting worried about people not turning up. She didn't have to worry - over the next hour, the place was getting quite full and had a good party atmosphere to it. Bob, Rumit, Hemal, Shifty and Chong were also there. Between E2 and myself we took it in turns to get behind the Technics and play the tunes.

The boys ready to party although looking at this picture
you'd think we were ready to go home!

The creative team got, er, creative!

Touchdown.

16

Rumit's law &
Shifting around town!

There's always someone at a party who doesn't like the music and does all they can to disrupt the show. This time some bloke walked up to me and started mouthing off. He was saying things like "change the music man" and then, as he got more agitated, would start to get abusive. Since we'd been DJ'ing for a while now we were accustomed to this and didn't say anything back - if we had done a full blown argument would no doubt break out and we didn't want to spoil Sunita's birthday. Little did I know that Rumit was watching close by and could hear everything that was being said. Rumit is a simple person, he doesn't like conflict and he doesn't like people taking the piss. He knew this guy would keep coming back and when he approached the DJ booth for the 4th time Rumit stepped in.

Calmly, he took the guy to the side and told him that it was a *private* party and '**my man**' could play whatever music he liked and since the birthday girl was not complaining, everyone else could get lost and he ended his conversation with him by telling him '**in a bit**'. Rumit then continued to tell the guy he should either shut the fuck up or leave. The other guy, quite taken aback by what Rumit said didn't know what to say or how to react and promptly retreated and never approached the DJ booth again. *There was something about the way Rumit stepped in that night and I knew this guy would turn out to be one of my best friends and he did.* Sunita, unaware of the commotion was having a good time, she was surrounded by friends and family and really enjoyed herself so that was good. During that party E2, Nee and myself got to know the other lads - Bob, Shifty, Hemal and Rumit much better and to this day I am thankful we did.

My mum, back from India was pleased to hear that I had passed my degree but she then started to tell me that I needed to get a job. She would often say "what do you do all day except sit around?". Unfortunately, my mum didn't realise that I was trying very hard to secure my first job. The CV was fine-tuned and I would trawl through the job section of the Leicester Mercury but I just couldn't find anything. In the first 2 months alone I must have applied to 80 blue chip companies in the vague chance that they had jobs going but the response was the same - they thanked me for my interest and would keep my letter on file just in case 'something came up' - it never did.

The job situation didn't improve, my mum wasn't interested in all the rejection letters and I was starting to get frustrated myself. I was putting so much effort into finding a job I liked but my mum simply thought I was messing about and not trying hard enough. As the summer drew to a close and the winter set in, she would tell me to find "any kind of job" but I refused. I wanted to wait for the *right* job; the one I had spent many years working for and I was not going to risk getting into the trap of finding any old job for fear of sticking with it for the rest of my life. This didn't go down too well with my mum and the tension was pretty high at home. I opted to stay out of my mum's way whenever I could because whenever I switched on the telly to take in the daily news, I knew she was thinking "oh, you've got time to watch TV but no time to find work" and I didn't need this at all.

Shifty, one of my new found friends had his own car and was the only one out of all of us who did. As I got to know Bob, Hemal and Rumit better, they would come round to my house and pick me up in the evening - they had nothing special planned but they had a car and that was good enough. I could always hear Shifty's car before I saw it - he had a Vauxhall Astra 1800 GTE and it was black. With a performance tuned engine, racing suspension and a full performance exhaust this car was *really fast*. As he turned into Lancaster Street he horned twice and once I was outside I had no idea who else was in the car. With tinted windows it was almost impossible to see inside Most often i'd be the first person he'd pick up. He lived fairly close by so after he had finished working for the day would head home, have a bite to eat and then head out.

When I first met him and he was introduced to me as "Shifty" I did wonder how on earth he got that nickname. His real name is Iftikhar which was shortened to "Ifti" and then "Shifty"; thankfully his nickname has no bearing to his character! One thing that I could never understand is how he managed to buy a car, park it yards from his house and drive it all round Leicester without his family knowing - they really had no idea he had his own wheels! During the holidays (Christmas, Easter, summer etc.), all of the lads would be together and shifty would come and pick us up one by one. Often he'd have to make several trips and we'd usually end up near a place nicknamed "Menzies" which was close to E2/ Chong's and Bob's house. Once there, we'd usually just chat about all sorts or take the piss out of each other, Shifty would do hand brake turns in his car whilst we captured it on video whilst on rare occasions we'd play football. Most of the summer days were spent in his car driving around Leicester. We had no nothing to do and nowhere to go but somehow we would be out till 2-3am and would probably cover up to 60-70 miles each night.

Shifty never got tired of driving no matter how many hours we were out that night. After driving around for a while we'd need some food and drink and would drive to the Jet petrol station near Abbey Park. It was quite strange - a black car with us inside would pull up and all the lads would pile out. The guy behind the cashier desk would often look quite worried; I guess it was car with its loud music and blacked out windows that made them feel edgy. Inside we'd buy all the cheese 'n' onion pasties and ask the cashier to warm them up for us. He never did get the temperature right and we would then have to spend the next 10 minutes trying to eat a blistering hot pasty and avoid it burning our hands at the same time. Once fed we were raring to go so would jump back into the car and head off into the night. Shifty's car stood out big time and there was always someone else who wanted to challenge him to a race. Most often it would happen at traffic lights. We would be waiting at the lights and then another car would pull up next to us. The other car had no idea who was inside the Astra but we could see them clearly.

One thing was for sure; no matter what car pulled up, no matter how fast or how new it was, there would be only one victor and that was Shifty. Shifty knew how to drive, control and outpace any other driver and the guy that pulled up next to us had no chance. As the bass line from the drum and bass track "Urban Shakedown" vibrated the windows of the car next to us, Shifty was in race mode and when the lights change, we were off. The engines would roar and in a matter of seconds we'd be well above the legal speed limit but as a corner or a roundabout came, Shifty didn't brake but simply steered into it and sped on. The other driver, playing it safe round the bend, was the loser and was well and truly beaten. This was the thing with Shifty and his car - others *thought* they could drive but he took driving to a new level.

On one occasion we were in town, close to the Holiday Inn and another bunch of lads pulled up. We were all used to this by now and knew what was coming. As the lights changed, the guys threw something at Shifty's car - this was totally out of order and

Shifty was having none of it. As we tore around St. Nicholas Circle, both cars headed towards the bus station and all of us were very angry by then as the other lads were hurling racist abuse too. Knowing that they couldn't shake us off, they did whatever they could to lose us but it failed miserably. We ended up on the A47 Humberstone Road where we were hitting speeds of up to 60 MPH. By the time we reached Uppingham Road, the guys must have realised that there was 5 of us in the car and that they were heavily outnumbered so the speed increased further.

Just before we reached Scraptoft Lane, the guy in front actually veered onto the pavement in a bid to get away from us and it was at that point that we decided to stop the chase. I'm the first to admit that what we did was stupid and dangerous but we were young, naive but still decided this was getting out of hand and let them get away. This is how we spent most of our holidays and as a bunch of friends we loved it. Shifty's Astra was previously owned by a company who race tuned cars; this would probably explain why his car was so fast. Sometimes we would drive out to Bradgate Park and Swithland Woods where we would cause a real stir. We drove to Swithland Woods one day and slowly turned into the car park. It must have been just after midnight and the silence was eerie. Around us we could see several cars and it was obvious that the occupants were not there walking their favourite pets! Instead they drove out there for some peace and quiet and to have some quiet loving! Disappointing for them, this was about to change.

All of us would sit in the car, music off, lights off and in the distance you could hear owls tweeting away. We'd sit there and let the other cars think we were just another couple but after about 10 minutes, and armed with torches, we would venture out. One by one we'd get out of the car and once out would choose our target car. Slowly we'd walk towards it, each of us separating as we got closer to the car. Though we tried our best not to laugh, it was useless and the occupants must have heard our sniggering and sounds of "sshhhhh" echoing through the woods. You have to remember that it was so dark here that you really couldn't see your hands if you put them in front of your eyes. We were all in place now and surrounded the car; the occupants inside were either too busy to notice us creeping up on them or were so petrified they stopped what they were doing in anticipation of what would happen next...

After a collective "3-2-1-GO!!" we'd jump up and start shaking the car whilst shining torches onto the unfortunate occupants. Most often, those inside the car had *no* idea we were there and the looks on their faces had us in tears of laughter for ages. In a state of shock, the occupants had no idea what was going on; one minute they were probably engaging in loving duties to the sound of Barry White whilst the next the inside of their car was lit up, their car was rocking and 5 Indians were staring inside. I truly think we must have scarred many people for life but it was one of the funniest things ever. The driver, still recovering from the torch shining directly into his eyes would desperately try to start the car but would forget that the seat was so far back that he could hardly reach the clutch. This meant more pain for them - we would just stand there looking around the inside of their car whilst the guy desperately tried to get his trousers on, move the seat and find his keys at the same time.

On one particular occasion, the driver shouted out "piss off you paki's" and this meant we had to take it to the next stage. As we stood there watching this guy hurl abuse at us, Shifty would switch into race mode, get the car and we'd all pile in again. We'd then follow the other car through the winding lanes around Bradgate Park and Swithland woods and this *must* have been traumatic for them. Not only had they been embarrassed beyond belief but they were now being chased and the chase continued for at least 4-5 miles after which Shifty decided enough was enough This wasn't a one off either - throughout the summer we'd do the same thing over and over again, choosing different victims and switching locations too. Bradgate Park had its fair share of night time loving so just as we'd done many times before, we would surround the car and jump out when the occupants least expected it. Sometimes we wouldn't harass anyone but would simply go for a night time stroll through the woods. This was *very* scary and with our torch batteries failing, things would get quite difficult. One particular night it was extremely dark - the sky was full of dark clouds and with no moon visible we stumbled around trying to find our way into the woods then frantically trying to get out of them.

After about 30 minutes the clouds broke and a little moon light shone into the woods and ahead of us we could see something moving. There was no noise except the noise of my mates trying to avoid falling over each other but the thing we could see moving seemed to get bigger and bigger and before long there were moving things all over the place. Suddenly one of us screamed in terror and the reflex action caused the rest of us to panic not knowing what had happened. As quick as the shouting started it died down and I remember calling out to my friends by name and one by one they all answered and I breathed a deep sigh of relief. It was like something out of Predator; all of us waiting for something to pick us out of the woods but thankfully the predators turned out to be cows who seemed to be more startled than we were. With that panic over, we'd had enough excitement for one night so we called it a night (if you know what I mean and hurried home...).

Despite all our night time antics, I made sure I continued my search for a programming job and as the days turned into weeks and weeks turned into months, I started to get extremely frustrated as the letters of rejection flooded in. Unfortunately, this was nothing compared to what my mum was thinking. Despite applying for almost 230 jobs in 9 weeks, scouring the local and national papers and spending countless hours at the job centre, my mum seriously thought that I spent all day and night dossing around. Whilst I was in the house I simply couldn't do anything right. Whenever I wanted to go out I would get sarcastic comments such as "You go out; don't worry about finding a job - you can't drive around all your life can you?"

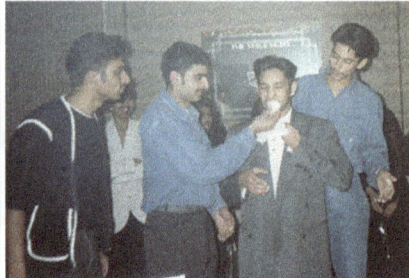

Shifty finally had his cake and ate it.
After these pictures were taken
things got very interesting...

Young Rumit & Hemal on
cake duty to the left...

I *knew* I was doing the right thing by holding out for the *right* job. I was confident I would find the job but didn't know when that would be whilst at home it really felt as if I was running out of time. That week I rebelled big time - I had taken great offence at being told I dossed about all day and even more offence at being told I should go to the Mandir (Indian temple) to pray for better luck. Not being religious at all, I thought this was a load of nonsense and one of the first things I did was go to McDonalds and ordered a Big Mac. Despite never being religious, I had always avoided beef because it was the 'right thing to do' and Hindus 'don't eat beef' but this time I thought "stuff it"; I didn't believe in it so why shouldn't I eat it? So I did and it didn't make me feel any better afterwards - I just did it to prove a point. In hindsight I now know that my mum only had my interests at heart but at the time it didn't seem that way at all.

Whilst on the topic I always hated the way I was told that I should go and pray. I didn't believe in any of it yet to go into a Mandir, pray and then eat the sacred food was simply wrong, hypocritical and I didn't want any part of it. If you are in any way religious and want to pray and follow the religious rituals then that's fine but what I can't stand is having other people's opinions forced upon me and I wasn't having any of it. Since that day I vowed I would never step into a Mandir and after that I only went into one the day I got married and never after that. Some of my friends may not like what i've just written or the fact that I openly ate beef but it's the truth and this book is about the truth. Eating beef hasn't changed the person that I am or the beliefs I have - it's a choice that I made, I have to live with and others will just have to accept it.

The rebellious streak didn't stop there either and it turned fairly nasty one particular week. Shifty came to call for me on a Monday and that night we drove up to Wycombe. After staying there till the early hours we drove back to Leicester and it was just after 4am by the time I got into bed. The next day we did the same; this might sound crazy but driving 200 miles nightly became routine and was hardly any effort at all. That night my mum woke up as soon as I walked into the house. The following morning she would always ask me what time I got in; even though she knew the time anyway - she wanted to check if I told the truth or not. With no need to lie, I told her that it was 5.10am when I got in but I was not finished yet. Bang on time, Shifty came to pick me up on the Wednesday and then again on Thursday evening but by the time we pulled into my street on Friday morning (it was now 5.30am) my mum flipped and as I tried to get into the house as quietly as I could, she must have heard it and came downstairs.

Just as I was about to turn the key, she opened the door with a half asleep and extremely angry look about her and I knew I was in trouble. All she said was "If you want to mess around then don't do it here" and with that she snatched the door key out of my hand. With no key, my mum figured that I simply wouldn't go out or if I did I would be back very early. Despite being very angry over this, I didn't want to make things worse and for the next 6 days I kept myself to myself. When shifty or any of my other friends came round I told them I was staying in and I did just that. I tried to avoid eye to eye contact and would leave the room when my mum walked in. It may sound daft but I actually did it to keep the peace and with no signs of this stalemate ending I grabbed my folder of rejection letters, came down stairs and threw all of them onto the floor. Before my mum had the chance to say anything I simply told her what these letters were and that I *was* trying to find work whether she believed me or not. I think this hit home and she realised that I was telling the truth, my door key was returned and normal service resumed.

Around this time, E2's dad had a Ford Sierra 4x4 which was pretty rare in those days and whenever it went into the local Ford garage for repairs they would get a car to run-around in. E2 would then come to pick me up and we'd go out cruising as well so sometimes we'd have 2 cars tearing around Leicester. Most often i'd be driving the car but at the end of the night we'd drive back to Lancaster Street to drop me off. As I put the key into the door to let myself in, all you hear was the high revs of an engine as E2 roared away only to pull a hand brake turn just before the end of the road! These hand brake turns turned into a routine occurrence and on some nights the hand brake turn simply wasn't good enough. E2 would always look back at me standing in my door way and I would often tell him to do it all over again. He would then reverse as fast as he could and then try another hand brake turn which would always be better the 2nd time around!

One particular evening there was only E2 and I in the car and we were driving in the Rushey Mead area of Leicester. With nowhere in particular to go, we simply drove around and whilst I was turning the car around in a Cul de sac, we noticed a wheelie bin close by (wheelie bins are bins with wheels for those of you that don't know!). I can't remember which one of us suggested it but E2 then grabbed the handle of the bin whilst I tried to manoeuvre the car closer. As we turned out of the Cul de sac and onto the main road, I began to build up speed whilst E2 was holding onto the bin. By this stage we were both pissing ourselves with laughter; we'd never seen a bin go so fast but we weren't finished yet and once we'd reached about 40 MPH E2 let go of it.

The bin spun out of control, fell onto its front but skidded along the road for ages spilling its contents as it did so. E2 was now looking backwards in his seat whilst I could see this large black thing in the car's rear view mirror. As it skidded along it made a racquet and eventually we heard a loud bang as it crashed into the side of the road and emptied the rest of its contents. We drove out of the area quick time; from that moment onwards we were hooked and over the course of many weeks we did the same thing over and over again. Often when there were 4 or 5 of us in the car, we'd grab 2 or 3 bins and drive even faster before letting them go and watch as they hurtled along the road like a missile then exploded as they crashed into something. As an experiment we wanted to see what would happen if we let go of the bin around the corner so we grabbed one and drove as fast as we could and let go of it just as the road started to bend to the right.

As the car veered towards the right, the bin veered completely out of control and instead wobbled around a bit, then headed straight for a parked van. Within 5 seconds, the bin had crashed into the van and just as it did we saw 2 people pop up from the front of the van. The couple had obviously chosen to grab a romantic moment for themselves but we soon put a stop to that - they now had someone's rubbish strewn outside the van and yet again we made a sharp exit. A few weeks later 5 of us were out with Shifty in a hired car and we spotted a bin in one of the side roads in the Forest Road area of Leicester. Not sure who grabbed the bin this time but Shifty was in racing mode and as we tore down the road with the bin inches from the car, the road veered to the right (we'd been here before!) but the bin slipped and continued straight towards a parked car.

Everything seemed to go into slow motion after that; Shifty slowed down and we urged the bin to slow down too but it wasn't to be - the bin crashed head on into the back of a car (I won't say which for obvious reasons) and completely smashed the rear window. We panicked and started to drive out of the area quick time but just as we got to the end of the road, a police car came into view but thankfully it drove straight past us and with that we knew we'd all had a lucky escape. We were extremely sorry for what we did to that car but we weren't going back there to own up - far from it. Shifty dropped us all off home and that was the last time we messed with bins again.

17

Last night a Renault saved my life...

During one of our regular nights out in Leicester, we were in yet another hire car. This time it was a white Vauxhall Nova and with 5 of us in car, those sat in the back were well squashed. It was a lovely summer's evening and that day had been exceptionally warm so we cruised around with all the windows and sunroof wide open. With Shifty driving all over the place, we found ourselves in Churchgate (a small lane in Leicester City Centre) and just as we got to the bottom of the road he pulled into a small parking space. I was in the back of the car, Hemal was in the front and I think E2 and Bob were in the car too. Just as we came to a halt, another car pulled up next to us and judging by the way Hemal spoke to the driver, it was obvious he knew him.

In the back we just started chatting away ourselves, completely oblivious to the conversation going on in the front. After a few minutes, we started to get quite hot and bothered in the back - it was a warm day and with no air conditioning and the fact that we were parked up meant there was nothing keeping us cool. I just wanted Hemal to stop chatting and shifty to start driving so we could get some cool air! Just as I was about to tell Hemal to let us out (it was a 2 door car), he suddenly shouted "drive!", "drive!" and shifty did as he was asked and sped off.

Not knowing what was going on, we all started to ask Hemal what had happened but he couldn't keep a straight face and was laughing uncontrollably. He didn't stop either and just kept laughing and after a while it was one of those moments where we all started laughing even though the rest of us had no idea why. As Shifty's driving got more and more erratic we were soon out of the city centre and shifty once more pulled into a parking lane. Thankfully Hemal had calmed himself down now and revealed what was so funny and we couldn't believe it. He threw an egg out of the Nova's open sunroof and with the accuracy of a missile, the egg somehow worked its way through the other cars sunroof and landed on the guy's head who then had raw egg dripping from his head.

In an instant it all made sense and we knew why he asked shifty to drive! We all thought he was speaking to a mate of his but he wasn't - he knew the guy but the friendliness stopped there. We pissed ourselves as we imagined the guy sitting in the car with egg on his face not quite knowing what had happened. I was still shocked with the Hemel's accuracy and we all had a great laugh at his expense. None of us even knew that Hemal had eggs in the car so he obviously pre-planned this or there was some other reason. Anyway it didn't matter, the incident was over and after another hour's driving we'd all had enough and decided to go home. That night Shifty asked me to take the car home; I was insured on it so didn't mind at all.

As we did most nights, we dropped everyone in a certain order - the furthest away first and by the time I had dropped shifty off it was almost 1am and I was yawning every other minute. I didn't drive straight home and took a longer route instead and after a few minutes noticed a car that seemed to be taking the same turns as me. Thinking it was pure coincidence, I just kept driving but when I drove twice through the same roundabout and circled around Freemans Common twice (an industrial estate), the car was still following and I knew that something wasn't right. I remember thinking that this was something out of the movies - I was being "tailed" (ok - I was in the UK so it should have been "followed") but "tailed" sounds better!

I could feel the adrenaline pumping through my veins and when I had no choice but to stop at a set of red traffic lights, those chasing me were right behind me and all of a sudden I felt slightly sick. The reality of who was chasing me dawned on me - it was egg-man. Oh yes; the person who had egg dripping from his face a few hours earlier and who we laughed at was back; he was angry, there were 2 of them and I felt very alone. My thoughts turned to Hemal - he was probably fast asleep whilst I was probably about to have the life beaten out of me! I had 2 choices; either pull over and see what they wanted or try and lose them. I would either be beaten to a pulp or caught by the police as I tore around Leicester trying to evade the egg man. There was no choice and as soon as the lights switched to amber, the little Nova engine screamed as I floored it and tried to get away from them. I don't remember what car they had but I do remember that the guy was a crap driver and before long, whilst on Victoria Park Road, I could barely see them in my mirror.

As the roundabout approached I hit some traffic even though it was early in the morning and I lost lots of ground but soon I was on my way again. Yet again I was stopped in my tracks by red traffic lights and even if I risked going through them (albeit very carefully), my decision not to was made up automatically with the sight of a police car right in front of me. The egg man pulled up behind me and I was quite surprised that they didn't even get out but he looked angrier than ever. As the police car vanished into the night, I knew I had to do the same and when the lights changed again I knew that the only way I could get away from them was to park up and hide but the question was where?

The tyres squealed as I sped off yet again and raced along East Park Road; by now I was desperate to get away and decided that I would drive down Clumber Road. Now, Nee lives on Clumber Road and there was no chance at all that he'd be awake - far from it - you could guarantee that he would be in stages N3 or N4 of the sleep cycles (you might want to look that up!) so I knew I couldn't knock on his door. Anyhow, I raced down East Park Road and past Spinney Hill Park at around 60MPH and made a sharp right into St. Saviours Road. As I got about 200 yards up this road I could see another car making the same turn. Without thinking I turned into Kitchener Road, then onto Clumber Road and drove as fast as I could. I parked the car about 100 yards before Nee's house, quickly unbuckled the seat belt and then ran as fast as I could towards Nee's house and quickly hid underneath a Renault 11 that was parked in Nee's drive. The car belonged to Nee's cousin "Kaba" who was also a good friend of mine. The rear end of the car was partly jacked up (a good thing as it meant I could squeeze underneath it). Fractions of a second after getting underneath the car, the other car pulled up and I could hear the sound of heavy footsteps coming towards Nee's house.

I could hear them mumbling to themselves and hoped they wouldn't spot me. Unfortunately they kept walking and luckily walked straight past Nee's house. After presumably looking around for what seemed an age, they slowly walked back past the house again and towards their car. I was expecting them to get really pissed off and smash the Nova or do some kind of other damage to it but I breathed a massive sigh of relief as they drove off. Rather than crawl out, I stayed put just in case they decided to drive round again. I was there for ages but in reality it must have only been about 30 minutes which is still a long time anyway. In the end I *had* to get out, my legs were cramping up and I was starting to shiver. It wasn't the cold but probably a mixture of adrenaline, fear and cramp all rolled into one. I stood up ever so slowly and decided I would leave the car where it was; there was no way I was driving it now - the last thing I wanted was another chase! Slowly I scanned the area and it seemed clear so I legged it home as quick as I could. As I got my door key out of my trouser pocket and shakily opened the front door I quickly stepped inside, closing the door firmly behind me - I was home; I had survived.

The next morning I recalled the events of the night before and the truth is that a Renault saved my life. Kaba's Renault was *always* breaking down and when I needed it most, the car helped me out by giving me a life line. Ironically, when I spoke to the others about what had happened, they found it funny and it was but at the time there was nothing funny about it at all. I wanted to know - why me? When I mentioned it to Nee, he surprised us all - he actually woke up because he thought he heard noises outside. The thing was you see, his bedroom overlooked the front road and he actually looked out of the window but not seeing anything went back to bed. Little did he know that I was hiding under a car in his drive way and 2 guys were on the hunt for me.

When I graduated from university, the last thing I thought was that i'd be still searching for work almost a year later. For some reason I just thought i'd find work pretty quickly but here I was, a year later in the summer of 1993 still unemployed. I had already been through a turbulent time at home trying to fend off the temptation to jump into any kind of job. I knew my mum was steadily losing her patience but I stood firm in my determination to stick it out for the right job and I did just that. By now my fortnightly trips to the "dole" office were just routine and i'd see the same faces week in and week out. I wasn't the only on struggling to find work either. Raj was keeping himself busy by working in their family business whilst Gee was working in Oxford Street.

During one particular visit to the unemployment office, I was called into a side room and the lady explained that I needed to attend a weeks' course on 'looking for work'. As she explained more about the course, it was clear that I had to prove to them that I was actively searching for work too otherwise they may stop my unemployment benefit money. So, not only was my mum giving me a hard time but now I had these guys on my case too - didn't anyone believe me? 2 weeks later I took a huge bag of rejection letters with me and when asked for this proof, emptied the entire contents onto the desk of the unfortunate person who had to deal with me that day. I was fed up of having to justify myself to everyone and if they wanted proof I would give it to them. They thought I was some kind of nutter and after checking no more than 5 letters I think they got the message and realised I was trying hard - real hard.

The pressure was on and I had to step up another gear. I didn't want to move out of Leicester but I had no choice and started to look for work wherever I could get it - location was not irrelevant. Recruitment firm were useless; one minute they'd raise your hopes with "an exciting position" but you'd never hear from them after that and all I did was leave endless voice mail messages that were probably just deleted. I went for an interview at TNT once where I felt like I was being questioned like a criminal. Before they even asked me a question I knew they didn't like me - this was fine, I didn't like them either but the worst thing about it was that I never heard any feedback from the recruitment firm that arranged the interview.

I got my own back several weeks later when someone at the "head office" of the recruitment firm called me to get feedback on their employees and in particular anyone that I had dealt with recently. When asked the question "Do you have any feedback?, my answer was a definite yes. I then spent the next 10 minutes at *their* cost telling them how they never call me back, never reply to my voicemails, never give me feedback and I would never use them again. I think they were quite taken aback by my comments and she assured me this would be fed back to the recruitment team. Hopefully my comments made some kind of difference and if it was up to me I would have sacked the team - useless gits!

One evening whilst we out cruising in the car again, we got onto the subject of holidays and we reminisced about our egg throwing incident at the Ritzy the year before. Despite that incident we all had a great laugh so we knew we had to do it again. Little did I know that the lads wanted to go somewhere in the next few weeks. Once we got talking, we couldn't leave the subject alone and before long everyone had their own ideas of where to go and after about 30 minutes the decision was made to go. Without a job, I knew my mum wouldn't be thrilled at the prospect of me going off on a jolly but to be fair it was quite understandable. This time we would give the south a miss and Blackpool was the destination.

On the morning we left it was a warm summers day in August 1993, we picked up the hire cars and we (Hemel, E2, Rumit, Vip, Shifty, Bob, Nee and myself) dumped all our stuff in the back and the journey started. This time we were going away for 5 days and the boot was packed of stuff. Hemal had been shopping, he had more lotions, creams, moisturisers and cleanser than anyone I know and one thing was for sure - regardless of what happened on our journey, we would all have baby soft skin!

Rather than drive straight to Blackpool we ended up in Leeds first and on the lookout for a decent night club. Each time we went out at night, something always happened and I really hoped to have an incident free first night. Ironically the best club in town seemed to be the Ritzy. We all hoped we didn't get the racists again but thankfully there was nothing to worry about. Once we got to the entrance there was a sign that said "free entry with a banana". Now, for young lads like us, money wasn't tight but if there was any way to save money we were interested so we went away and came back with bananas!

Once inside the atmosphere was totally different to our last experience in a Ritzy. Everyone was friendly, up for a good laugh and if you bumped into someone by mistake it was "sorry mate" and that was the end of it. I definitely think it's a northern thing; people *are* friendlier further north and even when we left the club and searched for a kebab shop, all the locals inside were cheery and friendly. Once we'd eaten, it was around 3am and with the others intoxicated with alcohol and kebabs, Shifty and I drove straight to Blackpool where we arrived on a clear and beautiful morning.

Accommodation during our 5 day break was something we never discussed so we had nowhere to sleep except the car. At the time it really didn't bother us at all and when we look back at this it's hard to believe we managed to get any sleep at all. At the end of the night we would drive around and search for safe place to rest for the night. Most often we'd find ourselves in a car park and it would take about 90 minutes before we finally dozed off. With 4 lads in each car coupled with the crazy things we got up to, there was pushing and shoving, constant piss taking, taunting, snoring, some wanting the car warm, others wanting it cold and so on. There was no time to waste and no time to sleep either despite all of us being really tired. The first thing we had to do get food so it was off to a cafe where we had a great English breakfast. By the time we'd eaten Blackpool was coming alive, I think we'd picked one of the warmest weekends and it was really busy.

After heading straight for the beach, E2 was thrown into the water and got soaked and the joker among the pack (Bob of course!) started spitting at us as we tried in vain to grab hold of him and chuck him in too. I've mentioned this before but Bob plays jokes on everyone but doesn't like them being played on him but soon it *will* be payback time. We were then forced into the arcades by Rumit, Hemel and Bob so that they could show us their gambling skills. The rest of us watched as the machines spun their reels and lit up just like the Blackpool illumination. When the machine gave 'nudges', these 3 knew exactly where the matching symbols were even though you couldn't even see them. The rest of the day was spent doing pretty much the same until we stumbled upon a shop that sold plastic masks. We bought 8 of them and decided to liven things up. With the masks securely strapped to our faces we drove around Blackpool. The funniest part was Hemal sticking his head out the sunroof and the looks he got from young kids.

When we stopped at traffic lights we would pick out a car and all of us would stare into it. With the loud music pumping out from our car's stereo, that alone would grab people's attention but when the passengers in the other car turned and looked at us they got an almighty shock at seeing all the occupant's wearing masks. The masks generally got a smile from most people that set eyes on them whilst others looked at us in disgust. After a few more days of Blackpool sunshine we needed to get out of there but not before a trip to Southport, where we decided to drive our cars onto the beach. We were having a right laugh until the tide came in and both cars got stuck with the water approaching rapidly. We asked a local for help and he just refused - nice man. Anyway, we dug the car out in the end, good job really otherwise we wouldn't have anywhere to sleep...

Whilst we in Southport we ran out of things to do and someone (can't remember who) thought it might be a good idea to recreate some kind of reconstruction of an event that happened in Southport a few weeks earlier. Looking back at it now what we did was plain stupid but at the time we found it extremely funny so I may as well tell the story - i've admitted everything else after all! We bought a load of stockings and parked our cars around the corner from a line of shops. With the stockings in our trousers, we found somewhere quiet and then pulled them onto our heads and then ran around the corner as quick as we could. Shouting "start the car, start the car" as loudly as we could, we ran as fast as we could towards our getaway cars!

As robbers, we weren't doing a good job; we didn't have anything with us to show we'd stolen anything but that didn't matter. The fact is we caused a real commotion - local residents, too shocked at what they were witnessing, stood still and watched as we jumped into our cars. The looks on their faces said it all - they were terrified and I knew then that we had done something really, really stupid. There was no going back now, we got out of there as quickly as we could and we're pretty certain someone must have called the police. Thankfully, nobody saw us get into

Original crew...

Drinks on the beach!

Nothing bad happened here, this picture was purely for the camera!

the cars but we didn't hang around. Any plans of staying for a few more hours went out the window - as did our stockings and we headed straight for the M6 as quickly as we could.

Over the years we've had many close shaves but this one took the top spot and we all decided to never do anything like that ever again. I knew, however, that this is what we agreed on - whether we kept to our word was something else. With a few days of our break left, we decided to drive to Scotland - up until then none of us had been there so we had a long drive ahead of us and we arrived in Edinburgh late in the evening. Luckily for us, we had our accommodation pre-booked in advance - our hire car so it was a matter of finding a good place to park up and sleep for the night. With a full day ahead of us, we asked the locals what there is to see in Edinburgh and off we went. We did a whistle stop tour of Edinburgh covering the city centre, Calton Hill and the Forth bridge where trouble came looking for us. About a half mile before the approach to the bridge, a car pulled next to us and the occupants started the usual racial taunts; it didn't seem to matter where about in the UK we were - racism was evident all over the place.

We tried to ignore it and common sense told us to ignore it but after a few minutes they would not let up. None of us had a mobile phone so we waved frantically to the lads in the other car and somehow they understood that the car next to us was causing trouble. In a flash, Shifty pulled alongside the car and the 'racists' now had 2 cars to deal with; one on each side. The racial insults soon stopped when they saw the other car and they then started to drive faster. The hunters were being hunted and there was to be no let up. For several miles, we followed them but tried not to speed or drive erratically. We just followed them and eventually decided to let them go... we really couldn't afford to get into trouble over something so petty so we called it a day. To end the night off, we thought we'd have a little more fun with our masks which was a great laugh... unfortunately that was the end of our trip and the only thing we had to look forward to was planning the next one!!

Calton Hill, Edinburgh. A great place to visit if you're ever there.

Left to right: -
Chongy, Shifty, Bob, Sandip, E2, Rumit, Hemal.

Back in Leicester, life returned to normal as the regular search for work continued. Even though I was keen to find work anywhere, there was simply no jobs going for graduates. It didn't help that I graduated without any experience at all. On my degree course half of the students, including Raj, Gee and myself, struggled to find a placement. Most companies were laying off full time staff let alone take on students - no matter how cheap we were! Irrespective of that I *had* to continue my quest for my first job so it was onwards and upwards as they say. In Leicester, the 'house music' scene was more and more popular, clubs were staying open until 5 or 6am and they were attracting a different crowd altogether. The louts and drunken yobs were replaced by those who simply loved the music - well house music to be exact. Some clubbers were just happy dancing whilst most others, fuelled by ecstasy, were *really* happy and spent a large proportion of the night telling each other (& strangers) how much they loved them.

It was a strange phenomenon; no violence, no dirty looks when you bumped into someone by mistake - just happy music with happy people and it was a great place to be. The best place in Leicester was a club night called "Splendid" at a place called Starlite 2001. The club's statement was "quality house music" and they stuck to this policy rigidly. The DJs didn't try to cut or scratch the records but chose to seamlessly mix the tunes to the wonder of the crowd. Old club classics met latest upfront house tunes and the atmosphere was electric. At about the same time my sister, who was always keen to expand on her skills, embarked on another course which involved lots of extra research and white papers to write. I tried desperately to get my sister to type her work straight into the advanced typewriter she had just bought but I fought a losing battle and in the end muggings here got all her hand written notes and then typed them up for her.

I say 'muggings' here but I don't mean that in the bad sense at all - it's my sister after all and I was just happy to help. I didn't mind the hours and hours I spent typing it all up, the endless time spent proof reading, countless hours fixing mistakes and so on! All her work would then have to be printed (it was too much work for her to read it directly on the typewriter(!) and i'd then have to make some final amendments and print off the final copy. Trust me, it was a long drawn out process and boy oh boy, some of those papers were well long and I struggled on some nights just to keep my concentration going. Thankfully, I haven't had to do this for many years but even if she asked me, i'd just do it - she is my big sister after all!

By the time 1994 had arrived I was I *still* jobless and was starting to wonder if I was destined to find a job at all.

The pressure at home was intense and something had to be done about it. It was clear to me that i'd tried my absolute hardest to find work but you can't get a job if there are none in the first place and something had to done pretty fast. Back in Wycombe, E2 and Sunita were the only ones left in their rented house - both Alpa and RT had finished their courses and were back home in Leicester. With a spare room up for grabs, I decided that the best thing to do was move in, albeit for a short while, to search for work down south. I thought my mum wouldn't like the idea of me moving out but she said it was a good idea and by September had arrived, I was all packed and ready to go. I didn't want to go but it

Fat friends!

"Hello, is Alpa there?"

Minny.

247

Hair ok.

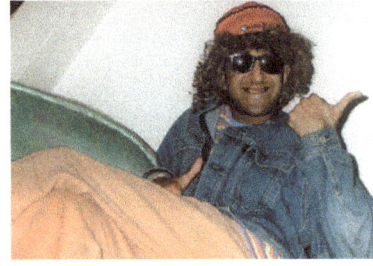

Paresh (Grandmaster P in the place!)

Priya stopped by and
decided to cook.

was tough and I just had to get on with it. Sunita was just about to start her final year on her course whilst E2 had just graduated and was looking for work as well. It was quite strange for me living there; i'd stayed there many times but I knew i'd be going home after a few days.

This time there was no going back - well not in the short term anyway. The first few days there were spent registering with the local unemployment office and answering all the standard questions again. When it came to "sign on" day, E2 and I would stroll down to the dole office and then nosey around town. On our way back we'd often stop to see Paresh who was working in a clothes shop at the time. Every time we went in he was always with the women - chatting to them and giving them advice on the pair of jeans they were trying on. When the customer's back was turned, he'd give us a cheeky grin. That's one cool thing about Paresh, no matter when you see him, no matter what time of day it is, he is *always* smiling and he's always up for a laugh. You'd also hear quality music in this shop - it was always Kiss 100 on the radio or Paresh or Munsha's own FBI DJ Mix - either way, it sounded great.

With our little chat over, we'd slowly walk back to Ogilvy Road and back to the house that was in dire need of a serious makeover. The proprietor "Mo" as he liked to be called was a down to earth kind of person. He spent many years in Blackburn, had a strong accent to go with it and spoke very fast. At first we struggled to understand what he was going on about. He sat there reiterating the house rules and the do's and don'ts. Before long he turned into more of a mate than a proprietor and he would sometimes pop by just for a chat. When the house needed some kind of repair, we would often accompany him to B & Q and then help him whilst he fixed whatever was broken. During the day, Sunita was usually the first one out the door. She would walk into town where she would then catch the mini bus that took students to the Amersham campus that was about 20 minutes' drive from Wycombe town centre. Meanwhile at home E2 and myself would scour the papers for work but there wasn't much going. It wasn't that bad for E2; after all, he had just started looking for work whereas I had been looking for 2 years and I was getting desperate. Money was very tight too; it's quite hard to survive on about £60 per week, especially when the rent was close to that anyway.

Martin, a friend who we met through Paresh, worked for a company that sold gun cabinets. Knowing we could do with earning extra money, he asked if we wanted to "earn a bit on the side" by making some deliveries now and then. We didn't need any time to consider it and just said yes. It seemed easy work and it would probably be a laugh but little did we know what was *really* involved. At random times during the day, we'd get a phone call - there was a delivery to be made and in a flash we'd be on our way back to town for duty. Martin met us there, introduced us to his boss and in minutes we were on our way. At first we didn't even

"Can't be bothered..."

look at what was in the back of the Citroen minivan and E2, not wanting to drive, sat in the passenger seat armed with the London A-Z. We made deliveries all over London and although it may not sound like it, it was quite good fun actually. One of the deliveries we had to make was in central London; it was in a small narrow road and there was just enough space to get the cabinet out of the van. It didn't seem heavy but that soon changed as we tried to pick it up.

This thing was *really* heavy and worst still it had to be delivered to the 5th floor and the lift wasn't working. This was bad and by the time we dragged the stupid cabinet to the 2nd floor, we were hot and very sweaty. It was at this precise moment in time that we wondered why on earth we were carrying this huge lump of metal and busting our backs for about £15.00? No, you haven't mis-read this, that's all we were paid for driving up to 5 hours in the car and carrying these damn things up and down stairs. Despite all this hard graft we carried on for several weeks but after a while the "workload", if you could call it that, soon dwindled away. To make matters worse, the £15.00 pounds we got was the maximum we received and we often got a measly £10 for our mighty efforts. After forking out for food during our travels, we sometimes spent just as much as we earnt so at the end of the day all we did was drive, almost break our backs and then walk back home!

18

The man @ Parametric...
he said yeah!

One day whilst scouring through the local Wycombe paper I noticed a job advertised that looked pretty interesting. It was a software testing role based in Bracknell. It wasn't the type of job I was looking for but it was a job nevertheless and up until then i'd never even heard of Bracknell let alone considered a job there but this opportunity seemed too good to miss. It was advertised as "ideal for new graduate" and I just wanted to get my foot through the door. Ignoring the advert's request to phone them, I wrote to them instead but went for the "honest" route. I basically wrote a detailed letter explaining my history; that I had graduated without experience and I was keen to learn even if it meant working for nothing.

The thing is I actually meant it - I was desperate to find work and I *really* would have worked for nothing simply to get some kind of experience. As I sealed my letter and headed off to post it, I walked along in a pretty dejected way. I resigned myself to getting yet another rejection letter or not hearing from them at all. Thinking about it now, I think this must have been the best letter i've ever written because it actually got me to the interview stage! Either that or the company; Parametric Technology Corporation; were so desperate that they wanted to take on anybody!

When the letter arrived asking me to go for an interview I felt that a milestone had been reached, akin to sailors passing Cape Horn or climbers reaching Mount Everest. Ok, ok perhaps being asked to come for an interview can't really be compared to circumnavigating the world or reaching the highest point on it but for me it was the best news in several years and I was going to make the best of it. After reading the letter came the realisation of what I had to do. With no work experience, no real job interview experience and nothing concrete to talk about on what I had been doing for the past 2 years, I felt very alone yet again but this had to change... and fast! By the way if some of you are wondering what "Cape Horn" is then look it up - go on, you know you want to!

Surprisingly for me, I was quite calm on the day of the interview which is totally out of character. When I finally found the Parametric Technology Corporation (PTC) building, the first thing that stood out was the sheer size of it - it was huge. Once through the doors, the calmness ended and panic creeped in again and I could feel my heart start to race as the receptionist told me that "David will be down in a minute". It was a long minute and I finally got to meet the person who had offered me a life line. David, the manager of the development team was a tall guy with a very calm look about him. Quite a contrast to myself - I could feel the sweat dripping from under my armpits and was just glad that my suit jacket covered the evidence. We walked across a huge expanse of floor space where there was a hive of activity until we finally got into his office which was about the size of our rented house in Wycombe. From that point onwards I started to calm down. I think it was the way I was being spoken to and the fact that my answers to his questions came out clear, accurate and impressive (even if I do say so myself).

I had this feeling that interviews are all about trying to catch you out but there was none of that at all. I completely opened up and openly admitted that I had been searching for work for a few years and that I had no experience to brag about. Whether it was my honesty that appealed to him i'll never know but I felt secretly confident when he thanked me for my time and showed me out. I must admit something told me the job was mine but i'd that feeling before so I tried to put it out of my mind. Two days later I got a phone call and I was just thankful I was in. With no mobile phone and no answering machine, I hate to think what would have happened if the man at PTC was unable to get through to me. The phone call was to let me know that the job was mine if I still wanted it. With that, I clearly remember my hands starting to shake and somehow I managed a "yes, i'd love to accept the role". A day later and the contract had arrived. I was employed - yippee and would be earning the grand total of £12,500 per annum. However, more than that was the fact that I had secured my first job; it may have taken 2 years to get it but at least I didn't cave into the pressure to get any old job and stood my ground. This was just the start of things to come - I was back...

PTC actually wanted me to start as soon as I could but I needed a few days to sort things out. The job application, interview and job offer came so quickly that I had no idea how to get to Bracknell by public transport and worst still I didn't even know if was possible! I told PTC that I could start in another week and my official start date was 31st October 1994. I then looked into how I would actually get there and got hold of the bus timetables from Wycombe. There was a slight problem - *none* of the Wycombe buses went directly to Bracknell and the only way to get there was a bus from Wycombe to Maidenhead and then another from Maidenhead to Bracknell. The logistics were horrendous; I had to catch the 6.40am bus from Wycombe which arrived in Maidenhead at 7.30am. I then had to walk to another bus station across town to catch a mini bus that would take me to Bracknell and arrive at 8.45am. As for the return journey, well the mini bus would arrive in Maidenhead for about 7.00pm after which I would have to trek back across town to catch the *last* bus back to Wycombe - by the time i'd get back to the house it was close to 8pm.

At my interview I forgot to ask what the dress code was. No, I wasn't planning to wear a dress (you know what I mean!) but rather than phone them to ask I bought a few shirts and some ties to go with it. By now, I was all set to start work and was looking forward to it although as the days passed by I was getting more and more nervous. The weekend before starting work, we (Paresh,

Munsha, E2, Sunita and myself) all went clubbing in London for an all-night session. We didn't get in till about 5.30am and the entire Sunday was spent half asleep and half awake. By the time evening had arrived, I knew I couldn't risk getting to bed too late. How I managed to get to sleep that night i'll never know but when the alarm went off it took me a few minutes to realise why it had gone off. Getting a wakeup call at 5.30am was unheard of and by the time the green LED digits on the clock radio showed 05:34 I was out of bed and changing into my work clothes. I then fumbled around for about 5 minutes sorting my tie out. Ties are horrid things and I just couldn't get the hang of doing them properly. Forget a neat triangle shape; I always ended up with something lop sided looking like a rectangle. After about 4 or so attempts, I managed to get it looking half decent and then, too nervous to eat breakfast, I was out the door and on my way.

It was a cold morning, the stars were out and I seemed to be the only one awake. Slowly I headed down Ogilvy Road and onto Green Street past Paresh's shop. As I walked past i'd pop into see my aunt (Paresh's mum) who was also starting her day by getting the newspapers sorted ready for the morning rush. It was a cold walk into town, this was only my first day and I couldn't think how on earth how I would cope with doing this journey for the foreseeable future. By the time I arrived in the Wycombe bus station, I found my bus and then waited for the bus driver to arrive. As soon as he arrived, he started up the bus and in a matter of minutes, I was trying hard not to breath the nasty black diesel fumes coming out of the bus's exhaust. Once on the bus i'd desperately rub my hands together. Despite having gloves, it was freezing outside and it seemed even colder inside.

Thankfully, the bus left on time and I soon realised why it took almost an hour to get to Maidenhead. The bus went right through to the countryside where amazingly people would get on at the least remote bus stops imaginable. As the journey progressed and darkness slowly switched to daylight, I was beginning to think the journey wasn't that bad. Feeling quite refreshed, I hopped off the bus as it pulled into Maidenhead and then, after a 20 minute walk through the town centre, found the next bus stop. By now, it was a cold but bright and sunny day and my nerves had all but gone. The mini bus pulled in and I settled down for another long bus ride. I soon realised that this bus service was mainly used to pick school kids up and take them to Bracknell. It went down some lanes that were so narrow, there was no way that 2 vehicles could pass each other. One of the "pick-up's" was so remote that once the bus got there, it had to carry out a "U" turn in the passenger's own drive way. Being a mini bus, it wasn't that bad but I was just amazed at the service offered to the kids. Don't get me wrong, I thought it was excellent but it was so shocking to see.

It didn't stop there either, throughout the journey, we went in and out of farms, down slightly flooded lanes and after about 30 minutes later, there was standing room only and the peace and quiet inside the mini bus had been transformed into a noisy and lively atmosphere as the kids talked about what they got up to over the weekend and what they saw on TV. Finally, at about 8.45am, the mini bus arrived at Bracknell bus station and I was glad to get off; the journey *was* bad and I had been jolted in all directions as the little bus ran over potholes along the country lanes that nobody could be bothered to cover up. With map in hand, I found Bracknell train station which was only a few minutes from the bus station and once I was over the train track bridge I was at the doors of PTC again and ready for work...

Reception made a call to my manager and then I was led up to the development area yet again. Once i'd met my fellow colleagues, I was beginning to think i'd have no fun at all. They all seemed so serious and they were all typing ferociously. One of them, Gary, was pleased to see me but as I was about to find out, this was mainly because hiring me meant he could concentrate on his primary role there (he had been doing almost the job of 2 people up until that time).

The first day was hectic to say the least, I had a very intensive introduction to the company, what it does, where it stands in the market and what the Bracknell office did. PTC wrote and sold a suite of software modules to companies that helped them design anything from a tooth brush to a Boeing 777. The flagship software was called Pro/Engineer and was one of the most popular and cutting edge pieces of software in the CAD/CAM field. The head office was based in Boston, USA and the UK division (i.e. the Bracknell site) supported the US development team. In short, the UK team wrote and maintained a UI (User Interface) toolkit that was used by the US team to actually enhance the software. It actually meant that we, as the UK team, was in charge of the building blocks of the entire application so the work we produced would be scrutinised on a daily basis.

Although I wasn't initially hired as a programmer, I loved the job and I loved software testing, In a matter of weeks, my job title was fully explained and I slowly but surely got to grips with new people, new offices, new software and I loved, *really* loved my job. I began testing the software in such meticulous detail that within 8 weeks of being there, I had found and raised over 243 software bugs. These were *real* bugs that would then be prioritised and resolved in future versions of the software. My impact to the company was virtually immediate and the recognition for it came straight from the top. I received a phone call from the R & D manager in Boston congratulating me on my work which was followed up by a "Thank you" in the monthly PTC newsletter that covered everything about PTC including team members of the month.

The bizarre thing is it didn't feel as if I was doing anything special; I was never trained in software testing - it just seemed fit in place. The staff were friendly and the perks were phenomenal. I held a respected position; had full Bupa cover, non-contributory pension scheme and the company ran an incentive scheme where they would issue stock options to employees in recognition of hard work. The way it worked was simple - you were given stock options which you could begin to cash in a year after receiving them. You would effectively make a profit at the time you sold them provided the share price went up. Trust me, they went up all right and after being there for 5 months, I soon realised why most of the sales staff had TVR's in the car parks. I also found out that in the previous year, over 20 employees had turned into paper millionaires simply because they had been working there for about 12 years and had been sitting on their stock options. If they sold up, they would make a million pounds - straight and without any messing about. That's what I call a *real* company and one where they really do invest in their staff...

One of my characteristics is that I always look at ways to improve the way I do things. For now, I was doing well and PTC were more than happy. My probation period was well and truly over and I was a full time and permanent member of staff. The software we wrote in the UK was tested by me and me alone (in comparison to the Boston team where there was over 20 full time testers) but this wasn't good enough so I thought to myself "I'll write our own testing tool to test our own software'. In English, this meant that I would use the UI tool kit we developed and supported and write an independent test tool using the *same* tool kit. The idea was simple; by using the test tool we could run automated tests and be able to test the tool kit much more effectively and furthermore, it could be run by anyone in the development or test teams.

Sandip
Patel

With a rough plan of what I wanted to do, I approached my manager with the idea and at first he sat back and gave me a look as if to say "What on earth are you talking about?" I actually thought I was in trouble or something for wasting his time with an absurd idea. He went all quiet and slowly swivelled around in his expensive looking leather chair. After several minutes he looked up at me and said "You know what? That's a fantastic idea, tell me more". Relieved that he actually liked the idea, I began to explain how it would work, the time we would save and that it would be time well worth investing and he agreed. With that I was given some time per day to design, code and test my first piece of *real* software.

After such a long break without programming at all, I slowly got back into it and really enjoyed myself. Putting code together and producing my own piece of work was so rewarding that I wished I could work extra hours just to continue with it but sadly, my working day was fixed rigidly by the bus timetable. At the end of the day I would walk back over the railway bridge and jump onto the mini bus for the reverse journey back to Maidenhead. Once there it was a stroll across town again where I had to wait for the bus back to Wycombe. As the days turned into weeks, I learnt that the bus service back to Wycombe was unreliable to say the least. On many occasions I waited there well past 7.30pm which was the time the last bus was due to leave for Wycombe.

On the days that it didn't arrive I had no choice but to catch a taxi all the way back and the worst thing about it was that i'd already paid for the return bus fare and I couldn't really afford the taxi but what was I supposed to do? I could have asked my cousin Paresh to pick me up but he would often be at work till late and I didn't fancy hanging around Maidenhead any longer than I had to. In comparison to what I was earning, the taxi ride home - a whopping £25.00 was a big deal, and I hoped there wasn't many more times that this would happen. Unfortunately, this wasn't the case and in the 9 or so months that I made this journey from Maidenhead to Wycombe, the bus simply didn't turn up at least 8 times. Writing to the bus company was no use - I was simply fobbed off but worst was still to come...

After one particularly tiring day at work, I was looking forward more than ever to get home. The mini bus from Bracknell always arrived on time and as I did each workday I strolled across town to wait anxiously for the Wycombe bus. Hooray, here it was - by now I *knew* when the bus would arrive because I could hear the engine's acoustics'; a bit sad but true! Thankful it had arrived; I got on and made my way towards the back of the bus. On most days about 10 people in total would hop on and hop off the bus in the hour long journey but by the time we were half way to Wycombe, there were only 2 other passengers. This is what happens when you get accustomed to static journeys day in and day out. You start to recognise people, their habits, when they get on, when they get off and immediately know when a regular isn't on the bus. When the bus stopped at the next bus stop, a scruffy looking man got on and right from the start there was something about him that was strange. It wasn't the fact that one of his trousers had a massive hole in it just above the knee or that he had a hood covering most of his face. It was the way he continually walked up and down the aisle and stared at the passengers including me.

It was one of those really horrid looks and it scared me big time. He would often walk quickly then stop, put his hands in his pockets as if to check what he'd put there was still there and would then start pacing around again. He then started chatting to the bus driver and they appeared to be giggling together. By now my mind was working overtime and I had visions of a crazed killer going berserk and hurting the passengers. I *really* started to panic when I caught the driver staring at me through the driver's mirror. Perhaps I was thinking too much into it but as time went on I had this gut feeling that something was about to kick off big time. I had to do something and fast so I raised my hand and pushed the red button to let the driver know I wanted to get off.

If I was the only one left on the bus, i'd be even more worried but I wasn't and I breathed a sigh of relief when I could feel brakes start to slow the bus down. As the bus doors opened I literally leaped out and almost felt guilty as I caught a glimpse of an elderly man staring at the strange person on the bus who was still pacing around. In an instant, my heart beat began to slow down but as the bus drove off and eventually went out of view, I was left in almost darkness in the middle of nowhere and I really do mean nowhere. There were no houses, no lights, no nothing - just a bus stop in the middle of the Buckinghamshire countryside and when things couldn't get worse, the rain came down. I slowly walked on; I didn't have a mobile phone so I had to get to a phone box so that I could ring Paresh to come and get me.

Twenty minutes later and I was relieved to see a red telephone box in the distance and thankfully it worked too. I called Paresh and after another 20 minutes he had arrived to pick me up. He did wonder what I was doing in the middle of nowhere but once i'd explained what had happened he said I did the right thing. By the time I got back to our rented house and explained everything to E2 and Sunita they too agreed that I had a real close shave. Two days after this event, the local newspaper ran an article where some passengers had been "terrorized by bus thief". Yes - this was the *same* person and it turned out that about 10 minutes after I jumped ship (or bus!), the man threatened the other passengers and then pulled out a 10 inch knife and apparently swung it as passengers and eventually stole all their money. Thankfully nobody got hurt and I was grateful I followed my instincts - something I always try to do now.

Luckily, this incident never occurred again but there were many more times after when the bus just didn't arrive. I'd have to catch a cab again and again and it cost an absolute fortune. When the bus did arrive, i'd get to Wycombe at about 7.50pm. I would then have to walk it back to the house which was ok in the summer but terrible in winter. By the time I got back home, it was around

8.30pm and to say I was tired was an understatement. It was a full 15 hours from the time I woke up to the time I got back and after having a quick shower and something to eat, i'd have about 30 minutes to chill out after which I had to get into bed.

Not long after I found work, E2 found work too and he bought his first car. The grey/blue Astra made a huge difference to our lives. For me, it meant that as soon as I stepped off the bus in Wycombe, E2 would be there waiting for me - thanks mate! Little but important things like the weekly shopping trip to Tesco or Asda was made so much easier and it was just having a toy! It also meant we could drive back to Leicester rather than trek via the bus or train. One warm summers evening, we were on our way back to Wycombe and were on the A45 near Warwick Castle. Suddenly, we heard a loud banging sound and it sounded as if something had become tangled in the engine. The noise was horrid and E2 stopped the car as quick as he could. The car actually ended up on the grass verge that separated the slip from the busy dual carriageway to the right.

Fearing the worst, we opened up the bonnet and expected there to be a huge hole or something but on initial inspection we couldn't see anything wrong. However, using our basic skills, we realised that one of the spark plugs was missing. This would explain 2 things; the noise of something loose in the engine bay and the noise - the engine had been firing on 3 cylinders for about half a mile. It was a Sunday evening, we were in unfamiliar area and it would be a struggle to find a car parts store. Unfortunately, there was no AA cover either so for the moment we were stranded. Having locked up the car, we walked up the slip road in search of shops and at first it didn't look good but as we walked further along we saw one of them big petrol stations - the ones that are like mini supermarkets and sell virtually everything.

We were hoping they would see spark plugs too and as we walked towards the "car" section, I could see the words "champion" and I knew our luck was in. Hanging up on the wall were a small range of "champion" spark plugs and in a matter of minutes, they were paid for and we were heading back. With no tools in the car, we had no choice but to tighten the new spark plug with our hands and hoped that it would be ok until we got back to Wycombe. As E2 got into the driver's seat to start it up, I took several steps back from the car - it was almost as if I was expecting something to go wrong. The Astra started and seemed to be idling and revving ok so it looked as if we would be alright. To this day, it's still a mystery how that spark plug worked itself loose and the changing of that single spark plug gave E2 and I the confidence to give his Vauxhall Astra a full service ourselves!

I always enjoyed going back to Leicester; it was our *home* and I missed the place. Once we were back the weekend was pretty much planned out already. Sunita would spend all day with her family and go out shopping with her mum. E2 would go into town without fail and I would often meet him there. Most often though, i'd walk up East Park Road and visit Nee/Dee at their first shop. Both of them had worked in the car audio field for a few years and between them decided they would open their own business to see how it went. They rented a small unit at the top of East Park Road and the business started to take off. It was a small place, there was no garage and inside the shop it would only take 3 or 4 customers to walk through the door and the place would be full! With limited stock, customers who wanted to buy anything browsed through brochures and Nee or Dee would then jump into the car and buy it from another car audio shop. An hour or so later, the customer would come back and they'd fit it *outside*.

Slowly but surely the business really took off and they started to get a really good customer base. True, there were many other car audio shops in Leicester but unlike Cartronics, the others were just out to rip you off or couldn't be bothered to spend time with you. Dee was a seasoned expert in electronics full stop and to this day I am amazed at the skill he has for diagnosing electrical faults. Mind you, Nee isn't that far behind either, but Dee has to take the crown! Armed with a test tool, i'd watch in amazement as he would remove panels from cars revealing yards of multi coloured cables. Within a few minutes he would have an idea of what the fault was and often would end up at the car's ECU. At the end of it, he could either fix the problem or give you a definite on what the problem was. There's no messing at all with Dee; he just tells you straight. Nee on the other hand is a little more customer focused but between the 2, they have a great working partnership which works very well.

19

Beats, breaks and clubbing

Back in Wycombe, the weekdays were spent working and we all looked forward to the weekends. With Paresh and Munsha still in Wycombe, we knew the weekends would be busy from partying and trust me, we partied hard. The clubbing scene across the UK was going through a revival, clubs were open longer, the crowd wanted to party longer and the clubs obliged with late night licences and headline DJ's most weekends. Musically, I had always been more into drum & bass than house but at the end of a day, good music is good - whatever it is so with that I just went along with the flow and enjoyed every minute of it. One of the clubs we started to visit frequently was "Club UK" in Wandsworth, London. On a Saturday night, Paresh or Munsha would call us up and ask us what we were doing that night. Most often our answer would be "nothing" and on hearing that, the Wycombe boys told us to be ready for around 10pm.

We would start to get ready about 9pm, it took me a few minutes to get ready. I mean, it doesn't take long to put on a pair of jeans and a shirt does it? Sunita and E2 however, took much longer. They had to decide what they were wearing, what shoes to wear, sort their hair out and on and on - it all seemed too much work! Paresh would normally drive which was a journey fraught with danger in itself. He's the original Patel "chevvy chase" (look this up for those of you not familiar with this name!) because no matter what he does on the road, he always seems to get away with it. Many times whilst he's been driving, we've drifted across 3 lanes of motorway whilst he fumbles around looking for a lighter that has fallen under the driver's seat. Whilst the rest of us were holding on for dear life, he would be casually looking everywhere *except* the road and miraculously when he finally looked up, he always seemed to be back in the correct lane.

The journey to Club UK took about an hour, mainly due to the London traffic which was just relentless and busy as ever even at 10-11pm. Once the car was parked up, we'd head down the stairs holding our breath for as long as we could; i'm sure it doubled up as a public urinal too! As we walked around the corner, we were always met with a mass of eager clubbers forming an orderly queue. The door policy was quite relaxed but there was strict rules on club capacity. This meant that once full, you had no chance of getting in unless you were prepared to wait and wait and wait. In the summer, when we had a summer that is, waiting in the queue didn't seem that bad but in winter there was no way you could last it out.

The waiting game was never a problem though because Munsha was with us. The pattern was the same - we'd join the end of the queue and Munsha would walk up to the front. You could see him share some quiet words with the door staff and after a handshake he would call for us. The first time this happened, we all wondered what was going on. The clubbers were also wondering what was going on as we hurriedly walked past them and were ushered into the club by the doormen. Munsha *knew* the door men and that alone was enough entry into the place. Outside the club you could hear the bass line murmuring behind the walls but as we walked up the stairs the bass grew louder and louder and the heat was intense. In the summer it was so intense that even the air conditioning couldn't keep the club cool and you'd be surrounded by sweaty clubbers punching their hands in the air to the beat.

One things for sure, if there was a club that had atmosphere, fun clubbers, good music and one of the best sound systems in the UK, then this was it. Club UK rocked hard and clubbers knew how to party. Munsha and Paresh had become great friends with a bunch of other clubbers from the Kent area and after a few weeks, they became good friends of ours too. Always happy to see you (wonder why!), they were a great bunch of people and Saturday nights at this club was something we all really looked forward to after that and 1994/1995 really was the year of Club UK. Inside the club there were 3 rooms, the main one where pure house music was played to the masses, the middle room that played more experimental and garage tunes and the dark, "special" room. Moody and loud, this room had a totally different atmosphere to the rest of the club. Inside, the music policy was different - it was faster, more trancy type music with a bass line so heavy that our internal body organs vibrated as each beat kicked in. Even the people looked different, they were all straight faced and showed little emotion.

Scattered around the room were huge objects such as dice and packets of Wrigley's chewing gum - they were so big that you could sit on top of them. I'm not sure who or where they got the idea from but it pretty cool. One of the best nights I had at this club and in this room was on a Friday night visit to club UK. Only 2 of us went that day - Paresh and I and whilst waiting in the queue we watched as Carl Cox strolled past with a huge grin on his face, a huge bag of records over his shoulder and an entourage of 3 or 4 people. Carl Cox has become one of the most famous DJs across the globe for his skills on the turntables but also for being a general nice guy who took the time to speak to you. Some of the DJ's i've seen over the years are stuck up arrogant gits who think they are above everyone else. Anyway, that particular night, we paid an early visit to the dark room and positioned ourselves close to the DJ booth which was a huge area surrounded by a metal front so that the clubbers and DJ could see each other.

As the clock slowly ticked away, we watched as Carl Cox approached and then entered the DJ booth. The look from the crowd said it all, everyone was watching his every movement. For a seasoned clubber and one who knew of this DJ, you couldn't have been in a better place to witness what was about to unfold.

As he prepared himself, the DJ before him slowly turned the music down. There was no MC, no mention of DJ's, no nothing. As one record faded away, the introduction track started playing and the big man was on. As the clubbers tried desperately to shake his hand through the gaps in the metal enclosure, the atmosphere stepped up a gear. The music gradually picked up pace and everyone was waiting for the bass to kick in and then it happened, the awesome bass line shook the place to bits yet again and for the next 2 hours we all witnessed why this man in my opinion is the world's best DJ.

He seamlessly mixed in tune after tune, mostly using 3 turntables and teased the crowd, feeding off their vibes at the same time. I have no idea where he got his tunes from but each one seemed to be better than the previous one. As Cox danced around himself, the sweat poured from his face and really looked as if he was enjoying it as much as the crowd. That night Paresh and I hardly left this room but 3am we had tired ourselves out and headed back home - definitely one of the best club nights we ever had! Most of our visits to this club were on Saturdays. We even had our own section in the club where no-one else would go. Mind you, when everyone turned out in full, there was about 20 of us in total and everyone else in the club seemed to know we would be arriving soon... We'd gather at the far end of the club where you could buy tip tops (or "Mr. Freeze") lollies which certainly helped to cool you down. Clubbing was a tiring thing and after a few hours, i'd make my way back to the tip top man who would bring out his other box of goodies - the chocolate bars. I'd then stand there munching away on a Mars bar - all this to the disgust of all the other clubbers - eating was the last thing on their mind...

The logo of "Club UK", one of the finest house music venues ever to open.

Usha busting her moves in our static caravan.

Paresh – mash up!

Me!

Thirsty?

Party people.   The *original* FBI soundsystem.

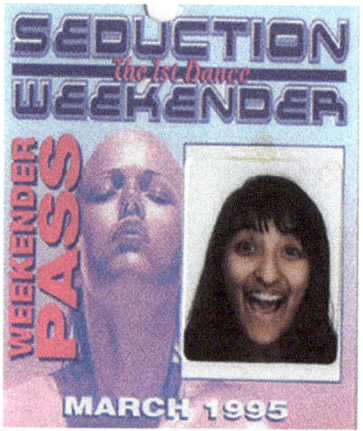

1995!!

The night always flew by and before long it was 3 or 4am and we would start to tire. The club was open till 6am and I think the latest we stayed there was around 5.30. Staying in a club so late was a real experience but leaving the club was even more bizarre. As we walked down the stairs, our legs felt as if they would give way due to sheer tiredness. As we got closer to the ground floor, the light was so intense that it made my eyes squint. In the height of summer, it was light at around 3.15am but here we were emerging from an all-night session in the club. In a flash, we were taken back down to earth - there were people walking their dogs, others who had been out early to fetch the papers whilst a big group of people stalked the exit asking everyone "mini cab?". Most of them were unlicensed idiots who figured they could make a fortune by charging extortionate rates to clubbers too out of it to know better.

We didn't need a mini cab; just a bed but before that we had to climb upstairs back into the urine filled car park where we left the driving to Munsha or Paresh (thanks guys!) and the tiring drive back to Wycombe. On the way home which seemed to take ages, we would head back up the A40 Westway and always made a pit stop at the huge BP station en route. Munsha or Paresh or sometimes both of them would then head into the shop and come back with several cartons of blackcurrant Ribena. I'm not sure what it is about Ribena but it's one of those drinks that helps you to recover after a night out. I don't know whether it was just me, but my ears used to "ring" all day from the pounding they took in the club.

There was no let-up however; the music in the car was turned up too and it felt as we were in the club all over again. Finally about 25 minutes later, we saw the signs for Wycombe and a few minutes after that we were back home. Despite being unbelievably tired, we rarely went to bed and the whole day was spent lounging around where we would often fall in and out of sleep. Paresh and Munsha would normally hang around for a few hours and then come back in the evening and we'd all tuck into our Sunday takeaways before getting ready for work. Mind you, it was only me who had to really get bed on time because getting to bed late didn't do me any favours when I had to get up at 5.30am!

The drive back to Wycombe in the early hours was great on a clear and beautiful summer's morning and Paresh and I would sometimes head down to Rye Park in Wycombe after dropping everyone else off. It may not sound like fun but walking along the waterside with the sun beating down with an eerie silence was *really* relaxing. A few feet away from where we were standing, you'd see an array of fish in all shapes and sizes. There were huge pike in these waters too and they'd just sit (or float!) motionless waiting for their prey to swim past. On the rare occasions we saw them in action, it was a phenomenal experience. This huge pike with razor sharp teeth would stun the fish as it swum past and devour it so quickly that it was over in seconds.

Ok, as I mentioned before, it may sound quite boring to you but if any one reading this has ever had an interest in fishing then you know what I mean. The waters here attracted many fishermen including ourselves (I don't really come under the fishermen category but you know what I mean...). In the evenings we'd come armed with deck chairs, a tub full of maggots, some sweetcorn, bread, beer (for Paresh, not the fish!) and lots of patience. It was peaceful, tranquil and even if we didn't catch anything, it really didn't matter. We could pass hours this way and it's just a shame we didn't fish more. Trust me, when I caught my first fish (a tiny Perch), it was great fun. I'd sit on my chair watching the float at the end of my fishing line. You *had* to keep your eye on it and if it went under the water a few times you knew you had a 'bite'. It was a miracle that I actually got my float in the water. As I swung the whole fishing road behind and then launched it forwards, it got it caught in the overhanging trees that grew by the waterside.

When you thought there was something on the end of the line, the trick was then to take up the slack of the fishing line and then slowly yank the fishing rod towards you. This action was meant to propel the hook into the side of the fish's mouth. I knew I had caught something and as I gradually reeled it in I could see it splashing around the surface of the water. With the rod in one hand, the landing net in the other and Paresh on standby, I slowly netted the fish. I then took instructions from Paresh and carefully tried to hold the fish in one hand whilst trying to release the hook with the other. I dropped the fish several times and my hands were often covered in slimy scales or whatever it was as I went to war with this fish. I did manage to get the hook out and after a good look at the fish, put it back into the water. Many people, Sunita included, often say "you wait hours for a fish, catch it and then put it back - why? Well I don't think you can ever explain why you do this. Apart from the fact that most fishing lakes/rivers or whatever have stringent rules on putting fish back, we're only catching them for fun. I mean, we weren't going to bring the fish home and stick them in the oven - the fun, as they say, was really in the catch!

Fishing – Rye Park, High Wycombe.

Back at home, dinner times for me at least were no fun. Whilst Sunita & E2 could rustle up something fairly quickly, I was, and still am, pretty useless in the kitchen. Mondays and Tuesdays were ok because after we had been home for the weekend, we had home cooked food that lasted a few days but sometimes deciding what to eat at the end of the week was a struggle. The kitchen in this house faced directly into the neighbours' lounge and we had scary neighbours. The bloke living there used to spend most of his time in his shed or something where he would fiddle with the countless electronic gadgets he had in there. On several occasions we would catch him staring out the window - he looked like that crazy guy from psycho. Mind you, his wife or whoever she was, wasn't that far behind and she was just as scary. Whenever we saw them, we made sure we smiled - the last thing we wanted to do was annoy them in anyway; we didn't want *any* psychos on our case!

The clubbing nights continued and on a few Saturday nights, we started to try out alternate clubs. We were soon hitting the dance floors of London's Cafe De Paris in Leicester Square where we DJ'd once alongside Munsha & Paresh. Camden Palace was a great night out with several floors of clubbers having it large whilst one of the funniest weekends we had was when Munsha, Paresh, Sunita & I spent 2 days and 3 nights in a holiday home in Great Yarmouth - it was a true clubbing weekend! It was February 2005 and the holiday season was over. One of the club promoters decided to make the most of the empty holiday homes and organised a huge party. All the clubbers stayed on site and in the complex itself, the main room was transformed into a clubbing haven. The music played virtually all day and into the early hours of the morning. When you needed a break from clubbing, all you had to do was walk out the main room and head for the caravan / home. Having said that, you could see camera crews knocking on doors and then video recording whatever was going on inside the holiday homes. Within minutes, images of what was being recorded were transmitted onto the clubbing channel that was being aired.

Over the next few months, we partied all over the place. In London, the regular haunts were Club UK and the Chunnel club. We also partied in a small town called Lydd in Kent which was a 2 hour drive from Wycombe. The club was packed to the rafters and during the winter we'd often sit outside on frost covered benches. It was a real shock to the system; one minute we were inside sweating from the intense heat whilst outside the temperature was well below zero and the sky was filled with millions of stars. When we wanted a different clubbing experience we would sometimes drive south to Brighton or Bournemouth where most of the parties were held in big rooms at the end of the pier.

For drum and bass sessions, there was only one place to go and that was "Total Kaos" nights in Leicester. It was always good partying at "home" and the nights were run by DJ SS and the Formation Records crew. There's no hiding the fact that DJ SS and Formation Records are my favourite DJ / Record label and I have been an avid collector of their music for many years. It was an era when drum and bass music or "junglist massive" to those in the know was *the* music that was causing a massive stir in the music industry.

Kits wedding – 'looking here please'.

20

Guns and bass

One night, E2 and I drove up to Leicester for a drum and bass (Total Kaos) session at the Starlite 2001 club where an A list of drum and bass DJs would be touching down for an all-night session. We got to the club for about 10pm and although we didn't plan to stay all night, weren't planning to leave early either. As the night wore on, the club started to fill up and the crowd was starting to feel the vibe. The beats and breaks filled the air as the DJ's started rinsin' out the sound and the party was in full flow. After a few hours of dancing around we were desperate for a wee and headed downstairs. We'd just got into the toilet when a group of around 8 people followed us in. A few of them looked as if they were stopping anyone else entering the toilet. We *knew* something was about to kick off and in a matter of seconds questions were being fired to us from several of them.

"Where you from?", "What you doing?". I felt like saying "We're from Leicester having a piss" but I didn't. As "we're from Leicester" came out of my mouth, one of them lunged at E2 who tried to protect himself but the others pushed his hands away. In the meantime another stepped towards me and started feeling around my neck. I figured they weren't gay and were after something else and they were. With a hard tug, he pulled on my gold chain that was around my neck - it broke in 2 pieces and the others scrambled to find the other piece on the piss stained floor. They retreated slightly as if they were about to regroup themselves. I could see them staring at us intensely and they started to shout at us but we struggled to hear them. Outside, MC Warren G was doing his thing on the mic and as he listed all the other big name DJ's that would be playing later, he finished his rhyme by saying "big ting's gwaan".

I was furious but what could we do? We were outnumbered and we had no idea if they had any other weapons on them so we did the best thing - absolutely nothing. Having stolen the gold chain that my mum gave me, they left laughing whilst I was in shock and extremely angry at what had happened. After an experience like that there was no point hanging around - what was the point? They had stolen something precious from me for the sake of money. Yet again, that damn thing called money had caused more problems. I'm a big believer in what goes around, comes around and I honestly believe that these bastards who stole the chain from me, got some kind of punishment in return. In no mood to party, we decided to leave straight away - it was one of the best decisions of our lives. A few days later I found out that it was a gang from Manchester that had turned up that night and terrorised many others, including us. The gang were serious too; they were armed with guns, yes guns and when I heard about that I was so relieved we didn't retaliate in anyway; if we had done, things could have been very different...

Most of the MCs at jungle / drum and bass events often used words that some of you reading this may not even have heard of before. "Nuff respect seen" would come blaring out of the MIC as the MC introduced the DJ. "Brejrin" was used to acknowledge a close friend - for example "ezee brejrin" - this doesn't mean that something you've done was easy (i.e. simple) but actually a way of greeting someone - a bit like saying "hello". Some people often used to say "safe" to mean "ok" or another way of greeting you. You might speak to your mate and arrange to meet at 6pm at which you might say "safe". Back to the MC - some of them would ask the crowd to "show their appreciation" to the DJ by saying things such as "nuff respect - wicked DJ".

As 1994 turned into 1995, the clubbing phenomenon continued to rise and rise at an unbelievable pace. New club nights seemed to open up every week, you could leave the club at 6am on a Sunday morning then walk a few streets and head into another club that opened at 7am. You could then spend a few more hours dancing away only to walk out the door ready for Sunday lunch! It just goes to show that the era of all weekend clubbing was really starting to take off. At the time I used to listen to Kiss 100, a dance music station in London and also read various DJ magazines including Mixmag & DJ. Outdoor music festivals aren't a new thing but slowly such events were getting more and more exposure and the promoters started advertising them big time through the dance music stations and music magazines.

One of the outdoor festivals 'Tribal Gathering', was billed as an outdoor dance music festival and it was taking place in Oxfordshire on 6th May 1995. The capacity was around 30,000 people and there were to be many different music "tents" including house, trance, down tempo, garage, break beat and drum and bass. There was no question of whether we were going or not - we were and that was the end of that. There were lots of us too - E2, Sunita, Paresh, Munsha and a whole load of others would be heading down there. With our tickets booked we anxiously waited for the big weekend to arrive - we knew this would be something different. On the 1st day we woke to a bright, warm morning and got ready. We knew it would take a while to get there; 30,000 clubbers would definitely add traffic and we weren't wrong.

As we got closer to the venue the roads were getting busy and we moved a few yards every 3 or 4 minutes. Soon we were so close the festival that you could hear the music pounding out from the speakers which clashed with the clubber's car sound systems that were being blasted out at the same time. By the time we got there it must have been around 3 in the afternoon and most of the people were just lazing around in the sun. As the day wore on, the sunset and the tribal lights lit up the whole place beautifully. As we walked around the festival, we'd head into the tents one by one and stay in there to catch a bit of the action. Some people who liked a certain type of music stayed in "their" tent and never moved from there.

One of the liveliest gatherings was in the drum and bass tent where the sound systems were subjected to the gruelling bass from record labels such as Formation and Ram. Everyone insider was up for it big time and the place was packed. The heat inside was phenomenal and every 20 or so minutes it was really refreshing just to get into the fresh air where the spring breeze would cool you down. I clearly remember many times looking around and watching happy people just having a good time. There was no trouble that I could remember and everyone just seemed to get on. The time just seemed to fly by and when things got too hot inside we could go out and get ourselves an original 99 ice cream from the Mr. Whippy vans that were scattered around the place.

As Saturday turned to Sunday, there wasn't a cloud in the sky and millions of stars shone brightly. I know this because I laid down on the grass & stared at them for around 30 minutes. It was a wonderful experience, the music, the people and just the whole atmosphere made it *really* special. It was almost impossible to dance all afternoon, evening and night. We'd sit down on the grass that was now starting to feel wet as we tried to catch our breath back and regain our strength. For those of us that were hungry, it was a trip to the countless food vans scattered all over the venue but to be honest the food didn't look too good so we ended up just eating snacks. I stuck to the soft drinks whilst the others went through countless bottles of beer & wine! Slowly but surely, we somehow managed to get through the night and soon it was starting to get light again.

You could see small crowds of people heading for the exit but on the whole the tents were just as rammed as they were 12 hours previously and the party people didn't want to go home. I think it was around 10-10.30am before our bodies couldn't take anymore and it was time to head home. This wasn't an easy job - there were 1000's of cars parked all over the place and it was quite funny watching people struggling to find their car. I'm sure some clubbers tried to find their car and then realised that they didn't actually have a car (that's the class A!!). I actually came up in E2's car and we managed to find the car fairly quickly but Sunita & Paresh went home with Munsha. We must have queued for about an hour before we got onto the main road and along the way 100's of people were jumping into and out of the bushes as they couldn't wait any longer and were desperate for a wee! The journey home was a tiring one but the sun shone brightly and it was a wicked end to an excellent night out. It must have been about 2pm when we got back to Wycombe but as it hit 4 and then 5pm, there was no sign of the others. When they finally arrived home, they told us that they were stuck solid in a mass of cars trying to get out and at one point didn't move at all for around 2 hours!

Well life trundled on; work was tiring, the weekends were even more tiring whilst the weeks and months seemed to fly by so quickly. At work, things were good, I was learning all the time and I loved every minute of it. A memo was sent around the office letting the employees know of a Parametric Technology night out - something they did regularly. Unfortunately, they were planning to meet for dinner at 7.45pm on one particular evening so I had to decline the offer. When David, my boss interrupted my work to ask me why I declined, I explained that I wouldn't get home till about 8.30pm so there was no point attending at all. Not quite understanding why I got home so late, I then explained my journey and he was absolutely amazed. He really couldn't understand how I sustained that journey and on hearing that offered to drive me home so that I could change and actually come to the dinner too.

I felt very bad accepting his offer as I didn't want to put anyone out, especially my boss but he was very insistent so I accepted. Driving from Bracknell to Wycombe, I explained to my boss that my working day started at 5.30am and ended at 8.30pm which was the time I got home and he just couldn't believe it. The dinner itself was fantastic, there was a real buzz amongst everyone and they even handed out awards for 'employee of the quarter' and well as other departmental awards. The employers and employees were totally committed to each other and the business and I really felt part of a team - at this stage I could never think of leaving. At the end of the night, my boss drove me back home and by this time it was well past 11pm. As I closed the car door, he jokingly shouted "get to bed - don't be late for work will you?"

The only thing that kept me sane with the long journey to and from work was my Walkman; well Sunita's Walkman to be exact. Every Wednesday on Kiss 100, the drum and bass show would be aired between 8 & 10pm and I would get my cassettes ready to record the show. With almost 2 hours of drum & bass to listen to (or the radio if I wanted something different), my journey was made slightly easier. After that, the Walkman became an integral part of me and I got to a stage where I had spare headphones and spare batteries - I couldn't leave anything to chance! For me, one of the worst parts of the job wasn't the job itself but the fact that I had to wear a shirt. Most people there wore shirts and I just followed everyone else but ironing was the real issue here. One day I was trying to iron out some creases but as soon as I turned the shirt over I created more creases and this went on and on and on. After around 20 frustrating minutes, I was so pissed off with my damn shirt, that I stood on the arm and pulled as hard as I could. The result was inevitable and as the shirt's arm detached itself I breathed a sigh of relief. Yes, ok, i'd done something *really* stupid and I was a shirt down but I felt all the better for doing it! The other downside of the job was my initial pay; after paying for transport costs, my rent, Sunita's rent and food, I was left with £90 to my name.

My issue with wearing shirts was soon to be resolved with a change in management. My boss, the person who hired me and gave me the chance I was so desperate for, announced he was leaving and one of the team leaders - a person called Paul Hackett was taking his place. I was shocked at first and wondered how i'd get on with the new boss. I didn't have to worry; all I had to do was get used to a *different* style of management. David was straight to the point, rarely laughed and expected results. Paul laughed all the time, relaxed the dress code (I swapped formal trousers and shirt for jeans and t shirt instantly!) and headed off to the pub on Friday lunchtimes - this was an exciting change! Just before my old boss left I had a little chat with him and told him I just wanted to thank him for offering me the job - he was pleased at that and I sometimes wonder what happened to him...

Around the same time, the head of R & D (or Software Development) for the entire PTC group also moved on and was replaced by another David - David Hall to be exact. He flew over to the UK and spent several days at the Bracknell office and I knew straight away that I didn't like him. It was just the way he spoke to us. He made sure he drilled it into us that he was one of the main men in the organisation (perhaps he thought we were too stupid and couldn't read the memos!). He was abrupt, rude and made several changes to the way we worked even though there was nothing wrong with our procedures. Several weeks later I was working on a new software release and noticed several blatant software bugs creeping into the product. This was rare for PTC and the output of the US software quality team was always good so this was a bit of a shock. Any software issue was tracked by our own bug tracking software but some of the blatant bugs weren't logged. I spent quite a while searching for them but they simply weren't there. I then called a fellow colleague in the Boston office who confirmed that the issues had not been raised at all.

Well, an issue is an issue so I raised the bugs myself and in total I must have logged about 15 in a matter of 30 minutes. Later that day when the Boston office were on-line, things changed. I got a phone call from the David Hall questioning why I raised these bugs. Now, I had to keep my cool at this stage at being asked such a stupid question but I gave him the simple answer of "they are bugs - that's it" and surprisingly he said ok and put the phone down. Over the next 60 minutes I received a further 6 phone calls from him asking about more bugs that I had raised and I knew at that stage that things were going to get heated. I then received several email alerts telling me that the bugs I logged had been downgraded in severity. I wasn't happy about this because most of the bugs I raised were obvious ones that our customers would see in a matter of minutes. So, looking at it from a customer's perspective, I changed the severity back to their original ones together with a comment on why I had done this.

The next day my boss, Paul, came into see me and asked me why I did what I did and I when I went through the issues with him, he was happy enough but I could tell that his character just wasn't strong enough to stick up for me against the big David in Boston. There was no way I was giving in, I had valid reasons for the severity I used and I wasn't going to let someone who was more concerned with employee status get in the way of releasing poor quality software. The big boss, or DBC as he was known, didn't like it one bit and then sent my boss the following email: -

Paul,

I dispute more software issues from Sandip Patel than the entire QA team here in Boston. Please ask him to change the severities back to their original values. He is meant to work for you, not against you.

Thanks

DBC

Rather than speak to me directly, I think he simply got fed up and realised that I wasn't going to give in. It was a bit of a cop out and to be honest my own boss caved in too because he asked me to change the severities back as well. However, there was no going back so the severities remained as they were. The issues got fixed and I had made a point to the entire development team that you really must stand up for what you believe in. From that day onwards, DBC rarely spoke to me which was fine because I couldn't be bothered with speaking to an idiot like him anyway.

One of the things that I disliked in the Bracknell office was my office - if you call it an office that is. It was a tiny place with no window and hence no natural light and it became very hot as my Silicon graphics machine worked overtime as I ran regression tests on it using test scripts that used every ounce of CPU processing time that was available. Due to expansion, the development team in Bracknell moved to another big office over the road that PTC has just purchased and my office was around 8 times the size and the difference was massive. I had space to move in my air conditioned new office and had a 270 degree view of the surroundings thanks to the high & wide panes of glass that adorned the front of the building.

One of the best days I had at PTC was during the summer months when they organised another one of their staff days out. This time, they chartered a huge boat which was waiting for us at the side of the River Thames. That day I didn't have to worry about getting to Windsor as E2 kindly lent me his car. It was a perfect summer's evening and after parking the car and walking towards the river all I could see was this huge boat that looked like some kind of millionaire's yacht straight out of Monaco. My fellow colleagues were in good spirits; helped along by the countless bottles of wine and beer that was being consumed. Whilst everyone else was knocking back their drinks so fast, I was eating the food just as quickly. When they announced that the entrees were being served, I thought great but when I got to the area where the food was laid out, I wasn't quite sure whether to look at the food or eat it - and i'm not joking either.

The thing is you see (as I learnt in later years), there is a certain etiquette to adopt when eating certain types of food - unbeknown to me at the time! Rather than make a fool of myself, I just waited for someone else to turn up and I just followed their lead. As we cruised up the Thames, we started to meander through some extremely affluent areas. We passed house after house or should I say mansion after mansion and most of them had their own boats moored at the bottom. This was where the *high rollers* really lived and i'm never seen houses quite like that before. The noise levels on the boat seems to get louder as those on board got more and more drunk and when the music was cranked up, most of the people living along the river heard us before they saw us. We cruised along for about 90 minutes and then turned back and it was really strange watching those I worked with and the way their behaviour changed now that they were intoxicated. By the time we arrived back in Windsor, it was just after 10.30pm and the PTC day out had been another great success.

21

The European
Adventure - July 1995

During those weekends when we were in Leicester, E2 and I would often meet the rest of our mates at "Menzie's" (a road close to Bob's house). The area was just an industrial estate where we'd meet up, have a chat and sometimes play football. We'd talk about anything and everything, take the piss out of each other and it was where we'd do some of our holiday planning. On this particular day as we discussed where we'd been over the years, it all dawned on us that another adventure was long overdue. We'd been to many places in the UK and someone mentioned Amsterdam, then Germany and also Paris as destinations they wanted to see. Over the next 2 hours, daylight turned to night time and we were still there, discussing, debating and still excited as ever. Finally, we made the decision to head to Amsterdam and basically take it from there. On our previous trips there was 7/8 of us so we needed 2 cars but now only 5 of us could make it; myself, E2, Rumit, Bob & Hemal. We had the people, the date, the destination and all systems were go. It was July 1995 and we hired the car, a brand new Ford Mondeo from Euro dollar and right from the start, I was glad that we had "unlimited" mileage as part of the deal - we would be doing a fair few miles!

Well, the journey began with a trip down to Dover and then a ferry onto Calais. By the time we got into Calais it was around 2am and quite a few of us were already getting really tired! Our first destination was Amsterdam and the plan was to drive through

Brussels and hopefully get there early in the morning. Apart from E2, no-one else was insured to drive the car and I don't think anyone would have enjoyed driving a right hand drive manual car on the right hand side of the road. It *is* surprisingly easy to get used to and it never bothered me one bit. We eventually got into Amsterdam and got quite lost in all the little side streets that are scattered everywhere. As we were planning to stay here for at least one night, we decided to get a hotel but sharing a room with my mates is fraught with problems.

You can't go to the toilet in peace, you are scared to go to sleep as you don't know what changes they'll make to your face and if you try to have a shower, the towel or even your clothes will go missing. How we survived that first night i'll never know. Amsterdam is a real eye opener for obvious reasons and for those of you reading this who have no idea what i'm talking about then take a trip and all will be revealed. The following morning we ventured out & to check out Dam - Amsterdam. We strolled around the tourist areas after visiting several cafes along the way. It's amazing what you can actually buy from these coffee shops and after a short stay in one of them, some of us were very relaxed indeed - enough said.

A very cosmopolitan city, Amsterdam was full of life and the best way to see the main parts of it were by foot. Mind you, its bicycles, not cars you have to worry about. They are an extremely popular mode of transport and you have to keep your wits about you and look out for them otherwise you'll get hit by one. After a fair amount of walking it was time to take it easy and view Amsterdam via the waterways that line the entire city. Opting to join fellow tourists on a boat cruise, we stepped on board and in the back of my mind I knew one of the lads would get up to no good. Still reeling the effects from the coffee shop, we watched as a man climbed down the stairs and banged his head on the sign that said "Mind your head". This was the catalyst; Hemal just couldn't control himself and pissed himself laughing and the laughing was infectious to such a degree that soon we are all at it.

That wasn't enough for Hemal; he decided to sit on the right hand side of the boat close to the rope that stopped it from drifting away. We all watched as he slowly un-hooked the rope around the huge metal thing that it was fastened to and instantly the boat started to move away and head further out into the water. Yes I know it was silly and for others it may not be funny at all but this was one of those moments that we'll never forget. The look on the fellow passengers as well as those trying to get onto the boat was priceless and as for the captain or whatever they're called, the look of desperation was even funnier. By now, Hemal just couldn't laugh anymore and as the captain desperately regained control over the boat, I thought we'd be in serious trouble and could see us spending a night in jail or something. Amazingly, the boat was simply pulled back and tied up tightly and that was the end of it - we never got kicked off it because they didn't know it was Hemal that did it! I think i've mentioned Hemal and his antics before in this book but you really have no idea what he is going to do - that's what makes him one of the funniest people we know - thanks Hemal!

Crew in Amsterdam...

Stopped for a coffee!!

After just over day in Amsterdam, we left and headed for Switzerland. Our journey would take us through Luxembourg, Germany and the Swiss Alps. It was quite a long journey but we were a lot younger then and needed very little sleep. As we powered our way through Europe, we stopped along the way for a well-earned rest before continuing our journey and finally checking into our hotel for the night. Well, I say hotel - what I meant was our Mondeo hotel - we were sleeping in the car and after finding a quiet parking space we tried unsuccessfully to get to sleep. A few hours later, with everyone totally exhausted, we drifted off. The following morning we head off quite early and it wasn't long before we were at the Swiss border where the officials decided to search the car. We were all hoping that they wouldn't find anything, especially after we'd left Amsterdam if you know what I mean but after an hour of looking through a boot full of clothes and Hemel's stash of cosmetic gear, they let us continue.

Zurich.

Lausanne.

The scenery along this stretch of our journey was breath-taking; it was warm and sunny but as we climbed 1000's of feet up, we saw snow on the sides of the road and crystal clear water poured over the side of waterfalls and crashed onto the rocks below. As we climbed higher and higher, some of the inclines were so steep, that the Ford engine could only cope if we drove up in first gear. We arrived in Zurich, looked around, had a bite to eat and then continued along our way towards Luzern. The driving and distance was catching up with us and soon it was time to settle down for the night again. Our hotel for the night was a car park, quite high up a long and winding road. I think I was one of the first to wake up the following morning; it was the sound of bells that woke me up. In the distance there were cows with bells around their necks and each movement seemed to echo around the surrounding area and at the same time magnified the sound as well.

As we did each morning, we found somewhere to freshen up, had a bite to eat and then continued our journey. Soon we were in Luzern where the locals suggested we take a ride on the cable car to Mount Pilatus where the views were meant to be spectacular. We arrived at the cable cars to find that it was really expensive getting to the top. However, the tariff was a tiered one and you could ride the cars to different heights; each having their own price. We decided on the cheapest so we hopped on and slowly made our way up the mountain where we'd hopefully see the world's steepest cog railway system. To say it was scary was an understatement; the incline was phenomenal and lush green areas of Swiss land soon turned into pure white snow. It didn't help that I was sharing a car with Hemal and Bob who both decided to add a little excitement by shaking the car from side to side.

If we weren't so high it wouldn't have been that bad but we were *very* high indeed and it was scary. Below us, the ground seemed incredibly far away and cars were minute little things. We got to one of the "tiered" viewing platforms where everyone has to get off and then back onto the next set of cars. We felt cheated as our ticket had only given us a taster of what was to come. Even from this height the view was fantastic but as we looked up at the mountain, our thoughts turned to what the view would be like at the top - we *had* to see it. We now had 3 options; pay and go up; don't pay and go up or just go back down. With a bunch of lads there was only one option and that was to try our luck and see how far we could get up without paying. An old man was in charge of getting people off cable cars and then onto the ones that took them higher into the mountain as well as checking their tickets.

Don't mess...

Services at 4000 feet !!

A few of us went up to him and asked him some questions we knew he wouldn't be able to answer quickly and we used that time to sneak behind him and were just about to get inside the cable cars when he looked around and spotted us. He must have had 6th sense or something but he caught us good and proper and as he came rushing over to talk to some of us, the rest tried to get on. It was no good, this guy was well on the ball and there was way we were getting up there. It was very expensive to ride the cars up to the top so we decided to head back down; a real shame really because i'm sure the views would have been spectacular. With no time to waste, it was farewell Luzern and time to hit the road again for our onwards journey to Geneva. With a tight schedule ahead of us, we looked around for a few hours before preparing for the long, long drive to Milan, Italy.

This was one of the fastest legs of the whole journey and the motorway network helped us to get to Italy in record time. As the trip meter on the Mondeo approached 1800 miles, I couldn't drive anymore and needed a break - bad mistake. With the windows wide open as we pulled into the services, the buzzing of mosquitoes filled the car and before long, the inside of the car was swarming with them. Outside, the temperature hit 36 degrees and E2 was bitten quite badly by them and his arms were full of bite marks - not pleasant at all. The sheer number of mosquitoes cancelled our planned rest break and we hurriedly got back into the car, driving off with the windows wide open hoping the nasty bugs would fly out and not come back.

Several hours later and covered in bites, we entered Milan where the temperature was still around the 35/36 degree mark. It's a busy city with bikes, busy people and lots of small Fiats driving like made all over the place. By now, all of us were shattered and the heat and bites made it 100 times worse. We quickly found somewhere to park and as the evening drew in, the temperature thankfully dropped and the breeze picked up so at least it felt cooler! Where better than Italy to have a pizza we all thought and found ourselves a "traditional" looking pizzeria (whatever they are!). Inside, with no air conditioning, we battled with the staff who took one look at us and asked us about India and started spurting out random words such as 'chapatti' and 'curry'. We weren't impressed but smiled back - you *never* upset restaurant staff before you get your food - remember that... All the items on the menu looked the same and weren't in English which didn't help us and we just said we wanted "pizza".

20 minutes later and piping hot pizza was served and we all tucked in not really knowing what we'd ordered. Our choice of food, or rather the toppings was appalling and by far, we all agreed that was the worst pizza we'd ever tasted. So, after getting hot & bothered inside the restaurant where the staff were more about our ancestral traits and eating the worst pizza we left sharply. We actually considered legging it *without* paying but our luck was out that night and it just wasn't the risk although it would have been quite funny. Next stop along our route was Genoa (a mere 70 miles away), a town on the coast and we arrived there fresh and in a better mood than Milan. The sun was shining, it was warm and we were at the coast so things were looking good. We actually managed to do nothing at all here, a real achievement really because up until now, we'd only had a few hours here and there to really look around. All 5 of us sat on huge rocks close to the beach and just sat, talked and had a laugh - a real "friends together" moment...

With the sun setting is the distance, we piled back into the car for the 438 mile drive up to Paris which was our last stop before heading back home. This was a mammoth journey and we literally drove all night. Bob, E2 and the others took it in turns to sit in the front with me - probably scared that I might fall asleep whilst driving or something. They needn't have worried; if ever I think i'm too tired to drive, I would never risk it, opting to pull over whenever I could. A few rest stops later and we were on the edge of Paris and as we got ever closer to the city, the famous Eiffel tower leapt out at us and looked stunning in the early hours of the Parisian morning. It was an extremely tiring day and one of the best moments captured was when we drove up the Champs Elysee and then onto the Arc de Triomphe, allegedly the world's largest roundabout! We even managed to get off it too which, if anyone has ever seen it, would agree that this was a mammoth feat in itself!

We then drove to Champ de Mars, 75007 Paris where we stood side by side and got a local to take a picture of us standing in front of the Eiffel Tower with the sun setting in the background - a great way to end our journey. Well I say end our journey but that wasn't quite the end. We had to drive back to Calais and then catch our ferry back to the UK. The crossing itself just flew by and we only woke up when we were about 10 minutes from Dover. Tired and in dire need of more sleep, we slowly made our way down to the car deck below and prepared ourselves for the drive back home. Luckily for me, right at the end of this journey, E2 decided to take over the driving so I managed to get some more rest. Arriving in Leicester, it was straight to the car rental place and when the lady asked me what the mileage was she thought she was hearing things. We'd actually driven just over 2500 miles in about 6 days. The car looked battered and tired as it sat there in the car park and before they hired it out again it would need a severe clean. With our deposit returned to us that concluded our European adventure which was a truly memorable experience...

Living in Wycombe was ok but not really exciting so Sunita, E2 and I began considering a move out of there. Work logistics meant we had to choose our new location very carefully. Only E2 had a car and although he could obviously drive himself to work, he didn't want to spend half his life in the car so we looked for somewhere within reasonable commuting distance. Windsor was a firm favourite but we were concerned about the cost. At the time we hadn't even looked at the rental prices - we just expected them to be high but were spent a few Saturday afternoons in Windsor speaking to agents and getting prices. In contrast to Wycombe, Windsor was totally different; in the summer it was an awesome place to be - you could chill out by the river, grab a drink under the shadow of Windsor Castle or just casually walk along the town centre mingling with the 1000's of tourists that would drive into the town on a daily basis.

We found one flat which was around £650 per month and went to view it. Once we got to 24a Upcroft, we found ourselves in a quiet street around 2 miles outside the main town centre.

We seemed to be under the direct path of planes landing and taking off from Heathrow and I clearly remember hearing an almighty roar which was getting louder and louder. As we looked up into the clear sky we were expecting to see the red arrows fly past but it wasn't them - it was the 11am daily Concorde flight from London Heathrow to New York. None of us had ever seen Concorde in the sky and the noise was deafening. As it flew into the distance, the rumble of its engine could be heard for several minutes as it flew supersonic to the USA in 3 hours flat!

The flat itself was on the first floor and it was owned by an old lady who still lived below it. Many houses along this street had been converted - they were split into bottom and top floors to fill the booming rental market. Inside, it was clean, tidy and immaculately prepared and we all liked the place and knew we'd be happy here. Both E2 and I had turntables and our concerns (even we didn't share them with the agent) was how loud we could turn it up before someone complained! It even had a garden which was also split into 2 and everything seemed ok with the flat. It was decision time; we all liked it and although the rent was more expensive, we all decided to go for it - the flat was ours!

The paper work was signed along with all the conditions that came with it. We had to keep the garden maintained including cutting the grass, pruning, weeding and disposing the waste. None of us had ever looked after a garden and it would be a miracle if we managed this but we didn't worry about; we were just too excited at living in Windsor. Prior to the move, I looked into how I would get to work and thankfully, my journey was about to be made *much* simpler. There was a bus service that ran every 30 minutes from Windsor to Bracknell, it took 45 minutes and there was no need to change buses!

Back in Wycombe, we gave our landlord the news who was fine about it and over the forthcoming weeks, we all started to pack our things into boxes ready for the move. On the day itself, we had a hired van and E2's car to move all our belongings. In the end I think it only took 2 trips but at the end of the day we were exhausted. As we sat upstairs, worn out from taking boxes into and out of the houses, we still had the task of unpacking everything and it must have been 9 or 10pm by the time we'd finished. It took a while getting used to live in a different place and for Paresh & Munsha it meant a 30 minute / 20 mile drive to come and see us. Mind you, if we needed to go to Wycombe then we'd have to make the same journey too so we never saw the FBI boys as often as we did before.

The next morning I could see the dramatic impact moving to Windsor had made. Firstly, I got up at 7am rather than 5.30am, managed to have breakfast and then walked for about 5 minutes until I got to the main road and then waited for the bus. The bus arrived on time and I was sitting in a warm, comfortable bus which didn't stick of diesel. By the time it pulled into Bracknell, it was 08:45am and I had spent around 50 minutes on it. When I travelled from Wycombe, i'd normally have to stand outside the PTC office for some fresh air as i'd start to get quite tired and needed something to refresh me. However, travelling from Windsor meant I was fresh all day for the first time in 9 months.

At the end of the day, it was a short walk over the railway bridge from where I could see the bus waiting at the bus stop. 50 minutes later i'd be off the bus and walking back towards our flat and on most days i'd be inside the flat no later than 6.30 - a full 2 hours *earlier* than before. The worst times for getting back home were during Royal Ascot because the sheer volume of traffic in and around this area caused major headaches for anyone travelling around there. Mind you, Legoland which had recently opened was also a huge tourist attraction and in the summer, the traffic from here could delay my journey back by up to 30 minutes.

A few weeks after moving into the new flat, Sunita got a car. She was working for BT and needed her own transport so her dad got her a Maestro. I'm pretty certain that Sunita didn't know what kind of car her dad was getting her and I don't think she cared anyway because it proved to be cheap, reliable and took her wherever she wanted to go. A large company like BT makes sure they train their staff well and she had to undergo intense training on dealing with customers under various scenarios. Mind you, she really didn't need any training on how to talk - she does that professionally!!

22

Get off my bus!

One particular morning I left our Windsor flat a few minutes late but this wasn't a problem because I usually left early anyway just in case the bus arrived earlier (I couldn't miss the bus at all so didn't want to take any risk). As I walked faster towards the main road, I thought I could hear the bus in the distance and I was right. I turned onto the main road and could see the yellow "Bee Line" bus coming my way. I ran across the road and stuck my hand out hoping the driver would see me. He was driving quite fast and when the bus came to a halt he didn't look too pleased. I couldn't give a damn what he thought - he shouldn't have been driving so fast.

As I stepped onto the bus, I dived into my pocket and pulled out a bag of coins. I was saving odd bits of change for weeks and weeks and decided I would get rid of them. You always see signs on buses telling you "Exact change please" so I was simply complying. Ok, I may have had about 100 coins in total but it was still money and I never expected there would be an issue. As the 'clunk' of the coins rattled around the bus, the driver looked at me in such disgust, you'd think i'd insulted his mother or something. Within seconds "Are you joking or what?" rang out of the driver's mouth and when I replied "No", he got angry. After telling me he doesn't have the time to count the money and more importantly that he can refuse to take me on board, he promptly decided to show his authority and promptly told me to get off the bus unless I "paid properly".

Unfortunately, I had no other money with me so against my principles I got off the bus. As the driver closed the door he gave me one of those wry grins and sped off. To say I was embarrassed was an understatement but this was not the end of it - no way. I then walked to a shop a few hundred yards away and the kind shopkeeper, grateful for the change, converted the money into pound coins for me. The next bus came along on time around 30 minutes later and I finally got to work albeit 40 minutes later. Paul, my boss, was still too chilled to say anything about my lateness which I was grateful for but all I could think of was that twat of a bus driver. I logged onto the internet and found the phone number of the Bee Line bus company and in a matter of minutes was talking to someone about it. I explained *everything* and surprisingly the lady on the other end was quite understanding. I just expected her to tell me that the bus driver was right and that they would not be expected to count all that money. In the end she took details of the driver (driver 0143 that is - yes, I made a note of his driver badge and yes I could still remember it!), the bus number and route and said she would get back to me.

It didn't take long for her to look into it - less than 10 minutes later she rang me back and apologised profusely, further explaining that this attitude from the driver was unacceptable and she assured me that the driver will be spoken to. She then asked me for my address and that was the end of it for now. A couple of days later I received a letter from them summarising the incident and they also included a 5 day free bus pass which was very welcome. In the letter it clearly said that the driver should have taken the money and he was totally wrong to refuse me travel. I knew from past experience that the morning bus drivers often worked the same route for several days and on rotation too so it would be a few weeks and then I would see the toss pot again. True to my word, I saw the same driver a few weeks later and this time I was prepared for battle. As he pulled up, he didn't even know who I was and then I pulled out my huge bag of coins for the 2nd time and shoved them in front of him.

Before he had a chance to say anything I stopped him and asked if he remembered throwing me off the bus a few weeks earlier. "Yes I do, and i'm not counting all that; give me something else." was his reply. Since he wanted something else, I was more than happy to oblige & slowly pulled out the letter from the bus company and shoved into his fat face. His expression totally changed, he knew he was defeated and I watched as he counted the mixture of 2p & 5p coins. It took a while to check them during which I gave him the same smile he gave me when he threw me off a few weeks earlier. I enjoyed that journey to work that day and just to rub it in even further I gave him a similar bag of coins the next day and I probably would have done it again but I never saw him after that - that taught you didn't it you fat twat! That's the thing with me you see, I don't like it when people try to screw you over because they think they are somehow superior to you. There is no place for rudeness in this world and it's a shame more people can't see this.

We all enjoyed living in Windsor, especially during the spring and summer months. During the warm days we'd head into the town centre and just wander around the shops as we mixed with the tourists that came to visit from all over the world. At 11am, the familiar sound of Concorde roared overhead as yet another plane full of elite passengers were being whisked off to New York in record time. During 1 or 2 weekends in the month, we would drive back to Leicester to see friends and family. Mind you, out of all of us, E2 went home the least; I think he just liked chilling out and I was always grateful when he lent me his car so I could drive myself back to Leicester. The weekend clubbing wasn't showing any signs of slowing down either and the trips to Club UK were regular as ever.

For Sunita & I, it had been ages since we'd been anywhere different so I decided to surprise her by booking flights to Paris. Yes, we'd been there before but hopefully a day trip would be less taxing for both of us. Rather than tell her, I decided to make it a surprise and E2 and I told her we were driving to Heathrow to pick someone else up. Whether she believed it or not I have no idea but when we got there and stood around waiting and waiting and waiting, she was starting to get fed up. To make it even more realistic, I told Sunita to come with me to one of the check in desks so that we could enquire about our missing person. As we approached the desk I pulled out the tickets without Sunita noticing and handed over the passports too. As the check in clerk started to ask questions like "Do you have any baggage", Sunita soon realised what I had been scheming and within a few seconds she knew exactly what was going on.

Thankfully, it was a total surprise to her and before long we were 1000's of feet up in the sky heading for Paris. We arrived in around 50 minutes - much better than the 9 or so hours it took us to get there on the coach. After passing through customs it was a short trek to their underground (well Le Metro actually...) and onto a fast train that took us to the centre of Paris. The weather was on our side too - it was a mild, sunny day as we took in the famous sites of this famous city. By the end of the day we were both very tired and ready to head home. The funny thing is, as the plane approached the runway at Heathrow, I could see E2 in his car driving below us on his way to pick us up. Admittedly, it may not have been him, but the car, the colour and even the white bit of paper that was wedged to his front tyre for the last few weeks could be clearly seen. It was around 9.30pm by the time we got back to the flat and moments after slumping into the welcoming sofa's the phone rang. It was Munsha and judging by E2's reaction, I knew we were going out. I wasn't wrong - he told E2 that he was coming round to pick us all up and we were going to Club UK ... again - so much for a quiet night in.

Job wise, E2 seemed happy enough with his work and I was definitely happy with mine but Sunita was looking for permanent work and to get away from her current BT job too. It didn't take long for her to get an offer either. A firm in Slough "A Plus" offered her a position of "HR Administrator" and she snapped it up. The pay was ok, the location was excellent and the prospects were good too so all in all things were looking good.

Another crazy picture – this time outside the flat in Windsor.

Ready for a night out.

Downtown, Windsor.

I always maintained that we were good neighbours to have even though we were really 1st floor neighbours! Some of the people who lived in the street were getting annoyed at the fact that we (Sunita and E2 that is) would sometimes park outside their house. I mean, if someone parks in front of our flat, then you have no choice but to park where you can right? Well, according to certain neighbours, this wasn't right and was in fact totally wrong. At first, it was just dirty looks we'd get but after that the notes would start to appear on the cars. "Can you park elsewhere please", "Can you park in front of your own house please?". Er, actually get stuffed - no we can't park outside our house because there's no room. Furthermore, nobody had any special parking rights so officially we could park where we wanted. In the end we resorted to using taxis but I must explain this. I don't mean *we* started to use taxi's per say - what I mean was we got our own back by calling taxi firms and giving the address of the idiots who were telling us where to park.

We'd dial a whole heap of taxi firms remembering to prefix with 141 and then put on all sorts of voices. Both E2 & I would piss ourselves laughing as we tried to keep straight faces. Sunita used to sit on the settee telling us that "we're mad and you'll get caught one day". When the taxi arrived, they gave the usual horn but after a few minutes would actually get out of the car and knock on the door. The twat of a neighbour would then look perplexed at this cab driver standing there asking him if he wanted a ride to Heathrow airport. We made sure we were well out of view and both of them would then look up and down the street in case they spotted anyone. In the meantime, we'd be hiding behind the curtains with tears of laughter streaming down our faces again. Ok - it may not have been *that* funny but it was to us.

Unfortunately, the notes on our cars continued so we decided to take our battle to the next stage. Rather than sending taxis to his house, we decided Pizzas would be sent too. After a few days of pizzas and taxi's arriving at the house, the notes on our cars finally stopped. I have no idea if he knew who had sent them but we'd taught him a lesson nevertheless - rightly or wrongly. Keeping our garden "maintained" was in our rental contract and gardening was something new to all of us. None of us were too fussed about the garden. Yes, we liked sitting outside when it was warm but none of us spent any time in there apart from that. The garden itself had lots of rhubarb growing in there and one day a neighbour who lived at the side of the house was looking at the sheer amount of rhubarb growing.

You could tell he was dying to get his hands on it but never asked for it outright until we asked if he wanted some. "Ok - i'll have a small bit if that's ok." Small bit?" - get stuffed, if you want some you'll take what we give you and with that, we pulled out as much rhubarb as we could. The less that was growing, the less maintenance we had to do - simple really! By the time we handed over the rhubarb the neighbour could just about hold it and the plant itself looked as if it had been hacked to death. Miraculously, the rhubarb plant survived and whether he wanted it or not, that neighbour, got *all* our rhubarb from that day onwards!!

The year that was 1995 seemed to go by really quickly. Part of the reason may have been that we always seemed to be busy at the weekends. Cooking days were always a good laugh - except for me. Both E2 and Sunita took pity on me and allocated something like Tuesdays & Fridays as my cooking days. Given that we'd head back to Leicester quite often, I got out of cooking on Fridays whilst they ended up with kitchen duty - thanks guys! Mind you, saying I had cooking days didn't mean anything. I just wasn't capable of knocking up a decent meal at all and it was simple food all the time. E2 & Sunita always tried to cook something decent and in hindsight I should have tried a lot more.

Often, whilst sitting in the flat watching TV, one of us would venture into the kitchen looking for some good. The food of choice was cheddar biscuits and after unwrapping the seal on the pack we would offer them to each other. I must say right now that Sunita wasn't part of this but in a matter of minutes we wouldn't be passing 1 or 2 biscuits to each other but would egg each other on to each 4/5 biscuits at a time. In a matter of minutes, the pack of cheddars was reduced to an empty packet as we looked at each other looking very smug. This wasn't a one off either, the routine continued for a few years after that which no doubt contributed to my weight ballooning up to a massive 14 stone.

As well as stuffing myself at home, I continued the habit at work too. PTC held many training courses and with training courses come lunch time buffets. My work *always* ordered more food than they required "just in case" and once lunch time was over, the food was free to anyone who wanted it. I didn't need to be asked twice and would head over to the kitchen area, grab a big plate and shove trifles, cakes and anything else that was on offer onto my plate. At the time I hardly followed any kind of exercise routine so the weight piled on and there was nothing to take it off.

We were only in the Windsor flat for a year and in September 1996, we moved to Slough. Yes, this was a backwards move but it was unavoidable so that was that. Luckily, the place we found was in a quiet Cul de sac and there were only 4 houses in total. Our direct neighbours were an elderly Irish couple who kept themselves to themselves but the man loved talking. In fact he loved talking so much that once he caught sight of you, he wouldn't let you go until he'd rambled on for at least 15 minutes. One of the other families were ok too - a couple with 2 kids - they were a right laugh but the chap that lived opposite us didn't like us from the start - all because of car parking space.

You see at the front of our house was a grass area and it was ok for him to park on the grass but not anyone else. If any of our cars were on the grass it would *really* wind him up and he would write messages and leave them on E2's / Sunita's car. Most of the time the message would be "Please don't park your car on the grass." It was quite annoying, especially as we'd just moved in - I mean the last thing we wanted to do was upset the neighbours. I couldn't believe it, in Windsor we had a car parking problem with idiot neighbours and the same thing was happening all over again.

For E2 and Sunita the move to Slough didn't make any difference to their commute to work but for me it made things slightly difficult. The bus I used to catch from Windsor actually departed from Slough bus station so that was a good thing but the down side was that the nearest bus stop was about 2 miles away. Unfortunately for Sunita this meant that she had to drop me off to the bus station each morning whilst in the evening either E2 or Sunita would come and get me. Sunday mornings in this house were quite chilled out. I was usually up quite early but then again none of us really had lie ins and most Sundays were spent at our local Asda which was close enough to walk! E2 would always get a newspaper and then spent the next 3 hours reading every word. Sunita would grab the cooking supplements whilst I would read the real life articles in the accompanying magazine.

One evening whilst watching TV, one of us (i'm sure it was E2), said something about having a house party. We'd been to loads in the past but never hosted one ourselves. So, within a few minutes of talking about it, we decided to have one and the party plans were in full flow. We set a date, Paresh was going to bring his PA equipment down and we would DJ ourselves. I can't remember how many people we invited in the end but it must have been around 50 or so. Thinking about it, it wasn't one of those mad, anything goes, type of parties but one where we invited real friends to have a good time - the last thing we wanted was to trash the place! A few days before the party we told our neighbours about it and they were ok about it. On the night itself, we had a good crowd, we danced loads (helped along by the excellent music selection) and everyone seemed to have a really good time. It was a late, late night but the great thing about it was there was hardly any mess to clean up in the morning - what a result!

Sam, Sima & Fay getting
ready to party.

Miyura had to be told –
smoking in the garden (!)

Alpa dancing – there's a surprise!

On the decks.

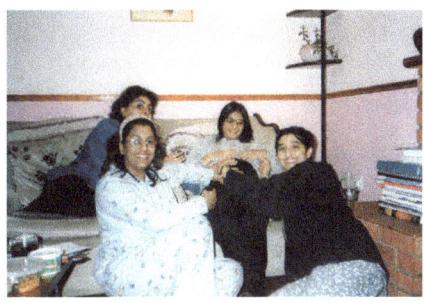

Miyura had something in her tummy.

The morning after the night before.

Cheers.

Cheers again!

E2 with Sunita's pyjamas...

Sunita with her pyjamas –
whose pyjamas were they?

Bond theme definitely going on!

At the end of a hard day's work, all 3 of us looked forward to chilling out together in the evening. It was just like the US sitcom "friends" except there was only 3 of us there. When we'd finished eating our dinner, we'd all get changed so we could relax.

E2 would sit there with his black jogging bottoms, white t shirt and baseball cap, Sunita would be chilling out in her polka dot pyjamas whilst I would slouch into the sofa in my shorts and t shirt. My recently purchased video camera would often come out in the evenings too and we'd leave the video rolling as we talked, took the piss out of each other and generally clowned around. On Sunday evenings when it was time for McDonalds, I would drive whilst E2 took the video camera along and added running commentary.

Ok, it was hardly exciting driving to a McDonalds in Slough but we had a laugh as he recorded random things along the way and the staff at McDonalds (understandably) gave us strange looks as they tried to figure out why on earth we were videoing them. In a matter of months we had footage from trips around Slough, at home, in town, driving back to Leicester and other countless places. Trust me, we spent many hours doing this which may have seemed pointless but looking back now, I have invaluable footage of us doing crazy things many years ago which we can cherish and laugh at when we watch again.

23

Away in the USA and Sunita's "big" decision

By now it was September 1996 and during one weekend when I was in Leicester, I was in the car with Nee & Rumit. They were talking about a trip to America - they must have been discussing for several weeks because they seemed to have a fair idea of where they wanted to go. It sounded as if they wanted to go but couldn't quite make the decision to actually go for it and needed that extra push. I was being dropped off first and as we made our way to my mum's house on Lancaster Street I asked both of them "Do you want to go to America?" Neither of them hesitated at all and both said a reassuring yes. When I asked them what was stopping them they said "nothing". Without a care in the world I then said "let's go then" and that was that.

At the time, they probably thought I was joking but I wasn't. None of us had been to the USA before, I was owed lots of time from work and Nee was just in the middle of getting a bigger shop for his business so the timing was almost perfect. Well, I say perfect but it wasn't quite - Preeti, his wife was expecting their first child a few weeks before we planned to go so Nee would get to see his baby and would then jet off! As we turned into Lancaster Street we were all very excited about the trip but it was still hard to believe that we'd actually decided to go. During the next 90 minutes we talked more and more about the trip as we eagerly listened to each other's ideas. There was lots to organise - time off from work, flights, accommodation and all the rest of it so it was game on!

Many months before the USA trip was even on the cards, Sunita and I had been talking about our future together. In fact, it seemed to be the main topic week in and week out and quite right too. I mean, time was ticking (albeit slowly) but ticking nevertheless and we had to decide what we wanted to do. I was clear on what I wanted; I wanted to marry her - simple really. Sunita on the other hand faced a big dilemma. She felt torn between me and her family and in the end actually decided that she wanted to respect the wishes of her parents by getting married the "traditional" way by means of an arranged marriage. When I told her we could "arrange" our wedding (& therefore have an arranged marriage), she didn't see the funny side of it - oh well, at least I tried right?

On a serious note though, I *respected* her wishes 100% as I had done many years previously when she didn't want to see me anymore. She was certain that she didn't want to upset her parents and although it wasn't what I wanted to hear, family comes first and there was no way I was going to try to talk her out of it. She knew what she was doing and was the only one who could make that decision. All I knew was that if we were going to break up then it had to be soon. I mean, what was the point of carrying on endlessly? So, it was virtually decided that the relationship had to end - nothing more to say really.

Within a few weeks of talking about the USA trip, holidays were booked, arrangements were made and flights were sorted. For Nee & Dee, they needed a bigger premises as their car audio business was really taking off now. They took over a shop on Green Lane Road but the paperwork was still going through and the way things worked out, they would be able to move into the shop shortly after we returned from our trip. The only thing left was the accommodation but we decided to sort all this out when we landed! The trip would be a full on coast to coast adventure and we'd be leaving on 1st November 1996. We'd be gone for almost 17 days which was the longest Sunita & I would have been apart since we first got together. I could have sat at home dwelling on our future (or should I say NO future together) but was the point? I'd be a liar if I wasn't hurt by what had happened but you just got to keep going so I tried not to think about it. I was going to the USA with my mates and were all *really* looking forward to it...

On November 1st, 1996, we boarded our American Airlines flight from Heathrow to Los Angeles. A gruelling 12 & a half hours later, we touched down at LAX Airport. We didn't pre-book any hotels or hire cars so we took a bit of a gamble (as usual!) and booked everything along the way. We got out of the airport, got ourselves a hire car and headed for Santa Monica which is one of the most famous areas of Los Angeles. After getting a little lost we eventually found a comfortable and cheap hotel for our stay in L.A. Eager to head out, we dumped our stuff in our hotel room and started roaming the streets of LA. We paid particular attention to where we were heading because when we picked up our hire car from the airport, the assistant told us to steer well clear of the areas he had circled on the map he was giving us.

Interestingly for me, he had told us to stay away from "Compton" & "Inglewood" which I could relate straight away to music lyrics from various hip hop artists including NWA. To Nee and Rumit, they were just names and collectively we made sure we didn't head towards these areas at all. We drove around for around 30 minutes, got something to eat & were too tired to do anything else so drove back to the hotel. One of the main attractions in LA has to be the legendary Universal Studios so we went straight there the next morning. The entrance to the park is pure American - big and bold and definitely in your face and after strolling around for a while, came face to face with memorabilia from some tv and film sets over the years. We saw "KITT", the car from the Knight Rider TV series, the De Lorean car from the film 'Back To The Future' and even drove past the Clock Tower (the one stuck by lightning!) featured in the same film.

As we continued along the tour I turned to Nee and said "You talking to me punk?". He gave me a puzzled look and wondered what on earth I was going on about. A few seconds later and with telling Nee to look to his right, he knew very well what I was going on about! The "A Team" van was parked right in front of us which was very cool indeed. For those of you that don't quite get the connection, "You talking to me punk" was a catchphrase of "Mr. T" - the gold heavy character in the series who hated flying! As we continued along our journey, we saw other props from Jurassic Park and took in a fantastic view of Silicon Valley & the surrounding areas. The next day we took a half day tour of LA

Remember this from
Back To The Future?

Time travel anybody?

End of route 66.

including the bay area, the famous Hollywood Hills, Sunset Boulevard, Hollywood, Beverley Hills and Bel Air. In the evening we got back into our hire car and drove to Santa Monica beach where we just chilled for the rest of the evening.

One evening, as we headed out to grab a bite to eat, Nee decided that he'd like to drive for a while so we swapped seats and he started driving out of our hotel car park. Just as we got to the main junction, things were going ok but he suddenly forgot he was in the USA and rather than looking left to check for traffic, he looked to the right and was just about to pull out as a car hurtled towards us. He only stopped because both Rumit & I were screaming at him!! That experience was enough to put him off so he reversed, yelled "sod that" and got into the back of the car - normal service was resumed as I got back in. It never bothered me driving anywhere in the world - it was quite exciting really but the strangest thing was driving a left hand drive manual car on the right hand side of the road. After visiting Malibu with its picturesque mansions dotted along the coast, our stay in LA had come to an end and it was time to head back to LAX for our short flight to our next destination - Las Vegas.

We actually tried to book some accommodation for Las Vegas whilst we were in LA. but because of the Tyson V Holyfield fight, we were told that all accommodation was full and that we would be flying into Vegas without anywhere to stay - great! Well, the flight into Las Vegas was wicked because one minute you can't see anything and the next you see this mini city with millions of lights appear from nowhere. We found accommodation in the end and we were staying right opposite the Mirage Hotel. Our first trek took us to a place called Red Rock Canyon which we later found was home to plenty of snakes - good job we never saw any! Our first evening in Vegas was an awesome experience. Nothing prepares for the sights and sounds of walking up the Vegas strip and watching in awe at the size and sheer wonder of the hotels and casinos that line both sides of the road. Each hotel has to be bigger and bolder than the others and once you're inside these hotels, you see the true scale of them. They have 1000's, yes, 1000's of rooms, indoor shopping centres, roller coaster rides and every other conceivable luxury you could think of.

Red Rock Canyon, Nevada

The strip –
Las Vegas.

Hoover Dam (Nevada, Arizona).

Rumit was next to the pilot of our tiny plane for our flight over the Grand Canyon...

After we'd looked around one of the casino's, Rumit took his place at the table and started to play crap (the game that is!) and looked like a true professional. With a small flick of his wrist, a tender nod of his head and a subtle shake of the hand whenever it was necessary, the card dealer understood exactly what Rumit was telling him. This was table talk on a grand scale whilst Nee and I were totally lost and headed off to find the slot machines instead. Whilst Nee sipped on strawberry daiquiris and man like Rumit chilled with his Jack Daniels, I stuck to good old Coca Cola as we shoved coin after coin into the 'slots'. At one point, I got the video camera out and started filming but I was soon pulled to one side by security who literally appeared from nowhere. I wasn't aware that filming was illegal but the security team stood there whilst I rewound and then recorded over the footage I had just recorded.

Amongst other highlights in Vegas were a trip to the Hoover Dam followed by a flight over the Grand Canyon in a tiny Cessna plane. Whilst we were on the flight, we hit some turbulent air pockets which sent the plane into an upward then downward movement. In a commercial airliner you would have barely even felt this but in this tiny plane we felt it good and proper. As for Rumit, who incidentally, had never flown before this trip, he was shocked beyond belief and probably wondered if we'd make it back safe. Within a few seconds (although it seemed much longer), we were cruising high above the Colorado River where you could see the brown, mud filled water cascading its way through the rocky earth below us.

The scene was wonderful and I had the video camera on hand to capture the moment - well I could if it wasn't stuck. As I switched it "on" I pulled it up so I could look through it but it was stuck. I tugged again and again but it was no use and eventually managed to turn around a little (it was a tight squeeze). As my eyes focused down onto the camcorder strap, my heart jumped a little as I realised what I was doing. I was actually tugging the door to the plane because somehow the camcorder strap had worked itself around the door handle. If the door had opened I would have been the first Indian man to parachute into the canyon (without a parachute!!) - this was pretty scary I can tell you - I didn't share it with the others though! By the end of the flight we'd had a fun filled day and one we wouldn't forget in a while. Rumit was scared to death, I nearly fell to my death whilst Nee was bored to death and actually fell asleep amidst the beauty of the Grand Canyon below us!

That evening, with one more full day left in Vegas, we were driving along the Vegas 'strip' and waiting for the lights to change when we could see a car heading towards us from the other side of the road. In a matter of seconds, the driver crashed into, and drove over, the barrier that separated both sides of traffic. The car then crashed into us and sent us crashing into the car next to us. It was all over in a matter of seconds and as we all got out, a bloke clambered out of the offending car and started murmuring all sorts of things. We had no idea what he was going on about but he wasn't quite with it and at first we thought he was probably pissed or something. 2 others then followed him and were quite annoyed by it all; so much so that all 3 of them ended up trying to fight with each other.

The police (well one of them anyway) arrived a few minutes later and dealt with the whole situation using his authority to maximum effect. No-one questioned him, nobody talked back, we did what he asked and you could see that the police there had *real* control over the situation and the public respected this. After looking at the carnage, he knew exactly where the blame lied. He then filled out various forms and handed one to the innocent parties which basically told the insurance companies that the other party was to blame. The downside was that although it was no fault of mine, the local car hire policy meant they couldn't give us another car and our plans to drive to Death Valley the next day had to be cancelled.

With the Vegas experience behind us, it was back to the airport for a 4 hour flight to Orlando via Dallas. The next morning there was no hanging around; we had our discounted theme park tickets and got into hire car number 2 and headed straight for Walt Disney World resort. It's quite strange driving into this place - you hear so much about it; the adverts on the tv, friends and relatives who have been there and just the general hearsay about it. We were there and determined not to waste a single minute. The car park was as big as a city and stretched as far as the eye could see. It was so big that the cars themselves looked like little matchbox toy cars!

Everything about this place was big; there were about 5 parks in total and it was as if they were all competing with each other to be bigger and better. One of the things that *really* stuck out was the size of the Americans - it might be stereotypical but it's definitely true and we were surrounded by young kids twice the size they should be walking with parents wider than freeways. They were all doing the same; eating burgers, stuffing their faces with huge chips (or fries!) and washing it all down with gallons of coke or anything fizzy they could get their hands on. It was horrible seeing this but never mind - we weren't there to watch them.

After some pretty nifty 'virtual queuing', we went onto the first ride @ Disneyland - *Jurassic Park* and then onto 'Back To The Future' which was excellent too. A trek around Disneyland really takes it out of you and at the end of the day we were looking forward to a well-earned rest. There is no denying it - Disneyland definitely lives up to all the hype and is definitely worth a visit if anyone is considering a trip there. With 2 days left in Orlando, we

spent one day driving east and looked around the John Kennedy Space Centre to see the space shuttle and learn a bit about space travel! On our final day we joined the crowd @ Gatorland where you can watch live shows where crazy people shove their head into the mouth of a crocodile whilst the crowd clap and cheer! Listen, there's nothing clever about that whatsoever - it's just stupid.

Too tired to head out that evening, we decided to chill out at the hotel and order in a pizza. We got the number for the pizza company from the hotel itself and it was "highly recommended". After the order was complete we just sat in our room joking around and our room phone rang about 30 minutes later. "Pizza for black bastard" came screaming down the line as soon as I picked up the phone. Taken back by what I heard I said something like "what?" The person on the other end then repeated it over and over again but before I had a chance to say anything hung up. I remember standing there with the phone in my hand trying to understand what had just happened. It just caught me off guard totally. We had never had an issue with racism so far but could it be the pizza company? We were all fuming by now and the hotel wouldn't even give us the address of the pizza company because they could see something was about to kick off. We stood by reception and refused to move until they gave us the address and in the end they gave in. At the time I wasn't feeling too good either; I had a really nasty cold, a headache and simply didn't need this type of crap.

We rushed outside, jumped into our hire car and made our way to that address. 10 minutes later and we were inside the pizza place. We asked for the manager straight away and in the distance we noticed someone looking very suspicious who also appeared to be eavesdropping subtly although he wasn't doing a good job. The manager finally came out and was far from co-operative at first but as we explained what had happened his mood slowly changed. Perhaps I was too quick to judge him but he was shocked by what he was hearing. Meanwhile, the eavesdropper was still trying to listen in and I was adamant he was our man. Unfortunately, none of the staff admitted to anything and luckily for them Rumit was in a reasonable mood. We left the place with a full refund, our pizza order and some extras to go with it. I just hoped for their sakes that they learnt a lesson there.

Our days in the USA were drawing to an end now but we still had one more place to go! The next morning we landed at New York's JFK airport and straight into the vibrant city that is New York. Having picked up another hire car, we found that the hotel rates were extortionate and there weren't many rooms available anyway. In the end we found accommodation some 15 miles out of the city which was a bit of a pain. With only a day to explore the city, we saw what we could including Times Square, the infamous Macy's, the Empire State building and the World Trade Centre. Our last night in the big apple was spent tucking into the biggest meal i've ever eaten and then we caught an afternoon flight back to the UK rounding off a wicked holiday. When you spend almost 3 weeks with friends, you *really* learn lots about them - more so than meeting them now and then for a few hours. Well I learnt a great deal during the time we spent together; I learnt that with Rumit and Nee, friendship was *unconditional* - they were there for me *all the time, anytime* and that meant the world to me. When I looked back at the fun times we had I knew then that I had true friends...

I'll never forget the look on Sunita's face when I got back home after the USA trip. To say she was pleased to see me was an understatement - it was almost as if i'd been gone for a year or so. I was puzzled though - before I went she decided we had no future so perhaps she was just pleased to see me and nothing else. Perhaps I was reading too much into it? The next day she wanted to talk & bear in mind she continually told me it couldn't wait, I knew something was bothering her. Anyway when we finally got time to have a chat, she explained that during the time I was away she had time for lots of "thinking" and decided that she couldn't let go. Meanwhile I couldn't let go of the cheddar biscuits

Twilight @ the top of the World Trade Centre, NYC.

(I missed them during the 3 weeks away!) but after a few harsh words from her I was back, focused & trying to listen...

She explained that she had changed her mind and wanted to get married. I was waiting for her to ask me properly but she didn't - it was kind of assumed that I still wanted to marry her too. I sometimes wish I called her bluff and said "No". Ok - it would have been cruel to play such a joke but it would have been fun! The truth is I was shocked, surprised and overjoyed at what she was telling me. I was waiting for this day and here we were basically deciding to get married. I always gave her the space she needed and never got in the way of her family and their beliefs and it must have been a huge decision for her. Neither of us actually asked the "Will you marry me question" - it was sort of assumed so there we were. We had made finally made the decision that would change our lives but we now had the task of telling our parents. We told E2 about our plans to marry and as expected he was overjoyed and really excited. With Christmas fast approaching, we decided to tell our parents in the new year which gave us some time to think and plan out what we were going to do. For me it was quite strange, it seemed that I was moving up the ladder of life and taking the next big step. Hopefully, things would work out ok but neither of us knew what would really happen and what 1997 had in store...

A day trip to Chessington World of Adventures, 1997 – would this be our last adventure?

24

Hand me down cars
& the hand in marriage

January 1997 and during a visit to my sister's, she mentioned that they were getting a new car and I was taken aback when she said I could have their current car - an F registration Vauxhall Cavalier. At the time, all I could think of was being able to drive to work and not have to catch the bus. I didn't need time to think and agreed to the hand me down car. Most people get hand me down clothes but this was much better. At the same time, thoughts of the wedding were constantly on my mind and I spoke to my sister about it.

To be honest there was nobody else I wanted to speak to anyway; it *had* to be my freckle faced sister. She knew we had been together for several years and told me not to worry about it. Easier said than done - but she said she'd speak to my mum for me. Looking back now, I can't believe I got my sister involved. There was no need to and I should have done it myself but she spoke to her and although my mum wasn't over the moon about it, she eventually came around to the idea. Paresh's mum, who I always felt was my "other mum" played a big part too - she knew Sunita really well and spoke to my mum and put in a few good words! I still remember the day I actually spoke to my mum about Sunita - we were sitting in the lounge and I pulled out a photo of Sunita - the photo was taken from a wedding / engagement or something and my mum looked at the picture quite blankly at first.

She then put it down and walked off - by this time I thought things had taken a nasty turn but in a few seconds she came back into the room with her glasses on! She then studied the photo like a forensic scientist. After what seemed like an age she looked at me and said "if you want to marry her then fine - you have to live with her, not me". At first this seemed quite abrupt but if you think about it, it's true so I guess it was a fair comment. Again, my mum never really approved or disapproved - I just assumed she approved so that was that. There was no point speaking to my dad about it - he never had any objections at all. In fact, he hardly had any objections about anything except for working. With the Patel side giving approval, I now had to concentrate on Sunita's dad. Just like my dad; Sunita's mum was ok with the whole thing; she just wanted Sunita to be happy and although her dad obviously wanted her to be happy, there was protocol to follow and I had to follow it correctly.

I think it was a Sunday afternoon that I plucked up the courage to finally go and see Sunita's dad. It was quite a good day as I had my new hand me down car; I was just hoping the imminent meeting wouldn't spoil the day! I was nervous, really nervous in fact; her dad was a proud man and I had to prepare myself for a verbal battering which I was expecting. As I rang the doorbell, I think it was Sunita who answered the door. She didn't say much and I followed her into the room where her dad was sitting in his chair. I say *his* chair because it looked as if that was his seat and nobody ever dared sit in there! Sunita's mum was in one corner and Sunita joined her and I walked over to her dad and shook his hand. It wasn't a firm handshake at all but it didn't matter - I was there to get the job done and I had to do it properly.

I had prepared myself for this weeks in advance but I couldn't speak. In the corner of my eye I could see Sunita & her mum sitting quietly but anxiously waiting for someone to say something and the first minute of silence felt like an hour. In the end, I just took a deep breath and looked directly at her dad and said "The reason i'm here is that I want to marry your daughter and I want to do it properly. I'm therefore asking for your daughter's hand in marriage...". Phew, i'd done it; I was relieved and everyone (except her dad) seemed to be relieved too.

I was quite taken aback when he looked back at me sternly and said "Do what you want - why have you come here?". Without thinking I repeated the fact that I was serious and that I wanted to marry her but only with her dad's blessing. He never said anything after that and I found it quite difficult to figure out what he was thinking. He just stared at the television and I sat there for another minute or so before getting up shaking his hand and leaving. I was glad to get back into the car and eager to get home so I could get out of my sweaty top. That afternoon we all drove back to Slough and the 3 of us had a good chat about the day's events. Sunita was just glad we'd told both our parents but I was still worried about her dad.

A few weeks later, we all went back to Leicester but this time I took Paresh's mum & dad with us. They stayed at my mums on Saturday night and on the Sunday, Sunita's mum & dad came over. As it happened, I was worrying for no reason; her dad had obviously thought long and hard about it and must have realised that deep down if it was what Sunita wanted then it's ok with him. I saw a different side to him that day - far different to the man I met a few weeks earlier. He was joking around and just having a good time which helped to break the somewhat tense atmosphere. Throughout this, my dad kept himself to himself but soon joined in when they (the men that is), had a shot of whisky as a toast. I guess the toast was the 'official' acceptance or agreement that we could get married. I often think that it's pretty daft how we had to get our parent's approval to get married but it's just an Indian thing. Up until then I knew and had met the rest of Sunita's family but only as Sunita's friend so the next visit would be quite strange knowing that this friend would actually be her husband.

In the Hindu culture, setting the date for a wedding can be a tiresome process. It's just not as simple as picking a date because there are "good" & "bad" days and you must only get married on a good day. You actually have to get a priest involved who takes the bride & grooms date of birth as well as the suggested wedding dates and looks at the Hindu calendar. At the end of it, he either approves or rejects the dates and from that you can either come up with new dates or use one of the 'good' ones. I know for a fact that we changed the date several times for this very reason but after a few days, the wedding date was set - 18th October 1997.

For me anyway, the thought of getting married was pretty scary and to be honest it really was a complete turnaround of events. I truly believe that if I hadn't been in the car that day when Nee & Rumit were talking about America, then the marriage would never have happened. I wouldn't have gone on the trip and Sunita would never have given the idea any thought at all. Thankfully, everything seemed to be working out smoothly and now the wedding plans had to begin. Sunita & I are both Hindus but she speaks Punjabi whilst I speak gujerati. The wedding ceremonies are subtly different too; traditional gujerati weddings are formal events with no alcohol or meat served at all and a long religious ceremony too. In contrast, a traditional wedding for Sunita would mean a full on party, meat & alcohol and a reduced religious ceremony. It would be quite difficult to fit both types of weddings so in the end we decided on a hybrid wedding! The agreed plan was to have the formal registry wedding in the morning and then have a party in the afternoon.

One thing we both agreed on was to help out financially wherever we could with the wedding costs. Weddings aren't cheap but Indian weddings are something else; you could easily spend upwards to £100,000 on them quite easily. The venue was in Leicester town centre and whilst Sunita's family sorted out the venue and food, Sunita & I paid for the DJ and whatever else we could afford. It wasn't expected of us, but we wanted to help & although it made not have made a huge difference, it helped, nevertheless. For the day itself, we had hired a DJ and some dancers. The DJs were Calibar Roadshow - the *same* DJ's that Munsha & Paresh DJ'd with years before and the same DJ that rocked Leicester during the days of our legendary daytime gigs. For now, there wasn't much else to do but as the date grew closer we'd have to design, print and then distribute the wedding invites. Having 700 people at an Indian wedding can be quite normal but our wedding was a cut down affair and between us decided we'd have no more than 400 guests!

Back in Slough, the wedding became the focal point of our discussions as we chilled at home after work. E2 would sit there asking how we both felt about it as well as other questions that were meant to put us on the spot. If we could be bothered, we'd also get the video camera too and start videoing these 'question time' sessions! Sunita would constantly tell him to get the camera out of her face and tell him he was stupid at which E2 would rendition "Stupid Girl" by Garbage - i'm not quite sure when this started but it was always a good laugh.

At Parametric Technology I was doing really well and finally having a car made a huge difference to my journey to work. However, the company outgrew their Bracknell office and moved to Fleet in Hampshire. The new location added about 30 minutes to my journey which was a bit of a pain but I soon got used to it. The new office was massive and I shared an office with James, one of my colleagues. This was no ordinary office - it had masses of space, huge desk areas and half of the room was covered from ceiling to floor with glass. Unfortunately, our outside view was of the M3 motorway (the office was right next to the motorway) but never mind.

The months soon crept up on us and by the time both of us had picked and bought our wedding outfits, the wedding was just around the corner. When Sunita asked me who my best man would be, we both knew the answer straight away - E2. There was no question at all, he was one of the people that got us together so it was fitting to have him by my side. An 'Indian' best man doesn't have to go all out and do the usual stuff of speeches but deep down I had a feeling that E2 was planning one even though he didn't really comment on it at all. One thing I did want to sort out was the honeymoon and neither of us had many days of holiday we could take. In the end we decided to go away for a week only; we were going to fly to New York and then onto Niagara Falls...

I have no idea where the terms 'hen' and 'stag' actually come from and how or why they relate to pre-wedding celebrations. I even asked Google to get some more information but there's nothing solid out there - all just hearsay. If you read the web posts, many of them talk about the Stag night being held in "honour" of the groom or "stag". "Honour?" no way man; all your mates want to do is inflict as much pain and humiliation that they can think of and that's the real truth.

Anyway, we were expected to take part in a "stag" and "hen" night; it *had* to be done as our friends kept telling us so we just went along with it. We actually decided to arrange the stag and hen on the same night; we had many 'mutual' friends so it seemed to make sense to do it this way. Our friends drove from all over the UK to Slough and we'd hired a mini bus, well more of a mini coach actually, to take us into London. Once there, the lads would go one way whilst the girls would go the other and we'd meet up at the end of the night... we hoped.

The girls had an adrenalin fuelled party at Salsa clubs in the West End and were definitely helped along the way with lots of alcohol. The guys on the other hand went into a 'normal' club in Leicester Square where there was also lots of drinking and banter. The night went so quickly that before those heavily intoxicated were stumbling back to our meeting point to get back onto the bus for the journey back to Slough.

The journey into London was a rowdy affair as everyone was all geared up for a good night out. On the way back everyone was unusually quiet; probably because of the alcohol and everyone just wanted to sleep. There was one person, the one they call Bob, who had other ideas. All the way back, he just harassed us all, waking us up when we were asleep, asking us daft questions and generally just being very annoying! For Bob, this was normal and in fact quite expected but it really pissed everyone else off. I then found out that Sunita had a bit of an incident at one of the clubs - she fell or something but hurt her ankle. I don't think it hurt that much at the time but it swelled up and she was a little worried that it might not get better before the wedding day!

As the mini bus arrived back in Slough, Bob really turned on the pressure; I was tired, had a headache and just wanted to get to bed. I didn't care about anyone else and headed off to sleep making sure I locked the door firmly behind me. As I got into bed I could hear lots of commotion downstairs and I knew that Bob was at the centre of it. For a few seconds I could smell something nasty in my room but I was so tired I must have dozed off. The next morning, or later that morning I should say, the smell was back and this time was really pungent. As time went on, the smell got stronger and stronger but I was too tired to care so I turned over to get more sleep. As I did this, the stink smelt as if it was coming from my pillow. I jumped out of bed so fast that i'm surprised I didn't pull a muscle and then proceed to life the pillow up - there was dog food under my pillow – that certainly explained the smell and guess who put it there? Yup, our man Bob - who else could it be?

I couldn't sleep after that and slowly headed downstairs not knowing what i'd find. As I walked into the lounge, the room looked like a camping site; our friends were sleeping all over the place, there were bits of clothing and shoes scattered all over the room but then I noticed something looking very white outside the house. It was Hemal's Datsun Sunny which had suffered at the hands of our Bob. It was covered with what looked like fresh cream and Hemal didn't even know about it but believe me it was a right mess. For the next hour or so, all those sleeping down stairs were all whinging about Bob and all the annoying things he did whilst the rest of them were trying to sleep. Bob - all I can say is that sooner or later, all those things you did will come back to haunt you! By midday everyone was up, cleaned up and ready to make their way home. Mind you, Hemal had a few words to say to Bob about his car and once the cream was wiped off, he was ready to head home too. It was a good hen / stag and the only real victim was Sunita who had hurt her ankle. Mind you, the dog smell lingered in my room for days so thanks Bob!

Prior to the wedding, both Sunita & I had taken a few days off to help out and finish off the last minute preparations. For me, there wasn't awful lot to do and for several days I really felt the wedding nerves. I don't know why, it wasn't as though I was worried about anything but it could have been the simple fact that I was about to take the next big step in life. Rumit, Nee, E2 and the rest of the lads came round when they could and it was good to see them. We would just hang around outside talking and just having a laugh. Meanwhile at Sunita's it was a different atmosphere altogether. They were partying for days before the wedding, her house was full and the alcohol was flowing. Her mum gave her strict orders to relax - Sunita still had her ankle bandaged up from the fall during the hen night!

25

Lagan, Shaadi, "the wedding"

Already tired from pre-wedding nerves, the night before the big day was even worse and I think I got little more than 3 hours sleep. It was about 6am when I got up but my mum was wide awake already (she was always up early and would take time out for her prayers). That morning she said "big day today" - she said it in gujerati and she had a strange kind of smile on her face. I'm sure deep down she was thinking that her youngest 'baby' was no longer a baby and was getting married which for her and most parents was a big deal and I guess an emotional one too. Although I wasn't hungry I made sure I ate something and as the hours ticked by, more and more friends and family arrived and there was a buzz about the place. A few religious ceremonies later and after having the piss taken out of me, I was finally ready to get my wedding gear on and get married. My outfit was a traditional Indian one and was quite expensive; about £300.00 pounds in total and in hindsight I should have hired it instead - it's a lot of money for something i'd wear once.

E2 had arrived now with the wedding car and I was getting worried about the time. The registry was booked for 10am and we were still at home at 9.35 so we had to get a move on. In Indian households, timing is notoriously bad and it was a real effort getting people to get a move on. Lots of people told me "don't worry, it's your wedding, let others worry". Not sure about that statement, we *had* to get there on time because there were many registry weddings that day and you were only allowed so much time to arrive! Finally, we were all set and we drove to the registry

office with the roof down. It was October 18th, 1997, and it was a sunny, warm day (18 degrees to be exact) so we had no complaints about the weather whatsoever. Sunita was arriving via horse and carriage so they left earlier as they were travelling from her parent's house in Wigston, Leicester to the town centre.

Thankfully, we both arrived at virtually the same time and the first thing we both noticed was that our outfits matched - hooray! We all then strolled inside, walked up the stairs and waited outside the registry room. The registrar (or whatever you call those that get you married), called us into a room for our pre-marriage talk which basically involved making sure we were ok, understood what was about to happen and to make sure we hadn't forgotten the wedding rings! Around 10 minutes later and the moment had arrived; Sunita & I were standing at the front with friends and family behind us. The room was quite noisy but as each second passed by, it quietened down and soon the registrar was asking everyone to quieten down. This was it, the time had arrived - my or should I say our lives were about to change. Well, actually they weren't - ok we'd be married but nothing major would change in the short term and all we'd really have is a piece of paper making it all official.

We both confirmed our names and the formal proceedings began. We came to the bit of the wedding where he asks if anyone has any reason why we should not get married. Sunita then looked behind her; first to the left and then to the right looking to see if anyone had objections! The friends and family laughed when they saw this which was good as it took the tension off just a little. With no objections, we continued and first up to repeat the wedding vows was yours truly. The registrar spoke v e r y s l o w l y y y y y y and moved his head around lots in the process. I then repeated one line of the vow in the same way as the registrar - very slowly and moving my head. I didn't think anything of it and I didn't really plan to do it but the guests reacted and laughed out aloud. By now, all my nerves had gone so it was probably good that I did it! Sunita then repeated the vows effortlessly and with a few more lines from the registrar, it was all over. He uttered those words, "I am pleased to announce that you are joined together as husband and wife...." to the rapturous applause of all our guests.

To this day I am still amazed at the whole process of getting married. The registrar says a few words and within minutes you're married - it just seems too simple to be true. Mind you in places like Las Vegas, you can get married in your car via a drive through wedding chapel - shame I didn't know about that earlier as it would have saved lots of time & money!! After the signing of the book, we looked around and the room was empty! Everyone had left the building and were now waiting outside armed with confetti and as we slowly but surely made our way outside and started to walk down the steps we were showered by handfuls of the stuff and it looked wonderful as it blew all over the place; helped along by the breeze.

I don't know what it is about Indians and especially Indian weddings but the mandatory photos can be a real pain sometimes. Whilst the rest of the guests had some time to relax and make their way to the wedding hall / party hall, Sunita & I had to get our photos taken. This usually involved driving to a park and spending an hour or so taking lots of photos in various poses. By the time we got to Castle Park (a photographer's favourite place!), I knew we'd be here for ages. The photographer wasted no time at all and in seconds we were forced to pose here, there, Sunita looking at me, both of us looking at the sky, walking down some steps, poking our heads behind trees and on and on. After a while none of us were really listening to the photographer and we'd sometimes look aimlessly around is - he would then say "looking here please" (meaning look at me!). At the same time, E2 and my sister were standing there amused by it all and all 4 of us were relieved when all the photos were done (well for the time being anyway!).

We couldn't make our way into the wedding hall until they were ready for us so although we arrived there in plenty of time, we were told to drive around for a bit whilst the last minute rush to get the place ready went on. I think the DJ's slowed things down as they got there late and after driving around several times it was getting quite frustrating and we just wanted to get inside. Finally, we were given the green light so we pulled inside the car park and slowly walked towards the entrance. We'd also hired some Indian dhol players (drum like instruments), traditionally used to mark the arrival of the bride/groom/both. As the dhol kicked in, it felt like a wedding and the guests inside knew we had arrived.

We had both invited many of our work colleagues; I know for sure that my colleagues were overwhelmed by the whole occasion and it had only just started. For now, they were enjoying the Indian hospitality to the max! We proceeded slowly inside the venue and all around we saw the great sight of friends and family and it was very daunting. All eyes were on us or it certainly felt that way but Sunita being Sunita could clearly see that some of the wedding plans were not done properly. For one, the champagne glasses were nowhere to be seen and I knew this was bothering her! Nothing we could do about it now; we just had to keep on moving until we finally made our way through the tight entrance and were soon standing behind the table with the wedding cake. The dhol players seem to go for ages but eventually their routine ended and one of the DJ's from Calibar Roadshow welcomed us in.

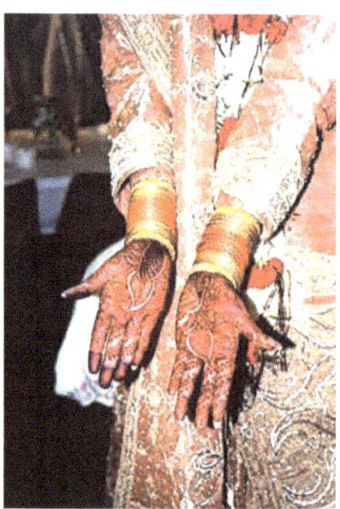

Didn't even wash her hands!

I was handed the bottle of champagne to open and i'm sure someone gave it a little shake before passing it over. As I popped the cork, it went flying in one direction whilst the champagne gushed out in another. Trust me, it *really* flew out and you should have seen how fast the immediate family stepped backwards - the thought of getting it on their clothes was unthinkable! With the champagne out of the way, it was time to cut the cake and with the 5-4-3-2-1 countdown, the cake was cut. I must admit, I do like a bit of cake but with so many people coming up to us and feeding it to us, I was sick of it at the end. We had to endure about 30 minutes of this and the photographer was back too and ready for action. I know it was our wedding day but it's pretty tough smiling whilst being force fed cake after cake!

That's how you open Champagne!   Time for a picture with the boys!

Sharmil, Bob Hemal.

Finally, the cake table was taken away and it was time for our first dance. I'm pretty certain it was Sunita who picked the track - it was Indian track called "Pehla Nasha" and then the real pain started. The thing is you see, nothing prepares you for the first dance, the time when *everyone* @ the wedding has their eyes focused on you and I didn't enjoy a single minute of it. My legs were all over the place and I just felt extremely pressured. Yes, I know, it shouldn't have bothered me at all but it did. As I looked out amongst the crowd there were some faces that were smiling at the sheer joy of seeing us married. Others, Munsha for one, was shouting "move your legs" - thanks mate. In my mind I was thinking "this isn't Club UK you know" - if it was i'd be moving my legs good & proper. I just wanted the first dance to be over and after an agonising 5-6 minutes it was...

As the DJ put on the next record, the dance floor slowly filled up and the party began. We could now start to enjoy ourselves and over the next hour or so, the DJ's mixed it up and created an excellent party atmosphere. Both of us finally had a chance to mingle and chat with friends and family. My work colleagues were really shocked by the whole occasion; they never expected it to be such a loud and colourful affair and the free alcohol was a real bonus for them too. The one thing about weddings, especially Indian ones, is that there's always a bunch of people who you've never met in your lives. The only reason they were there is that at some point they knew our parents and that was enough to get them an invite.

Anyway, as the crowd partied on, the alcohol was starting to take effect on the guests. Those that would refuse to dance whilst sober would be heading straight for the dance floor and nothing would stop them. Soon, the hands were in the air, people were on each other's shoulders (a common thing!!) and the atmosphere changed from a wedding to a real gig type atmosphere. It was actually a good thing that we decided to book some other entertainment too - we actually hired traditional bhangra dancers. Dressed in traditional outfits, the dancers got the crowd's attention but the party piece was something else. One of the dancers pulled out a long, sharp knife - well it was more of a sword and the one of the dancers announced over the mic that kids and young children should stand back and that parents must ensure they stay back.

As the dhol player (an Indian 'dhol' is a double barrel shaped drum played with a stick at each end) started his routine, the sword man stepped up and started swinging it around. At first it was a slow swing but as the dhol player stepped up the pace, the sword swung faster and faster and at one point swung so high that it actually shaved a bit off the ceiling files to the amusement of the crowd. On seeing this you could understand why he asked kids and younger guests to step back; failing to do so could have easily chopped off someone's ears! Whilst all this was happening, E2 was stone sober; he was driving the wedding car after all but my other friends (Rumit, Hemal, Bob, Sharmil etc.) were getting really pissed. Nee was obviously there too but I don't remember him having lots to drink - I think he was too full up from all the food. Meanwhile Rumit was having the time of his life; as he walked around the wedding hall, he kept getting stopped in his tracks and kept getting shots of Dimple whisky shoved into his hand.

One thing I have to say about Rumit is that when he's in the mood to drink then he can *really* drink and he was in the mood that day. He was so happy that he even started to drag me back onto the dance floor - something he'd never done before. One magical moment on the dance floor was watching Rumit dancing around and then bumping into Sunita's mum ("mum"); the look on her face was priceless. She gave one of those really dirty "what are you doing?" type of looks whilst Rumit continued to party on without realising what happened. No one noticed this at the wedding but we only saw it when we watched the wedding video and Rumit could hardly look at the screen when we kept on rewinding it!

Once Rumit gets merry, there is usually no stopping him but the drinks that everyone was giving him (& the ones he drank himself!) eventually took their toll. One minute he was there and the next he was gone. He was actually outside being extremely sick against a wall where Hemal, Bob and a few others were with him. There wasn't much I could do about it and the lads had to escort him back to a local hotel where he slept it off. A few hours later, the lads tried to phone him but it was no use; there was no way he was picking up his phone in that state... To this day, whenever all the lads get together and talk about weddings, Rumit and his drunken state always brings a smile to our face...

As WE All Know - We are here to celebrate the wedding of two people who are both so dear to us all.

Never before in all of these years that I have known both Sandip + Sunita would I have guessed we would be here celebrating one of the most happiest days of there lifes.

Sandip + Sunita are not only my close friends but also part of my family. Having lived with them for many a year I've got to say that Sandip has chosen the wrong profession as a software engineer he should have been a full time chef Mondays + Fridays evenings will never be the same.

As for our Sunita she should have been a popstar as her singing is out of this world. I am sure she will be more than happy to give us all a demonstration if we wish.

Anyway on a more serious note, Priya + I would personally like to wish them both the very best for the future + hope they have a lifetime of love, peace + happiness as two other people deserve it more.

On That Note Please Raise A Glass To The Lovely Couple.

Above – a copy of the original wedding speech that never happened!

26

West side & our honeymoon

Having been to the USA a year earlier and absolutely loving it, I selfishly decided to head way out west yet again for a trip to New York and then onto Niagara Falls for our week long honeymoon. Just under 7 hours after take-off, we were in New York City or NYC and heading downtown to check into the Howard Johnson hotel on 34th Street. The location couldn't have been better; Madison *Scare* Gardens was around the corner (it was close to Halloween so they decided to rename it for a short while!), if you looked up into the NYC skyline, the Empire State Building was right in front of us whilst Times Square was a mere 2 minute walk away. The buzz was amazing and I knew the location was a good choice. Ok, we may not have ended up on a beach but come on man, we were in New York City!

During our stay, we ticked off the main things to do including a shopping trip to Macy's which really does overwhelm you due to its sheer size. Next up was the Empire State Building which provides amazing views from the top. You get a superb 360 view of NYC and the surrounding areas and it's really worth spending an hour or so up there. Heading towards the financial district we walked through Wall Street and then got into the super-fast lifts of the World Trade Centre. The view from the Empire State building was pretty amazing but the view from the top of the WTC was something else. It was taller than the Empire State building (ok, officially 100 feet taller!) and the views out across the Hudson, Jersey and looking back towards Empire State were truly breath-taking.

To this day I cannot believe that the twin towers are sadly gone now and I am still amazed at the engineering feat of building such huge buildings. You are so high up that commuter planes whizz by underneath you which gives you an indication of how high you really are. One of the highlights of NYC was boarding the Liberty Island Ferry that takes you to the Statue of Liberty; without doubt one of the most famous landmarks of this great city. For me personally, the statue was unbelievably smaller than I expected. When you see it on holiday programmes or the news, it looks very tall but compared to New York "everything's big", this is quite small! Nevertheless, the ferry ride is the best way of getting superb pictures of this statue with Manhattan in the background. Once there you can actually walk into and climb up the statue but we gave this a miss, opting instead to sit down and watch the stunning views...

Bronx anyone?

Street level, World Trade Centre.

Top of the World Trade Centre

On board the Liberty Island Ferry.

Our remaining time in this city was spent walking around Chinatown, the markets and along 5th Avenue and just enjoying the hustle and bustle. Sunita loves "people watching" whilst I like record buying. One afternoon, she did her thing whilst I found a record shop (oh yes!) just around the corner and soon found loads of rare records I struggled to find in the UK. For me and my love of music it was quite a surreal moment; I was listening to music on Technics SL1200 turntables in New York City inside a record shop in Time Square. The atmosphere, the vibe or whatever you want to call it was something i've never experienced to this day and i'm pretty certain I never will again.

There's something very special about this city and you really do need to go there to understand why so many people bang on about it. Niagara Falls was our next destination and I had pre-booked our tickets on the Amtrak "Empire" service that would whisk us from New York's Penn Station through Albany, Syracuse, Rochester, Buffalo and then Niagara. The Amtrak trains are huge, very comfortable and quiet and although it was a 7 hour journey, we arrived at Niagara raring to go. We actually got off the Amtrak on the American side of Niagara (it actually spans America and Canada).

The first thing we had to get sorted was our accommodation; I can't remember where we stayed but as soon as the lady in reception saw the mehndi on Sunita's hands (mehndi is henna based temporary dye that is used to decorate hands and feet typically during an Indian wedding - not permanent), she asked if we were newlyweds and when we said yes, she upgraded our room and we ended up having one with a Jacuzzi - result! The hotel (I think it was actually a Ramada), was only a few minutes' walk from the falls themselves and outside the hotel you can clearly see the water vapour rising into the air.

With our luggage quickly dumped in our room, it was time to explore and as you get closer to the falls you can hear the sounds of the water falling into the vast basin below. As mentioned earlier, the falls can be viewed on both the American and the Canadian sides and the only thing that separates the 2 countries is a large bridge. This photo was taken from the American side; Sunita and myself are still debating which one of us took the picture below as i'm sure you'll agree - it's pretty well taken!

Niagara Falls (USA / Canada)

If you want to get up close and personal, the best place to be is definitely the Canadian side and it's quite strange strolling over the bridge. You get stopped by customs who then ask for your passport, stamp it and you walk off the bridge and into Canada! As you walk deeper into the Canadian side you can get really close to the Horse Shoe Falls where the real force and power of these falls can be seen - the volume of water is incredible but if ever you go there be prepared to get wet! For the ultimate experience, hop onto the 'The Maid Of The Mist', a boat trip which takes you quite close to falls where a poncho is optional but recommended and getting wet is guaranteed - check out the picture...

The 'Journey behind the falls' trip is also a great thing to do; you really do get a completely different view of the falls but don't bother if you're not prepared to get wet. You are guided behind the falls where you can look up and see millions of gallons of water crashing over the side. The sheer volume of the water and the spray it emits makes it really difficult to see properly but for a real adrenaline rush this is something you really should do if you're ever out there.

Having completed a guided tour of the area and our eye opening visit to Hard Rock under our belt, it was back onto the Amtrak for our return journey to New York where we'd catch our

Shower anyone?

flight back to the UK. Although our honeymoon only lasted a week, we made full use of the time. For me, the 2nd trip to the USA was wicked and for Sunita, well she simply loved it. E2 picked us up from Heathrow and 20 minutes later we were back in Slough. I remember thinking "great", a few hours ago we were in New York and now we're in Slough; what a reality check.

Both Sunita & I were back to the work on the Monday so that really was our wedding and honeymoon over and done with. At work my work colleagues who had been guests at our wedding were still really over the moon at being invited and were really humbled by it all! Life as we knew it just seemed to carry on and work became a routine task as it was before. The photos and video of the wedding arrived a few weeks later and it was quite strange reliving it all again. As we'd done many times before, Sunita, E2 & myself sat there in Slough watching it, laughing, taking the piss and eating lots of cheddar biscuits...

27

My new family

When you get married things generally change; you may live somewhere else, may start a new career and so on but one of the biggest changes is that suddenly you have a whole new family and you have to do your damn best to 'fit in'. For me the transition to becoming the brother and son in law was low key – I felt as though I just fitted in and it helped that I knew Rita for many years before that too. It is difficult to put into words the impact that family has had on me; they have always treated and welcomed me in a way I would never have expected and it is extremely humbling (either that or they needed someone to fix their computers!).

Location: India.

My "father in law", "dad" or "Mr. Leta" to his business partners is a real character; always smiling, always happy to see you, always telling you stories and always ready for a barbeque. He works hard and enjoys the fruits of his labour. It might be a pun but trust me he has the fruit trees in the garden to prove it! A Libran like myself I think we share many traits and have the same views on my issues but if someone were to ask me what makes me smile the most when I think of him... it must be his one liners or should I say his "take" on well-known sayings or items. To give you some examples: -

"I'm feeling on top of the world" (Dad days "I'm feeling on top of the moon")

"Bits and bobs" (Dad says "bobbing and bitting")

"I need some WD40" (Dad says "I need some DW40")

My mother in law or "mum" is simply one in a million; she may be retired on paper but her day to day life is anything but retired. She is busy, busy, busy all day long and is the string that keeps the family tied together. Always smiling, always wanting to feed me, always grateful for any help I give, I couldn't have asked for a better "mum 2" – and I can chat with her on WhatsApp – result!

Location: @ mum / dad house, Leicester.

Location: Sumo, Leicester.

Rita or "Aussie Rita" as she is stored in my phone is a laugh a minute. Often thinking one thing but saying another we're always laughing when she's around and she's been the same in all the years I've known her and it's been *many* years I can tell you! She's more like a best mate than a sister in law and I wouldn't have it any other way!

Isn't that right our kid?

Let's face it, Max can talk and I mean *really* talk. If someone brings up a topic that he is interested in then you're finished and you may as well say goodbye to the rest of the day...

What I want to know is..."Who broke my spade?"

Location: Unknown (most likely Hervey Bay, Australia).

She can transform a drab face into a head turning glamorous look in minutes and at the same time cook up a delicious feast with her culinary skills – trust me; this girl has some serious talent. Jasmin, the first born amongst the grandchildren is finding her forte in life and until she does, we're all enjoying the chocolate cakes!

Location: @ mum / dad house, Leicester.

We really need to go, we only have -3, 0, 4, 2, 1, 9 minutes before the show starts. Sorry – I was "acting" like Surita so *"get lost mate"*. Surita, definitely a girl who knows what she wants and will get it no matter who stands in her way is a crazy, mad and funny street dancer who likes spilling drinks on people just for the sake of it so be careful.

Location: Meridian, Leicester.

Location: Burrum Heads, Hervey Bay, Australia.

Raj / Ravi / Brejrin or whatever they decide to call each other; these 2 guys know how to work hard and play even harder. Ever since I've known them they have the ability (with their piss taking of each other) to liven up a room in seconds as witnessed by myself @ many weddings. Ravi, always on the receiving end of Raj's pranks is the quieter one; the one that likes to chill and take things at a nice, easy pace. All I can say is that i'm glad to be part of their family – definitely 'good guys' and let me tell you one thing; I don't say that about many people.

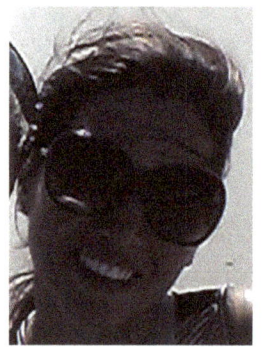

Sarita, the Indian wife transported from India to the East coast of Australia should be given a medal for coping day to day with Mr Good Guy Raj!

She's got a super sense of humour and juggles 3 kids, a husband, a business and hectic home life so she's definitely the good girl to the good guy!

Location: Woodgate, Hervey Bay, Australia.

Full of life, this crazy girl *loves* headbands and as you can see from this picture is always up to no good! She's no good at staring competitions though (I beat her every time – remember? December 2016!)

Location: Esplanade, Hervey Bay, Australia.

On the face of it Amar is a quiet boy but once you get to know him he is a fun cheeky little kid who loves his cars, Lego and drawing funny pictures. I had a super time meeting him for the first time and the cries of "Frank" make me smile to this day!

Location: Raj/Sarita crib, Hervey Bay, Australia.

Location: Raj whip, Hervey Bay, Australia.

The cheeky smile says it all – "Kiwi" has to be watched at all times. One minute he's here and the next he's gone...you *really* do have to be on your guard when he's around. He has no fear whatsoever and is a real aussie' - oh and whether you're a man or woman watch it down there – this kid goes for the parts that no other would dare!

Location: Piccadilly Circus, London.

Just like Sarita, Nisha flew over from India to start a life down under. Little did Ravi know that several years later, he would be *down under* his own car after a very bizarre accident but let's not talk about that!

On a recent trip to the UK she mastered the "shot" and was stalked by a clown!

This little bundle of joy is heaps of fun but cross him and they'll be trouble. A big fan of Thomas he knows what he wants (whether that's dad, Nana or all of them!)

Location: Ravi/Nisha crib, Maryborough, Australia.

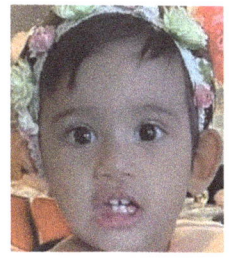

Niah is an energetic little girl who is not one for sitting still. You really have to keep your eyes on her! One minute she's here and the next she's gone. Ravi and Nisha have got their hands full with her!

Location: Maryborough, Australia.

351

28

My mate Sunita

"You're such an idiot" / "you're so stupid" - just a few loving things my wife Sunita says to me when I wind her up or throw her one of my super sarcastic lines. As I sit here writing this, she's sitting across the room from me watching EastEnders. The end of a long hard day and it's her time to chill out. I did ask if she wanted a cuppa but as I glanced towards the table close to her, the large glass says it all - her Tia Maria and Coke confirms she's had a hard day. A true Virgo at heart, Sunita definitely matches the characteristics of her star sign and I think that our journey to where we are now has lasted because of one thing and one thing only - we *talk to each other*. Perhaps this sounds bizarre but what I mean is talk, really talk. We can and do discuss everything and there are no secrets between us. Good job really because she is probably one of the world's lousiest "secret keepers" but jokes aside (yes, I can be serious you know!), I really do believe this is the reason we're still together whilst others aren't.

I've never understood whilst those in relationships keep things from each other and worse still, if you're serious about each other and can see a long term relationship then there shouldn't be any secrets at all. Trust me, i've seen, heard and witnessed marriages breaking up all around me to know that the "no secrets" approach works. In life, most people have a certain breaking point where their calm and cool exterior breaks and the volcano building up inside them finally erupts. I certainly have a very short fuse but one thing that is truly remarkable about her is that *nothing* seems to phase her at all. She doesn't angry, it takes a mammoth effort to get her annoyed whilst amidst total chaos she remains totally calm. Unfortunately for her, she has to contend with my ranting and raving and i'll be the first to admit that I can be extremely annoying but despite my moods, despite those moments where I don't want to speak to anyone and many other things that i'm sure she'd like to change about me, she never gets drawn into an argument.

Arguments are a strange thing in our lives. We just don't seem to have them however bizarre that may sound. Sure, we have disagreements; I mean I often get pissed off when she insists on putting the kitchen light on at the height of summer at 2pm in the afternoon when the whole kitchen is already brilliantly lit up by our closest star the Sun, but i'm used to it now and my efforts to "save our planet" just seem to fall on deaf ears. To her credit, even if it looked as if something might escalate into an argument she'd just diffuse it straight away. "Sunita", made up of the Sanskrit words "Su" meaning "good" and "nita" meaning "well conducted", is quite simply my "best mate". She's always there for me, always listens, puts up with my endless stubborn moments, will *never* say no to making me a sandwich at any time of the day and quite simply is the best thing that has ever happened to me. Cringe at the words i've written or laugh out loud, it's the truth, the whole truth and nothing but the truth - you get me?

Within a matter of months, 1997 was no more and as we entered 1998 Sunita and I had to seriously consider what we wanted to do in terms of where to live. At the same time, E2 who was now in a different relationship, was also considering a move out of Slough. One thing we did agree on was to leave the rented house in Slough during September which meant we had around 8 months to plan ahead. I definitely didn't want to live in Slough, we couldn't afford a place in Windsor and anywhere else was simply too far. Deep down, I always wanted to move back to Leicester and Sunita actually wanted the same too. Despite that we started to look at properties in the surrounding areas but the prices were simply out of our range and you didn't really get that much house for your money anyway.

Pravin has his hands full!

Valentine's day was fast approaching and I decided to surprise Sunita again with another trip away. A few trips to the travel agent and it was all sorted; we'd be flying to Rome for the weekend. I was hoping I could keep it a secret from her and thankfully, with the help of E2, I did. Early in the morning, I woke Sunita up and told her to get ready. Still not quite with it and half asleep, she didn't know what was going on and thought I was pulling her leg. I wasn't, I was pulling both as I tried to get her out of bed. Thankfully, 15 minutes and a barrage of questions later she seemed to be with it and quickly got her stuff together.

E2, who was by now our airport chauffer service, dropped us off to Heathrow and off we went. We arrived with glorious sun beating down on us and the forecast was for great weather all weekend; definitely a good start. Our hotel was in a great spot, the Coliseum was only a 5 minute walk away and as we got out our Rome guide, it was clear that we could actually walk around the city as most of the famous areas were pretty close to each other.

Whenever we go away, one thing we always do is walk or use the local public transport to get around - you really do get a better "feel" of local customs and the experience is simpler richer this way. Vatican City and in particular the sheer expanse of it, is awesome and it was really weird seeing a real confession booth for the first time. Sunita stepped into the confession booth and didn't surface for a *very* long time - quite worrying really! That evening we went for an authentic Italian meal where the singers and musicians were out in force. As they worked their way around the restaurant they finally came to us and the double act started their show. One of the guys started playing a banjo or something and kind of pretended to sing to Sunita. The other one looked at me in a "give us your money style" which I really didn't like but hey "when in Rome" and all that so I gave this stranger and his accomplice (who was crap by the way) some Italian Lira and off they went. Over the next day and a half we walked around the old Roman ruins scattered around the city, visited the Trevise Fountain and mingled with the locals @ the Spanish Steps.

Having just flown back to the UK from Rome, I left my travel bag out because 2 weeks later I would be flying out to Boston, USA for a business trip. Many people in the UK development team at Parametric Technology had flown out there to work with the other developers and now it was my turn. On the morning of my flight I was picked up in a top of the range Mercedes and chauffeured to the airport by an extremely posh speaking man. The way he spoke, the way he dressed and his stature was something else and I think he got a shock when he picked me up. I came out of the house dressed in my Nike trainers, my jogging bottoms and my Adidas top and he was probably thinking I should be travelling to HMP rather than the USA!

The object of the trip was simple, get out there and share software testing ideas, discuss how we can improve things and come back armed with great ideas. I arrived there late at night to a horrendous thunderstorm. I picked up my little hire car and somehow navigated out the airport and into the city but I was struggling big time. Due to the ever increasing volume of traffic, the Boston roads were clogged up with so many cars, trucks and vans that the local's daily commute was a very slow affair. Deciding drastic action needed to be taken; the local authorities planned the "Big Dig" which was a mammoth re-routing of traffic around the city. Basically, they were digging up a route around the entire city - a sort of Boston M25 and to date it has been the most expensive highway project in the US (or so Wikipedia tells me!) Anyway, there were diversions that went nowhere, locals who couldn't give me directions, I didn't have GPS navigation and the heavy rain kept on pouring down. Nevertheless, I persevered and after 50 minutes arrived at my hotel extremely tired and ready for bed.

I was only in Boston for about 7 days and it was good to put faces to names. The meetings I had were very constructive but the guys out there were far too formal for my liking. I felt you couldn't have a laugh with them but over the next few days, the Patel charm and comical nature came out for all to see and the whole mood changed totally. After discussing team objectives, ideas and how to make things better, we would spend the next 2 hour talking about fast cars, what we were doing that evening and why Americans were so fat. I'm not quite sure how we got onto that topic but it was self-explanatory - you eat too much - see quite simple isn't it. In the PTC canteen, the staff sat around stuffing themselves with steak, pasta, chips (I mean fries!) and washing it down with litres of coke. Most of them had trouble sitting down, getting up and their trouser belts were close to bursting. My plate and its contents looked miniscule in comparison and many asked me "You not hungry?", "You not eating?"

In my spare time, I strolled around the city, chilled at the Boston Red Socks football stadium, browsed around Quincy Market and visited the famous Aquarium by the docks. I really liked this city and when I got back to the UK learned that the US team really liked me too. In fact I was offered a full time job in Boston where they would pay for a flat and provide me with a car. I couldn't believe it and living in a different country was something i'd wanted to for years. Excited from the offer, I rushed home and asked Sunita what she thought of the idea. Unfortunately, she wasn't up for it because she didn't want to be 7 hours away from her family so sadly I declined the job offer. Looking back it was a real opportunity and I sometimes wonder what would have happened had I taken that role but never mind...

29

Not losing the plot? Plot 169

With no more international travel planned in the next few months, the focus for Sunita and myself had to be where we were going to live. We knew we had to get out of Slough but the houses we'd seen were just crap and / or too expensive. We weren't making any headway and it was getting quite frustrating. Nevertheless, life continued as usual and during another visit to Leicester we were at my sister's house when she mentioned there were some new houses being built close by. Although both of us would have liked to move back to Leicester, it wasn't practical because we were settled in our jobs and none of us even considered a move back. The houses being built were literally around the corner so we thought we'd go and have a look anyway but as we turned into the new estate, (or "Blackthorn Manor") as it was officially known, we fell in love with what we saw. The whole area was different to other "estates"; this one was spacious, the houses weren't crammed together and there was a really homely feel to them. Fair enough, this was just the outside view but when we stepped into both the show homes, we just as impressed. The decor, the layout and everything about them made us want to buy there and then but hold on, we only came here to look right?

We stepped out the house and into the sales office where we picked up some brochures, prices and had a general chat with the advisor. As we slowly walked towards the car, none of us said much but in our minds our thoughts were for one thing only - moving back to Leicester. I'm not certain but I think it was me that thought "sod this, let's move back". So, I asked Sunita what she thought about the house - daft question really and at that precise moment in time, our minds were made up. We had seen 2 houses, but the one we could afford or thought we could afford was £96,000 and surprisingly we only had to put down £250 deposit in order for them to secure the house for 4 weeks whilst we arranged the mortgage. Almost £100,000 was a lot of money for a house even if was in Oadby, as many people would tell me later. The cost of the house obviously mattered but we couldn't think of living anywhere. We carefully scrutinised the plots and with the advisor, worked out which house would be built next and where the house was physically positioned. The house we were after was a "Bromley" and built by Bryant Homes - a 3 bed detached house on a corner plot. There were many other Bromley's we could have picked but I wanted one with a corner plot and where the garage was attached to the house (thinking for the future and possible extension...)

There was no point messing around; the deposit was paid, the paperwork was signed and Plot 169 was ours. The reality of what we'd done soon sank in - we had just committed to buy a house for almost £100,000 in Leicester when we both worked down South. It meant getting a mortgage when we were both about to resign and hence would be back to Leicester without jobs.

Scared, apprehensive, worried - we felt all of these but there was no going back now. As for the house, well there wasn't much of it really - when we saw it close up for the first time, the foundation and part of the surrounding walls had been constructed but we did manage to customise it to our own tastes as it was being built. It would be ready at the end of September 1998 and there was lots to do in the meantime.

We told very few people about the house; in fact I don't think we told anyone. The main reason for this was we hadn't sorted out a mortgage so the sale could still fall through. The first thing we did was to get a letter from our employees that stated our current salary and that we were in full time employment. This was a risky game because surely the mortgage team would question why we work in the south but were buying a house in Leicester? With the letters sorted out, we applied for a mortgage through Yorkshire Bank; our primary choice of lender simply because they were the only ones that offered "flexible" mortgages. This new type of mortgage would give us the flexibility of increasing or decreasing the payments with no penalty and we'd also reduce the amount of interest we would pay considerably. I had never heard of such mortgages and it was Pravin that made me aware of it so thanks Pravin.

Both of us were quite surprised when the bank approved the mortgage but I think a big factor in their decision was that we were putting down a big deposit so we were probably classified as a "safe bet". Despite the down payment, we still had to borrow a decent amount of money and during this whole period, my mind often wondered into the past back to the day when I got home to 79 Mere Road to find our house has been repossessed. I was adamant that history would not repeat itself and together with Sunita focused on ensuring we could comfortably afford the repayments. With finances in place, the final signatures were completed at the solicitors and the house was ours but there was still several months before it would be finished and there were lots of loose ends to tie up for both of us...

Now that the house was officially ours, we told our friends and family and when we were in Leicester for our regular weekend visits, would take them to the construction site and point at the house. It was well exciting watching the house getting built but many friends and family commented on how expensive the house was. Yes, it was expensive relative to other similar houses but, our house was in a good area in a leafy suburb where prices were noticeably higher anyway. One thing I definitely learned as I got older was that people will always tell you that you did this wrong or you paid too much for that. Everyone thinks their experts at everything so you've just got to do what's right and trust your instincts as they are usually right.

July 1998.   July 1998.

September 1998.   October 1998.

A little Priyanka came to visit!

30

The resignation
& the last evening...

Nee & Rumit were very pleased to hear we were moving back to Leicester whilst E2 had a feeling all along that we would eventually move back. Now that we'd made the decision to head home, we let our landlord know that we were moving out. E2 made the decision to leave the house around a month before us but the bit I wasn't looking forward to was resigning from Parametric Technology. As the weeks rapidly passed, our house was nearing completion and we both had to give in our notice. I remember writing my resignation letter vividly because it took me 4 attempts to put together a simple paragraph.

It was quite strange; I simply didn't want to resign because working for this PTC was one of the most memorable experiences of my life. This may sound odd, but for me, this wasn't just a job; it was my *first* job, the company who gave me my first chance, my first real break and the company that allowed me to learn, develop and excel at my work. I had earned lots of money in a short time, they let me travel and gave me the freedom to make the difference. How on earth could I consider leaving? Well, there was no going back now and as I walked into PTC that Tuesday morning on a warm summers day in August 1998 I felt just as nervous as I was almost 4 years previous when I walked through the doors for my interview.

A few minutes after Paul, my manager walked in, I knocked on his office door, stepped in and handed over the letter. He then read my letter and asked if there was anything they could do to keep me there. They offered more money but money didn't come into it; it was family and being back in Leicester that swung the decision. From what I could tell, he seemed genuinely saddened by the news that I was leaving but understood the decision. As I stepped back into my office, I remember staring out my huge window and looking onto the M3 motorway but my quiet thoughts were interrupted as all my work colleagues came in one by one as they heard the news and wanted to hear all about our move.

At roughly the same time, Sunita resigned from "A Plus" where she had been working for several years so that was that and it wasn't long before the weeks creeped up on us and E2 was about to move out. The night before he moved out, we all sat in our usual positions in the lounge of our rented Slough house. It could have been any other day but that evening I went through many emotions which to be honest I probably won't be able to put into words. From High Wycombe to Windsor and then onto Slough, the 3 of us had been through lots of things whilst living together. The fun we had was insurmountable, the tears of laughter unforgettable and the friendship unbelievable but this *was* our last evening together and it was another sad moment. As we had done countless times before we had a right laugh that evening and talked about all the things we'd done together over the last few years. As the clock pushed past midnight, it was time to get some sleep and with that we all headed for bed - *can the last one switch off the lights please?*

The next morning, E2 walked out of the door for the last time; starting his own journey for his next step in life. For Sunita and I it was back to work for the final few weeks. At work, my workload gradually slowed down as they didn't want me to start on projects that i'd never finish. One of the best times at work was Fridays; not because it was the end of the week but rather that on Friday lunchtimes, we would walk to the pub for a slap up lunch. Just getting there and back took an hour in total so the whole lunch took well over 2 hours. There was no point in rushing around so as not to piss off the boss - he was with us so no excuses required!

We would order the food, get a round of drinks in and sit outside talking about everything from plants to the asteroid belt (honest!). After a while everyone seemed to forget we were meant to be at work until Paul would eventually say "well, I think we'd better get back now". If it wasn't for the fact that we supported the USA team over in Boston and the fact that they would be coming "on-line" soon, we'd probably end up in the pub all afternoon...

Over the next few weeks our home routine was the same. We'd get home from work and then spend time packing up bits that we were taking with us and to be honest there wasn't that much to pack up anyway. The most time consuming part for me was trying to get all my vinyl records off the floor and into strong bags. Paresh and Munsha popped around several times during this time and we would all sit there reminiscing on the clubbing days and the memorable moments we all shared together. Soon, the day arrived; the day we'd leave Slough, the day we'd leave our jobs and the day we'd be moving into our new house.

As I drove to PTC for the last time that morning, i'd already decided that today was going to be slightly different and parked my Cavalier in the reserved section that was allotted to the Sales team. I couldn't understand why this team had dedicated parking slots but I didn't care. For that one day, they would have to park their TVR's next to my car and just live with it. As I did every morning, I dumped my coat onto the seat in my office and headed for the kitchen where I made a huge mug of tea and helped myself to the biscuits on offer - it would be rude not to...

I did very little work that day as most of my colleagues spent lots of time talking more and more about the move and our plans. They were still shocked that we had no jobs to go to whilst for now I was just trying not to think about it. It was Thursday 24th September 1998 and for lunch we headed to a different pub out in the countryside. As we made our way there, the sun shone and we had a fun filled lunchtime; we had so much fun that 3 hours passed by without anyone realising! Even by our standards, this was a *long* lunch but my boss didn't care so that was that. Part way through our lunch I was handed a small package which consisted of a huge leaving card and a set of John Lewis vouchers which would be very handy indeed.

That afternoon I spent a few hours handing back stuff to PTC and discussing the projects I was working on so that others could take over. I backed up anything from my Silicon Graphics workstation, sent a final "thank you & farewell" email, signed off as "**skp@ptc.com**" and said good bye to the countless others working at PTC in various departments from HR to finance, support to Sales. As I walked into Sales, the place erupted into cheers; mainly because I had the audacity to park in "their" car park when no others would dare!

It was now time to go so with a deep breath I said my final goodbyes to my team. It was a horrible thing to do, I didn't want to say good bye and I still didn't want to leave. I spent considerable time with my manager who thanked me for the impact I had made on PTC and conversely I thanked him for all the support he had given me over the years. As I walked along the corridor, the entire development team stood there still saying their goodbyes, shouting obscenities (all in good taste), cheering and jeering! With one last wave from me, I turned towards the reception, said goodbye to Caroline on the front desk who gave me a big hug and a kiss and bid me farewell. At that moment in time, my eyes filled with tears and I had this feeling in my stomach that I had *never* felt before. I was leaving PTC and I just couldn't stop the tears flowing.

Ok, so you might be thinking "what an idiot - it's just a job right?" but no, this wasn't just a job but I wouldn't expect anyone else to understand anyway. I pushed the rotating doors for the last time and walked down the steps to the car park where the sales guys were standing getting their nicotine fix. Rather than have them question why I looked as if i'd been crying, I said "terrible hay fever today" and walked past them. As I looked towards my car, I started to laugh; my car was parked in between countless TVR Cerberas and Chimeras which gleamed in the sunlight. For one day only, their cars took the back stage whilst mine got the most attention! I started the car and revved it hard to the amusement of the sales guys and with that drove out of PTC for the last time; an era had well and truly ended...

That evening, the final bits of packing were done and the following morning all our stuff was loaded into the cars and we drove back to Leicester. As we turned left into Whitebeam Road, we passed huge 4/5 bedroom houses and as we drove down to the bottom parked outside our new house - 12 Whitebeam Road. Although we'd seen our house many times and at different levels of construction, it was so special looking at our *own* house even though it was for now at least directly opposite a noisy construction office and the whole area was covered in slushy mud. Before unloading everything, I met the site manager who gave us the keys and took us around the house, handing over all the paperwork at the same time. Inside, the place was immaculate but it looked so bare as there were no curtains, no sofas, no TV, no beds - virtually nothing! The site manager told me that I would find some minor defects which I should make a note of and they would then fix them all. I didn't need to be told that; i'd be doing that regardless of what they said. We'd paid close to £100,000 for the house and I would make sure everything was fixed sharpish.

We followed the site manager around each room and as we did so, I could already see a few things that weren't quite right. 20 minutes later and the inspection was over, we had the keys, the manager closed the door behind him and it was just us. The actual reality of what we had done had sunk in and it was quite scary. We were back home which was what we always wanted but we had to get ourselves sorted with jobs quickly. As we looked out the house and looked at our cars packed with our stuff, our focus changed and we spent the next hour or so unloading the car. Most of the stuff was packed in boxes so it was ok but the heaviest items by far were my records and I was well relieved when they were safely upstairs in the "music room". Not quite sure why the back room got that name - it just seemed right!

Although the house was clean and tidy, the same couldn't be said for the outside area. Our house was among a group of around 12 being built at the bottom of the road and ours was one of the few finished. What that meant was diggers, trucks, fork lifts and other construction vehicles constantly driving up and down the road as they moved supplies from one area to the next. This left the make shift pavements and roads covered in thick mud which would ultimately get into our house unless we used a few basic rules. The rules meant we took our shoes off as soon as we got into our house. We had to put sheets down just to protect the carpets and these sheets stayed there for several months.

With all our stuff unloaded, I plugged in our tv given to us as a wedding present from Rumit, Nee, Bob and the rest of the lads. Unfortunately there was no reception even though it was correctly connected to the aerial socket that was neatly fixed to the lounge wall. Suddenly it dawned on me that I didn't see an aerial on the roof and thinking about it, none of us even considered it at all when we bought the house. I just assumed all new houses came with aerials - I guess they don't! That night was quite boring and uncomfortable - we had makeshift beds on the floor of our bedroom and had to cover the bedroom window with yet more sheets just to blank out the light.

In the first 2 weeks that followed there was some serious house shopping to do and slowly but surely we started to transform the house into a home as we added our own special touches to the decor. We could now watch tv and sleep in a proper bed but we still had the nightly routine of putting up our 'yarn' curtains. Now that the house was slowly getting into shape, we knew the task of job hunting was our priority. Sunita, always keen to get on with things, took the initiative and landed herself a temporary job at the Leicester Space Centre offices in Leicester City Centre. Though it wasn't her ideal job (there isn't many "people watching" vacancies in Leicester...), it gave us an income so that was good.

The Cavalier had a new home!

A young Preeya builds a snowman!

An older Sunita enjoying the snow (classic Austin Maestro in the background!)

As for me, well I had to spruce up my CV so I did this and then registered with a few job agencies. At first I didn't really hear much from them but out of the blue I got a call to say i'd been picked for an interview at TNT at their offices in Atherstone, Leicestershire. It was a real break so dressed in my suit and tie I drove there one cold October morning. The place was huge and I was led through department after department until I walked into an office where 3 interviewers were eagerly awaiting my arrival. I thought I did quite well in the interview but their questions were relentless and quick fired. I don't recall any kind of 'pause' in my reply so I was confident and very optimistic all the way home.

A few days passed and I heard nothing from the agency even though i'd left at least 3 messages for them to call me back with an update. This *pissed* me off because a simple phone call is all it takes to let you have some feedback and / or whether i'd got the job or not. I suspect that the company didn't think I was suitable and must have fed this back to the agency but the agency themselves or their employee was too lazy to give me a courtesy call. I had the last laugh though - several weeks after my interview, the head office of the agency called me. They were doing some kind of survey and wanted my opinion on how I had been treated. I made the most of it and told them that the agency was unprofessional and gave them the employee details of the person who washed their hands of me. I think I even told them that I would never recommend them to anyone and that they were a waste of time. A few days later the agency called and apologised profusely about the way I was treated so I took my chance again and told them what I thought of them - I felt loads better after that!

Though it was quite frustrating not having a job, I was enjoying the time off. You don't realise how much time you spend at work until you're not working and suddenly you have so much time to yourself. I certainly made the most of it - i'd search for jobs in the morning and then get into the car and just loaf around. I'd drive to my sisters, my mums, Car-tronics, head into town and anywhere else I fancied. The one thing I couldn't forget to do was to pick Sunita up. Yes, being out of work meant I did the space centre run, dropping her off and then picking her up and then telling her about my hard day. The weeks flew by and although I wasn't panicking at not having a job, I had done enough loafing around and I needed to find something.

31

The Magnetic Appeal

After the TNT episode, I switched to a different recruitment agency and it wasn't long before I got another interview. The sound of this one was even better; technically it was exactly what I was looking for and it was in Leicester! It was the first week in December, the Christmas explosion was well under way and it was cold. Looking very smart if I say so myself, I arrived at Magnetic North Software very nervous yet excited at the same time. The interview went well - I answered the questions confidently and it was more of an informal chat than an interview. That day I got a call telling me I was put forward for the 2nd interview which was to take place in a few days' time. When I went back for round 2 I was met by Dominic Gray. I didn't know at the time who this person was but as with the first interview, it went *really* well. There was a real flow to the questions and answers and my previous experience at Parametric Technology seemed to add an air of confidence to Dominic.

With the interview over and done with I couldn't do anything except wait for the call and after a few hours it came - I had been offered the job! The feedback from Magnetic North had been excellent and they wanted me to start as soon as possible. I could have started the day after I got the job offer but I thought about it and figured I may as well enjoy the time out so I did. I accepted the position and my starting date was first week in January 1999. The position itself was working for "Magnetic North", a spin off from the main "Checkmate Management" company which meant that I would be the first Magnetic North employee.

In the weeks leading up to Christmas, the UK was suffering from a sickness bug which left 1000's of people off work. In the first week of January 1999 I was very ill and had apparently caught the bug. The night before I was meant to start the new job I was still very ill; being sick, bad headache, shivers, aching bones and on and on. Nevertheless, I was not missing my first day at work - I had to be there no matter what so I went. I arrived there about 15 minutes early and walked into a heavily crowded reception area. As it was the first working day after the Christmas break, all the staff were discussing their festive antics with each other and discussing their new year's resolutions. Not knowing anybody, I kept myself to myself - on another day I would have tried to strike up a conversation but I felt awful, thought I was going to be sick and just wanted to get inside the main building so I could settle down.

Unfortunately, the staff were all huddled together because the security system and the swipe card system failed and wouldn't let anyone through the doors. There was nowhere for the staff to go and in the end, some of the ceiling tiles were removed and one person (Helen Brighton) climbed through, jumped to the other side and did something which allowed us to get access to the rest of the building. Once inside I was led to a small room which would be my office for the foreseeable future. I say "my" office but it wasn't exactly that. There was 8 of us in a room that was only big enough for around 5 employees. I was shown to my desk area and it was quite clear, given the 2 inches of space between myself and a crazy American to my left that working like this would be difficult. Unfortunately, being crammed in like that didn't affect me too much that week because an hour later I was too ill to stay at work. I ended up going home; my grin and bear it attitude wasn't working and I needed to go home. It was a good job I did go home as I was badly sick later that day and I needed rest.

The following week I was virus free and arrived at work ready to make a mark and show the company they'd made the right choice when they hired me. Despite sitting next to an American who spent all day eating and shaking his head left to right, I adjusted to having a small working space and just got on with the job in hand. In comparison, the software applications I would be working with seemed a lot simpler than Pro/Engineer (PTC's application) but it was clear that they *did* need someone to test their software. Within 1 hour of getting my hands on my first testing project I had found and logged 34 software bugs and by the end of the first week, we were into 100+ issues. There's no denying it, I had made a dramatic impact and as the managers ran their software bug reports, they thought the reporting was flawed as they'd never seen such high numbers of bugs! For me, it was great news, I was doing my job and doing it well but for the company, well they just needed to fix all of them as the software couldn't be shipped in this state.

There were several developers here but most of those in the office worked for Checkmate management. The prime software developer for Magnetic North's products was based 100 miles away in Manchester and worked from home. I had spoken to him many times, mainly discussing the software bugs i'd raised but about 6 weeks later I met Nick Gash for the first time. What a meeting it was too - over the phone you can only imagine what a person looks like but when you see them it's totally different. I remember the door to our office opening, closing and hearing Helen say "hi Nick". I remember thinking "aaahh, I can meet Nick now. As I turned to face him, I wasn't prepared for what I saw – he was so tall!. Even the American; still eating and shaking his head thought he was big and we were finally introduced to him. I was expecting him to batter me - I mean i'd logged well over 100 bugs against his software code - something most developers don't like. It didn't faze him though and I think he was quite pleased to see me too, or at least put a name to the face.

Although working at the Space Centre, Sunita also kept her eye out for full time work and it wasn't long before she found a position working as a Human Resources assistant for a big food company. Our worries had vanished now - both of us were working and we could get on with life. Sunita appeared to be enjoying her work which is obviously a good thing and with regular income coming in, we could continue getting stuff for the house. The Blackthorn manor estate where we lived was slowly but surely starting to take shape and the slurries of mud soon stopped as more and more houses were being completed. At the same time, I was on first name terms with the site manager. My "issue list" was handed to them and he arranged for 'remedial work' to be carried out to our house - as i've said before, everyone else may have been happy to put up with a few things wrong with their house, however minor, but I wasn't and soon everything was resolved. In fact, after that I only had to make eye contact with the site manager and he would get worried - he'd immediately assume that I needed to talk to him even if I simply wanted to say hi!

Life outside of work was a mixture of just chilling with friends and family and Sunita and I were extremely pleased we followed our instincts and came back home. At least one day in the week, we'd arrange to meet up with our friends and just go for a drink. Most of these were just casual drinks - one or two and then it was back home. On some nights things were different and a whole night of drinking and partying was planned. Whilst the others were preparing themselves for an alcohol fuelled marathon, I had to pace myself. As a teetotaller, I always found that soft drinks tasted quite nasty after you've had 3-4 and learnt to consume my drinks *very* slowly.

The worst part of the entire night for me was having to "get ready"; I disliked the fact that you had to wear shoes and a shirt to get into the numerous bars and clubs. I just wanted to go in my trainers, jeans and t shirt so I just changed and we all met in town. At first the drinking pace was quite slow but as the night wore on, the pace picked up. Often Rumit would say he didn't want a "heavy" night and often he'd be working the next morning. However, once the Jack Daniels and Coke were flowing he soon got into the mood and after that there was no stopping him. Our nights out were great fun though; I was with Rumit, Nee, Bob,

Hemal, E2, Wongy and of course not forgetting Sunita and sometimes even aussie Rita.

Not to be left behind, Sunita managed to keep up with the boys drinking and as soon as her Tia Maria and coke was almost empty, Rumit made sure another one was on its way! As midnight came and went we would now be in the 5th or 6th bar and trust me the lads were well and truly hammered. Hemal would be making us all laugh, Rumit would be taking the piss out of everyone, Nee would have stopped drinking (he knows exactly when to stop!), Bob would look sober and Sunita would constantly be laughing. In fact, to this day she sometimes gets into fits of laughter for no reason. When you ask her what's so funny, she has no idea which just makes her laugh even more. As for me, I couldn't drink anymore soft drinks and wanted to head home as the hours of standing around left me tired.

It's much different when you're drinking - the time just seems to fly but when you're sober it's a totally different thing. Just when I thought the drinking had stopped, someone would shout Tequila or Aftershock. Soon, a tray would appear from somewhere with tiny 'shot' glasses and everyone was literally forced to take one and shove it down at the same time. The looks on their faces said it all - it looked and probably tasted disgusting but it was the thing to do. That wasn't the end of it either but after the 3rd or 4th shot most of them couldn't drink anymore. By 1 or 2 am, I was ready for bed whilst the others were ready to party on. After finally getting everyone out of the bar and repeatedly saying our good byes it was time to head home.

On one memorable night, Sunita and Rumit were partying hard and I lost count of the number of tequila shots they had. By the time we got out the bar, Sunita was feeling the effects and had to be carried out! It was a real effort getting her into the car and then look after her whilst trying to drive at the same time. Sadly, this wasn't the end of it either; at home the vomiting started and she was so out of it that she couldn't even hold her own head up. Rather than leave her to sleep it off, I chose to sit by her side just in case she was sick again. Thankfully, around 2 hours later, the sickness stopped and I put away the video camera (er, yes I did video it!) and then made sure she was comfortable. I'm certain that I played the video clip back to her and she was shocked at what she saw. Don't get me wrong, I didn't video it to take the piss - far from it. I did it to show how dangerous drinking can be. Yes, I know I probably sound like an old boring git but it *was dangerous* and I didn't want that to happen again. The following day she nursed a serious hangover but I think the lesson was learnt..

Music had been an integral part of my life from a very early age. I've mentioned before that my sister was very, well 'musical' shall I say when we were younger and music was always playing in the house. When the DJ scene exploded, I spent lots of money on vinyl and I was really hooked - something i'm still into today. At the weekends I would head for 5HQ, a record shop in Leicester town centre where i'd spend a few hours listening to all the promo/ white labels (unreleased records...). The shop was part of the Formation Records group and you'd often have DJ SS mixing it up live and soon the place was heaving with drum & bass crew nodding their heads as they got drawn into the sound. There was no pressure to buy anything and I could take a pile of records and listen to them in the numerous listening booths scattered around.

Soon I was a regular and my Saturdays were planned out - in the morning i'd head into town, buy records and then go and see Nee & Dee in the afternoon. The whole day went so quick it was unbelievable but the best part of the day was getting back home where I could immerse myself into my own world. I would go upstairs, head into the 'music' room and hurriedly pull out the new vinyl i'd bought earlier. One of the benefits of living in a detached house was soon to become very clear - I could really **pump up the volume** - we only had neighbours on one side and the noise didn't travel at all. In minutes i'd be in my own world and escape from it all and for the next 90 minutes or so i'd play new and old vinyl, switch musical genres, cut, mix and scratch it up. Some of the tunes i'd play reminded me of a certain time, place, people or event - there was always something to relate my music to. Nobody could tell me what to play; I was in full control, in fact I became my own **selecta'**...

For me music is a huge release - I can let off steam when i'm behind those phenomenal Silver Technics turntables. The greatest single thing about turntables and being able to mix is that I can literally go on my own musical journey. People often talk about travelling as they wanted to "find themselves". Well, I had no need to find myself - I knew exactly where I was and at that moment in time, I didn't want to be anywhere else!! Sometimes i'd be sitting downstairs with Sunita watching TV or something and an old "tune" would pop into my head and more often than none, i'd have to go into the music room, pull out the record and listen to it. I guess many people like to have a drink to calm down or let off steam and for me it has to be music - end of story.

Occasionally, i'd go on the decks (aka turntables) late at night. Whilst Sunita was fast asleep, i'd listen to the music through headphones rather than the speakers and once again enter my own world. In the middle of winter, on those cold frosty nights, I would often open the blinds in the music room and be star struck (er, sorry - pardon the pun!) by the beautiful stars that glittered in the night sky. I've always been intrigued by our solar system and i'm truly fascinated by the world above the earth. I wish, truly wish that one day I could blast off into space and view the earth from outer space but i'm a realist and sadly, it is highly unlikely that this will ever happen.

Everyone tends to have their own favourite foods, films or destinations but I have found that few people have a favourite song. Go on - ask yourself that question - what's your favourite song? I bet you're struggling to find the answer to that... Mine is easy; without doubt it *has* to be "three times a lady" by the Commodores. Perhaps it's because it was one of the earliest songs I recall listening to - it was released in 1978, the time when we lived in Halstead Street but I think the reason I love this so much is because of the words and the simplicity to it. So there you go, music for me is something that makes you happy. I think too many people get stuck up on not wanting to listen to music because of who produced it ("it's too cheesy"!!). What a load of nonsense - if you like it then who really gives a damn by who made it or who sung it? More importantly, it is one of those subjective things so there isn't a bad or good track so don't let it bother you ok!

Now that we were married and settled with jobs in Leicester, the idea of starting a family was firmly lodged in my head. The thought of having kids early appealed because you could enjoy the whole process whilst still being relatively young. I'm not saying that the enjoyment dwindles as you get older but time is on your side the earlier you start. Sunita wasn't ready for this just yet and preferred to wait a little while longer so despite having different views, agreed to delay things for a while. With kids out of the way for now, I switched attention to a mini holiday. Early in October 1999 I remember watching a holiday programme that was showing San Francisco and it looked great. I've always said that one of the things i'd love to have done is to take time out to see the world so this would be a great start...

With this vision in my mind I made a spur of the moment decision and headed off to book flights to San Francisco. I booked time off work and rang Sunita's boss as I wanted to make this trip another big surprise. Her boss agreed to giving her the time off but in the office where she works, nobody can keep anything secret so I was concerned that someone would say something and my plans would be revealed. Meanwhile Sunita who is extremely curious by nature, would not let up if there was any kind of gossip or rumour in the office and would do whatever she could to get the truth. Everything was set - I didn't tell anybody as I just couldn't trust anyone else to keep it all quiet. The night before we were flying out, I left the passports alone. I knew that if Sunita had an idea that we were flying somewhere, she'd check the passports.

Early in the morning, exactly as I had done the previous year when I took her on a surprise trip to Rome, I woke her up to tell her to pack her things. Slightly annoyed at being woken up, it took a few minutes before she knew what I was telling her. She confessed she knew something was happening but had no idea it was a trip to San Francisco. I've never seen her pack her stuff so quickly and it didn't help that I stood there and made her hurry up. 30 minutes later, Rumit was at the door - he was dropping us off to Heathrow and 2 hours later, I gave Rumit our house keys. He headed back to Leicester whilst we headed through customs whilst 90 minutes after that, we were heading West on the American Airlines Airbus bound for Los Angeles where we'd take another short flight to San Francisco.

It was a long flight - almost 12 hours and just before we touched down in LA, I noticed the famous Hollywood sign. I'd seen it before but Sunita found it quite strange to finally see something you'd only seen in films. Yes I know, it's just a sign but she'd never been to LA before so I guess it was quite exciting. Mind you, we didn't have time to stop and look around L.A - we quickly transferred to another flight and about an hour later we were on our way to our hotel in San Francisco. As we did in most of our trips abroad, we had already planned where we wanted to go so without wasting any more time we ventured out. During the first 2 days we wondered around the Bay bridge area and Fisherman's Wharf. It's chilled out here and life trundles on at a very relaxed pace but one of the highlights had to be the trip to Alcatraz.

Having watched "Escape from Alcatraz", it was quite surreal stepping onto the Island and matching real life images with those from the film. Inside, the place was surprisingly clean but I guess the tourism boom had a big part to play in that. You get one of the best views of San Francisco from Alcatraz Island and as the sun starts to set, the reflection on the water with the Golden Gate bridge in the background is a really good photo opportunity. The Golden Gate bridge is another great place to visit and has again featured in many films. When we arrived at the bridge, it must have been around 11am and the mist hadn't quite cleared so we were quite shocked that we couldn't actually see it at all.

We'd heard that the mist does tend to clear pretty quickly so we wondered around the area and it wasn't long before the full expanse of the Golden Gate was visible. It was massive and continued further than the eyes could see; the number of vehicles using it was phenomenal and once you actually stepped onto it, the slight vibration and movement of it could have easily put off someone with a nervous disposition. I'm certain Sunita was pretty impressed but it stopped there - I mean it's just a bridge right? For me, it was something different - an engineering marvel, a technological achievement but above all I was finally standing on the Golden Gate Bridge.

The view got better and better as we walked across it and trust me it was a *long* walk. If you include the approach to the bridge, it is 1.7 miles in length! We stopped half way and stared at the picture perfect view back across the San Francisco bay area with Alcatraz Island to the left. Finally, we reached the other side but to be honest there wasn't anything special to see so we simply turned around and started our long walk back. Before we jetted back to the UK, we took a ride on a cable car which was a memorable experience and one i'd recommend - you can't go to San Francisco and not do this!

With our trip over, things at work were very hectic primarily because the whole world was worried about the "Millennium bug" or "Year 2000 bug". Most software vendors had to verify their software was "compliant" so that they could reassure their own clients. I always thought the whole thing was overstated and simply hyped up by the press. Countries with little resources fared no worse than those with million pound budgets and as the clocks rolled over from 1999 to 2000, I don't think anything major happened. However, I spent a huge amount of time ensuring Magnetic North's software passed all the year 2000 software tests and we did with no problems at all.

I was at Nee & Dee's for the Millennium celebrations; Rumit was among the 1000's in London's Trafalgar Square whilst Sunita and her cousins were out in force in Leicester town centre. At their house, we tucked into lots of food and got out the good old video camera. We had a right laugh there that night and so was the rest of Leicester if the number of fireworks was anything to go by. The Leicester skyline was filled with rockets, air bomb repeaters, star fountains and numerous other types of explosive fireworks. If Nee had it his way, he would have made his own fireworks (trust me, Nee's firework experiments were something not to be messed with!!) but he was very sensible on that day.... As time rolled on, there were minutes before 1999 was out and 2000 was in.

The TV was switched on and the countdown began - 10,9,8,7,6,5,4,3,2,1; the year 2000! was here. The place erupted, everyone was hugging each other and jumping in the air. The noise was something i'll never forget and to be honest will unlikely hear again. For a few minutes the entire country felt as it was united in its celebrations and it was awesome. The video camera captured all these moments and I added my bit - pretending to be a news reporter or something. Whilst others could blame their antics on the drink, I was sober so I had no excuse at all. I tried to ring Sunita, Rumit and E2 but as with most New Year's celebrations, the GSM network just couldn't cope with the sheer volume of calls and for the next 3 hours I would slowly get text messages as each operator cleared the back log...So, a new year, a new decade and a new century was here...

32

Work ethics and
the 20 20 20 man...

By now "life" was quite ordinary; we went to work, we came home and that's about it. On my way to work rarely a day went by when I didn't think "there's more to life than this". This was often compounded when the weather was miserable. I'd be stuck at the traffic lights and as I looked to my left and right, i'd see other people looking well miserable. They were all like robots going about their daily life and sadly I was among them. Admittedly, most people *had* to go to work but I was always scared of getting stuck in a routine that i'd never be able to break out from. I wanted more than this, more for my family and I stuck to that dream - the dream that one day we'll be in a position where the hardest choice of the day was to decide what to do that day.

Despite this dream, work was great, I really enjoyed it and always gave 100% each and every day. One of my characteristics is that I seem to have a knack of knowing when something is likely to go wrong - I guess this is a good thing in the software world right? On one occasion our team were working on a new version of the product which, for Magnetic North, involved the use of new technology, new ideas and would provide us with a real challenge. Stepping up a gear I threw all my efforts into it until one day the Managing Director (a certain "Dominic Gray"), the boss of Magnetic North decided to look at the new software we were releasing. In the particular version of the software he was using, there must have been a few bugs he wasn't expecting but he was in a particularly bad mood...

He called me into his office - at the time I was the primary software tester so I was in charge so to speak. Within 10 minutes I realised how much of a bad mood he was in. He picked out certain product features and questioned why this and that didn't work and just let off steam. Shocked at what I was hearing I was speechless; i'd never experienced an outburst such as this and it was awful. I was very proud of what we were developing as a team and a company and yes, the software did have bugs but we hadn't finished the software so bugs were to be expected. More than this however, it felt like I was being personally attacked and that my work was being questioned which for me was the worst thing about it.

I left his office feeling down but that wasn't to be the end of it. I had immense pride in my work and I was going to let him know. So, I compiled a straight-to-the-point email telling him what was what. On pushing the "send" button I left the office. I was angry, really angry and just wanted to head off home. Little did I know that he read my emails minutes after i'd left and tried to catch me as I walked out. The following morning I came to work and read an email from him in which he basically said that I had misunderstood what he said and that there was no issue with the work I was doing.

Since that episode I think Dominic and I *really* got to understand each other better. He knew that I wasn't someone who would keep quiet if anything could improve and also that I would make myself heard. At this point i'd like to say that Dominic is without doubt a real character. You often hear about 'characters' who can liven up a room in seconds or are generally one of those people that you love to be around. Well, over the years i've certainly had my 'running's' with him. Many times i've questioned company policy and how we do things and more recently made lists of all the things that have gone wrong together with a list of things we can do to ensure things don't go wrong again. I do have the utmost respect for him because despite his position, despite that he is the MD, he never, *ever* speaks to you disrespectfully. He might speak to you with true sarcasm but we're all entitled to do that.

He will always make time for you and watching him "in action" at customer meetings or sales pitches is awesome. With most sales people, they learn what they are selling parrot style. They know what their products do but not how they do it. This man is different, in a room full of business executives, managers and so called IT experts, Dominic always tends to have an answer for each question. When highly paid IT "experts" are struggling to answer how to re-route DNS traffic from one ISP to another or a phone system expert is struggling to get a piece of equipment to work, my man Dominic will have the answers himself and I have seen him being a piece of equipment to life right in front of a customer's eyes (when the customer's own IT expert said the equipment was faulty).

In September 2000 Sunita found out that she was pregnant - we were having a baby! The news was fantastic; I was going to be a dad - this thought kept going through my head repeatedly. For me, it was special because I had the opportunity to look after my son the right way. During my childhood I had experienced too many things that should never have been witnessed by anybody let alone a small child (me that is). I would not make the mistakes my dad made; I wouldn't make promises I couldn't keep and I, well both of us, had the opportunity to bring up a child the way they should be brought up - with love and laughter...

It took quite a while to get used to the idea of "being a dad" and I would have certain moments - in the car, walking during my lunchtime - anywhere really when the reality would rain home and my mind would be filled with all the things that I wanted to do. In the meantime, Sunita was as healthy as ever; she was always one of those people who rarely got ill and as the weeks flew past she seem to take pregnancy in her stride. As the weeks slowly passed by her tummy grew ever so slightly and it was *really* strange to think that in a few months we'd be parents! I remember when we told everyone they were so happy and my sister gave us both a great big hug when we told her.

Time check - November 2000 - Knowing full well that in a few months Sunita wouldn't be able to fly anywhere, we decided to take a trip to the USA again. Her cousin was working out there and we planned to stay with her and do some travelling together so with tickets in hand and bags packed we headed back to Heathrow in my blue Cavalier. Almost 7 hours later and we in New York. For Sunita it was her 2nd visit there whilst I was on my 3rd! As ever, the city was vibrant and exciting as it had always been in previous visits and the atmosphere, buzz, excitement - call it what u want, was wicked. Her cousin lived across the Hudson in the Jersey area with about 5 other girls. Although we were very grateful for them "taking us in", I sometimes wished we had booked into a hotel - there was just too many of us in that room.

In the mornings, the smell of deodorant and perfume from 5 girls mixed violently creating a strong smell. In addition to that the constant drilling and banging of workers building a new office about 20 metres away didn't help and most mornings we'd get up before everyone else anyway. The location was stunning and I didn't realise how stunning until the next morning when we ventured out to get some breakfast before heading into NYC. As we got out of the lift, we walked for a few minutes and as we turned around a small corner, downtown Manhattan came into full view. In glorious technicolour, the breath-taking NYC skyline was right there in front of us. The view from the Statue of Liberty was excellent but from here it was even better. The night time view was just as amazing; all the millions of office lights lit up the NYC skyline and it was picture perfect.

For the first few days of our trip, we ventured into the heart of New York again; Times Square, 5th Avenue and all the other tourist spots. One of the highlights was seeing the legendary Grand Central Station - home to many fine New York based movies. In the evenings we would stroll around the city and go for dinner at many of the countless restaurants on offer. After a hectic day it was back to the block of flats where the smell of perfume still lingered in the air. Later that week we drove to Washington DC - home of the US President. The drive wasn't bad at all; helped by the 8 lane freeway that linked the 2 cities. As we entered the city we saw a glimpse of Capitol Hill; it was *really* strange finally seeing an iconic building you read and see so often on TV and in the press. I was quite shocked at quite how close you can park to it. I expected lots of security around it but surprisingly there wasn't. There were a few security guards but we got up, close and very personal and had a good look around the place.

Central park.

Meena & Sunita – Washington Monument in the distance.

Capitol Hill...

Time to move on; directly in front of Capitol Hill is a wide expanse of road (the National Mall) which is much longer than it looks. As we walked up towards it, we saw this huge thin structure in front of us which we later learnt was the 'Washington Monument' - all 169 metres of it. The walk along the Mall took ages and I mean ages. By the time we got to the Washington Monument we were ready for a sit down. There was, however, no time to waste and before long we were looking directly at the White House. Out of all the sights we saw, this had to be the most impressive. Sadly, the night was rapidly drawing in and with that so was the light. The photos we took came out crap to say the least; we never had a digital camera, the zoom was useless and all we got was a blurred outline of the president's home.

After taking a final look close look at the Washington Monument and the White House, we made our way back along the National Mall to find some place to eat. By this time it was around 7pm and the locals that stood around the street corners and just "hung around" were quite frightening to be honest. Thankfully we all agreed on where we wanted to eat, promptly tucked in and then walked as fast as we could to the car. We were all shattered by this stage and I had the task of driving us part way back. It was a long drive back to New York; made worse by sheer tiredness and we were thankful when we set eyes on the towers of the World Trade Centre as they came into view. After another day of exploring around NYC, it was time to say our farewells and head back to the UK...

In the time that we were in New York, a cold weather front seemed to linger over the UK and remained that way for many weeks - it was freezing. Mind you, it didn't bother me. I quite liked the cold weather and I loved the cold, crisp UK winters. As the daylight hours slowly diminished and we edged into winter, the days were clear, sunny and cold whilst at night, the skies were clear, the stars were out and it was even colder. In the mornings, a sharp frost would cover the area - cars, roads, trees - you name it, it was covered and looked beautiful as they are glowed up in the morning sunlight.

Yet another Christmas came and went and the reality of becoming parents dawned on us as the year turned into 2001. In just a few months' time, we'd have a new family member and although there wasn't a great deal of preparation to do, the nursery for one had to be sorted out. We never had any extravagant plans for the nursery. All we did was paint the walls, put up a few shelves and add a few stickers around the room but the result was great. Sunita was still as healthy as ever, simply got on with it and planned to work for as long as she could - it just seemed to make sense to continue working and take more time off after the baby was born. Our baby "stash" of stuff soon got bigger and bigger - our garage was also becoming full of buy 1 get one frees which would save us a fortune in the long run and everything was set for the arrival.

People often talk about birth "plans", having babies at home, practising the route to the hospital and loads of other things. We certainly weren't planning on having the baby at home and I knew the way to the hospital so that was that. At work I had booked 3 weeks off - one thing was for sure, I wanted to spend as much time at home with the baby; it was very important for me to do this and I wanted to give Sunita all the support she would need. The big day, the "birth" date came and went with no real fuss - the baby wasn't quite ready to emerge just yet! As the days progressed there was little activity and we were then given a "date" to come into the hospital.

With the original due date behind us now, the hospital gave us a new date which basically meant that if the baby hadn't arrived by this date then Sunita would have to be "induced" and the baby would definitely be arriving then. Almost 2 weeks went past and there was still no sign of the baby. During this time I often walked into the newly decorated nursery and just stood there thinking to myself how our lives would change. As I looked around the room at all, it felt as if I was being stared at. I was - the cuddly toys always seemed to stare right at you; even those on the slightly wonky shelf that I put up.

Well the time for the baby to arrive "naturally" had well and truly run out and on the date we were given, we made our way to the hospital. It was a strange journey; 2 of us were going there and 3 of us would be coming back. Once there, after her notes and various other things were checked, we were led to a private room. I had my video camera with me and tried to take some footage where I could. Sunita on the other hand who sternly told me that "her dignity had been dropped off at reception..." was in no mood to have a Sony Camcorder shoved in her face so that was my cue to switch it off. Good job really because shortly after that, the medication they gave her started to take effect and she looked to be in real pain.

The pain was the labour contractions and judging by the reaction on her face they were *really* painful. Feeling totally useless I did what I do best - joke around but I think "Dr, Dr" jokes weren't quite appropriate! Time just flew that day and by early evening the contractions were happening big time. Outside the room, Sunita's sister and mum had arrived to check out what was happening and I think they wanted to be in the delivery room. For me, however, this was a *personal* thing; it was our baby and I wanted to be the only one in the room with her so I simply said "no" to letting others in the room. Call it selfish, call it cruel, call it what you want - this was *our* moment and I didn't want to share that intimate moment with anyone - it was just so personal that it had to be the two of us. Sometimes in life you have to follow your instincts and do what you "feel is right" so I did.

As the minutes ticked by, it was clear that despite being "induced", the baby still wasn't quite ready to pop out. Sunita needed to kick start the labour process and there are various ways to do this including eating spicy foods and going for a walk. With that in mind I told her to go to the canteen and get me a sandwich; it was the least she could do after all! Another way is to use "complimentary therapies" such as acupuncture, massage and even herbal teas. Not quite sure about Sunita but I could certainly have done with a cuppa right now - this was hard work! Apparently a tried and tested method of getting the contractions to speed up is to drink a mixture of Castor Oil and Juice. Known as the "midwife cocktail", this is meant to be a sure fire way of moving things along nicely. Mind you all Sunita would have to hear was "cocktail" and she'd probably down it in one!

To be honest I don't think it would have made any difference if she had Castor Oil or Castrol GTX - things were just not happening. In the end they gave her some more medication and the results were phenomenal. Her mood totally changed, the contractions got closer and closer and she was clearly in lots of pain. The TENS machine (a machine that sends electrical pulses throughout the body and helps to reduce pain), didn't do much and as I held her hand for comfort i'm amazed she didn't break any of my fingers considering how hard she was squeezing them. Looking at Sunita you could tell and I mean *really* tell that this was one experience she'd never forget and I realised i'd never forget it either. I don't think i've ever seen her in so much distress and I could tell that she just wanted it to be all over.

She was continuously pushing as she had the "urge" - a common thing apparently. I still had an urge for a cuppa but I kept my mouth well and truly shut! Meanwhile the delivery staff were desperately trying to control her urges to push and kept telling her to *only* push when they told her. As I watched helplessly as Sunita struggled, the cries of "push, push" filled the room and as time ticked on she was getting really tired. Having been administered with an epidural earlier, the pain relief was starting to work rapidly but a natural birth was looking less and less likely. It was no good, the staff were getting worried the baby would be in "distress" as they put it and they wanted to carry out a "Caesarean section". There was no time to waste and the option to proceed with the C section was left to me - presumably because Sunita was too out of it to make the decision.

No sooner had the consent form been signed, they grabbed the form out of my hands; no one checked anything, no one asked me if I understood what was happening. I could have written "Santa Claus" on the form and it wouldn't have bothered anyone! Sunita was wheeled out of the room as fast as possible. I was told to "get changed" and was led into a side room which was white walled and worryingly had plenty of blood stains on the floor. My immediate horror at seeing the red stuff splattered everywhere soon gave way to the fact that this *was* a delivery suite and I guess seeing blood was to be expected. Armed with blue gown, head scarf thing and a rapidly beating heart, I was then led into yet another room - this was where the real action would take place.

33

Blood, sweat & tears

Inside the delivery room, all seemed pretty calm at first; hardly anyone spoke and all the staff got on with their duties in virtual silence. As I walked towards Sunita, she was pretty calm which I assumed was the work of the medication she'd been given in preparation for surgery. Goodness, just the word "surgery" scares the life out of me. Mind you, it would probably help to scare the baby out of Sunita! Within 30 seconds, it was as if someone flicked a switch, the silence turned into noise and as I sat trying to comfort Sunita, a drape was placed between her head and her stomach - most pregnant women don't really want to see what's happening below. Always curious, I was keen to know what was happening and in a flash I saw them slice open the stomach. Yes, I know, it sounds awful and let me tell you something - it *is*. Nothing and I mean nothing prepares you to watch someone take a scalpel and use it!

Whilst all this was going on, Sunita (still calm as ever), was also wondering what was happening and even asked me "have they made the cut yet?". She never felt the incision at all and when I told her "yes" it must have been pretty alarming for her knowing she was wide awake whilst a medical team were poking around her stomach. Whilst Sunita lay there I was focused good and proper on what the team were doing. When the medical team weren't discussing last night's TV or their plans for the weekend, they were pulling here and pushing there. They were so calm about it you'd never have thought they were trying to get a baby out. Just as I was about to look towards Sunita, I saw one of them dig deep and pull hard and then we, or should I say I, saw our baby.

Stunned and most definitely lost for words, I had just witnessed something spectacular and our baby boy was here. Sunita was asking "what is it?", "what is it?" and she was dying to see him. After cleaning him up a little, the **obstetrician** brought him to us and we had our first look at our baby. Our baby, 'Rishi' was taken away and I was asked to leave the room. Once outside, they had wrapped Rishi in the blanket we'd given them earlier and I managed to spend about 10 minutes alone with him. I had the video camera rolling and I was just so happy, overjoyed, surprised, grateful and watched in amazement as he opened his tiny eyes and moved his little fingers.

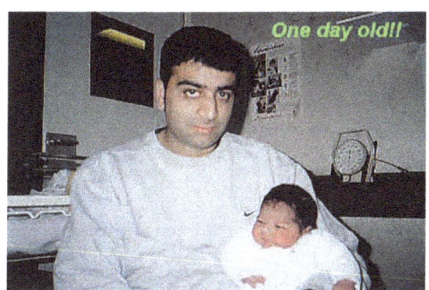
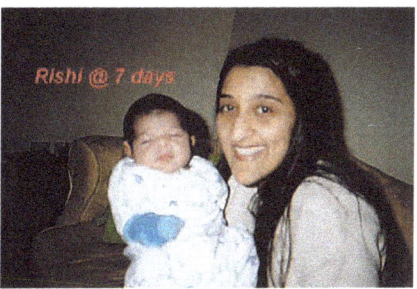

After a while, I was getting anxious myself; I was worried about Sunita. When I thought of what she had been through that day, I just wanted to make sure she was ok. Watching the C section was horrific but interesting at the same time and I breathed a huge sigh of relief when she was wheeled out. Unfortunately, she was shaking like mad and felt extremely cold. She looked so tired and I wanted to do something to help but there wasn't much I could do. After a while, all 3 of us (that sounded strange!) finally got back to the ward where Sunita could finally try and get rest - that's what she thought anyway. After the C section you're hooked up to all sorts of things, catheter, drip and as Sunita has said many times, you don't quite pick up your dignity just yet.

As time drew on, she was clearly in pain as the medication wore off. The pressure to feed didn't help and I think she felt bullied in there. I remember leaving the ward for a few moments whilst I rang everyone to tell them the great news and after doing so rushed back. Rishi was born at 9.46pm on April 26th, 2001, and both Sunita & I were now very happy, but tired new parents. Time went pretty fast and it wasn't long before I had to leave as the visiting time had run out. That night I could hardly sleep; the fact that I was a dad, a parent to someone and that a new journey had begun was too exciting to put into words. I had plenty to do the next day and headed straight to work. I was officially on holiday now but I popped in to see everyone and give them the news too. On my way back home, it was a brief stop at Fosse Park to pick up an outfit for the baby photos and it was then straight back to the hospital.

When I got there I soon learned that it wasn't a good night for Sunita. I think the previous day *really* took it out of her and in the early hours of the morning she cried several times as emotions ran wild. Still, I was there now and as the day progressed she seemed to get better. The streams of visitors certainly helped and trust me, we had loads of them. As the C section was basically open surgery, they keep you on the ward for a few days "just to make sure". The following Tuesday we were told there was a possibility that they could both come home. We had to wait for the doctor to do their rounds which always took ages. In the end, the doctor agreed they could leave and I went off to get the car because before the hospital staff let you go, they always check you have a baby seat and it's fitted correctly. Now, the nurses work at the hospital, not Halfords so i'm not quite convinced of what they check but nevertheless I guess just checking you have a child seat is a good thing...

Unfortunately, we were down to one car, a few months earlier, a crazy driver drove straight into my trusty Vauxhall Cavalier; a car that had just hit 201,000 miles and up until then was mechanically perfect. Anyway, for now, we were cruising around in Sunita's Austin Maestro and she was relieved to finally leave the hospital and head home. It's a short drive - literally 10 or so minutes from the hospital to our house and as we pulled into our drive, it just felt weird. Within a few minutes we were back in our house much to Sunita's relief and the moment we both recall so clearly is walking into the lounge, sitting down with Rishi still strapped into his car seat. Sunita and I looked at each other then looked at Rishi; it was one of those "what now" moments. The last time we left the house together there were 2 of us and now there was 3. Our world which we knew would change *had* changed and this was the start of things to come...

I was off work for 3 weeks which was good because Sunita needed plenty of TLC and rest. At times, the C section stitches didn't look as if they were holding and little bits of blood would seep through the wound. Thankfully, the initial panic was soon followed by relief as she was checked out and it was deemed to be "normal". I think we adjusted pretty well actually, the night time feeds were taken care of by me. Sunita could hardly sit up unaided so when Rishi cried for his milk, I took him downstairs and enjoyed one on one moments feeding him during the early hours of the morning. Changing the nappies was a bit of a wakeup call but I soon learnt to control my breathing whilst on pampers duty. The trick was to take lots of little breathes through your mouth - this meant you didn't have to use your nose as much because trust me, the smell was *really* awful at times. As the days turned into weeks, we had adjusted very well, Rishi's sleeping patterns weren't that bad, Sunita was getting back to her good old chatty self and I was loving every minute of it. I wanted to do everything; feed, bathe, change nappies, take him out for a stroll and so on.

As an Indian, one of the worst things about having a baby is being told to "do this, do that". I know other people mean well and really only have your interests at heart but I just got fed up with being told how to bring up our baby or told to do things differently. Some people said that when feeding Rishi in public you should cover up the feeding bottle because if 'others' see it back luck could head your way. Others said you should keep the baby in our room for 6 months whilst traditionally you're not even meant to leave the house for 4 weeks after giving birth. Well, let me tell you something; if YOU want to do this then fine but we weren't going to bow down to pressure from anyone. We would go out if we wanted to, we would feed him openly without covering up the bottle and after 2 months Rishi would be in his own room. To all those who said otherwise, nothing untoward has happened but let me make one thing perfectly clear. I am not saying that these superstitions are wrong or there is no truth in them at all. What I am saying is you should do what you feel is right, not what others think is right but above all, you should make the decision yourselves...

My 3 weeks holiday was over real quick and in the 2/3 weeks that followed I used to come home at lunchtime to see them both. Things were made a little trickier since we only had one car and it was about to get worse as another driver, at the *same* roundabout, piled into the back of us one afternoon. Thankfully, I knew we were about to have an accident. I was waiting for traffic to pass on the roundabout and I could see the car in my rear view mirror coming fast behind me and braking hard at the last moment. I told Sunita to hold on tight and then the car hit. Luckily, the impact wasn't that bad and no-one was injured. Our one car was now damaged but still driveable so that was a relief - the Maestro was still alive. You know what, that car despite all the bad hype and press was a solid car for us. It never broke down once, always started first time and just kept going.

At work one guy was always taking the piss out of the car. "Car started ok then?", "Do you drive the car at night so no one can see you? Aren't you embarrassed? ... and so on. One day after work, I could hear the sound of an engine cranking (or 'turning' for those of you not mechanically minded) but not actually starting. As I turned to see whose car it was it was the piss taker himself. Yes the person who kept having a go at our car had his own car troubles. In the end his car just gave up; it sounded as if the battery was dead. Pretending I didn't see this I walked to the car, got in, started it and was just about to pull off when he came running over and made gestures for me to open my window. He knew he needed help, I knew he needed help and when he asked if I could give him a "jump start" I said "oh, you want a jump start from *this* Austin Maestro? He felt like a twat at that point and I made sure he understood not to take the piss again. That day he learned a harsh lesson and he never made any jibes about the Maestro ever again.

For lots of people, taking pictures is just part of life; we take pictures at birthdays, weddings and so on. When you have a child, most of us are very trigger happy and you end up with 100's if not 1000's of photos typically in a short space of time. Nowadays with the digital camera era you are no longer limited to 24 or 36 exposure films and can take 1000's of photos and just delete those you don't want anymore! Although there is no substitute for the good old photo album, I decided to make use of the world wide web and put together my own web site. The idea was simple - construct a "Rishi" section and update as the months and years progressed. When he gets older, he can see his life in pictures all with a click of the button.

Furthermore, friends and family around the world could access and see the pictures too. I also wanted to dedicate part of the web site to my close friends and put up things such as holidays we've been on, parties, weddings and anything else like that. Unfortunately for me, all the photos that I wanted to get onto the web site were printed photos and not in digital format. This meant I had to scan them first; a simple task I thought to myself but as I started to scan them in I soon realised this was going to be a very slow process. It took around 1 minute to scan each photo but that wasn't the end if it; photos that are scanned don't scan with great accuracy (well our scanner didn't anyway!). I now had the task of tidying up each photo, making it lighter, darker, swapping from colour to black and white, adding comments and so on. I spent so much time doing this that Adobe Photoshop was my new best friend!

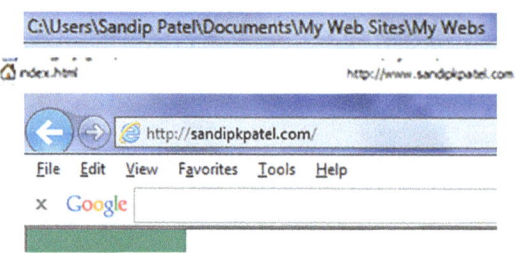

Trust me, I spent many, many hours scanning, fixing photos, adding web pages, adding web page commentary, testing the web site, fixing slow web pages and on and on. The web site progressed at a good pace and after a few weeks I was extremely pleased with the result. It would be an on-going process but I kept telling myself that I had to allocate time every 2 weeks or so just to keep up with it and thankfully I did just that. The weeks turned into months and by the time June 2001 had arrived we decided that it was time for Rishi to sleep in his own room. That night we tucked him into his cot in his own room and it was very strange not having him in the room with us. I'm not so sure about Sunita but I was awake on and off for most of the night and I clearly remember getting out of bed at around 4am just to check on him. He was fine and I was just being over cautious but there was no way I could sleep unless I knew he was ok. The good old baby monitor reminded us of everything he did; you could hear him breathing; greatly exaggerated when he had a cold, you could hear him moving around and even making noises when he was awake.

For us, life was moving on at a leisurely pace and we just got on with things as we'd done before Rishi had arrived. Things obviously change; before you could make sudden decisions to go out for a meal or nip to the cinema to watch a film but now we had to consider the baby (or young infant!). When we went out and what we did revolved around Rishi but one thing I do think both myself and Sunita agreed and stuck to was the fact that having a baby wouldn't turn us into recluses. Yes, things did change and you have to adapt and make sacrifices but we made sure we got out and about. I for one don't like to be stuck at home for too long and can always find something to do or somewhere to go.

I may have touched on this before but especially in Indian families there seems to be this belief that the women look after the children whilst the dads just work and don't get involved in the daily (and nightly children's duties). There was no way whatsoever that we were doing this and I could never understand why others chose to live their lives this way. Of course mums look after kids but is everyone so blind that they forget about the dads. Parents is plural not singular and the thought of not being "hands on" with Rishi would simply horrify me. In fact, it was quite the contrary; I made sure I was involved in everything because I *wanted* to.

As we entered deep into the UK summer, Sunita's work colleagues had arranged a night out away and it would be the longest time so far that she would be away from Rishi. For me there was nothing to worry about; if a dad can't look after the children because they are so reliant on their wives or partners then this is a sorry state of affairs in my opinion. I do say "my opinion" because others may have their own reasons for raising children in a different way so I don't want to upset anyone ok? As it turned out there was no drama, Sunita had a great, well deserved time out with her friends and I had a great time at home. Ok, Rishi did scream his little heart out for a while in between feeds and changing his nappy but it was all under control...

34

My V6 and the long, long party...

As we only had a single car, getting around town was proving to be a little difficult especially when we both needed to go out. If Sunita needed the car then i'd have to drive home at lunchtime and then she'd have to drop me back to work and then she could do whatever she needed to. For a while it was ok and we just learned to live with it; after all, you just learn to live with what you have right? In the end though, this simply wasn't sustainable, it was too hard work and we decided that we did need to get another car. For many weeks, my evenings were spent looking through car adverts and looking at what we could buy comfortably. It was all very confusing, so many cars, so many choices and stepping into the main dealerships was quite daunting as you can easily get hooked into their mesmerizing sales pitches.

One day however, we drove into a Vauxhall dealer; no particular reason why but we thought we may as well look anyway. Having seen several cars and not being particularly impressed by them (I think it was the cost rather than the car!), the salesman led us outside to a gleaming black Vectra. It was fast, had a big V6 engine and drove beautifully and I was certainly won over. The cost however was putting me off but Sunita simply said "We can afford it; if you like it just get it!" It was very tempting and in the end I just couldn't resist it so the deal was done. Interestingly, when we filled out the paperwork and added our address, it turned out the salesperson lived around the corner from us. He knew that if I had any problems with the car there would be no escape; he thought I was joking but I wasn't!

It was quite exciting picking up the car; when we went back to the dealership, it had been fully serviced, it was sparkling clean and ready to go. Inside the car it was so clean you'd think no-one had ever set foot inside it but within minutes of getting there, I was in the driving seat and on my home. I was well pleased with the car; fair enough it was *only* a Vectra, it wasn't going to turn heads but who cared about that? It might sound daft but for the first few weeks I hated it when the car got dirty inside. Every 2-3 days I would get the hoover out and get the car back to its show room condition. Anyway, the main point is we had 2 cars now and our transport problems were solved.

Rishi's first trip to Twycross Zoo.

Time check; well it was now November 2001; Rishi was around 7 months old and one of my sister's legendary parties was around the corner. She was soon to turn 40, the big 4 0, the day "life begins" or so they say. This time my sister wanted the party at home, the invitations were sent out, the DJs were booked (i.e. myself and Paresh) and all other arrangements were done. A few days before the big day I spent ages sorting out the records. DJ'ing to a varied crowd wouldn't be tricky but would be challenging. I may have mentioned this before but any party that my sister or Pravin hold are always wicked; the crowd is always up for it and everyone has a great time. Having the party at home would make it much more personal and being able to DJ was wicked as far as I was concerned so roll on the party...

On the day itself, there was the traditional sound check hiccup. We hired some kick ass speakers but the volume was only coming out of one of them. I didn't realise but the house was slowly filling up with people and I was getting quite worried about the speaker. I checked and double checked everything but couldn't find the cause. After another frantic 20 minutes passed I found the cause - one of the cables had a slight kink in it so a bit of black tape soon fixed that and it was all systems go... Everyone was at this party, my sister's lifelong friends, work colleagues, my mum, brothers, cousins and my friends too. As the night drew on there was no sign of anyone getting tired.

The dance floor (yes we had a real dance floor!) was packed for most of the night. After the cake was cut I tried to make my sister say a few words but there were so many people it was hard to get across to her. Anyway, the crowd just partied on and on and fuelled with drinks I knew this would be a long night. At 3am, the party stepped up a gear with fireworks being let off outside. It was November so I guess the neighbours were used to hearing them but many were probably well pissed off at hearing them at 3 in the morning! By the time it was 4am, most of the people had gone and only the diehard party goers were still there. Looking around, it was my 2 brothers, my sister, Paresh, Pravin, Divya and just our close family.

On the decks, I had a great night but night had turned into morning and by the time the clock struck 5am I had been playing music for about 7 hours and couldn't do it any longer. I was so physically tired that "the last record" was the last one. When the last tune faded out the rest of them jeered and wanted more but it wasn't to be and that was the end of the night (or as it turned out - morning!). It had been a great night, a great party and a real family affair which made it even more special...

2001 felt like a long year and when Christmas finally came, Rishi got to see Santa for the first time. Well, it was just some bloke dressed up in town but he didn't know that so it was ok! As we rolled into 2002 we'd already decided that we wanted to get

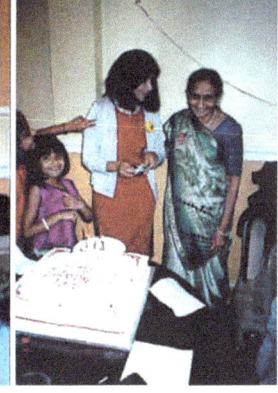

My big sister turns 40!

Priyanka, Preeya, Bena
& Mum.

Rishi had his eyes on the cake!

Kiran the joker!

away and have a well-deserved holiday. Destinations, flights and their duration, heat and all sorts of other factors and their impact on a young child made it quite tricky to decide where to go. In the end we just headed off to a travel agent and just looked for some bargains - a few hours later and we'd booked a week's holiday to Malta. An added bonus was Rishi would turn 1 year old whilst we were on holiday so it would be a special birthday away from home...

As the months creeped on, our little boy started to show his fantastic character; he was energetic, playful, rarely cried and was quite simply the best thing ever. Yes, all people probably say that about their own kids and quite rightly too. The one thing that

All smiles – Rishi was a very smiley kid...

drives me insane is those parents who opt to have children but then decide that they can't spend time with them - what is the point in having kids if after you have them you do everything you can to avoid spending time with them?

As we left the house for our first holiday together, we were all excited. For Rishi, it was just another trip in the car for now. Little did he know that in a few hours, he'd be sitting in our laps heading east 30,000 feet in the air. We had no idea whatsoever how he would cope on his first flight but trust me, we found out the hard way. As we sat around the airport lounge waiting to board the aircraft, fellow passengers played with Rishi and asked how old he was and did the usual "aaahh - cute baby thing" that people do. 90 minutes later the same passengers were probably swearing at us; Rishi, our mild mannered affectionate child had turned into a monster. He screamed the place down, didn't want to sit still, was agitated at the cramped seating (thanks JMC!), was tired, hungry and his ears were probably hurting like mad.

With no sign of him calming down, there was only one thing to do - walk around. My first problem was getting out - we were sitting next to the window and so Sunita and another passenger had to get out first, navigate their way around the 2 people that were also standing in the aisle trying to get stuff out of their bags at the same time that the airline was trying to push around the duty free trolley. After squeezing out, we were free but the screams didn't stop and as I walked towards the front of the plane I hoped he would settle. When I reached the front and turned around, I could see the passengers with their angry looks on their faces, I could read their "bad parent, bad parent" thoughts and many were red eyed having been woken up by this screaming kid.

Still, not much I could do about it so I just walked and walked and walked and started annoying the rest of the passengers at the rear of the plane. Eventually, Rishi had cried so much that he just fell asleep and you could see the relief on everyone's face. Thankfully we managed to get back into the seat without him waking up and he slept the rest of the way. The return journey wasn't bad at all and he slept all the way - phew! The holiday was just what we needed; it was warm (bordering on hot actually), it was sunny, the choice of food and places to eat was varied and the scenery (particularly around Gozo and the Comino islands) was spectacular.

With just the 3 of us there, his birthday was quiet but he had his cake and ate it! We asked the hotel to make us a small cake, making them fully aware that there was only 3 of us eating it. I was shocked to find they had made a cake that would feed 20 people and there wasn't much we could do with it; it was far

Rishi's 1st birthday in Malta!

Cooling off with his mum.

too big for us to finish and in the end most of it ended up in the bin. With the help of Sunita, Rishi had a few attempts at blowing out his single candle before getting bored and deciding to eat the cake instead. The next day we flew back to the UK where Rishi, who never showed any interest in walking, started to take his first, very wobbly steps.

For the Cartronics boys; aka Nee and Dee, business was booming and they were rapidly outgrowing their shop in Green Lane Road. They would have been even busier if they had a bigger garage and better parking at the side of the road. Sometimes they had so many customers that they virtually blocked the road and we'd watch as other drivers struggled to get through. Their shop had 2 garages but one of them was smaller than the other and it was quite a struggle to get a car in there so they just made do with one of them. In the winter it was freezing and if a large car was in the bigger garage there was no way you could close the shutters and the heating would have to be left on full time.

They needed a bigger place and had been looking around for a bigger premise for a while. It was quite difficult; there wasn't many places close by that were big enough for their needs and had plenty of customer parking space. Luckily a building formerly used as a garage came onto the market and they snapped it up. It was only about half a mile away and was further up Green Lane Road so the location was excellent. Better still was the space; customers could park their cars on the road without worrying about traffic wardens whilst they also had plenty of space on their front drive. Inside there was lots of work to do - the place had been run down and the back end of it looked as if it would fall to bits if there was heavy wind. Nee and Dee knew they had to fix it up properly so plans were drawn up to sort it all out.

A few weeks after they got the keys to their new shop we were planning to head to Wales for a lad's weekend as our other friend, Hemal, was getting married soon. However, Nee and Dee said they couldn't go anywhere as their builders were relying on them to clear the inside of the premises before they could start work. There was no way we were going anywhere without Nee and Dee and they could only go if we all played builders, demolished several walls and left the place in a state so that the real builders could start their work. Time wasn't on our side so we decided that we all had to pitch in and get the job done as soon as possible. Early one Sunday morning, I arrived at their shop with my "ready to work" clothes on whilst Rumit arrived ready to demolish anything.

Nee, Rumit, Dee, Mr. C & myself taking a tea break!

With all of us on the case, we made good progress. In a matter of hours, walls were ripped down, huge piles of rubbish were removed, unsafe piping was removed and the place was transformed. We looked the part too; our faces were black from all the dust; our clothes were ripped to bits and there were empty cups (previously filled with tea) all over the place - true builder traits! Around 6 hours later we'd reached our goal and the real builders could now come in and start the main renovations. This also meant that Nee and Dee could relax... our trip to Wales was on!

We planned to do some quad biking in the Snowdonia Mountains; something that Rumit and I had experienced several times before (the views were awesome). The quad centre itself was run by a lady who lived in a small town close to Portmadog in

North Wales. The little town of Criccith was busy all year around and there was no available accommodation at all. Feeling dejected we called up to cancel the quadding but our luck had changed. The lady said we could camp out in her garden! With all our stuff packed into Nee and Dee's Toyota space cruiser, all 5 of us started off on our long journey to Wales.

Once there, well once inside her garden, we quickly set up camp for the night. Rumit and Hemal were planning on sleeping in the tent whilst the rest of us would sleep in the cruiser. We had a great evening, it was warm, the sky was blue, all around us was rolling countryside, we had a barbeque that sent the smell of chicken into the air causing Bruce (the quad lady's dog) to hang around with us hoping we would send some meat his way! Later, we were joined by the quad lady too and she seemed to have a great time chilling with us and stuffing her face with Indian style chicken. It was quite late by the time we went to bed and had a great night's sleep. The next day we were all up early and eager to get quadding. We packed up all the stuff, headed off for breakfast then came back ready to go. After the safety brief, we were led out into the mountains and after around 20 minutes we were racing along slippery tracks, trying to get into each other's way, skidding around and pulling 360 degree turns.

For Rumit "need for speed" Kotecha, he had gone a little too fast on one stretch of the track and came face to face with a low hanging branch causing him to swerve after which he lost control, slid down a ditch and was halted by a tree. Thankfully he was ok; it could have been much worse so we all breathed a sigh of relief. Rumit wasn't fazed by it all; he was just eager to get quadding again so we all stormed off again going higher and higher and avoiding the sheep that would jump out in front of us... After several hours of quadding we were shattered and it was time to head back to Leicester. We all had a great weekend and since then we've not found any quad centres as good as that one.

Inside the Toyota with Nee & Dee. Inside the tent – Rumit & Hemal

Hemal up to no good! Rumit and the
smashed up quad.

Hemal & Yamini @ their
registry wedding. Thirsty work!

For many years now my Saturday routine has been the same; head off to see Nee and Dee at Car-tronics. I love it there because it's just so different; there are always new gadgets to mess with, all types of cars with various things that need fixing and most of all was the fact that I could have a real laugh with my friends. The type of cars that came into their garage ranged from old Mini's to brand new Ferrari's. One thing is certain; the way these boys interact with customers is straight forward. There is no bullshit, no nonsense and they simply tell it to you straight. They're not out to rob anybody and are always there to help. It's for these reasons that they've become so successful and the fact that many customers trust them with their expensive cars rather than the dealers!

With so many customers walking through their blue doors, it was inevitable that some of the things you hear bring a smile to your face. Over the years there have been so many but some of the best were: -

- One customer who came in with a MG sports car asked if they could out his stereo because his speakers weren't working at all. When they drove his car into the garage, they found that the customer had cut off the magnetic part of the speaker to fit them into the doors (presumably as they were too big). Physics aside, you don't need to be a Mensa member to work out that you probably shouldn't cut things off randomly if you don't know what you're doing. Common sense in this case clearly wasn't followed and if they hadn't seen it for themselves they would have never believed it. I have no idea how they kept a straight face whilst explaining to the customer that the reason the speakers don't work is because he has cut off the core part of it! I mean honestly, cutting off the magnets.... It's like removing the screen from a TV and then calling in the repair man because you've got no picture.

- Another customer enquired about the gear stick accessories. You can remove the original "top" of the gear stick and replace it with a customised one but they are only for manual gearboxes. The customer, clearly interested in it, asked whether it would work in "5th gear". Now, some of you are probably thinking "what's wrong with that question?" Think on, think on and it will come to you eventually....

Many customers though say the same stupid thing time after time. They'll come in with a broken stereo and choose to have a new one fitted. Once done, Nee or Dee would call the customer over and say "Right, your car's ready...". Almost immediately, the customer would reply with "Does it work?". I mean come on, they've just had a new stereo fitted which Nee / Dee would obviously check but customers repeatedly asked the same daft question. Of course, it bloody works... I hoped that one day either Nee or Dee would say "No it doesn't" - what would the customer say to that?

35

November 2002 – Rumit & Rita's wedding

Weddings are generally good fun, especially family ones but for me, it was a very special occasion when Rumit said he was getting married towards the end of 2002. His wife to be; 'Rita' or "I'm from Dudley Rita" was a young, enthusiastic budding solicitor and was a fun person to be around. The first time we (Sunita and I that is) met her was quite strange as we didn't actually meet her. We were at a wedding and saw her from a distance. I remember Rumit discreetly pointing to one side of the wedding hall and describing the colours she was wearing and finally, after filtering out all the other women wearing similar colours we saw her! I think the first time I spoke to her was in my work car park; Rumit drove over as I had to give him something so I managed to chat to her for a few minutes. I think she knew quite a bit about me but she wasn't shy or anything which is good – in fact she talked so much I got bored – only kidding Rita!

They were going to get married over 2 weekends; the registry and Indian ceremony one weekend and the wedding reception the following week. One evening when I was out with Rumit and Nelesh, he asked which one of us would be the best man. To Rumit it was quite simple; it *had* to be one of us and suddenly Nee said "Let Sandip do it, I don't like making speeches!" So there you go, I was the best man for the second time! Yes, I was E2's best man several years earlier and I was actually quite pleased to be chosen again! Mind you standing up in front of 100's of people and delivering a speech would be quite daunting but there was no way I'd let one of my best friends down so I just had to get on with it!

"Being late for a wedding is a woman's prerogative" – this is what you hear time and time again. For Indians, this is nothing new; most Indians are late for everything and is commonly referred to as "Indian timing" or lack of it. I was very proud of being the one who would pick Rita up and drive her to the registry hall to get married. Picking her up in my black Vectra wouldn't have gone down well so I borrowed my sisters Mercedes convertible. On the morning of the registry wedding, I had one thing on my mind – "Don't be late for the registry". It was quite simple really; get ready, drive to Rita's, pick her up, drive to the registry. It surely couldn't be that hard could it? The night before I was adamant that I would not be delayed at all the next morning. I must have done Sunita's head in. Is my suit ready? Is my shirt ironed? These were just some of the questions Sunita tirelessly answered. There was no need to panic though; Sunita is one of the most organised people I know so yes, everything I needed for the next morning had already been sorted out and was ready to go.

That night I set my alarm and then set another one just to be sure. Yeah, yeah I know, a bit crazy really but I didn't want to start the day off by getting up late. There was no need for either of the alarms; I did sleep that night but not much and as many people who needed to get up on time have experienced themselves, got up just before the alarm went off! I got myself sorted and set off to get Rita - it was their wedding day! I got to Rita's very early which I guess isn't a bad thing and then waited for Rita to get ready. As time ticked on, many of her friends and cousins arrived and I wasn't worried about the time whatsoever but 30 minutes later with no sign of Rita I was worrying big time. To the others there I put on a brave face and a few minutes later Rumit called me to check we'd be on time. Not wanting to worry him at all I said "No problem mate, we'll be there..." I found myself pacing around and round whilst I eagerly waited for the bride to arrive but I got the horrible feeling that things were starting to go wrong.

One of her cousins came downstairs and I asked her what was happening. She wasn't worried at all; "she'll be a few minutes" - to be honest I didn't believe her. By now, the woman's prerogative to be late was wearing a little thin and I had visions of a furious Rumit standing in the registry room waiting for her arrival. I think the registry wedding was booked for 10.15am and it was now 9.45am; although that still gave us 30 minutes, we had to get from Melton Road into town, park the car and get inside. Rumit phoned again and I told him "we're just leaving mate..." If only he knew the truth; we were far from leaving and I had to do something about it. Just as I was about to make my way upstairs I heard the fantastic "clunk clunk" sound. It was the girls making their way downstairs and the sound I could hear was their high heeled shoes pounding on the stairs.

Within a few seconds Rita came into view - totally unaware of the nervous breakdown I almost had, she said "Let's go" so as quick as I could I got her into the car - here comes the bride (and she was dressed in white!) By now time was really against us; if my memory serves me well we had 9 minutes to get to the registry office so we were up against it big time. As it turned out, the traffic lights were green all the way which helped us to get there with about a minute to spare; I cannot express how relieved I was that we weren't late. I must say that I felt extremely honoured and proud to have been the one to bring Rita to Rumit that morning; it felt really special so a little message to both Rumit and Rita: "Thanks for letting me play a special part in your wedding guys..."

The formal registry ceremony took place and a few minutes later, one of my best friends was married - wicked man! After showering Mr & Mrs Kotecha with confetti it was time to head off to the next location - the temple where the Indian wedding ceremony would take place. I'm the first to admit that I had no idea what would happen at the temple. All I knew is that I would be sitting next to Rumit and swapping places with Nee from time to time (Nee was back on best man duty once again!). The ceremony was performed by a priest who recited verses from the holy book and got the married couple to perform various rituals whilst friends and family looked on. The whole ceremony would take quite a while and everything was going ok until I thought I heard my name booming out the speakers. I quickly shrugged it off, I must have been hearing things. I mean why on earth would my name be mentioned?

As I slowly looked out into the crowd I could see smirks on the faces of many. Not quite sure what the smiles were about I just continued to sit there as there wasn't much I had to do anyway. A few seconds later I was certain that my name was being said and this time the reaction on the crowd was overwhelming. They were in fits of laughter and as I found out a few seconds later, my name was basically added in verse as the best man. In short they were singing happy wedding vibes but taking the piss at the same time. I must have looked like a right plonker; I was so preoccupied with the priest (just in case I was summoned to do something) that my concentration on the singing lapsed. The crowd were laughing more as to them it appeared I was unaware of what was going on – and they were right! Anyhow, it was all good fun (well sort of!) and a few hours later it was all over. That day my nerves took a right battering but the main thing is that everything went smoothly...

The wedding reception took place the following weekend. I know for a fact that Rumit wasn't too keen on the first dance. Mind you being forced to dance with Rita would put most people off; seriously though the "first dance" can be quite uncomfortable and Rumit didn't want to be up there for too long by themselves. He didn't need to worry; about 30 seconds after their dance started, the floor soon filled up as other couples took to the stage; you could see the nerves drain from his face which was good and the Jack Daniels that flowed afterwards soon helped to calm him down. It was a great reception; friends and family having a great time. Rishi looked super in his little Indian outfit but he was only 18 months old and part way through the reception I dropped him off to my mum's so he could have a sleep whilst we partied on...

Very cute!

Rishi saw a bus – look how excited he got!

By the time Rishi was approaching 2 years old, he'd been in nursery for almost a year and a half. The hours worked out well for Sunita, she'd drop him off at 8.30am then start work. She opted to work part time instead which made sense as she could then pick Rishi up once she finished work so she got the best of both worlds. Rather than send him to a nursery we could have left him at my mums but figured it would be much better to have him attend a nursery where he would interact with other kids -it would be much more beneficial to him in the long run. The one thing we weren't quite prepared for was the cost of it all - the cost of sending him part time per month was close to £500 - an unbelievable amount of money but if we wanted to send him there

416

then that's the price we'd have to pay. In total Rishi was at the private nursery for 3 and half years - it doesn't take much to calculate what it cost us over that time!

Rishi was so much fun, he had a super cheeky smile and was a happy child. For his second birthday we weren't sure what to do. I didn't want the typical "Indian" thing of having a massive birthday party in a function room somewhere because you end up not celebrating the birthday but instead have to make sure you look after (free food and drink!) for the adults. Well, no way was that going to happen; it was a kid's party not an adults but as the date got closer and closer we still weren't sure what or how to celebrate it. In the end it was decided that we'd celebrate it @ home and Sunita then started looking through the yellow pages for a kid's entertainer. We'd left it late; very late in fact and we were quite surprised at how quickly the entertainers get booked up. Thankfully Sunita found someone who was free on that date so we made the booking quick time. So there you go, "Bo Bo the clown" was booked, and the marquee was sorted whilst most of the food and drink would be arranged closer to the day.

The weather report for the party day wasn't too good; showers and heavy winds were predicted so it was fingers crossed that they'd get it wrong and it would be a warm and sunny day instead! Soon the marquee that we'd put up in the garden was packed with people; the adults were at the back whilst the kids were all sat very excited at the front. Bo Bo the clown had made an entrance, a rather lack lustre entrance but an entrance nevertheless. With most kid's entertainers, you know if there good or not within minutes simply by the way they interact with the kids but there was something about him that just wasn't right. As the party got into full flow, the kids looked as if they were enjoying themselves and were amazed at the animals being made from balloons...

Bo Bo then started to tell jokes but the nature and innuendos associated with them weren't kiddie friendly at all. For quite a while, his jokes didn't get the laughs with the young ones - they just looked at him with blank faces whilst the adults at the back were feeling quite embarrassed. As for us; Sunita and I that is, we didn't know what to do; we'd hired a kid's entertainer and were witnessing a stand-up routine from Jongleurs instead. I was quite pissed off and angry at Bo Bo and felt like confronting him. What I *really* wanted to say to him was "You some sort of clown? but I knew he'd say 'yes' so I didn't... Instead, we told the kids it was time to have something to eat so for now, they were safe.

After having a quick bite to eat, the clown only hung around for a little while and then we were glad to see the back of him. I don't think the kids suffered too much in the end and they all seemed to have a better time chasing each other around the garden. Unfortunately, the weather prediction was spot on; it was clouding over and the wind was really picking up and within about 30 minutes we had to get everyone out of the marquee as it was too dangerous to be in there! With that the party was over; the hyperactive kids went home and we cleared up. Mind you, now that the kids party was over, the adults one would begin. That evening we'd invited all our friends around and trust me we had enough jokes that day and it was a great finish to Rishi's 2nd birthday even though he wasn't around to see it!

In the summer that followed Rishi's 2nd birthday we never managed to get away at all and home life plodded on as "normal" if such a thing exists. To be honest nothing stood out, well nothing life changing anyway but things were good. Work was stable for both of us, which is obviously a good thing, Rishi was settled in nursery and happy to be there and for me at least, the best thing about each day was simply watching our boy grow up. Each day was different, each day he'd say something that made us laugh and each day he probably did something that annoyed us! Regardless of what he did though, we wouldn't have had it any other way - try as you may, you simply cannot put in words what your kids mean to you. It's something i've heard others say but somehow never thought i'd be saying the same let alone putting in into words.

Rishi was always losing his toys; quite understandable considering some of them were quite small and could easily end

Sunita clowning around.   Rishi doesn't look too happy here!

Big panda from Sharmil kaka
& Rina Kaki!

A young Rita!

up being shoved under the sofa, fallen behind the radiator or shoved into the VHS player? What? Yes, it's true, one evening when we were trying to play a VHS tape.... hold on, just hold on. Before I carry on I want to talk a little about VHS tapes. Now, when you consider that they first came out way back around 1980, it's an absolute miracle, an amazing feat, a technological mishap that they still exist today. With all the technology surrounding us, how on earth has VHS lasted so long and continues to do so? Interesting question eh? No? Well it's just me then so back to what I was talking about before.... I was saying that we were trying to watch a VHS tape but the tape wouldn't fit into the player. I tried several times but there was no way it was going in.

There was something in there and as I looked into the player, I could see something orange firmly stuck inside - would you believe it, Rishi's flute that was lost a few days earlier had been found. The little monster did what many kids do and shoved it into something. It was only a small flute and to be honest I was just relieved that he managed to shove it in without getting hurt - it *is* electrical after all and anything could have happened. I managed to get the flute out and the video player is still playing happily today. Unfortunately for us, Rishi hadn't quite finished with his tricks. We had been given a DVD player as a present and one day he decided to eject the DVD because he wanted to watch one of his movies. Things for him went to plan, for us it was much more expensive. Ejecting the DVD tray was easy for him, he found the button and hey presto, the tray ejected.

He must have got bored or something after that because the next thing we knew he rushed back upstairs. When I came back down and saw the DVD ejected I just went over to close it thinking that someone had ejected it by mistake. On pushing the close button, I could hear a grinding sound and the tray appeared to be stuck. I tried to push it but it was no good and I soon realised why - the tray itself was bent to a degree that there was no way it could be bent back and that was that. He'd broken the DVD so I made him watch as I unplugged it from the back, disconnected the power, unravelled all the cabling, made him look at the bent tray and then made him watch me throw it in the bin. I'm certain my actions that day hit home; yes he was only young but I think he learnt his first real lesson that day and the proof is that to this day he is unbelievably careful with our stuff around the house.

Vip hits 40 – time to cut the cake.
Mind you looks more like
a more spade than a knife!

Rishi, Preeya, Ashish,
Priyanka & Rahul.

It took 2 of them to lift him –
Rishi ate too much cake!

Cry baby!

36

If only everything in life was as reliable as a...

Before we knew it, 2003 was almost over and it was amazing how fast the year had gone by. Obviously, the days, weeks, months and years pass by at the same pace; it's just our way of life, the things we do and so on that merely give you the impression that time is moving at a rapid pace. Nevertheless, as a family we managed to take a short trip to Venice where we watched Rishi run across St Mark's Square as he chased away the hundreds of pigeons that lurked around the centre. Rishi was at that age where he was so much fun and we had a super 3 days away. We travelled around by bus quite a bit as our hotel was outside the main tourism areas and we often prefer public transport anyway because it's the best way to see a city...

In the same year Sunita was pleased too; her Austin Maestro, the car that everyone loved to take the piss out of, was finally put to rest and her new car; a VW Golf had arrived. She specifically said she wanted a silver one so she got it. We had to drive to Birmingham to pick up the car and I remember being at the wheel of the Maestro as we made our way there. The car, despite being a laughing stock amongst many was a reliable, dependable and cheap car whose days were unfortunately numbered. The car dealer offered a whopping £10 for the car which seemed insulting but Sunita wanted her new car regardless and the deal was done.

Soon after buying my Vectra I decided to splash out on a private number plate. Luckily I found the perfect one and after parting with hard cash, I was the owner of "V6 SKP". I say perfect because the car was a "V" registered car, it also had a V6 engine and SKP are my actual initials "Sandip Kumar Patel" (in case I hadn't mentioned it). Now that we had another new car (well nearly new anyway), I thought I may as well get a private plate for Sunita too. I knew exactly which plate she'd be happy with and a few weeks later, having parted with close to £400, "V5 SKP" was registered and belonged to Sunita.

Just for the record, her car was a "V" registration too, her lucky number was 5 and her full name is "Sunita Kumari Patel" so as you can see, it all worked out perfectly.

I don't care what anyone else says, having "**V5 SKP**" and "**V6 SKP**" plates was very cool and they looked great on our cars parked outside. Throughout the years, about 6 people have offered to buy the plate off me and most of them thought I would sell; they probably assumed that being Indian, I couldn't pass the offer of making some quick money! Well sorry to disappoint but the answer was no. I wasn't interested in selling and I wasn't interested in their offers either so that was that.

37

Parenthood

Watching Rishi grow up was priceless and as weeks turned into months and months into years, it was quite frightening how quickly he grew up. When you have one kid, the busy bodies often wait a few years before saying things like "it's time Rishi had a brother or sister" which used to wind me up. Ultimately, it's no-one's business except mine and Sunita's so I wish they would just shut up! I say "they" in the singular sense of the word because after having Rishi, both of us were adamant we didn't want any more kids. Well, if the truth be known I did want kids but would have liked to have 2 within a few years of getting married. Sunita on the other hand wasn't quite ready for it which was fine. Anyway, despite what either of us wanted, we had a child and for now there would be more additions!

As Rishi grew up, he was still as active as ever and it meant that we could start to do more things with him. He loved riding his tricycle and we took many trips to the parks where he'd race along like made along the paths. Over time, he outgrew the trike and switched to a bicycle with stabilisers but once he saw other kids with just 2 wheels, he kept wanting to take the stabilisers off. This, as you can imagine, was easier said than done. Had I simply unbolted them, he would have ended up on the road and in tears no doubt! There was only one thing to do; I *had* to teach him to ride a bike for himself. I was looking forward to this moment because to me it was a proper father and son thing. That's not to say Sunita couldn't teach him, far from it but I don't think she could run as fast as me and there would certainly be lots of running....

So on one fine spring morning, the stabilisers came off much to Rishi's surprise. He gave me a "what are you doing?" look and was petrified at the thought of riding his bike without his tiny wheels to assist! As we got into our car and drove out of Whitebeam Road, he looked even more scared but dad was on hand to reassure him which seemed to do the trick. Within a few minutes we were at the park and ready to go. Before we set off on our pilot "run", Rishi kept saying "don't let go of me dad...". "Course I won't" came my reply, knowing full well that if the plan came together that's exactly what i'd be doing. I grabbed the back of the seat, Rishi grabbed the handle bars and I told him to look straight ahead and to pretend that I wasn't there.

The first run was brilliant, Rishi pedalled away and I held onto the seat to stop him veering to one side and crashing....and then I let go. Rishi had no idea that I wasn't holding on and each time he appeared as if he was about to look behind him I made sure I grabbed the back of the seat which gave him the reassurance he needed that I was there. We must have been in the park for about 30 minutes and in that time he was getting more and more confident and each attempt was better than the previous one. He progressed so well that at times he managed about 10 metres before he started to wobble like made and fear turned into joy much to my relief! Just as I was about to tell him that it was time to head home and that we'd practice another day, we thought we'd give it one more go. This time something changed, I held the seat for a few moments and that's it - he was on his own.

Yes, he swerved all over the place (sorry to the old lady whose little dog almost got squashed!), yes he nearly crashed into the park bench and yes it was tiring but he'd done it. He suddenly shouted "Dad - let go of me" at which I replied "i'm not holding you!". He didn't quite understand but I ran a little faster and once he saw me he soon realised that he was riding solo - yippee! The look on his face; that magical expression of sheer ecstasy; that sheer delight and amazement was awesome and something every parent should witness. Rishi started off by not believing he could do it and we proved he could; it may only have been a bike but to a 5 year old, this was a big thing and one which boosted his confidence no end...

Over the years we've always made a point of making sure we do things as a family, from simple things like going for a walk to riding our bikes and even going for a leisurely swim. This was *real quality time* and something we all looked forward to. All too often you can get entangled up in life so much that you lose focus of the important things. I was guilty of this for quite a while and to be honest it was only until we had Rishi that I understood how precious time is. Life moves fast and you need to make the most of it. This is probably the reason why I like to get out and about so much. I'm sure Sunita used to get fed up with me whinging about boring Sundays and those evenings when we had nothing planned.

I must admit that on some days it is good to have nothing planned so you can just chill out but in general I hated the thought of wasting time. I was always itching to get out, go somewhere, do something, visit someone, anything as long we did something. In hindsight, I think that's one of the reasons why Rishi's a well-travelled young boy, the travel bug has definitely spread across the family.

38

Weight a minute

"Get me a chocolate as well..." I used to say to Sunita whenever she walked out the door on her way to Asda. I've always loved chocolate; I can't believe how anyone couldn't like it and i'd always readily take the opportunity of getting some when I had the chance. Mind you it wasn't just chocolate that took my fancy; ice cream (especially Strawberry Cheesecake Haagan Daaz) was another favourite and something i'd eat weekly. At work i'd often go the breakfast van that occasionally parked further up the road and get myself a huge breakfast bap even though I wasn't really hungry. 10 minutes later and I really wished that i'd done a 'Zammo' special and "just said no!" (if anyone doesn't get that it's a famous line from Grange Hill - look it up!). The bap was well nice but totally unnecessary but I just couldn't say no. Over the course of the week, this became a regular thing and the fresh cream cakes (another addictive thing!) at lunch time were just too irresistible.

At home our eating habits were totally different; Sunita was big on fruits and salad whilst I was big on anything else. Over time, the weight slowly but surely piled on but I never looked like one of those "fat" people and the weight never really bothered me anyway. The fact that I needed 36" waist jeans and extra large T shirts was totally irrelevant until one day my sister invited both of us to one of her "health road shows" which was basically an open day on health related matters. Once there you could check your blood pressure, get cholesterol levels checked and really get your own MOT so to speak. We went along but for me it was just to make up some numbers and to give my sister support. Once there, there was a real buzz in there; perhaps it was because of the location. It was held at the Belgrave neighbourhood centre on Melton Road in Leicester; home of the infamous "Golden Mile".

Bit of trivia for you now - most people think the name "Golden Mile" comes from the vast number of gold and jewellery shops that adorn this road but in fact in the early 60's/70's a short stretch of Melton Road had so many traffic lights, it was said to give off a golden colour hence the name. Recently, however, the name has been attributed to the gold shops and the traffic light influence has been long forgotten... Anyway this part of Leicester has strong Asian influences and a large proportion of Asians live there. This was good for the health road show; inside it was packed and there was a hive of activity as people hurried around the various stalls, discussed health matters with the professionals and got their bodies checked out. My sister was really busy that day so never really got to chat to her that much but one of her colleagues asked if I wanted my blood pressure and weight checked.

I never thought twice about it so headed off and within 20 minutes my mini MOT was over. When the results came back, I was shocked and I mean shocked. Being told that I was overweight took a little getting used to. Ok - she never said "Listen fatso, you need to cut back on the pies right?" but she gave it to me straight. Basically someone of my age and height shouldn't weigh as much as I did and I was told to lose weight now. At the time, I was glad that neither my sister or Sunita were there to hear it because Sunita for one would have probably said "told you so" which was something I didn't want to hear. There was no point hanging around now but just before we left my sister said "Did you have a good time?". In my mind I was thinking "yup - had a great afternoon thanks" and with that we left.

Though I say it myself, I have a tremendous amount of will power and knowing full well that I had to change things made me even more determined. It would be no easy task though; I weighed in at a hefty 14 stone, some 3.5 stone above the "ideal" weight of someone my age and height but how on earth was I going to even start? Well as a kid I loved to go swimming but never really got the chance to go that often so I decided i'd make up for lost time now. Oadby swimming pool is only minutes from my house so that was the first step - get back into the pool! Sunita was a little shocked when I said i'm going swimming and I was more than shocked when I actually went. The pool "length" seemed very long and at the end of my first length I was extremely short of breath, my muscles ached and knew exactly that I was well out of condition.

However, I would not be defeated and knew that you can't just expect to swim loads of lengths when you haven't done any real exercise for years. That day I struggled big time and had to cling onto the side of the pool whilst young kids and super fit adults swam past effortlessly. When I got home, Sunita could clearly see I didn't have a good time and when she said "who told you to go then?" that didn't go down particularly well either! Over the next 6 months I made radical changes; swimming was a twice weekly thing and I even went in my lunch times! I would also go for a brisk walk around the business park where I worked not just to get out of the office but to get exercise and a bit of fresh air - it was wicked.

The high calorie, high fat content diet was overhauled and I virtually cut out all chocolate (except Fridays which was my chocolate day!) Fresh cream cakes were still naughty but nice but were restricted to once a week. Whenever I felt a snack attack coming on, i'd eat fruit rather than tucking into a Yorkie or something. I stuck to this regime for many months and the results were astounding and I don't use that word lightly. I felt better generally, was less susceptible to colds, could swim for one hour non-stop and was in the condition of my life. The weight literally fell off and I was down to a lean 10 stone 2 lbs; i'd lost over 3 stones in weight! The only downside was that I had to buy new clothes; the ones I had were massive. I could get into 30 inch waist jeans; a far cry from my 36 inch waist I had before and t shirts were now "small" fitting as opposed "large" or "XL".

Most people look at "diets" and get pressured into cutting out all the things they like such as chocolate. It doesn't have to be that way; it is all about moderation and being sensible. Provided you eat sensibly and exercise regular, you can have the "treats"; just don't eat too many of them! My blood pressure was checked at the doctors 6 months after that health road show; my blood pressure was in the doctor's words "text book", my cholesterol was "text book" and my BMI was 21.2 which is perfect for my height and weight - that ladies and gentleman is how you do it...

39

My work family and
hospital billing - July 2003

At Magnetic North (the company I worked for in case you'd forgotten), work load was as hectic as ever and as new projects kicked off, the work was more and more challenging. In short, there was far too much work for a sole software quality assurance engineer and I was given the go ahead to recruit a placement student to assist for a year or so. The process was fascinating and I was involved with all aspects including liaising with the placement unit at Leicester University, CV screening, arranging interviews and the actual interview itself. It may not seem much but for someone like me who had always been the one being interviewed, I was on the other side of the table so to speak. The interview process and how the candidate "performed" was quite relaxed and not like the very formal procedures you often must follow in some companies.

One of the best questions, not for its complexity, but for its simplicity was "What weaknesses do you have?". This *catches* people out and they often sit there pondering over why we would ask such a question. Depending on the answer, the follow on question would be "What have you done to overcome your weakness?". Anyhow, the range of answers was truly mind boggling and you had a pretty good idea of who you'd want back for 2nd interviews. For the second interviews, I wrote a software test and would secretly smirk to myself as I watched all of them battling away to finish all the questions in the allotted time. Over the years we hired a number of students and several of them have indeed stuck in the profession. Naturally having me as their manager, gave them the best start to their career but I would say that, wouldn't I?

Each month I would "sign off" their work which meant summarising what they'd been up to in the preceding 4 weeks and I was also tasked with meeting their tutors to discuss their progress. For me, the placement scheme was brilliant, I knew how difficult it was to find work and just being able to help these students was extremely rewarding indeed. Although we trained the students as much as we could, there was always some aspects of the business that required senior staff. On one such occasion, a customer of ours had bought our software and wasn't prepared to pay off the remaining balance until we had carried out a formal "UAT" (User acceptance test) at their premises. Basically, this means that before they would pay Magnetic North what they owed, we had to prove to them that the software we had deployed did work and "did what it says on the tin!".

I knew of the customer and clearly remember overhearing various discussions on "how we're going to get the rest of the money...". I was then called into Dominic's office (in case you've forgotten, he's the MD of Magnetic North). Dominic being Dominic started off by saying *"Listen S, I need your help... ever been to Philadelphia?"* You see, the customer I am talking about were based in the USA and we literally had a week to turn this around. I'm certain we discussed this on a Tuesday and within minutes of hearing the plan, an E ticket had been booked for the following Sunday. The schedule was set; I would fly out alone to Philadelphia via Toronto and would be met there by Dominic and Susan (another colleague who had secured the initial deal...).

Unfortunately, it meant flying from Heathrow and it was a very early start on that Sunday. I think I was up for 4.30am, drove down to Heathrow, parked the car and checked in. First of all Air Canada decided they "couldn't find my reservation", then told me "I may have to fly the next day" and after kicking off a bit told me they'd found the booking. I didn't need this so early in the morning and already I hated this stupid airline. The flight out was uneventful but Toronto airport was "interesting" for the wrong reason. You land in one terminal, go to another to pick up baggage then have to go back to the original terminal to catch the next flight. I managed to board my onward flight with minutes to spare thanks to the crappy airport and a few hours later we touched down in Philadelphia. After loitering around the baggage hall like a criminal I soon realised that I had a problem; I may have arrived but my luggage didn't!

At the lost property booth, I was met by an American; ok it was a big American who asked me about my luggage, gave me a lost luggage reference and assured me they would be in touch. She refused to take my mobile number so how on earth she thought she'd get hold of me was anyone's guess. So, I was hungry, tired, had no luggage and now had to make my way to "Delaware" as I was heading straight to the customer's premises. Oh yes, we had little time, well only 3 full days so there was no time to waste. Inside the rental firm's office, I was confronted by a lady who seemed to take a liking to me. She asked loads of questions, none of them particularly relevant to anything and to be honest I was too tired to care. She kept going on about a free upgrade. "Fine" I thought, just give me the damn car so I can get out of here...

The paperwork took ages and she could see I was getting frustrated so said "you wait outside if you want, the car will be outside soon...". With that, I stepped outside; it was hot and humid and dark, gloomy clouds filled the sky -it was going to chuck it down hard real soon... 10 minutes went by and the car hadn't arrived but I was too tired to argue anymore so just waited. A further 10 minutes later and I was really pissed off; it didn't help that a brand new Chrysler C300 was parked right in front of. Now these cars are common now but in 2003, they were extremely rare, and i'd never seen one before. It was a huge car and looked more like a presidential limousine! Reality kicked in and I remembered I was stood there with no car so I stormed back inside.

A few minutes later and I was back outside; the gleaming new Chrysler C300 *was* my hire car! I had been standing in front of it for over 20 minutes like an idiot but I was just glad to get inside. There was no time to waste; I had some directions but with no navigation had to rely on my navigational skills and a level head - i'd find the customer's premises.... eventually. After a few minutes i'd found my way out of the airport and was on the freeway; it's amazing how quickly you adjust to driving on the other side of the road but i'd done this plenty of times before so it was fine... About 45 minutes later, I pulled into 118 Lukens Drive and was soon in the car park of HBCS (Hospital Billing and Collection Service. I was met by 2 members of the "quality" team (basically those involved in the deployment of the software).

I tried to keep the introductions and small talk to a minimum; time really was tight and I was keen to get cracking. With that, the HBCS team opened up the phone lines which basically meant that we could dial into call centre and test the software we had installed. Teething problems meant progress was slow and a few hours later I got a call on my phone - I had to go back to the airport because Dom and Susan had just touched down. An hour later and the pick-up was done and we headed back to HBCS once again. On our way back I gave them both an update of where I got to and we discussed the plan for the next 4 days. The thing is we were all flying back on Thursday and hence the pressure was really on to get the job done.

Dominic was keen to get the job done and the last thing he wanted to do was get lost. Within minutes of getting into the car he'd switched on his laptop and then stuck a small aerial to the windscreen. A few clicks of the mouse later and his laptop was filled with an area map of the Philadelphia area - he had GPS on his laptop! By the time we arrived back at HBCS it was getting late; we did manage to get some more work done but everyone was tired and we decided we'd done enough for one day. By the time I got into bed, i'd been awake for over a day and was totally shattered but the next morning, we were raring to go; our team talk had been done and we headed back to HBCS. It was Monday morning now and what a difference... their huge car park had a single space free which meant there were lots of people inside, the call centre floor was incredibly busy and for me it was awesome seeing such activity. My job was basically to run through about 50 separate software tests over the next few days and to basically get "sign off" which meant that HBCS agreed that the software was working correctly.

However, getting to that point would be quite tough. I loved it though, I met so many people: managers, supervisors and I even spent considerable time sitting with the agents as they talked to their customers and tried to get them to pay their medical debts. For me it was a real buzz seeing the software we'd developed used in real life. You're always aware that many customers have your software but it's not until you see it in action do you get that great sense of satisfaction that all the hard work you put into it had paid great dividends and HBCS, in this case, were benefiting from the software. As the hours slowly ticked by, I felt a huge adrenaline rush as I rushed around playing back calls, checking audio content and discussing the UAT with the customer. Slowly but surely, the blank spaces on the UAT form were filled in with tick after tick; we were making great progress!

By the end of the day, I was ready for bed but we had to eat first. All 3 of us decided to head off to get a bite to eat and then come back to work! Dominic had managed to persuade the customer to give us access to their building. This wasn't a small building or a small company either and i've said it many times before but Dominic has a phenomenal way with words and his rapport with the customer is exemplary. I can't remember where we ate that evening but it was jokes all round and it really was a laugh a minute. Rested and fed, it was time to head back; we managed to get inside the building ok but it was pitch black and we couldn't find the light switch. Picture the scene; 3 of us who have never unlocked this building in our lives had let ourselves in with no idea of where the light switch was, we had no ID and looked really suspicious. All we could do was use our hands to feel our way around which was hilarious but eventually saved the day again and we had light.

When he looked closer at the light switch he had just turned on, he noticed he was inches away from what looked like a live power cable; instead of putting the building lights on; Dom could have put his own lights out! That was a real close shave but we had the building to ourselves now and had full control over their phone system, hundreds of their desktop PC's, their server room and of course the coffee machine! That evening, despite us all being very tired, was an extremely productive one and we managed to carry out a "dry run" of the software tests we'd be performing over the next few days.

We'd make phone calls to each other and put as many different accents on as we could. Instead of "can you hear me?" we'd piss ourselves as i'd start to talk in slang and then Dominic would join in with "here me now, here me now..." as well as "big up selecta'". Anyway it was well funny but I don't think we even deleted the call recordings. I can just imagine the reaction when the HBCS quality monitoring team listened to those calls. The tests passed but i'd have expected that anyway - it was just easier running through these tests in a controlled environment but the next day we'd be running them again in the hectic call centre environment so it was fingers crossed...

By Thursday morning our work was virtually done but the final "sign off"; that signature that meant the software was ok and that Magnetic North would get paid, was still elusive and the only person who could ensure we got it was me! After a brief meeting with the customer to let them know our "plan" for the day it was straight to work. That morning I rushed around all over their call centre; running tests, checking audio yet again, running through real call scenarios, waiting anxiously as the call centre supervisors listened to the calls and fed back progress to management. By 2pm in the afternoon we'd done it, I say we because it really was a team effort. That final signature was on the form and our work

436

was done. Rather than speak to their management individually, a meeting was called and a summary of our 3 day work was explained in full. Everyone involved was happy, the customer knew they had software they could rely on and knew the effort we'd put in whilst we got paid and could move on.

For me this trip was the most memorable at Magnetic North; I had an experience i'd never forget, I went there with 2 colleagues who made the journey fun and without doubt, the moment Susan starting to wind her window up frantically just as we pulled out of a "Gas" station because she thought a local was trying to steal the car, was one of funniest things i've seen. As it turned out, there was no misdemeanour here; the local was actually trying to complement her on the Chrysler C300 because as I said before the car really stood out and looked special. At about 5pm that day we said our good byes to HBCS, headed to the hotel, picked up our stuff then drove back to Philadelphia airport where we went our own ways. I was flying to the UK via Toronto whilst Dom & Susan had an alternate flight plan and with that we all headed home.

The flight back to Toronto was boring and I by the time I got into my seat for the transatlantic flight back I was exhausted. Unfortunately, I could feel a headache coming on and asked the flight attendant for some tablets. 15 minutes later, my head was throbbing and the flight attendant had disappeared so I asked for tablets again - how bloody hard can it be to get a few pills? By now I was getting agitated and despite getting the pills eventually, my frustration with Air Canada didn't end there. Unbelievably when they served the evening meal, everyone seemed to get in except me. What the hell was going on, was I invisible or something? Was there some kind of vendetta against me? Did they realise anyone was sitting in this damn seat?

I was even more furious when we finally landed at Heathrow - "I'm sorry Mr. Patel, you're bags aren't on this flight..." Yes you guessed it, Air Canada lost my bags - again. I was lost for words;

losing them once was bad enough but twice was inexcusable. I just wanted to get home now and I still had a 2 hour drive ahead of me so once they assured me that it would arrive and that it would be sent to my home address, I got into the car and headed home... it was Friday morning and Dominic said I could take the rest of the day off which was quite nice so I just chilled at home for the rest of the day and looked forward to seeing Rishi and Sunita.

40

Rushed projects and rushing home

Working in a relatively small company such as Magnetic North meant that you're typically involved in most projects which is quite a good thing because you really do feel involved. Working in software can be a rewarding and extremely challenging career and one particular week in November 2004 tested my patience to the limit and led me to make a harsh decision. One of our customers was expanding and they wanted to use our call recording software in a way that it wasn't designed to. Business being business the customer placed an order and Magnetic North slightly reengineered the software to work as per the customer's requirements. There is no issue there provided the software development life cycle was followed correctly. Unfortunately time, as ever, was very limited and it was one of those situations where the software just had to be delivered on time. This meant rushed coding, sparse software testing and lots of support cases as the customer reported bug after bug. Firstly, I did understand the necessity to "please" the customer because customers are the heart of any business but I struggled to understand the logic in delivering software that clearly didn't work correctly.

Fundamentally, Magnetic North as a team pulled out all the stops to get the job done which is obviously very credible and I know for a fact that there were many late nights and extra hours over the weekend just to keep things on track. But, as the bug count started to rise, the customer's perception of the software must have taken a pretty big dent and it was this that really bugged me (pardon the pun!). Realising that we had an issue,

I discussed this with the managers but the feedback was simply that there was nothing they could do and that we just had to get on with it. Over the next 2 weeks, each day was the same, the customer kept finding more issues and pressure was on from upper management to get them fixed. The customer was losing patience quick, demanded to see proof that we did test our software and the relationship between the 2 companies was at an all-time low.

Despite airing deep concern yet again I just felt that nothing proactive was being done or even being discussed about and I decided that I could no longer be part of it. At around 11am on a Wednesday morning (the date and time stuck in my mind ever since), I went back to my desk, wrote up my resignation letter and left it on my manager's desk and went home. Perhaps that was the wrong thing to do, perhaps I was making too much of it, perhaps this was over kill? All I know is that I had immense pride in what I did at work and the basic software life cycle was completely ignored and we basically just released software that was un-tested. I didn't want any part of it, I felt let down and felt that this was the only way out...

As soon as I got home I got a call from work and agreed, reluctantly, to meet my boss to discuss the incidents leading up to the resignation. I went; I discussed everything on my mind and felt better for doing so. I went on to explain that although my resignation may have "come out of the blue", there were many factors that led up to it and I was serious about it. I then listened as my boss as he explained the reasons why the software was developed in that manner and although he agreed that it never should have happened, it was good that he was honest and basically told it as it was. Hindsight is always good after the event and at the end of our talk, we had agreed many things, put together an action plan and were confident we could put this bad episode behind us and ensure it never happened again. My resignation was retracted and the following day we kicked off our plan. I was then given time to test the software properly, we released a software patch which made the customer happy and more importantly injected some much needed confidence back into them.

At home, my father and his addiction to drink was still causing friction in the family despite years and years of us all pleading for him to sort himself out. In that time my mother still put up with all the abuse; the only difference now was that she had been through such emotional turmoil that nothing my dad said or did phased her at all. To her credit, to the rest of us, she was the same old mum, always pleased to see us and always looking out for us. Whenever I went around to see my mum in the evening, she'd be busy cooking dinner for my dad; heating food and then heating it again when he complained that it was too cold even though he never even tried it. He thought he could treat my mum however he liked and my mum had been through so much that she could see no way out and just put up with everything he did.

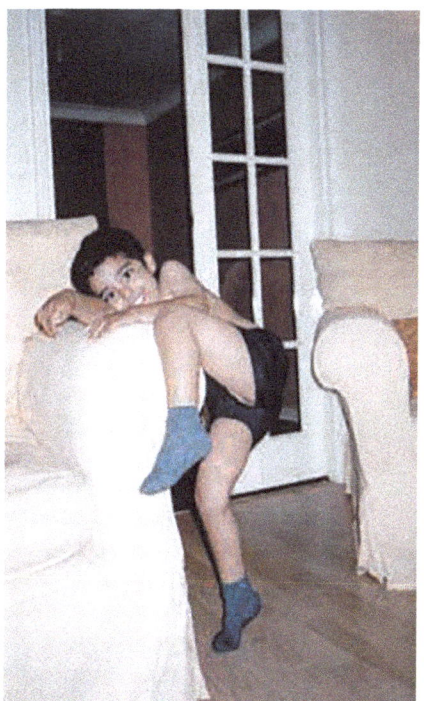

Rishi with one of his moves.

My wifey!

Smiley kid.

Camera tricks!

Rare photo of Max.

Kiran and Priyanka share the
same birthday − 8th December;
this time it was his 40th!

Raj & Rumit − glasee!

For a few months though, this was about to change. At the start of 2005, my mum went to India; a trip she made every other year and this time she was going for around 6 weeks. Whenever my mum went away, my dad was left home alone and my sister and sister in law would take it in turns to take food around. My mum jetted off to India for a well-deserved break in the hot sun and the rest of us just got on with it. Without my mum, there, I only went to the house now and then; I hated going there simply because every time I did, my dad would be extremely drunk, would swear nonstop and it was horrible to see. A few weeks after my mum went we all seemed to notice that the food left the day before was either still on the dining room table or only a little of it has been eaten.

Despite my dad's drinking habits, this was unusual because he always ate his food, even if it was late at night. Initially we thought he wasn't hungry but when the meat went untouched (given the fact that he always ate that), we thought something was wrong. He always seemed to be sleeping too but we knew something wasn't right when he slept right through prime "pub" time. I mean, it was unheard of that he'd be sleeping at 8pm but eventually night after night, he just slept and slept. I don't think any of us were overly concerned; I thought he'd had too much to drink in the afternoons and was simply sleeping it off but this wasn't the case. His condition worsened; we tried to wake him several times but each time he look very confused and although he was speaking, you could see he was struggling to get the words out which made it difficult to understand him.

In a few weeks, things got bad; he was admitted to hospital and the change in him was unbelievable. He seemed to have a vague recollection of who we were, kept repeating himself and slowly his body seemed to shut down. This was scary, i'd never seen anything like this before and in 6 weeks my father was given more medication than he had done in the previous 67 years. The prognosis was bad and terminal - he had that dreaded condition "cancer" or as the medical staff put it "Carcinoma". The cancer spread so rapidly that in a matter of weeks, my dad had no idea who we were, couldn't speak and had to be looked after full time and had no control of his own body.

Laying in front of us was a dying man; our dying father and if i'm honest sadness didn't describe my initial thoughts. It may sound awful but I was just relieved that this man who beat, punched, mentally tortured and inflicted year after year of pain on my dear mother could do so no more.

By the time my mum had returned from India, the hospital could do no more for my dad and he was moved to a care home in Wigston, Leicester. After that, we'd all visit in turn, taking food, sitting with him and making sure he ate. The staff, always looking on the bright side of things, did all they could to make sure he was comfortable but we all knew that the end was close. In fact, when we were told that he may only have a few weeks left, my mum rang our close friends and relatives who, slowly but surely, came to visit and quietly say their good byes. My father had a sister in Coventry and they never got on; whenever they met it was a short "hello" and that was that. When she came to visit, there was no emotion in her face at all. You'd think that knowing her brother was dying would make some sort of difference but it made none whatsoever. Mind you, I guess there was no pretence and I doubt if my dad would have been bothered about it anyway...

I remember the day as if it was yesterday; it was a bright sunny spring morning and it was May 2nd, 2005. It must have been around 11am and the phone rang; it was my sister to let us know that my father had died. In an instant, I recall shaking a little and little Rishi came running in asking who it was. I didn't tell him what happened but rang Sunita straight away as i'm certain she had to go into work that day. She was shocked but not surprised but then again I think it was the same for all of us. We knew it would happen but nothing prepares you for it and that day was one of the hardest of my life. Sunita came home and just before we drove to the care home we tried to explain to Rishi what had happened and he seemed to understand.

We had been to the care home many times before but this was different and my heart was racing. The car park was fairly empty and we were the first ones there. My dad's nurse met us at the door and offered his condolences leading us to his room as he continually said how sorry he was. Outside the bedroom door I froze for a split second and didn't know if I could go any further but in the end I just pushed the door open and walked in. Seeing my dad lying there brought out all emotions in a split second. I never thought i'd react like that and I just ran out of the room in tears. Despite all the things my dad has done over the years to our family, he was still *my dad* and it was just the shock of it all that I couldn't cope with. The person who never shouted at me, always cared for me and never told my mum whenever I got into trouble was gone. The care worker did his best to comfort me but what do you say to a person whose dad has just died? It wasn't long before the rest of my immediate family arrived and eventually we were all together in the bedroom; emotions running high.

When a Hindu person (like us) dies, there are some strict rituals that must be followed; one of which is putting some holy water into the mouth of the person who has just died. One by one we all did this and it was hard watching the kids, the nieces and nephews having to do this. To their credit they all seemed very grown up about it and got on with it without any kind of fuss. I remember Preeya, my niece, being incredibly upset at losing her grandfather. I can understand why; despite all the things i've said, my dad always liked having a laugh with the kids. Mind you the kids gave as good as they got; often laughing at my dad's unusual hair cut!

The doctor came shortly after that to complete the necessary paperwork and medically examine my dad for the last time. A quiet man, the doctor offered his condolences and left as quietly as he came. It was official, cancer had spread rapidly and was the cause of death. For all of us, our lives had changed in an instant but there was one person missing. My brother Vip was on holiday in Tunisia and we had to call him up to give him the news. Sadly, Vip's birthday would never be the same again - the thing is you see, my dad died on Vip's birthday.

My brother then struggled to get a flight and arrived back home a few days later. At home, my mum's house that is, friends and relatives started to arrive and join the prayers that were being said. Men and women sat separately, probably because it was the women who led the prayers which incidentally would last many days. The women wore white as this is the traditional colour of mourning whilst the men wore whatever they want. One thing that always made me laugh no matter the situation was the Indian men who looked extremely smart in their slick suits they'd put on. If it wasn't for the Adidas trainers, they decided to wear they would have looked cool!

For me and my brothers we just sat in the front room and greeted guests as they arrived. It's quite amazing how so many people surface at times like this; i'd never seen many of them before or if I had it was when I was much younger. "Don't you remember me?" "What are you doing now" "How much money do you earn?" - These were just some of the questions that the elder folk would ask me repeatedly. I felt like telling them to get stuffed, after all, it's none of their business but I had to be respectful so I gave them answers that just shut them up. After a while, my one word answers got the point across and the next time I spoke to them was to say goodbye.

One of the worst aspects of a Hindu death is having to prepare the body. I don't mean that in a nasty way but having to go to the funeral parlour and "dress" the body is hard hitting. A few days after the death my brothers and I had to do this very thing but for Kiran, the "middle" brother, it was far too much and he couldn't do it. Cleaned and dressed, my father was now ready for the funeral which took place a few days later. On the morning of the funeral, a Hindu priest comes to the house and performs many final rituals and many more prayers are said. For my brothers and I, there were many "things" we had to do, many things we had to recite and to be honest we were just like robots that day just doing what we were told.

Friends and family place flower petals around the body, incense is placed inside together with flower, butter and herbs and as a last mark of respect we touched the feet of my father. The funeral directors arrived and the body left the house and we made our way to the cemetery for the cremation. The priest reads out my father's life - it was just like "This is your life" except the person isn't alive anymore. Usually everyone must cram inside the small rooms and people often spill outside but this time there were plenty of spaces. I often thought this was an indication of how well liked someone was and if this was true then I guess the empty seats speak for themselves...

The cremation process is a key part of the funeral for Hindus and in particular the "Panch Bhuts" (the body's 5 basic components) need to be returned to the universe to help maintain "cosmic equilibrium". The components in case anyone is interested, are "Prithvi" (earth), "Jal" (water), "Tej" (fire), "Vayu" (Wind) and "Akash" (space). Cremations are also deemed to be the fastest way of releasing the soul. That's the theory at least but as far as I was aware cremations were simply a way to prevent the spread of disease. I mean if you think about it, cremation prevents infections and diseases from spreading because there is no possibility of soil contamination which is a real possibility from traditional burials. Anyhow, back to the funeral...once the priest finished talking about my dad's life, we (my brothers and I) were called up to the front where you basically finish this part of the ceremony by pushing the button which then closes the curtains and hides the coffin.

We were then led around the back of the building where you take the final step and watch as the coffin disappears into the fire. A few minutes later and it's all over; the friends and family step outside and offer their condolences once more to the family and with that everybody departs. Once you get home you're meant to have a shower and change your clothes and only then can you get on with things. At funerals, the elders, allegedly wise to the cultures and beliefs of our religion, often give you dirty looks if you so much as crack a joke or dare to smile. Well let me tell you one thing; our religion doesn't encourage crying at funerals because it is said this can delay the soul from departing. Thankfully, those idiots soon left and at home the mourning wasn't suppressed but we all shared laughter and it was a good time if that makes sense.

The following 3 or 4 days were routine; we'd get back from work and head straight to my mums and all eat together. It was a time when all of us as a family, stuck together and showed what families are supposed to do. Sunita, to her credit was a real trooper throughout it all. Unable to speak Gujerati

447

there were certainly some hairy moments when she was asked many questions by the "elders" and she dealt with them by speaking broken Gujerati and lots of nods! When the prayers started, each of the women often get urged to sing verses solo and unbelievably Sunita joined in and got quite a few compliments.

It was great watching all the ladies having fun in a strange sort of way but Sunita; if you're still reading this book and haven't got bored yet, "thank you" for being the tower I leaned on many times during this time. Following my father's death, Rishi often asked where he went and why he died. It's quite hard to explain this to such a young boy but we simply told him that he was unwell and he has gone to heaven. He often asks about my dad; his granddad and the one regret I do have is that we don't seem to have any photos of them together but thankfully Rishi has a pretty sharp memory and remembers him well.

The rest of the 2005 was pretty much uneventful but Rishi kept us busy as ever. He was growing up to be a curious, fun loving kid and was one of those that just couldn't sit still. As a family, we always tried to do as much together as we could. Often i'd finish work and would pull into the drive with Rishi eagerly looking out of the window with a huge smile on his face. Sometimes if I wasn't home on time he'd ask Sunita if he could ring me and then ask what time i'll be home. Many times I was far too tired to play football but I always found the strength to put that aside and have fun with him. Sunita wasn't very good at football and occasionally i'd pretend I didn't want to play but said his mum would. He would then give us one of those "are you kidding?" looks and would say "mum isn't good enough" or "I don't want to play football with mum...".

He loved and still does like drawing and painting and together with Sunita they would spend many hours creating things, painting, gluing and sticking. Sunita is quite creative and Rishi looks as if he's heading the same way.

Some of the many pictures Rishi has drawn! Some are very interesting, have lots of detail and intricate too...

When the weather was ok (basically not raining), we'd often swap the bus for the car and he would rush upstairs to ensure he got the front seat. He loved the bus too and I preferred it to taking the car. Perhaps it was the daily bus journey I made when I was given my first job that got me used it but practically, it was just easier. No rush to find a space in an expensive car park and no need to drive were just some of the benefits! My local bus company also lets you get into town and back for just £2.00 which is a bargain and I guess i'm doing my little bit for the environment too...

If Rishi wanted to do something he'd ask one of us and if Sunita or I agreed he would often say "promise?" I've mentioned it before but if I promised Rishi something then I would make sure I stuck to it. Sunita on the other hand made several promises but for one reason or another didn't manage to keep them which clearly upset Rishi. I was quite annoyed too but to be fair, Sunita had probably never experienced what a broken promise felt like as a child. Since then Rishi knows full well that a promise means just that and it works both ways (or 3 ways too!). If he promised to tidy his room then he knew we expected him to definitely do it. Trust me, there were of plenty of promises that summer and plenty of activity including more trips on the bus, coach trips to London, trips to Museums, train journeys and more worldwide travel.

For Rishi, this year would be an important one; in August he would start school and say goodbye to the nursery he'd been at for the last 3 1/2 years. By the time he finished nursery we had ploughed £21,000 into it. When we calculated the figures, it was unbelievable; when money goes out each month it's quite a lot of money but when you add it all up it was astounding. Prior to joining his new school, he had a couple of open days where kids could see the classrooms, playground and generally get a feel of where they'd been spending several more years. It was a good idea and helped the transition for many kids.

Luckily for us, his time at the nursery had prepared him well for school and towards the end of August in 2005 we took Rishi to school for the first time - his first day! He looked great, grey trousers, black shoes, white collared 't' shirt and red jumper. Many parents get quite emotional on the first day; their child appears to "have grown up suddenly..." but we were just keen to get him there before his nerves kicked in. His first day was fine and he seemed to get on ok which was obviously a good thing. We did, however, have one day where he did get upset and didn't want to go to school but this was a pure one off and since then we've never had a problem...

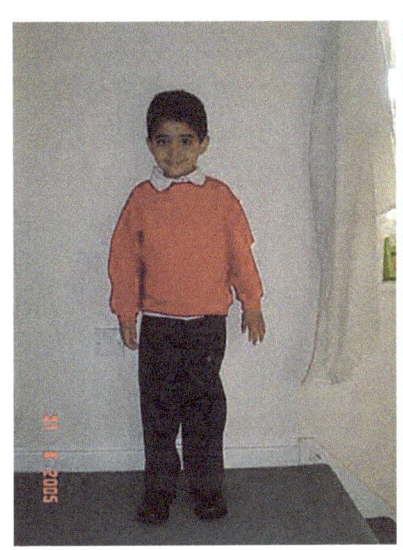

451

41

The TV conundrum and boys home alone

Let's face it, most of us like to plonk ourselves down in front of the good old "telly" (that's television for those "proper speaking folk!") after a long day's work or when you know your favourite program is about to start. Rishi loved watching cartoons; most kids do and I did as well so often we'd sit there whilst Pink Panther did his stuff, the Scooby Doo kids solved another mystery and Tom and Jerry did their cat and mouse thing. On occasions both Sunita and I would be pre-occupied doing stuff so Rishi would have free roam of the Sky control. I must point out that Rishi was very hands on with the remote control and loved to push buttons randomly. Unfortunately, this randomness often switched the TV channel to programs not suitable for kids and as soon as I first spotted this I made sure I added a pin code - one less thing to worry about.

Anyhow both of us would often come back into the lounge to check on him to find he was watching "How the Titanic was built" or "Invention of the steam engine" and many other programs like this. Once he switched to these channels and saw a few minutes of them, he was hooked and soon he loved them as much as his cartoons. For me this was great; I loved watching National Geographic and Discovery channel programs but Sunita would yawn sarcastically whenever there was a risk that I wanted to watch one. As he grew older, Rishi got more and more into these programs and wanted to know how things are made, how stuff works, how the biggest bridge in the world was made and so on.

452

In my experience, many fathers are horrified at the thought of looking after their own kids for a few hours let alone a few days. For some reason that I still don't understand, it seems that only women can look after kids. I'm not like that and I don't care what anyone says, fathers just don't want to or are afraid of looking after the kids in the same way their mothers do. Quite the opposite to this, I loved it and it was a good job I did because in October 2005, Sunita was heading east to India as her brother Raj was getting married. Family weddings are special and this was about as close as you could get so there was no way Sunita was missing out. Her sister "Aussie Rita" (she emigrated to Queensland, Australia earlier in the year) was flying to India too via the UK (long story - don't worry about it). So everyone in Sunita's family was flying out to India for the wedding except myself and Rishi. Sunita would be away from home for 3 weeks which was far too much time for Rishi to be out of school, especially as he'd only started a few weeks earlier.

There was a whole group of them going and on the morning of their flight, we headed off to Sunita's mums house to say goodbye. Aussie Rita had made the long journey all the way from Australia and was now flying to India - just think of the air miles! We said our farewells and prepared for our 3 weeks alone. My mum and sister fussed as usual and rang us up to make sure we were ok and whether we wanted to go around for dinner. There was no need to worry about us, we were fine and having a great time. I had loads of holidays left so took them in one go - it meant I didn't have to worry about work and could spend lots of time with Rishi once I picked him up from school. In that 3 weeks, we had plenty of father and son madness; trips to town, to the park; on the train, feeding the ducks, play fighting, drives in the car and loads of other stuff. The days flew past and before we knew it, 3 weeks had passed and we were on our way to Birmingham airport to pick Sunita up again. Aussie Rita was back in Australia and normal operation resumed at home...

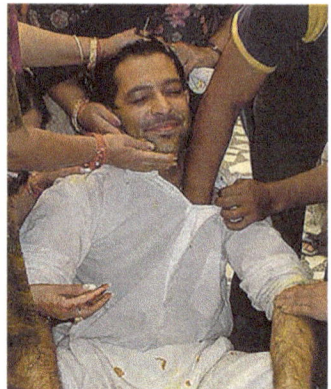

Time to get clean –
Indian style!

Raj "what have I done?"
Sarita "Nice shoes..."

As Rishi was growing up, he amassed so many toys he was literally out growing his bedroom and some urgent action was needed! The solution was simple; the "music room" would be Rishi's new room and vice versa. We had to move stuff in stages,

454

Mum couldn't take it anymore.

Newlyweds!

Sarita & Sunita
(look at those white teeth!)

there was no room in the house to move out all my records, turntables and rest of my music. We ordered a new bed for Rishi, put it together and with that Rishi's room was ready for him. He loved it, it was like having a new toy; albeit a big one. He had cupboards and under-the-bed storage space so his clothes, cars and other toys were put away neatly. Meanwhile, his old room would undergo a mini makeover; the stickers were removed from the walls, shelves taken down (... and the shelves *were* straight Sunita ok!), carpet removed, walls re-painted and laminate flooring was laid down.

My several thousand records were stored neatly in specially made MDF cabinets and I knew they'd fit in Rishi's old room but I never realised how tight the fitting would be. With both cabinets back to back, there was 2 inches of space either that – that's what I call a tight fitting. The transformation was complete- it did take a while to get used to having Rishi in the other room and I often walked into his room expecting to go onto the decks – doh! One thing I will say about Rishi is that he is (usually) extremely neat and tidy. All his toys are put away neatly, particularly his cars that are "parked" up at night. He knows where everything is in his room and if you move something.... "no dad, it doesn't go there..."

It was inevitable that Rishi soon got hooked into music. It's quite hard not getting into it when his dad is continuously filling the house with music from the record crates, especially the deep baselines from the drum and bass tracks. He loved it; when he was young he was small enough to sit on the turntable but as he grew taller, he'd sit to next to the turntables whilst I played the tunes. In the last few years, he's picked his own favourite records; learnt how to work the amplifier and mixer and I just leave him to it! On a few occasions, Sunita and I have crept up to the room and slowly opened the door to see him nodding his head to the beat and moving the cross fader left and right. For me, it was great seeing him take an interest in something different particularly as he enjoys it so much too. To this day i'm hopeful that with some guidance and assuming he still likes his music we could have a superb turntablist on our hands...

Most kids when growing up have the odd fall here and there; I should know as I had many of them and still have some scars to prove it. During playtime when the kids were left out, I knew for a fact that Rishi was one of those kids who'd constantly be rushing around. Playing "tick" and trying to get to "den" (i.e. the equivalent of a safe house!) was one of his favourite games. Unlike schools of the past, falling over in the playgrounds of today is a somewhat different affair. Kids are taken to proper medical rooms, forms must be filled in and a letter goes home to the parent informing

them of what happened, how it happened, what treatment the school gave and anything else. During one particular term Rishi had so many of them it was unbelievable. During one week in the summer whilst he was out on his new push along scooter he tripped quite badly and fell on his front. Luckily his knee took the brunt of the impact - better his knee than his face and blood spilled out. Rishi thought his world had come to an end but with some TLC from is mum he was soon ok.

Rishi was quite worried that the mark on his knee would stay there and others would laugh at him during the summer when he wore his shorts. It took a long while but I convinced him that the little people that live in his body and wake up when Rishi's fast asleep at night would ensure that no scar was left behind. It may sound like a daft thing to say but it's true to a degree. Ok, there are no little people inside that fight your cuts and bruises but your body does fix itself at night whilst you're resting so there is truth in it. There have been many nights when we've gone to kiss him goodnight where he's asked "Will those people come out tonight dad?" "Of course they will son" would be my answer every time.

Homework times were interesting, not because of the type of homework but simply having the opportunity to sit down with our child and help him understand something that he may not quite have grasped at school. Sometimes they'd learn fractions in their maths class but only do them for a few days. A few weeks later they'd get fraction homework and Rishi struggled on occasions. Bit of a daft way to teach kids really; what's the point covering an important part of the curriculum in a few days for the *first* time and then expecting kids to remember how to do them several weeks later? From an early age, it was clear that we'd had make sure Rishi did extra studying at home. Some of the homework he got was pathetic with no imagination from his school but perhaps this was simply because the teachers had no time, perhaps it was because of the cut backs or perhaps it was just because there were always a few crap teachers in good schools?

Anyhow, it didn't matter, we made sure we sat down with Rishi and slowly worked through the homework. Sunita did most of this as i'd get home several hours after but during those times where I helped it was extremely rewarding. There were many times when he'd sit there very quiet and often in tears because he kept telling us that "he couldn't do it". This was just a confidence issue and I told him over and over again that I didn't care if he got all the answers wrong or had difficulty reading words. What I cared about was that he *tried* and after repeating this again and again over many weeks, the message finally sank in. He tried his best and I was true to my word; I really didn't care during the early years if he messed things up and I really was only concerned with the fact that he always gave it his best shot.

Rishi loved talking; he got that from Sunita and many of his early school reports reflected this. "*Gets distracted easily*", "*talks a lot*", "*needs to concentrate*" were just a few of the comments on his report. His "attainment" scores were poor; typically an average of "3" which according to their scores was "normal". There was nothing normal about it; I genuinely think the teachers couldn't be arsed to give an accurate report. Unfortunately, the scores didn't improve much over the next year or so but in year 3 he suddenly moved up a gear and his school results were hitting "1" which is top marks although his attainment was still 2 - a massive improvement - well done son!

Over the years computers have had a massive impact on schools. When I was a young kid I didn't even know what a computer was. At secondary school we had BBC Micros and all my friends had computers but I didn't. It didn't bother me but the reason i'm talking about them again is that schools without computers nowadays is like Laurel without Hardy - impossible! From a young age, Rishi mastered how to switch the PC on, launch internet explorer and search using the world famous Google search engine - he even managed to customise it along the way!

RISHI PATEL, 4
I love you mummy

Mother's Day messages –
appeared in the
'Leicester Mercury'.

Trip to the Natural History Museum.

Holiday in Tunisia.

The sea was warm.

Sunita on a camel,
Sahara desert, Tunisia.

Salt plains, sunrise.

42

"Mum, can I have a brother or sister?"

I can't remember the circumstances that led up to it but one day Rishi asked Sunita if he could have a brother or sister. Sunita didn't expect that, *we* didn't expect that but it was a fair question from an inquisitive boy. It turned out that out of all the kids in his class, Rishi was one of the few who was the only child. Without trying to question him as if he was on trial, we tried to get information out of him to try to understand why he suddenly asked the question. It was clear that Rishi sees many of his friends being picked up by their parents together with their brothers and / or sisters and it obviously started him thinking on why he doesn't have one or both. Inside class Rishi also explained that one of the topics was "families" and all the kids were telling the teacher how many siblings they have. I must admit this kind of threw me a little bit; Sunita and I had discussed more kids several years earlier but we decided that one was enough.

As the years progressed I was quite content but it transpired that Rishi asking about a sibling got Sunita thinking about it more and more. Each time Rishi asked Sunita, she mentioned it to me. Up until then, Rishi never asked me about siblings but one day whilst I was walking home with the crazy boy, he said "Dad, can I have a sister?" It was at that precise moment that it hit home hard. Here was a 6 year old asking if he can have a sister and for a split second I didn't know what to say. I wanted to say "no" but I couldn't and I think my words were something like "we'll see". This was a cop out but I didn't want to lie to him so I told him the next best thing which I maintain to this day was as honest as I could be at that time. I didn't mention to it to Sunita until the next day; inside my head *that* question kept repeating itself and I just couldn't think of anything else.

Many times I was caught in deep thought about having more children. I could see the obvious benefits for Rishi; he'd have a brother or sister to grow up with but for me one of my life long ambitions kept getting in the way. From a young age, when it was clear i'd be lucky if I saw Skegness let alone travel the world, I made it my ambition that one day I would hope to travel around this planet of ours. I felt fortunate; I had a good job, a happy marriage and a wonderful kid - why would I want more? Well I say that but the excitement of seeing new places, experiencing new cultures and diving into history drove me on. I felt Rishi was at an age that if we did decide to take a break and see the world, he'd be ok and all I could think about was our travels....

In contrast, Sunita felt totally different and as each day passed, she thought having another child would be the right thing to do so Rishi would have a sibling. "Cousins are cousins but there's nothing like having your own brother or sister" - the exact words that Sunita said quite often during our numerous late night discussions on kids, travel and the future. Neither of us was right and the ironic thing about all of us is that I *did* want kids (yes, plural!) early on in our marriage but at that time Sunita didn't - in the end we did what good marriages do - compromise. In a twist of fate, we'd gone full circle except that this time we wanted different things. I never understood how much this effected Sunita until one evening when she was very quiet. Now, if you know Sunita, you know that she loves talking (and people watching!) so to go through an evening with her hardly saying a word is strange but that's exactly what happened.

Surita, Raj (Monique in arms) & Rishi).

Sarita, Sunita, Ravi & mum.

Rishi with grandmother.

It wasn't a one off either and over the next few weeks Sunita was getting upset more and more. It was a strange period, Rishi was relentless with his questions over having a sibling, Sunita was obviously upset about the whole thing and very keen to have another child but I felt different; or at least I thought I did anyway. One night, i'd just finished listening to vinyl through my headphones and decided to check on Rishi before I headed downstairs. Rishi had a real tendency to move around lots whilst sleeping so checking him an hour or so after he went to bed became routine. Often, the blanket would be totally off him, his legs would be sticking out or his pillow would end up in the middle of the bed.

We'd then have to carefully try and manoeuvre him back and / or rearrange the blanket and pillows again so he was nice and warm. That night was quite strange - Rishi hadn't moved at all, he was tucked in and fast asleep. I stood there longer than I usually do and just stared at him and all that went through my mind was how precious he was. In an instant, the thought of him growing up without having a sibling had a marked effect on me, it felt totally wrong and unbelievably my attitude towards having more children changed.

It was the same the next day and the day after that too and the more I thought about it I couldn't understand how I could have ever thought otherwise. I knew that my travel; well our travel plans could wait and that it was more important to have another child for Rishi's and his brother or sister's future. Don't get me wrong, the thought of having to raise another baby when it felt we'd got our lives back was daunting but it was exciting at the same time. I just had to be sure it was the *right* thing to do and once I was certain it was, I decided to tell Sunita which made her day and the old cheery Sunita was back! We talked, well Sunita did most of the talking but it was good just openly discussing the child thing and we were really looking forward to the new journey.

43

To the Punjab & back

Well the time line rapidly moves on; we're now into March 2007 and my work, always busy at the best of times, was busier than I could ever recall. To keep level pegging with our competitors, we had to incorporate many new features into our core software products but we wanted to go beyond that. We not only wanted to match our competitor's features but incorporate many more to give us that competitive edge - a crucial thing in our market place. Unfortunately, there was too much work for our development team and something had to be done about it and the answer to the solution was to set up an ODC or an **O**ffshore **D**evelopment **C**entre. These so called ODC's are basically outsourcing your work to another company where the workforce typically becomes an extension of your own development team. The real benefit at this moment in time was cost; the cost of one experienced software developer in the UK would probably pay for 4-5 equivalent developers in India.

The plan was simple; we had set up a fixed cost project to re-design and re-write the entire user interface of one of our software products whilst one of the most critical steps in the master plan was to ensure that the ODC knew how our software was installed, what features it had and how they worked and generally got to know the software as well as we did. This was not an easy task and it wasn't something that could be done remotely so I was sent to India for 2 weeks along with my manager at the time. We had 2 weeks to get the job done and I was looking forward to it. I hadn't been to India since I was 14 and was ready to meet the challenge.

The flight to Hyderabad (the one in India, not Pakistan) couldn't have been better; Business Class on Emirates - it doesn't get better than that. I've always enjoyed flying whatever class; there was something fascinating how these huge giants climbed into the sky effortlessly and planes in general just seemed an engineering marvel. Anyhow, fully reclining seats, on demand movies, a choice of 300+ CD's/DVD's, cake trolley, dinner on demand and not having some smelly drunk falling asleep on you or asking you to get up every 2 minutes so they could squeeze by you. Nah - this journey was class and I made sure I enjoyed every single minute of it and trust me I did. We touched down at the Rajiv Ghandi airport in Hyderabad at about 8am and on getting out of the airport terminal the sights and sounds flooded back. The constant horns "horn please!" and the sight of the classic 'Premier Padmini' and 'Hindustan Ambassador' was very welcome indeed. These cars were bullet proof; they must be to survive the harsh heat of India and the continuous start/stop the engines are routinely put through as they meander through the congested streets of India.

The ODC company sent a car for us and within 20 minutes we were at the entrance to a massive building. As we entered inside, we were met by an overwhelming welcoming committee and a garland of flowers were put around our necks - we were the guest of honours! As I looked across at the "What's happening today" board I saw both of our names which was a nice little touch! I made sure I hung onto the garlands and made sure my colleague did too. It's a sign of respect that you do *not* leave them behind... There was no time to waste; after the introductions to the team it was straight into the training rooms and to get on with the job in hand. As time slowly ticked on, Nick and I (sorry - didn't mention his name earlier!) were getting more and more tired; the long journey was taking its toll and it was time to call it a day. So, our first day was over, we headed to our hotel for some well-earned rest - we would certainly need it!

Our hotel was excellent; the Taj Banjara - part of the well-known and respected "Taj" group, known for quality and excellence. It didn't disappoint; from the moment we stepped in to the moment we checked out, everything was virtually perfect but the overwhelming factor was the staff -always pleased to see you and courteous beyond belief. You may think "well they work for the Taj; it's their job to be polite". Well you may have a point but it's the way they said it; I don't know, i'm a bit of a softy and was truly humbled by the whole experience. Over the next 3/4 days the schedule was the same; get up at 7am, get ready and down for 7.30am, breakfast (watching as the monkeys outside climbed the overhanging trees!) and straight to the office. You could see the enthusiasm in the ODC team as they got very curious about the software and clicked here, there and everywhere. They tried things we hadn't and managed to find many bugs which were quickly got the UK team to fix pronto!

Outside the Sonata Software
offices – busy!

Exploring the Golconda
Fort, Hyderabad.

The trip for me had a dual purpose; my 2 brother in laws, Raj and Ravi (Sunita's brothers) were in India at the same time (for a wedding) but didn't know I was in India. Mind you, none of my family knew either but there was a reason behind this - I was hoping to pull off one of the biggest surprises ever. Rather than spend the weekend in Hyderabad; I planned to head North to the Punjab to give Raj and Ravi the surprise of their lives. Would I get there? Would my big plan fail miserably? Would someone let it slip? Well I can tell you straight away that Sunita was a little pessimistic about the whole thing. She wanted me to pull off the big surprise but thought there were too many things that could go wrong. Furthermore, she was adamant that venturing into the Punjab alone when you don't know the area or speak the local language was just asking for trouble.

I must admit that on that basis it didn't look good for me; I had never been to the Punjab region. I could speak Gujerati but not Punjabi and although I could just about understand Punjabi that would be no use if I couldn't communicate back. Anyway, I pressed on, I hadn't travelled all the way to India to chicken out now! In between ODC duties, I booked the flights to Punjab and arranged for the train to take me from Jalandhar to Delhi where I would catch a flight back to Hyderabad. The ODC was hard work, long hours in the training rooms and constant question / answer sessions but it was worth it. I felt along with my boss, we were making a real impact and it was an amazing experience.

It was now Friday - our first week of ODC was complete and Nick and I were shattered. The ODC company took us on a sightseeing tour of Hyderabad and by the time we got back to the hotel it was about 7.15pm. I then began packing my things for my weekend trek to the Punjab region. I didn't get any sleep that night and was taken to the airport at 2.30am so I could check in for my Spice Jet flight to Delhi followed by an Air India Express flight to Amritsar. Back at home, Sunita had called Sarita (Raj's wife - she was also in India but staying at her parents' house for a few days). I got to Delhi with no problems at all so it was so far so good. I then hopped onto the bus which takes you to Delhi International airport so I could catch my Air India Express flight to Amritsar.

As the pilot carried out all his checks prior to departure, it was decided that a tyre had to be changed so the flight was delayed for 2 hours before it took off. On the flight to Amritsar I had my camera ready as I thought I might be lucky enough to see the Golden Temple from the sky. My luck was in and I managed to get a great shot of the temple - it was great to see it, just a shame I didn't have time to visit it. By now Sarita was at Amritsar airport and didn't know where I was. Unfortunately, the nature of the delay was not conveyed to those arriving at the airport to meet and greet so she had no idea if I was on the plane. She called Sunita who didn't know what to do either. My phone wouldn't "roam" correctly so she couldn't even call me but in the end Sunita decided that Sarita should stay there and that I will arrive.... eventually!

By the time we landed I had no idea whether Sarita would be there or not and after strolling through the main terminal I could see someone frantically waving — it was her and she was with her father too. Once i'd cleared passport control, I was free to go and finally met up with them in arrivals. Sarita had a barrage of questions; What was I doing in India? When was it arranged? Where I was staying and so on. A few minutes later and we were in the car and heading to Jalandhar; Sarita's home town. It was a 2 hour drive so plenty of time to answer those questions. I think Sarita was quite shocked at the fact that I managed to get there. For me, it was quite normal but I was incredibly excited at seeing the look on Raj & Ravi's face the following day.

As we drove South-East and negotiated sharp bends, cows in the middle of the road, local farmers hauling tonnes of farm produce on a cycle and trying to avoid massive trucks who constantly made the most of the "horn please" requests, I was loving it. The Punjab was lush, green and felt alive. Most people would have dreaded that drive but I absolutely loved it. It was a stark contrast to Hyderabad with its massive buildings and hi tech city and to be honest I was so pleased I decided to make the trip.

During the journey Sarita got a call on her mobile – it was Raj calling from Balachaur – another town in the Punjab. Once off the call, Sarita explained that Raj was sending a taxi to Jalandhar the following morning to pick Sarita and Monique (their daughter) up and bring them to Balachaur. Little did he know that there would be one more passenger – moi! As we arrived in Jalandhar there had just been some rainfall which was quite welcome; it certainly cooled things down a little bit and a short while later we turned into a small road – we were home! I'd seen lots of pictures of Sarita's house on their wedding DVD a few years earlier so it was quite weird as I stepped inside. Her mum, brother and sister were inside and probably wondering what I was doing there too. Tiredness kicked in big time but there was no time to sleep; I was just too excited so after freshening up and having a bite to eat we just sat and talked. Well I say that; the only person I could chat to was Sarita who became my translator for the weekend!

I must say a big thank you to Sarita (aka 'Good girl') – (private joke) and the rest of her family for the incredible hospitality they showed me whilst I was with them. Indian culture in general stipulates that you should always welcome your guests as if they are part of your family and the way they treated me was no exception. In the evening I thought we were just going to relax at home but her dad didn't want to waste the evening and decided we'd go out. We got into the car again and as I reached my seat belt I knew something wasn't right. Everyone else looked in amazement at what I was doing - people just don't wear seat belts in India so to see someone doing so was certainly strange. However, i'd been on that 2 hour journey from Amritsar and trust me there were many instances that reminded just why it's good to clunk click on every trip... you get me?

At Sarita's house with a very young Monique!

After negotiating our way out of the narrow roads, the size of the city soon became clear - it was quite a big place and much bigger than I thought it would be. The city felt alive, there were loads of people out on the streets, in their cars and it felt as if everyone had waited until night fall before they ventured out! As we headed towards our destination, we started to pass huge buildings all brightly lit up and each one we passed seemed to be bigger and better than the previous one. Curious as to what they were, I asked my translator about them and learnt that they were wedding halls. Wedding halls? They looked more like aircraft hangers - they were massive... In the distance I could see another brightly lit building with lots of activity outside. We pulled into the car park - I still didn't know where we were but if the noise was anything to go by this seemed like a fun place. You could hear laughing, music and lots of cheers with 100's of people all over the place.

We were in a place called "Haveli" and the only to describe it is a place where you they try to relive the traditional Punjab way of life. The staff are dressed in traditional dress, there are "fake" villages, the music is upbeat and the dhol is standard whilst the vegetarian food is awesome. Add to that various stalls, people telling jokes, musicians and singers and you have all the ingredients for a great night out. In the 2-3 hours we were there, I loved every single minute of it and I can honestly say that I felt more Indian that day than i've ever done in my life and to me that was an unforgettable moment. After about 2-3 hours I was really feeling the effect of all the travelling i'd done that weekend. I worked out that I had been awake for about 42 hours with absolutely no sleep in between; how I was still awake was beyond me but I really needed some sleep now. I think everyone else was tired too so after eating we headed back home.

Sarita decided to start cooking.

We're both Libran you know – ask Balan Singh.

Sarita met a friend.

It must have been around 11.30pm by the time I finally got into bed and the next thing I remember is someone repeatedly calling out my name. I was so shattered that although I could hear, or at least thought I could hear someone calling out to me, I thought I was dreaming and just wanted to go back to sleep. There was no let up though and eventually I realised that it was Sarita with my wake up call. Boy - that was probably the deepest sleep i've ever had but it had to be cut short. We had to get up early as the taxi would be coming to pick us up - I didn't realise that it was about 5.30am though! Wearily I dragged myself out of bed; usually I need very little sleep but I could have easily jumped back into bed and felt as if I could sleep all day. Anyhow what was I talking about? I hadn't travelled all this way to sleep; there was a big surprise ahead and there was no time to waste.

The taxi arrived at Sarita's house bang on time and as Sarita, Monique and I got in, I suddenly felt very nervous but nerves or not, our journey to Balachaur had begun. When I got into the taxi, I sat at the front which was a bad mistake once again as i'd probably shit myself from the scary journey that was ahead of us. I remember looking to my left for the seat belt and the fact that I couldn't pull it as it was stuck in the door. By the time I realised it was stuck, the driver was wondering what I was up to. Anyhow I opened my door, released the seat belt and started to put it on. As I did so I could feel I was being stared at and as I turned to the driver he had a look of amazement on his face. In the back Sarita saw the funny side of it too although I hadn't worked out what so funny at the time.

Eventually though I realised that the sheer fact that I put the belt on was highly amusing to the taxi driver. Never in his life had he probably picked up a passenger who went on to belt up. He probably thought i'd gone mad or something but undeterred I kept it on. The thing is you see the culture is totally different; with people hanging off over crowded buses and other sitting on top of trains, not wearing your seat belt wasn't strange at all - what was strange was putting it on! After about 90 minutes we arrived in

474

Balachaur - the big moment was almost here! The taxi driver stopped at the side of the road and once out of the car I spent a few minutes just looking around. I'd seen many pictures; heard lots of stories but I was here at last - let the fun begin!

I had no idea where I was going so I just followed Sarita as she led us down a small narrow path. There was no one around which I thought was strange but then suddenly I saw Sunita's aunt and I recognised her. I was expecting her to gaze in shock as to what the hell I was doing there but there was no look of surprise whatsoever. The reason was simple; she didn't know who I was which I thought was brilliant. She did look at me in a puzzled way but I guess this is because she was wondering who on earth I was and why I was there with Sarita. Now my understanding of Punjabi is miles better than my ability to speak it but I heard Sarita ask aunty whether she knew who I was. Aunty shook her head; even more puzzled before and I was loving it. However a few seconds later Sarita told her that it was Sunita's husband but it still didn't seem to sink in but then suddenly chaos broke it.

It finally registered, she finally *knew* who I was and screamed out loud, ran inside, screamed some more, came back outside, gave me a massive hug and started to pour mustard oil at the entrance of the house (the pouring of oil is basically a 'welcome' gesture). I was then led into the house where the screaming continued. In a matter of seconds Sunita's close family had emerged from their rooms and were staring at me - they were all probably wondering what the hell I was doing there. Unfortunately, we had a major communication barrier so my trusted translator Sarita did the language duties once more. It was great meeting them all; they seemed really pleased to see me and I was yet again made extremely welcome. In all the hysteria I wondered whether Raj and Ravi who were sleeping upstairs had caught on to what had happened. Did they know I was downstairs?

Well once Sarita explained what was going on, the others kept quiet and I slowly walked upstairs hoping that I wouldn't bump into the boys; well not yet anyway. As I got to the top I peered around the corner but could see nothing except a door that led to the bedroom. Quietly I walked over and then banged on the door - there was no response so I banged again. I could hear some muffled sounds coming from inside. I suspect Raj and Ravi were either hung over from the night before and / or had been up late and didn't particularly enjoy this unplanned wake up call. This was the moment of truth.... Slowly the door opened – it was Ravi who took one look at me, looked again and said "*What the f**k!!*". Meanwhile Raj, presumably awake also came out, rubbing his eyes – his response was "*Baal head*" – basically this is Leicester slang for "what on earth...."

The look on their faces was priceless and then came the questions: '*What you doing here?*' '*How did you get here?*' '*How long are you here for?*' As it turned out they weren't asleep but in fact getting ready for the wedding I mentioned earlier. With shirt buttons undone and trouser belts hanging on, they stopped what they were doing as I rapidly explained what I was doing in India and the events that took me to the Punjab region. They were shocked beyond belief and as they continued getting dressed all I could hear was "can't believe it man". We all went downstairs and I was led into a small room – it was time for a much welcomed cup of chai!

Time was ticking; we had a wedding to attend so it was good bye for now and back for another thrilling ride in the cab. The driver was late so for about 10 minutes we all stood around whilst

Raj made calls to the driver to find out where he was. I loved it and watched as the locals got on with their day to day chores – this was real Punjab life and yet again I took as many pictures as I could. Eventually the driver arrived; it was the *same* driver and he soon had a sly grin on his face as I got back in and proceeded to put my belt on again. Before I had a chance to tell Raj to belt up he beat me to it. "I don't have to wear my belt now"- he said as he explained to his other cousin the story behind it. So, we were all set, I was about to shit myself again much to the amusement of Raj so off we went. There were many scary moments on the road; too many in fact but this was nothing to compared to this journey and believe me I was glad I was securely strapped in.

We got to the wedding ok but that was after we almost crashed into a tree whilst overtaking a heavily loaded truck whose driver was too busy looking everywhere except the road; nearly killed a dog who was daft enough to walk on the pavement (yes the driver decided the use the pavement albeit briefly), nearly got squashed by melons that threatened to fall out the back of a lorry where the 10 year old sitting in the back was desperately trying to keep the melons in, nearly knocked a person over who decided to cross the road at the red lights – our driver must have been colour blind and last but not least I almost grabbed the steering wheel as the driver was trying to find a piece of paper that had fallen and as he did so, made the car swerve all over the place.

The day was a long one; exaggerated by the very early start and my body was letting me know that I needed to get some more sleep and quick! At about 6pm it was time to go and I said my farewells to Raj, Ravi and all the cousins i'd met for the first time. It was quite bizarre; i'd sneaked into their lives suddenly about 10 hours earlier and now I was sneaking out again. Raj, quite pissed now from all the wedding booze asked me many times whether "i'd be ok"; "do I have enough money?" and generally was quite concerned at the thought of me travelling alone back to Delhi. I assured him many times that i'd be fine but he was adamant that he'd get someone to drive me to Delhi. All I could think of was our taxi driver and the fact that i'd only just survived the numerous journeys - how on earth could I survive an 8 hour drive to Delhi in the dark?

There was *no* way I could sleep on such a journey and I *really* needed to sleep. I just about managed to persuade Raj that the train would be better and thankfully he agreed. As we piled into Sarita's car (all 6 of us!) it started to rain a little which was very welcome indeed as it cooled things down yet again and soon we were back home. The train station was minutes from their house which meant I could relax a little before heading off. I quickly changed, packed my stuff, had something to eat and then had to say more good byes. Sarita and her father drove me to the station where we navigated our way onto the packed platform. There was hardly any space to stand and the train was late - great! Eventually the Muri Express pulled in and it was time to say good bye to Sarita and her father who, along with the rest of the family, looked after me so well I was truly humbled. After waving good bye I was quite sad as it seemed my journey was over but it wasn't - well not yet anyway.

I was booked into a sleeper cab which meant I could finally stretch my legs and try to get some sleep. Each sleeper is individually numbered but I found it quite difficult to work out which one was mine. I'm sure I got into the right one and after making sure my valuables were secure I finally settled down to sleep. My travel bag doubled up as my pillow and a dark side curtain made sure the outside light didn't disturb me. The train was smooth, made very little noise and the rest of the passengers were quiet. Unfortunately, I was rudely awoken from my sleep by an angry looking man who kept asking me for my ticket. I must have been in such a deep sleep that it took a while to register what the hell was going on. He kept saying "you're in my seat; you're in my seat...". I couldn't give a shit whose seat I was in; in fact, I couldn't give a damn if I was on the roof - please just let me sleep...

Eventually the man realised that I wasn't going to trade places and gave up and I could hear him utter something as he walked away - he must have been pissed off. Thinking that would be the last interruption, I checked the time - only 1 hour had passed but it felt like I was asleep for hours and hours. There was still 6 hours to go so I turned around and settled down to sleep again. Just as my head hit the pillow; I mean travel bag; someone pulled back the curtains and by now I was pissed off. I was just about to unleash a torrent of abuse on the person who interrupted my sleep but I realised that it was one of the train porters offering me a pillow and blanket. This *was* a good interruption and I quickly tore off the pristine wrapping, covered myself with the warm blanket (it was unusually cold on the train...) and swapped the bag for the pillow and finally settled down for some uninterrupted sleep.

Being woken up once was bad enough but I was furious when I felt someone shaking me again. I quickly jumped up, almost banging my head to find someone asking me "if I wanted Delhi?". Of course I did I thought but before I had a chance to say anything he continued "this is Delhi..."

At first I thought I was hearing things; for us to be in Delhi around 6 hours must have passed. Surely I couldn't have been asleep for so long... could I? Frantically I grabbed my mobile and the time was 04.10 so this wasn't a rude awakening at all; it was a very welcomed one. Luckily for me, that person decided to wake me up otherwise I would have still been on that train heading East. I stepped off the train to what I can only describe as adrenaline fuelled chaos. The platform in Jalandhar was busy; this platform was nothing like i'd seen before. It was early in the morning but there was 100's of people everywhere; some trying to sell food and drink; others offering to carry anything for a few rupees, people sleeping close to the tracks and the rest of them just stared at me as I looked lost and tried to get my bearings sorted!

The exit sign finally came into view and I now had to work out the best way to get to the airport. The easiest way would have been to jump into a taxi but I was looking for a stand or counter where I could pre pay it so I didn't get embroiled in an argument over the fare afterwards - I just didn't need it today. All the taxis were lined up at the front but I soon gave up on that idea. In the distance I saw a rickshaw office and no sooner had I walked up there I was harassed by a mass of drivers wanting me to get into their rickshaws. I could understand as they shouted out "why pay more at the office; i'm cheaper..." but cheaper or not I wanted to make sure I got to the airport in one piece so I ended up paying in advance and was taken to my rickshaw.

It wasn't a good start; my driver looked pissed off anyway but the thought of having to drive me to the airport seemed to piss him off further. I got into the back, grabbed onto my bag and was pleased to be on the way. The hustle and bustle of New Delhi station soon faded away and just as I began to relax things started to become interesting. The roads were narrower and the street lights were non-existent - where on earth was he taking me? It started to rain a little and I was starting to shit myself. I was in a rickshaw with a pissed off local who was driving me through unlit roads; my mobile said there was no reception (thanks Orange) and my only weapon of mass destruction was my bag which was still being held firmly in my hands. The worst part was still to come; he decreased speed for no reason then made a right turn into an even smaller road. It was very quiet and I really thought I was about to get attacked, mugged, both or something even worse. My heart was pounding and all I could think of was whether I should bail out there and then.

"I know", I thought to myself, "i'll chat to him..." My Gujerati was excellent, my Punjabi useless, Hindi just about manageable and English good but whatever I said to him, regardless of language, he never replied. We continued; when was this guy going to stop? It didn't help matters when my brain decided to fill itself with the opening sequence to the film "Bone Collector" (the bit where the couple gets picked up from the airport and the cab driver locks them in) - not the kind of thing you want to think about! However, in the distance I could see what appeared to be a road; well it had lights on it anyway. The lights got brighter and brighter as we got closer until he eventually turned left and it was clear that we were on one of the major arterial roads of Delhi. I breathed a huge sigh of relief; the driver probably took a short cut or something and although we hadn't arrived at the airport yet, just the fact that we were in built up areas made me feel safe.

The journey seemed to go one forever and by the time we got there almost 40 minutes had passed. If any of you reading this have been in a rickshaw then you'll know that 40 minutes is a *very* long time to be stuck in one but it didn't matter - I had arrived safely. I didn't stop for anything and quickly proceeded into the airport, checked in and made my way to the departure lounge. My Spicejet flight departed on time and by the time i'd landed in Hyderabad and made my way back to the office for week 2 of my trip it was almost midday. Somehow I managed to work through the day despite being exceptionally tired but driving into the grounds of the Taj Banjara at the end of the day was a great site - the long weekend journey was finally over!

That night I had a really good sleep and the next day Nick probably got quite bored as I told him all about my journey. Whilst I was trekking around the Punjab, he was being shown around the infamous 'High Tech City' or **H**yderabad **I**nformation **Tech**nology Engineering and the famous Cyber Gateway that welcomes you with its masses of glass frontage. The last few days in India flew past and by the end of the week we'd completed all our tasks which meant it was time to head back home. The return flight was pretty uneventful but seeing Dubai from 1000's of feet in the sky was pretty amazing - all the multi million pound buildings came into view, glittered in the relentless sunshine and one of the most amazing things was actually seeing the infamous "Palm" come into view.

The airport itself looks as big as a small town and I remember thinking to myself that it would be great to get out and about and have a wonder around Dubai. Sadly, there would be no sightseeing this time so after a quick plane change and a brief stop in Duty free, we settled down for the flight back to Birmingham where I certainly made the most of the Emirates inflight entertainment.

I enjoyed my trip to India and couldn't wait to get back home to see everyone and tell them all about it - despite my adventure I missed home terribly!

The rest of 2007 was uneventful except for our week's holiday to Egypt. We flew out in the middle of July and it was hot, averaging about 38 degrees during the day and about 29 degrees at night. Our Sonesta Beach hotel in Sharm El Sheik was a great resort, right on the bay and within minutes of a private, clean beach with crystal clear warm water. Books, travel programmes and those that have visited Egypt talk about "the world's best snorkelling" together with the history and culture that goes with it. Rishi felt like he was in paradise; the hotel had about 7 pools whose water was warmed by the fiery sun and was perfect for chilling out in. For me it was a chance to finally give snorkelling a try. Ok, shoving glasses on and breathing through a tube may not be too taxing on the brain but it was the location that was exciting. Rishi and I practiced in the hotel pool before heading off to the beach so we could check out the underwater world!

Sunita wasn't too fussed about seeing fish, she was happy lazing around on the lounger. It wasn't long before Rishi gave up trying to master snorkelling. To be fair it is quite difficult to get used to the idea of breathing underwater - your instinct is to surface and grab some air. In the end, I continued to practice alone and eventually got the hang of it. There was fish everywhere, blue ones, green, small, large, multi coloured ones and they were all inquisitive and came right up to you. It was an awesome experience and I couldn't believe the variety of sea life that was literally a few feet from the shore. If you wanted to see something different all you had to do was swim off in a different direction. Somehow I managed to get Rishi to have another go but he found it too difficult and decided to put his goggles on and quickly dunk his head underwater for a few seconds, look at the fish and then surface again.

The swimming pool was awesome too, Rishi and I would jump in, splash around, chase each other, throw a small ball around and then when we got thirsty would swim up to the pool bar and enjoy a cool drink. Sunita preferred to chill out on the sun lounges but we managed to get her in the pool a few times! In the evenings, despite the temperature dropping, it was still incredibly hot so we'd walk along Naama Bay and listen as the restaurateurs did their best to persuade us to dine with them that night. One night we had a great meal by the sea; huge rugs were sprawled over the beach and then tables and chairs were laid on top. Our table was literally a few feet away from the calm water and we could see tiny crabs revealing themselves from the sand!

It was tiring but our day trip to Cairo was a super experience. From Sharm El Sheik there are various ways to get there including private taxi and bus but the 6+ hour journey wasn't an option in the relentless heat and we opted to fly there instead. We booked the trip through our hotel who arranged everything. To make the most of the day we'd have to be up early as everyone from several hotels had to be picked up first and then transported to the airport for the 60 minute flight. Cairo; the city of the pyramids and the Sphinx, was incredibly hot but our air conditioned tourist coach kept us nice and cool. First stop was to the Egyptian Museum, apparently home to the greatest number of Egyptian artefacts and antiquities in the world and although it was interesting, the sheer volume of people in there made it hard to really see everything up close.

As we left the museum and drove a long one of the main trunk roads, there was excitement on the 'right' hand side of the coach; everyone started to get their cameras out and then people started to clap and cheer. In the distance, you could see what appeared to be the pyramids; they just seemed to pop out of nowhere. I somehow expected them to be in the middle of miles and miles of desert but they looked as if they were on the side of the road. At first you could see one of the huge pyramids but as we meandered through the road, smaller ones could be seen behind them. The next stop was to a split level restaurant where we'd have our lunch. The waiters were extremely polite and they made damn sure that everyone there knew that you could see the pyramids from the upper floor. Once we'd eaten they shifted up a gear and started to home in on individuals asking them if they "wanted good pictures of the pyramids".

I knew exactly what was happening here; our few days in Egypt had taught us a few things already. They would lure the tourists upstairs, walk with them to the windows and then offer to take photos after which they would shove their hand out expecting to land some money for their efforts. Well, the waiter that took a photo of us probably wished he hadn't. First of all I wasn't going to pay him for taking a photo that a fellow tourist would have taken happily and secondly the photo he took was crap anyway. When he finished, he was quite gob smacked when I took the camera off him, said "thank you" and promptly walked off.

From the restaurant, we made our way to the pyramids which was only a short dash across town. The approach to the pyramids is off a dusty path where you get your first real view of the main pyramid and the place was well busy - coach after coach was parked back to back in the make shift car park. Tourists were there in their 100's all snapping away at the awesome sights all around them. In Sharm El Sheik it was very hot but Cairo was something else - it was boiling! The sun was super strong and the air was filled with billions of sand particles that were being lifted by the wind. It's only when you get up, close and personal that the sheer size of the pyramids can be appreciated. Saying they were 'massive' is an understatement; each individual block must have around 4' tall and 5' wide and I cannot imagine how heavy they were. 'How on earth did they get the blocks to the top?' I asked myself rhetorically.

In the distance you could see the other smaller pyramids and in the 40 or so minutes we were there, a considerable amount of time was spent trying to shake off the locals that were hoping you'd buy camera film, scarfs or water from them. One of them overstepped the mark with a fellow tourist and continued to harass him. The tourist told him politely that he wasn't interested but the local refused to take no for an answer. Our tour guide intervened, called the police and then explained to the tourist that if he gave the go ahead, the police would throw the seller in jail. Upon hearing that we were all shocked but our guide went on to explain that the Egyptian government relies on the financial contribution of the tourist industry and anything that might jeopardise this is dealt with swiftly - they did mean business!

One of the surreal moments for me was walking towards the Sphinx; as you do the area opens into a clearing full of chairs. For those tourists who hang around till dark, they can take a seat and then watch an epic light show with the pyramids in the background; an awesome setting or what? However, it was the fact that I had retraced the steps of James Bond in the film "The Spy Who Loved Me" that made it very cool - at least I didn't have to worry about Jaws! After leaving the pyramids it was a trip to a perfume shop and then straight to the airport for our flight back to Sharm El Sheik and some welcomed sleep. A few days after that our holiday was over and flew back home.

Towards the end of 2007 I remembered thinking that it had been a good year for travel but little did I know that soon I would be jetting back off to India for round 2 of an overseas project. This time the trip was shorter; a week to be exact but our route there was the same. The time out there was pretty much work all the way but at the weekend we (there were 2 of us) hired a driver and hit the tourist spots. At lunchtime, I asked the driver to find the best "road side" place to eat. My colleague thought i'd gone mad - it's fair to say that most of the roadside fast food places didn't look too good from the outside but I kept saying "it'll be fine, just trust me..." and soon he gave in. As we pulled into the dusty car park, the locals watched in amazement as 2 guys, one Indian and one white guy ventured into the building and sat down. To the locals we stuck out like anything but it didn't matter; it was all part of the adventure and as it turned out, the food was delicious so we gave it the thumbs up!

Outside our resort...

Enjoying the resort pool.
Rishi looks just like Jai here!

The pyramids – look how
big each block is!

Rishi wasn't too keen on the ride!

Sunita – the look suited her!

Thumbs up!   A local asked if they could
                              take a photo with me!

After a week in India I flew back to the UK whilst my colleague stayed in India for a few more days. The flight back on Emirates took the same route; Hyderabad to Dubai and then Dubai to Birmingham. Once I was in Dubai I couldn't stop wondering if I would ever get to see Dubai - I had been to this airport for the 4th time now and never managed to step outside!

44

Shaken and definitely stirred

In life, many people experience many scary things; for some a ride on the Nemesis at Alton Towers is scary whilst for others simply climbing up a ladder is terrifying enough especially those that suffer from a fear of heights. The bottom line is we're all different but at *00:56 on Thursday 28th February 2008*, I experienced the most frightening thing of my life and I sincerely hope I never have to go through that again. I think it must have been about 11pm by the time I got to bed; Rishi had been asleep for a few hours and Sunita had dragged herself back into bed after having a power nap on the lounge sofa; "you get the best sleep on the sofa you know" she used to say...

I must have dozed off quickly and then after what seemed an age, felt something shake. My first thought was *"am I dreaming?"* and I didn't know if I was or not. Dream or not, the shaking got worse and I knew this was for real. It's hard to explain what I was thinking and I truly cannot explain the fear that I felt that night. I was wide awake now and the bed was shaking violently. The noise was immense and strange; it felt as though people were in our house running about whilst at the same time there was a tremendous rumbling sound. The noise lasted for about 9 seconds and in that time, I was reduced to a nervous, shaking wreck. Rishi ran into our room crying; goodness knows what he was thinking whilst Sunita sat up in bed and didn't seem bothered by it at all.

"What was that?" she said in a calm manner - there didn't seem to be any reaction from her at all. As quick as the shaking and trembling started, it stopped but you could still hear the loud

rumbling fade away into the distance. I was speechless and didn't know what to do. If I was watching a Hollywood blockbuster the next thing that usually happens is that a phone starts to ring. The ringing alone was usually enough to scare the living daylights out of someone who was already petrified. The timing was perfect and bang on time our house phone started to ring. Clearly *something* had happened...but who was on the phone? It was Nee; he was shocked as I was and his opening words were "*What the fuck was that?*" I didn't want to say it but it felt like we had just experienced an earthquake but I always associated those with other countries.

I *had* to know what it was and I quickly powered up our Dell laptop and switched on the TV hoping the BBC's News 24 channel would reveal all. Never have I typed so fast into Google .... "earthquake UK" is what I think I entered but the only search results were for an earthquake that occurred a few years earlier which I never knew anything about. Nee was still on the phone but then Dee was trying to call him so he hung up. Whilst I continued to search, I listened out for the news - nothing. I was still quite panicky at this stage; Rishi kept asking what had just happened and was scared. He was in our bed now, comforted by Sunita who just kept telling me to "go to sleep". Although shocked at Sunita's dismissal of such a big event, I was more relieved that we weren't being burgled which was one the horrible thoughts that ran through my brain earlier.

Around 10 minutes later, the BBC changed their headline story and slowly the news that parts of the UK had experienced an earthquake was confirmed. This one hit 5.2 on the Richter scale with the epicentre in Lincoln which, geographically, isn't that far from Leicester and probably explains why we felt it so much - well that's my explanation anyway. Knowing it was an earthquake, Sunita settled down to sleep again but for me there was no way I could just switch off. I couldn't get back into bed, close my eyes and forget all about it; how on earth could I do that? In the end, the TV was switched off and the laptop was shut down but I hardly slept after that. To be honest I was worried about aftershocks; the smaller earthquakes that always tend to occur after the main shock has hit.

I didn't have to switch the alarm off on my phone; I was already awake; it was dark and the time was 5.30am. That earthquake spooked me so much that I was scared to even go downstairs but I plucked up the courage; got myself ready and ventured downstairs. My thought turned to damage and whether the house had suffered any at all but there wasn't. Outside it was still dark; we were still in deep winter and I was even nervous getting into the car. It was freezing outside but for some reason I had to drive with the stereo off and the windows down. It may sound daft but I just kept thinking that if there was another earthquake I want to hear it coming first. On a typical drive to work, things are pretty quiet; there's hardly anyone else on the road and just a few die hard people who could be arsed to get up to walk their dogs. *This* morning was different - there was an eerie silence about the drive and as I drove past our local BP petrol station, you could clearly see that this earthquake had left its mark.

One of its huge advertising pillars; a huge metal pole wasn't vertical anymore but horizontal as it laid across the petrol station exit and blocked part of the pavement. Across the road, some of the street lights were shining brighter than others - their glass covers were lying shattered over the road - presumably the shaking of the earthquake loosened them and sent them hurtling to the ground. Many alarms were triggered too; the sirens had stopped but the typical blue stroke could be seen flickering. I decided to listen in on the radio but kept my window open and it was clear that it was breaking news. As the news reports rolled in, it was clear that it was one of the biggest earthquakes to hit the UK for many years.

By the time I got to work it was still dark - it was only 6am but surprisingly the work alarm wasn't triggered at all. Later that day as the rest of my colleagues arrived, it was surprising to learn that many people didn't even feel the earthquake at all.

Others *"felt something move"* but that's it - I was really surprised; how on earth did they not hear or feel it? Thankfully there were no aftershocks and I sincerely hope I never have to go through that again; the whole experience was too terrifying...

2008 was an important year; predominantly because Ravi was getting married to Ruby. Ravi, for those who have become lost in all the names, is Sunita's brother. Officially they were already engaged, well "Indian" engaged anyway but this year the formal registry wedding and main Indian wedding would take place. Indian weddings are usually a big affair but Ravi was the last one in the Dhunna family to get married so it was special and if Raj (Sunita's other brother) had anything to do with it, everyone would remember this one. The plans, as ever, were made many months in advance but as the weeks slowly passed, the registry was getting closer and closer. Around the world, family members were sorting out their visas and getting ready for the big event. The actual registry took place on 2nd March 2008, a triple day for events as it was Ravi's birthday, it was their official wedding day and it was Mother's Day! Prior to the registry we all decided that the lads would wear formal suits and we had some interesting "fitting" days prior to the day. Even Rishi wore a suit and looked very smart indeed whilst the women were also colour coded in their blue sarees...

On the day of the registry, Ruby had the giggles and to this day i'm still not sure what was so funny. Despite the laughing fits, the vows went perfectly and they were pronounced husband and wife. With the formal duties over it was time for partying and not long afterwards Ravi was probably fed up with the constant mouthfuls of cake that were being shoved into his mouth. Wedding cake is bad enough but he had birthday cake to go with it too! As the day progressed people drank, ate and danced the night away - it felt like a full blown wedding but this was just the start.... As the year pushed on we were soon into April and friends and family were arriving from Holland, Ireland and Dublin - trust me, this was a wedding on a global scale. It's a good job that Sunita's parental home is big; it had to be really, at its peak there must have been at least 5 families staying there not to mention the countless others arriving daily to take part in the wedding festivities...

Aussie Rita and the kids were back in town. The GSM operators braced themselves for the additional load that would be put on their voice networks - everyone knew Rita would be jamming up the networks real soon! It was quite good fun having them stay at our house and I know for sure that Rishi loved it. The only downside was that he still had school which made him a little upset - he just wanted to say @ home and play! The wedding was split over several days, in the week leading up to the big day there was something happening at home virtually each day. On Friday 11th April, the standard "Friday" night party would be taking place close to their home. For the entertainment, a DJ is pretty much standard but this time Raj has gone and booked "Shinda" - for those familiar with the Asian bhangra scene, you know what a big name this is! At home (Sunita's dad house that is), each night was the same; music, food and getting pissed. Just as the lads got themselves sober the next day they had to do it all over again but there was no let up at all.

When we went over to the house you'd sometimes see Raj and Ravi looking battered with thoughts of "we're not drinking again". A few hours later and the shots were being poured into the glasses for round 2,3 & 4! The Friday night party crept up, everyone was excited; the venue looked great, the drink was ready to pour and the food was cooking - all we needed was the party people. On the night, things seemed to go quite slowly and Raj looked around and was concerned at the very few people that had turned up but he was panicking over nothing. This was an Indian wedding and the infamous Indian timing was to blame. A short while later and he chilled out, the place was getting packed and he was getting into the swing of things. Sukshinder Shinda's band was on stage performing their "Check 1-2" sound check - boy was their sound system loud!

Traditionally, the "Jago" ceremony is the one that families (well the girls anyway!) look forward to. Jago or "wake up" is literally where the girls/women and (and drunk men!!) dress up and dance through the streets. It's a sort of "there's a wedding, let's celebrate" type of thing and it's a great event to watch. In a secret hotel room, our Jago women, namely Sarita 'good girl', Aussie Rita and Sunita were getting ready for the big event together with some of the kids. They swapped their boots and jeans for traditional Jago attire and to the beat of the Dhol player, walked into the venue. Everyone, no matter how sober or pissed you are generally takes part, some just start dancing, others clap their hands whilst the majority simply look on. They made their way through the tables, tried to avoid falling over chairs and then made their way to the dance floor. They were dressed in colourful outfits and had pots on their heads; it was a great atmosphere and within seconds of getting onto the dance floor, it was packed.

The Jago was the ignition for the rest of the night. It just got everyone in the party mood and once the ceremony finished, the celebrations started and didn't finish until the early hours. In between we all tucked into the food, there was lots of drinking and when the DJ introduced the main live act of the night "Shinda", the place went wild. The singer started things off slowly but as the alcohol worked itself in, the lads emerged and the real partying started. Such is the stature of this singer that out came the mobile phones and cameras and soon the stage was filling up with young kids and their parents as they tried to get their picture taken with the man. Soon the kids were off and at one point Sunita and Aussie Rita were partying hard on stage. For safety reasons, the security had to limit the number on stage but one things for sure he kicked started the party and made sure everyone had a great night. The Friday night party lived up to the expectations; at the end of the night just a handful of people were left on the dance floor.

Friday night parties are hard on the system and we all needed a little time out to recover and thankfully the next day, Saturday, would be one of those. For Raj, Ravi and a whole host of others who woke up with a huge hangover the last thing on their minds was that they had to do it all again the next day. When we went round there, all the lads looked like zombies and were sipping at their morning (or afternoon!) tea and already reminiscing about the night before – well those that could remember anything about them anyway! The day drew on and the final preparations for the big wedding day were made. The wedding day was the culmination of months of planning and was *the* final party and almost certainly one that most would remember. We tried to get the kids into bed fairly early that night but it didn't quite work out like that. Sunita & Rita were busy checking and double checking their wedding outfits and painstakingly trawling through their box of bangles, bindi's and other accessories that "had to be right for the wedding". Everything that needed to be ironed was ironed and we were all set...

Our house, though slightly chaotic, was nothing compared to the parental home – it was total chaos in there; all those staying over were hurrying around the place trying to either get ready themselves, sorting the kids out (if they could find them!) and generally trying to get everything done on time. Strict time keeping was crucial that day; there were ceremonies to perform at home, we needed to leave on time so we'd arrive at the venue on time. In traditional style, Ravi was dressed up and looking sharp although not as sharp as me I must add... within 30 minutes he was transformed into his groom outfit complete with turban and swords. The video guy and photographer did their usual "looking here please" whilst Rishi had a big part to play himself. As the only nephew, he was Ravi's right hand man or little right hand man to be exact and earned himself a large amount of money during one part of the ceremony.

Outside there was lots of activity mainly because the D.E.A. had arrived. Before you start to panic, there wasn't a drug bust or anything but in fact the Dhol Enforcement Agency – a group of musicians that would provide the beats as Ravi left the house. The groom leaving the house *is* a big deal hence it had to be done properly. Traditionally as the groom exists, the music kicks in and everyone starts to dance around. In the Punjab this is quite normal but at 10am on Leicester Road in Wigston, it would to some seem pretty abnormal! However, Sarita, Rita and Sunita weren't bothered by that and started off the dancing (albeit mild!) as the DEA did their thing and Ravi walked out of the house and towards the cars. The cars were impressive, 3 in total; 2 limousines and a Rolls Royce Phantom and the kids loved it. Inside the limousines they were stunned by the luxurious seats, the drinks, the TV, DVD, drinks and they didn't want to get out!

At the wedding venue, we were met by a lady and her horse. 'What?' I hear you say.... Well again, traditionally, the groom arrives on a horse or even elephant but getting an elephant into Leicester town centre requires a bit of effort so Ravi settled for a horse. Thankfully the horse's owner had attended many Indian weddings before so she knew what to do and assured us the noise wouldn't scare or panic the horse in any way. Rishi on the other hand wasn't so sure – you see as Ravi's right hand man; he would be sitting on the horse too and let's just say he wasn't too keen.

We didn't drive right up to the venue as the groom and co had to make a grand entrance. The DEA were ready; Ravi and Rishi were sitting high on the horse and it was time to make some noise. We got a call from the bride's side of the family (who we could see at the end of the street) telling us that they were ready and that we could start to make our way up there. The dhol beats started and echoed through the narrow street and for those living around there, certainly gave them a wakeup call they'll never forget. The noise was *very* loud and coupled with our dancing and shouting livened up the atmosphere. By the time we'd danced our way to the front of the venue, Rishi looked as if he wanted to get off the horse whilst Ravi had no idea where he was (his face was covered by the "Sehra" - traditional head piece typically covered in garlands).

The dismount from the horse was simple enough but getting him into the venue and into the main wedding arena would be more difficult. Along the way, both sides of the family engage in some harmless banter. One ritual is where the bride and groom try to put a garland around each other's head whilst the other has to stop them. Sometimes the groom's brother lifts him up just as the bride tries to put the garland around the groom's neck. Unfortunately for Ravi, Ruby had a fantastic aim and managed to get the garland around him on the 2nd attempt! - well done! With the first set of formalities done, it was time to get a nice cuppa and some food - this went down well. After that, it was time for the priest to take control of the proceedings and perform the actual religious ceremony and get them married the "Indian way". Depending on the priest, the time taken to perform this can be fast tracked but typically it will take as long as it takes and there is no rushing them.

Most people at weddings love to drink champagne; well if it's in the glass anyway. When it was time to cut the cake, the bride's family were on the left, the groom's family to the right and there were a number of bottles at the front. Ravi's uncle picked up one bottle and gave it a shake. Sunita's dad egged him on to shake it some more so he did and before long the bottle was being shaken all over the place and when it was opened a mountain of bubbly flew out all over the place drenching those standing close by. This was *not* good and the stern looks from those that had champagne dripping off their suits and sarees was not a good sign at all! Worst still, it went over the cake and the floor turned sticky as the champagne started to dry off. In the end, the venue's owner had to step in and clean up the floor before anyone slipped and did themselves damage...

Soon it was time for the couple's first dance. Whenever I got to someone's wedding, it takes me back to our first dance - if you could call it that! Anyhow, the dance floor was soon packed - at most bhangra fuelled events everyone loves dancing and the time left was precious. The atmosphere was brilliant but was about to be taken onto another level as Raj had booked "Jazzy B" to entertain the crowds. Just like the Friday night guest, Jazzy B is one of the best known and popular Bhangra artists and upon arriving at the stage, out came the cameras and mobile phones again - "*gotto get my picture for Facebook innit*'. Over the next few hours, everyone enjoyed great music, great food and a wicked atmosphere and slowly but surely, the "lads", usually shy of hitting the dance floor unless they were pissed, were raring to go and then made up for lost time as they danced the afternoon away.

It was quite sad when the wedding was over, it just didn't seem right. The days leading up to the big day were just party, party, party and it was hard to believe that this was the last party. As tradition goes, the newlyweds go back to the bride's house where she basically gets ready to leave home. In virtually all other religions, this is a happy affair but for us, it's quite a sad part, especially for the bride and her family. It's a time where the bride says goodbye as she leaves the parental home and starts a new life with her husband. Sometimes the groom and bride live hundreds of miles apart, even in different continents but Ravi lived down the road - literally but Ruby was still leaving home...

By the time Ravi got home, he'd wished he hadn't. They (Sunita, aussie Rita, Sarita and a load of other money grabbing women, stood by the front door and demanded money off him before they'd let him in. The girls, adamant that this was tradition, stood firm and weren't prepared to accept small change either so for a while it was stalemate. After a few rounds of negotiation, they settled for £20 each and trust me by the time Ravi paid them all off, he must have spent around £160! Inside the house, the bride and groom then play a series of games that are meant to determine who is the dominant one in the relationship. If I remember correctly, Ruby was the victor and that just urged the girls on again. Unfortunately for me, the robbing instinct was still lurking around; I had to sit in front of Ruby and put some items in her clenched hands without dropping them. I passed the test but bizarrely had to pay Ruby £20 - ~~daylight~~ night time robbery or what!

It must have been around 8/9pm by the time the final set of games had finished - this was the end of the whirlwind wedding! Everyone was shattered; the long days and short nights was catching up with us all and over the next few days, the worldwide gathering soon dissolved away as friends and family flew home. Aussie Rita and the girls still had a few days before their flight back to Australia and they certainly made the most of the remaining time. Ravi and Ruby jetted off to Dubai, Thailand and then finished off their honeymoon in Australia where they'd meet up with Rita et al once again!

45

Dhunna Under

For Raj, Sunita's 'good guy' brother, the stress of the wedding was now behind him but he had another thing to deal with - his emigration plans to Australia. In the preceding 18 or so months, he planned to leave the UK and fly the 10284 miles or 8930 nautical miles to the East coast of Australia where along with Sarita and Monique he intended to settle down and make a fresh life for themselves. He wasn't the only one either; our newly married Ravi was also emigrating so it was all change. I vividly remember Raj being ecstatic when he got news that his Visa was approved. Ravi on the other hand was just chilled about the whole thing - typical Ravi really! Raj couldn't wait to get out of the UK; he'd had enough and needed a change of scenery. After a surprise leaving party which was messy to say the least the day had arrived for the 3 of them to go. There was no way his mates would let him go quietly and unsurprisingly on the way to Birmingham International Airport, they all stopped for a quick pint or 2 whilst Sunita, Rishi, Sarita and Monique and I carried on.

Eventually Raj and a van load of mates arrived at the airport and that's when the fun started. With the bags checked in, the lads headed straight to the bar where the pints, shots and anything else that they could think of came out. There must have been about 15 of us in total and for several hours that evening our group made the most noise! As soon as the glasses started to empty, shouts of "next round" bellowed out and it was straight to the bar ordering another mammoth round. As the friends started to talk about the things they'd done in the past, the funny stuff, the

not so funny stuff and the damn right stupid things, the place erupted in laughter but time was ticking and there came a point where even I had to say "time to go Raj".

By the time we got the section of the airport where only travellers are allowed, Raj knew this was it; this was the time to say goodbye. He went up to all his mates one by one; giving them a big hug in the process and whether they admit it or not, there were some sad friends that day. Little Monique was too young to understand what was happening and after saying our goodbyes to them all they headed off into the departure lounge. No sooner had they left the UK, Ravi and Ruby arrived back; fresh from their partial round the world trip. For them, there was no time to waste and within a few weeks they were heading back to Heathrow to catch their flights to Australia.

46

We are family...

Our plan to have another child looked to be dwindling away. Rishi kept on asking about having a brother whilst Sunita and I often discussed that if she didn't fall pregnant by such a date then we would give up on the whole thing. That date was fast approaching and I just had the awful feeling that it just wasn't meant to be. I then started to get the guilty feelings; just looking at Rishi and the thought of him not having a sibling was hard to take and I know Sunita felt the same way. Still, there was nothing we could do about it; we simply had to get on with life. At the end of a very long day at work, I came home on a fine summer evening to find Sunita and Rishi chatting in the kitchen. "Time for a cuppa" were the words that I often said as soon as I walked in and Sunita knew that was my way of saying "put the kettle on".

After hearing what Rishi had been up to, he ran upstairs to get onto his computer. I think I went to grab the tea bags or something when I heard Sunita say *"have a look at this..."* We had been planning a trip to Australia so I actually thought she had some ticket prices or something travel related to look at. She was holding a long piece of plastic in her hand and virtually shoving the thing in my face - my eyes focused on the word "pregnant". I didn't know what to say and Sunita looked just as surprised as me. In an instant I was ecstatic but a little sceptical. What if the reading was wrong? I think we both had similar thoughts because Sunita went on to explain that this was the second test she'd done and *both* results were the same - she was pregnant. The relief was immense, the joy uncontrollable and all we could think about was how would Rishi react when we told him the news.

That evening the reality of it dawned on us; we were having our 2nd child and it felt that our family would be complete. Sunita made an appointment to see the doctor after which we had a date for the first scan. Though the D.I.Y pregnancy kits tend to be very accurate, there was still a chance that the results could be wrong and although as adults we could cope with being wrong, telling Rishi he was having a brother or sister then having to tell him we got it wrong was unthinkable. Thus, we decided to wait until we were 100% certain before we told Rishi; we just had to make sure we didn't let it slip in conversation! On the day of the scan itself, Rishi was at school and I spoke to my manager about having a slightly extended lunch. This would give me the chance to drive home, pick Sunita up, get to the hospital, drop Sunita back off and then get back to work!

The scan was at the Leicester General Hospital; the same place where Rishi was born. When our, or should I say Sunita's name was called, we hurried into the small room where they tell you what's about to happen. After putting some special gel on the tummy (it helps with the scan), we could see our baby in glorious back and white; we *were* having our 2nd child! The baby was tiny but it was amazing to think that here we were staring at our baby

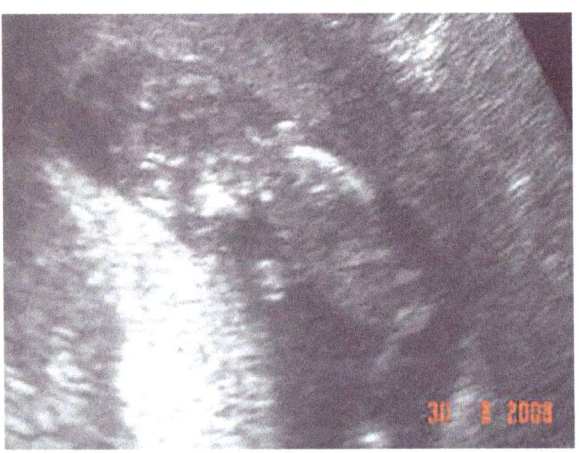

Baby Patel.

when between us we had lost all hope of having another child! After hearing how many "weeks" the baby was and whether we wanted some photos (of course we did!) we headed back home. I was so excited that I took the scan pictures to work and showed everyone. That evening we decided to tell Rishi the news.

We both called out to Rishi; "we've got something to show you" I think were our exact words. Excited at what it was, he came running down the stairs and we told him to open out his hands. We then put the scan picture in the palm of his hand. There was no reaction initially probably because he couldn't quite work out what he was looking at. I think one of us said "it's a baby" and there was a long pause but then Rishi said "is it our baby"? Once we said "yes, you're having a brother or sister" that was it. He has a massive grin on his face, ran upstairs then ran back down and was even more hyperactive (we didn't think that was possible!). Asking if he was happy was daft; his reaction said it all and I think both of us knew that we had made the right decision. It's a shame we didn't capture that moment on camera because let me tell you one thing - to this day *nothing* has come close to making Rishi's little face light up as much as finding out he was going to have a brother or sister.

It wasn't long before all our family heard the good news and everyone was very happy for us.

I remember ringing E2 who said the news was "wicked" but I had to tell Nee and Rumit too. I thought i'd do something different so I changed the home page of my web site and included the scan picture. I rang Rumit, pretended I was having problems accessing the web site and asked if he could check for himself. Always happy to help, he then connected to the www and at first said "can't connect". Now, this was *unexpected* and it looked as if there was a problem but it was just a glitch. For about 8 seconds Rumit didn't say a word; I think his eyes were fixed on the image and it probably caught him out! Once he realised what was going on, he was well pleased.... the same thing happened with Nee; he had no idea why I was asking him to check my web site but once he did, he was shocked but happy all the same - doing it in a style of my own!

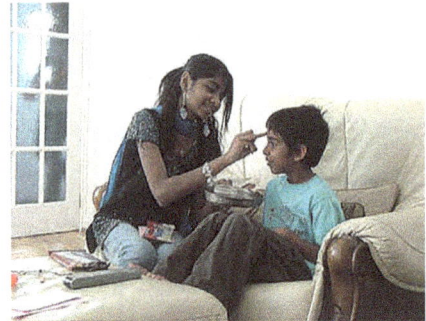

All smiles!

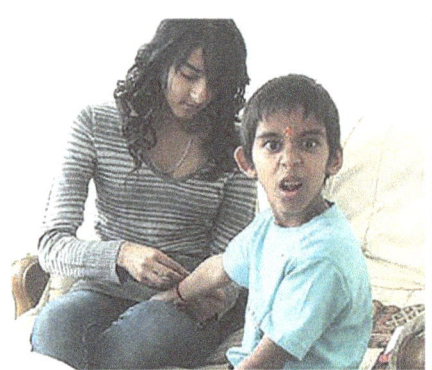
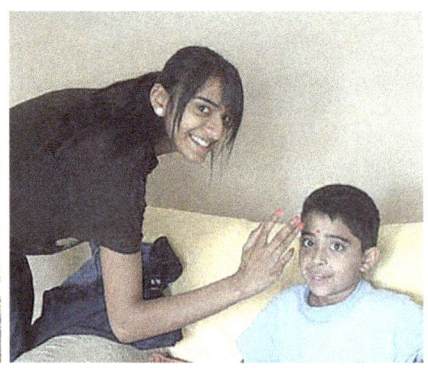

Nice look Rahul!   Rishi looked forward to the chocolate!

Preeya – full of drama!   My lovely sister!

504

47

G'day in Hervey Bay

Even before Aussie Rita emigrated to Australia, it had always been one of those places that I wanted to visit. Determined more than ever to go and coupled with the fact that we wouldn't be flying anywhere for a while once our baby arrived, we decided to head to Australia for just over 3 weeks. In fact, we'd decided to go down under before we even knew Sunita was pregnant and we had many things to do and so little time in which to do them. If you're lucky you can often pick up some real holiday bargains but we knew that this holiday would be expensive. The flights alone set us back £2800 and we still had a few things to buy and take a fair amount of spending money too. For Sunita it was planning heaven; she's a great organiser and does plan things to perfection. Her 'to do' lists are legendary even though I do take the piss out of her for it on occasions.

As each item on the list was done, she'd happily cross it off and it was onto the next one! Visas to Australia are meant to be straightforward - you can even apply for them on the internet. However, our travel agent said they'd "thrown in" the visas as we booked our flights through them. It would save us £45 pounds so we were happy for them to sort it for us. Both Sunita and Rishi had their visas sorted without any fuss at all but I wasn't so lucky. When I went to the travel agent I was told the Visa office needed more information about me - from the sounds of it there was another Sandip Patel who must have been involved in some dodgy activity which raised some alarms. Of course, it had nothing to do with me and all the Australian visa office wanted was some more information. Unfortunately, this was too much bother for the travel agent who decided to do absolutely nothing about it. I was told to come back in a week but despite giving them this time there was still no progress.

10 days before we were meant to be flying out there was still no sign of my visa and I was told that I needed to pick up my passport as the travel agent "couldn't do anymore". I was furious, they were the ones who said they'd sort it out and now they couldn't be arsed. I felt like going back and telling them what I thought of them but what was the point? The next day I managed to get the email address of someone at the Australian visa office in London; explained the current situation and the failings of the crappy travel agent. Within a few minutes I received one of those standard replies telling me that my email was received and it would be dealt with in a few days but to ring a number for more urgent cases. This was urgent and I was soon typing those numbers into a phone.

The lady I spoke to was extremely helpful; fully understood the situation, was annoyed with the travel agent and said to "leave it with her". About 40 minutes later I got an email from here, complete with visa number which was automatically assigned to my passport number - that's what I call efficient service. Instantly I sent her an email back, expressing my gratitude at the speed and quick service - it was the least I could do and finally we were all set for our big trip. Our journey to Australia was with Emirates, without doubt one of the best airlines in the world and our first leg was from Birmingham to Dubai. Yep, we were off to Dubai and yet again I would see nothing but the inside of the airport terminal. Rishi was excited as ever and hoping that during our trip, he might get to see an Airbus A380.

We left the UK on Friday 15th August 2008 landing in Dubai at around 7am local time where the temperature was already 34 degrees! As we walked down the steps of the Boeing 777, Rishi was amazed at the sheer size of the airport - it was like a mini city! The terminal is massive and we had to literally walk from one side of the

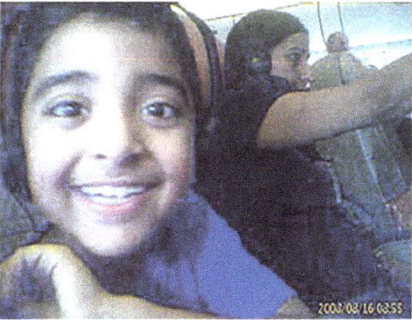

airport to the other to catch our connecting flight. Sunita was over 4 months pregnant now and although she was still active, the long walk did leave her a little tired so she was glad when we reached our departure gate. Our next leg of the journey would see us head to Bangkok and then after a brief stop head direct for Sydney. During the long, long flight Rishi had a wicked time. He had a massive collection of films to choose from, an array of games to play and loved making seat to seat phone calls. I must have answered about 20 calls from seat 26J during that flight.

Eventually, after spending about 21 hours in the air, our journey was almost over; we were about to land in Sydney but we still had one final flight to catch. After picking our bags up, it was straight onto the shuttle bus for the 20 minute ride to the domestic airport where we caught the Virgin Blue flight to Hervey Bay. The flight was short; well short in comparison to the ones we'd been on so far and as we approached Hervey Bay we flew over deserted beaches, vast expanses of land where the water looked a picture perfect turquoise colour and the sun was beating down. About 20 minutes before we touched down, my phone beeped; it was Aussie Rita letting us know that Max would be picking us up. I thought it would be quite strange seeing him for the first time in over 4 years but good old Max was the same and was eager to get us home - well that's what we thought anyway.

Surreal, strange, different, unbelievable - that's some of the thoughts I had as we drove out of the tiny airport at Hervey Bay. On a personal note it felt quite strange finally arriving in Australia; the country I thought i'd never get to. Yet we had arrived we were looking forward to seeing some of this vast country. As we turned into Riverheads Road, Rita and the girls were looking out for us; they kind of knew when we'd arrive home but our arrival was a little strange. Just as Max pointed out their house, we could see Rita standing at the front waiting for us to turn into the drive but in pure Max style, his excitement got the better of him and he drove straight by and he kept driving till we couldn't drive anymore.

Eventually we ran out of road - ahead of us was a sort of mini-roundabout and beyond that just a vast expanse of water. Max explained that this was the gateway to the famous Fraser Island. At the time it was just a name; it could have been called Fantasy Island and it wouldn't have mattered - all we wanted to do was to get home! Finally though, we headed back and turned into their drive; Rita, Jasmin and Surita were there waiting to greet us; we were home! Though we only saw the gang a few months earlier, it was great seeing everyone yet again and we chilled out for the next few hours and had a nice cuppa! I must say that they have a beautiful house, masses of land and an inviting swimming pool too. You could see Max was very proud of his work; Max being Max you knew he put plenty of time and effort into the build and it showed so well done mate!

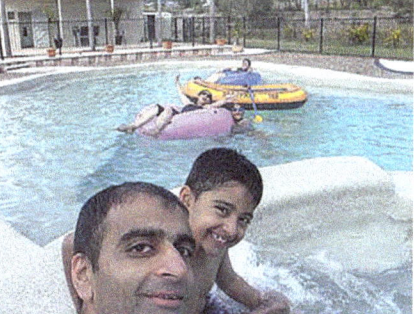

Sunita – chilling...   Beautiful pool & house!

After resting for a few hours it was time to meet up with Raj, Ravi, Sarita and Ruby as well as little Monique. In the few months that the boys had been out there they had found, made an offer and then purchased their own business and were busy running it. They all looked quite settled but as we later learnt, running the business was a huge challenge mainly because a large proportion of the income was from the fast food section of the shop and it was the multitude of things involved in that process that caused the stress. Their food menu was massive; I think I counted close to 50 different things that could be ordered and they were new to the whole thing. However, despite having a few mishaps along the way, they slowly started to sort things out and in the few days that we stayed there you could see things improving daily...

They say people need holidays to rejuvenate you but this holiday did that and more - it made us think seriously about moving out there. I've been on many holidays with my friends and even more with Sunita and Rishi but none of the places we've been too had the effect on us as much as Australia did. Perhaps it was the fact that Rita, Raj etc. were all over there now. After all, family *does* and always will make a big difference to the quality of lives wherever you are. However, above all was the fact that we felt so relaxed there; the people, the sights and sounds of Hervey Bay itself; the fact that you can jump into a car and drive to a deserted beach where the water is crystal clear; where you can jump onto a boat and head out to sea and watch Humpback whales, swim with dolphins or enjoy or enjoy snorkelling - the list goes on and on.

I just fell in love with the place; more so than the rest because i've always loved the outdoor 'thing'. Even Sunita who previously rejected the offer of moving to the USA and on the back of that thought would never want to move anywhere, was keen on a possible move whilst Rishi didn't even want to come home! The world heritage listed Fraser Island is a mere 30 minute boat ride from Rita's house and to put this into prospective, the Island is in the same category as both Uluru (Ayers Rock) and the Great Barrier Reef and is without doubt an area of amazing beauty. Keen to make sure we made full use of our time, Sunita and Rita had already planned things to do and by the time we left Hervey Bay we'd seen and done many things including chilled at the beach at Hervey Bay, went to Fraser Island where we passed the Moheno shipwreck as we hurtled along the 75 mile beach highway in our 4x4 bus and visited Lake McKenzie.

We then drove south to the Gold Coast where we spent a day at the Warner Bros film studio theme park before spending another fun filled day at SeaWorld. The beaches, just like those at Hervey Bay were clean and relatively quiet and on a few mornings I made the most of them by going out for a long jog along the beach! Brisband (if you're Rishi), Brisbane (to the rest of you!) was next on our hit list; the city has a real buzz about it, the sun was beating down and we lounged around the make shift beach area right in the heart of the city! The following week, we joined Ravi and Ruby and drove south yet again to Noosa Bay; this was definitely a playing ground for the rich and famous and it was a real eye opener looking at the $1,000,000+ penthouses and mansions that were scattered around the area.

However, one thing was clear; the quality of life and mood in general was upbeat wherever you went whether it was in Hervey Bay, Noosa or Brisbane - people generally just looked happy! Back in Hervey Bay we split our time between Rita's and Kawungan mini mart and we tried, where possible, to make sure we spent

End of a busy day at Kawungan.

Young staff.

Local beach – Hervey Bay.... perfect.

Enjoying a stroll along the promenade in the evening.

Lake McKenzie, Fraser Island.

time with everyone. One afternoon, with the help of Max and Rita, we headed to the Harbour to get onto a boat that would take us to 'Round Island'. The island was about 20 minutes away but on this day we had Brisbane's channel 9 TV station on board too. They were there to make a short promotional film about Hervey Bay and in particular Round Island - the best thing was that it would be aired on TV later that year - would we be the stars of the show?

On this day, Raj, Sarita and Monique were with us too but our first challenge was getting off the boat! To avoid the boat getting stuck on the sand embankments, it got close to the island but then all of us had to wade through several feet of water and with the sea a little choppy, that was proving to be quite difficult! Nevertheless, we were on dry land again and the first thing our guide (Murray) set up was the good old Barbeque. The spread was excellent and Pippi hunting was definitely an experience

SeaWorld, Gold Coast.

Waiting for the dolphin show - SeaWorld.

Surita & Rishi look tired after a long day – the others can be seen behind!

Gold Coast beach.

Noosa, Sunshine Coast.

Sunita & Rishi, Noosa, Sunshine Coast.

Collecting shells on the beach.

Aussie Rita & Sunita relaxing in the sun.

Round island.

Beers on the boat – Round island.

(using your feet you move the top layers of sand hoping to uncover some shell like things which open up when fried!). I didn't find them nice at all and preferred the sausages which were cooked to perfection. Lunch over and done with I had to find the loo and trust me, I found it alright. The loo or "dunny" as our guide called it was a short walk away and once inside you it was a loo with a view - there were spectacular views of the island and the beach area with the Hervey Bay mainland in the distance.

Raj and I were quite keen to find out how big this island really was so we headed down to the section of beach we arrived at. We then started to walk counter clockwise and it wasn't long before we saw a totally different side of the island. The sand was the softest i'd ever felt, the small streams of water were unbelievably warm and the wind speed totally dropped. We couldn't hear or see any of the others and it felt like a big place and in the running for a paradise island. As we continued to walk we could see the land veer to the left and after a few more minutes we could see the others; round island was round but very small too. Once back aboard the boat, the next destination was to see the Coral Reef, try to see dolphins and for those that were interested, time for some snorkelling. Our guide, Murray asked who was keen to do a spot of snorkelling and I wasted no time in saying "yes". I could see that Raj wanted to have a go and after much persuasion he decided to come join me in the water.

As suspected, getting into the sea and watching the colourful fish was wicked and as food was thrown into the water you got an amazing view as hundreds of fish gathered to grab some of it. Although he struggled at first, Raj seemed to get the hang of breathing underwater but whenever the fish came towards him, he went the other way - I think he was scared something might come and take a bite out of him Soon Raj thought 'stuff that' and got out whilst Sarita thought 'sod that' and got into the water. Unfortunately, a combination of not being a confident swimmer and a slightly choppy sea meant she couldn't keep her balance so she had to give up and get back on board.

Back on board, the TV crew were doing their rounds and looking for people to say a few words about the trip to round island. Raj declined straight away so they shoved the mic in Sunita's face. Being the talkative type, you'd think she'd have no problems reeling off a few words about the days adventure but she found it quite difficult to keep the momentum going. Raj then decided he wanted me to say something so kept on telling the presenter to give me the mic. Well, for what it's worth I did my bit and if I say so myself it went ok. However even after they said "brilliant - thanks for that", we didn't know whether their passing comment was just to please us - I thought they would take pride in editing us out. Keen to find out when the TV show would be aired, we discovered that it was due to hit the airwaves in October/ November 2008 so we'd just have to wait and see!

Sarita takes to the sea!   My turn now – look at the TV cameras...

2 weeks had already passed and we only had a few more days in Hervey Bay so there was no time to waste. We had already done and seen many things but a skydive was something i've wanted to do for years and years. In the UK the appeal just wasn't there but here in the warm coastal resort, the location was perfect. I had discussed this many times with Aussie Rita (who had already jumped out of a plane in the UK). She was up for it and we even managed to persuade Ravi to do it too. We asked the others; Raj said "get stuffed", Sunita said "you must be joking" whilst Sarita looked as if she wanted to do it but she changed her mind and said no. The rest of us were still keen and decided to go for it. On the day of the jump I wasn't nervous at all but just really excited - one of my ambitions were about to come true! We met our instructor at their office down on the beach and filled in the forms. The interesting part of the question was where it said you jump out at your own risk and there is a possibility you could die!

That didn't bother me at all; I figured jumping out of a plane with an experienced parachutist was several thousand times safer than driving down the M1. Paperwork done, we climbed into their van and drove to Hervey Bay airport whilst Sunita, Ruby and Rishi followed in the car. After a brief safety drill, it was decided that Rita and Ravi would jump out first and whilst they jumped aboard the plane, the rest of us drove to the landing point which was a short drive away on a different beach. The pilot of the little plane and his colleague down below kept in contact with their radios and once the pilot signalled that they were about to jump out, we were told to look up and they'd be a good chance to see them bailing out! Now - we were jumping at an altitude of 14,000 feet and I was sceptical about seeing them but unbelievably we saw 2 shining dots in the air - it was them! As the seconds turned into minutes we could see the tiny parachute fully opened and watched as they drifted back to earth and eventually made a safe landing on the beach.

Once free from their parachutes, the look on their faces said it all - it was wicked! It was my turn now so back to the centre to get strapped up. I decided to pay a little extra and have the whole experience put onto DVD so I had a camcorder shoved into my face at various times, before we got onto the plane and during our ascent. The view at 10,000 feet was phenomenal; in the distance I could see Fraser Island, Round Island and the curvature of Hervey Bay itself. The sea below looked beautiful with its myriad of blue and turquoise colours and despite thinking I would be shitting myself by now I wasn't at all. The pilot signalled something to the instructor who in turn signalled to me that it was time to go. The plane door was opened and I then had to manoeuvre myself in front so that I could be strapped to the instructor. Once I was hooked to the instructor, the next stage was to put my feet out of the plane and trust me, this was one of the best moments of the whole experience.

I sat at the door of the plane with my feet dangling off the side looking at the picture perfect view; we were 14,000 feet in the air, the noise of the wind was deafening and this was the moment I had been waiting for. With a 3,2,1 and a go, go, go we hurled ourselves out of the plane and immediately did a 360 as we raced to the ground. As we spun round I could see the plane above us and then enjoyed the view as we descended. I really cannot

All set for the jump – this is my ride!

The moment of truth.

Freefall! You can see the plane at the
top of the picture!

Hervey Bay was getting
closer and closer...

Incredible.

Thumbs up – great experience!

Time for a barbeque.   Evening out.

describe the feeling of freefalling towards the ground; the speed, the adrenaline rush and the incredible view all rolled in made this one of the most memorable moments of my life. After what felt like a few minutes, the parachute was opened and we were hurled upwards as the parachute filled with air and then slowly started to fall again. Rita and Ravi slowly came into view and my instructor shouted "feet up, feet up" and within a few seconds we had touched down. After sharing our experiences, it was back to the jump centre where the recording was transferred to DVD and then it was back to Kawungan!

A couple of days afterwards, our time in Hervey Bay had come to an end. It was quite sad saying goodbye to everyone; we'd had a wicked time with them all and enjoyed the 3 weeks we spent there. I remember dropping Rita off to work. going back to their house, picking up all our stuff and then heading straight to Kawungan. Before we said our farewells, it was time for Sunita to get her gifts; it was her birthday and she made sure everyone knew it! The celebrations had to be cut short as we needed to get going - our flight from Hervey Bay to Sydney would be departing soon and so we needed to make tracks. The goodbyes were horrible; it was awful leaving everyone behind again but we had to go. After getting into the car, it was one final wave before we made our way to the airport - Rita, Max and the girls would be meeting us there....

Hervey Bay comes across as a small sleepy town but it's far from that. In fact, it's quite a big place; surrounded by plenty of residential areas; plenty of sun drenched beaches and just a *really* nice place to be. One things for sure; the locals definitely know Max and Rita. In the 3 weeks that we were there, it became clear that these guys have really made their mark here. I managed to get my Australian driving licence; notably assisted by Max who knew virtually all of the staff in the office. Our trip to round island was swiftly booked because Max knew Murray; the owner of the Round Island cruise company whilst our skydive was managed by someone that Rita knew very well. One day Sunita and I went to a small shop in Hervey Bay to get some photos printed and to get a copy of a photo. The chap behind the counter took one look at the photo and said "I know her!" and to cut a short story even shorter (ha ha!), he knew Rita via the kid's nursery that she runs there. I even managed to open a bank account whilst there and it was no surprise that Max was on first names terms with the manager there!

Anyway, we arrived at Hervey Bay airport just as Max and Rita were parking up. We grabbed our suitcases from the back of Max's Toyota and headed inside. Whilst Rishi chatted with Jasmin and Surita (the little Surita that is!), Sunita and Rita were getting a little emotional at the thought of us leaving; it was one of those 'nice' sister moments. Meanwhile Max kept saying "when you moving over then?" to which I felt like saying "as soon as I can!". Not one for long goodbyes, I said we'd better go now and with that we parted. As Sunita, Rishi and I walked around the customs area, I couldn't believe it - Max was chatting with the custom guys - he knew them as well; was there anyone they didn't know? We waved goodbye and in an instant, it was just the 3 of us again.

Warm and sunny when we left Hervey Bay, it pissed it down as we touched down in Sydney. The taxi ride from the airport to our hotel was horrible; it rained even more and as we chilled in our hotel for the rest of the evening, there was no let up. The hotel handed out umbrellas as all the guests rushed around trying not to get wet but rain or not we were going out that night - it was Sunita's birthday so we had to do something. We found a great Italian restaurant pretty close by, had a super meal and then it was back to the hotel to chill for the evening. Our room on the 42nd floor was *very* high up and Rishi loved it; he spent ages looking out of the window towards the Opera House and beyond!

When my eyes opened the next morning, all I could think of was the weather. I didn't have to get out of bed; the whistling of the wind as it bounced off the buildings was enough to tell you there was a strong gust blowing outside. The sound of the rain as it battered the windows was enough to piss me off even more. Still, we were in Sydney so we had to make the most of it and with that we had our breakfast and ventured towards Darling Harbour; an area close to the hotel with many restaurants, the aquarium and numerous companies offering to take you on boat rides around the waterways or further out to sea to see the migrating whales. Sydney was a busy place, mad almost and reminded me of London and a far cry from Hervey Bay.

The location of our hotel was perfect; a mere 15 minutes' walk to the Opera House and the Sydney Harbour Bridge. After 2 days of rain, our last day in Sydney started off warm and with the sun beating down, Miss efficient Sunita got all our stuff and made sure everything went back into our bags and suitcases in a neat and orderly manner. With the bags packed and locked away in the hotel room downstairs we had most of the day to see some more sights. From our hotel, it was a short walk to the rock area, packed with small gift shops and pubs and then onto the Harbour Bridge itself. Sunita was getting tired quite easily now (pregnant and all that...) so whilst she sat on the Harbour bridge itself, Rishi and I paid our entrance fee and climbed up the 100's of stairs to the top of one the bridge's pillars. The view from the top was spectacular; the Opera House looked picture perfect as the bright light of the sun reflected off its numerous walls whilst on the bow of the bridge itself you could see groups of climbers ascending as they faced the challenge of the bridge walk.

We then doubled back on ourselves and made our way to the Opera House. Along the way the crowds started to gather big time; it had a real Covent Garden feel to it; there was one lady who was incredibly flexible and managed to fit herself into a small glass cube much to the amusement of the laughing and clapping crowd. In the distant you could hear the Didgeridoo (some claim that it could be the world's oldest instrument!) played by an Aboriginal looking man adorning full face paint. We took our time getting to the Opera House; it was warm, sunny and the place was lively so why rush things? Along the way we passed some water taxis which soon got Rishi's attention. The expected "can we go on one dad?" soon followed and the standard reply of "we'll see" was returned much to his disappointment. Still, a few minutes later the view was excellent; to the left the Harbour Bridge stood big and bold whilst to the right the striking features of the infamous Sydney Opera House was right in front of us.

In pure tourist style, we took plenty of pictures but to be honest the best ones were those taken from a distance. We climbed up the stairs of the famous Opera House and lazed around whilst Rishi, left with the camera, made the most of it and snapped away from all angles. We must have been there for about 45 minutes before we decided to head off. Not wanting to disappoint Rishi, the 3 of us stepped aboard the water taxi which took us on a rapid ride underneath the harbour bridge and then back to Darling Harbour which looked totally different from the rain soaked area we saw the day before! After having a spot of lunch we took a casual walk to the Sydney Tower, the tallest rotating restaurant in the southern hemisphere! We didn't go there for the food though; I signed up to take the Sydney Skywalk which is basically to get strapped up and walk around the outside of the tower on a special viewing platform. Whilst I was outside enjoying the 360 degrees view of Sydney from 1000 feet up, Sunita and Rishi were enjoying an equally great view from the safety of the inside using the numerous telescopes scattered around the place.

View of the Opera house from the
Sydney harbour bridge.

Warm and sunny in Sydney!

Sunita relaxing in the water taxi –
getting close to the
Sydney harbour bridge.

Outside the Opera house.

Whilst at the sky tower we kept a watchful eye on the time
and I had been dreading the words I was about to say. "It's time to
go" - damn, there they were; those words that signalled the end of
our holiday. Yup, we had no choice but to make our way back to
the hotel where we'd arranged for a taxi to take us back to the
airport to start our long journey home. The flight back took a
slightly different route to the one we arrived on. We flew almost
16 hours non-stop from Sydney to Dubai (back there for the
6th time!) and then after a change of plane, another 7 hours to
Birmingham. As the doors of Boeing 777 opened again, it was shit

being back - well for me it was anyway. I hate the feeling you get when you come back off a holiday; the thought of having to get back into our "normal" lives, the day to day chores and the repetitiveness of it all.

It must have been at least a week by the time we adjusted to being back. It took a while just to get back into a normal sleeping pattern whilst for Rishi, who had missed around 8 days of school, he had to get back into his school routine. As usual, I put together a web page of our holiday and then published it to the world for everyone to see. There was no doubting it; the effect of Australia on us was clear - so clear in fact that we decided to begin the long process of applying for an emigration visa to live and work out there. I just wanted to get there as quickly as possible but my time estimates were a little unrealistic (yes, ok Sunita; you were right...!) Over the forthcoming weeks, we had an endless flood of emails between us and the Emigration agency we were using and after being advised of the costs involved, the process started in earnest.

One warm weekend in the summer a bunch of my friends (some i've known since nursery school!) took the train into London to meet up with some of our other friends originally from Leicester

Family get together @ Kiran's house.

Rare visit by the man Chong 'rip' Rana aka VIP the man from China.

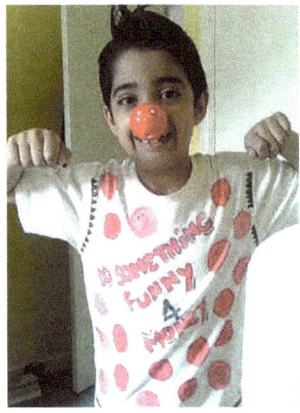

Rishi did something funny for money!

At a farm in Buckinghamshire.

Rishi - mixology.

too. In a matter of hours, Nalini, Nila, Bindy, Shanti, Bindi, Alka and myself were all reunited again and chatting about everything and anything. It was always great to meet up and a massive achievement given the number of years that had passed in between...

Nila, Nalini, Bindy, Me, Shanti.

It was now September 2009 and shortly after we got back, Sunita had a 'scan' appointment at the hospital where the staff could check the baby and make sure everything was ok. We both agreed it was important to keep Rishi involved throughout the pregnancy and it was great to see him watch in amazement as the staff made Sunita comfortable on the bed, applied the special 'scan' gel and within a few seconds showed us our baby / Rishi's brother or sister on the monitor. I think it was hard for Rishi to believe that the little thing in the middle of the screen was a baby. As this was our second baby and given the fact that it didn't bother us whether we had a boy or girl, I *wanted* to find out what we'd be having. Sunita and Rishi had other ideas and wanted another surprise so in the end I was the only one who found out. Whilst Sunita and Rishi looked the other way, I watch the monitor

closely as the lady clicked around the screen and then suddenly popped up a message that said "Male".

The one thing I will say about myself is that I can keep secrets; unlike Sunita who will spill the beans a few minutes after being told to keep quiet about something! That evening I had strange looks from Rishi who was excited as ever. It was as if I might give a clue or something on whether we'd be having a boy or girl but they didn't want to know and I would make damn sure they didn't find out. Shopping was interesting and so was the typical pregnancy rumours... whenever we were out and about Sunita reckoned that I headed towards the boy's section and, without realising, would give them clues that it was a boy. When she told me I just dismissed it as rubbish on the basis that as soon as i'd finished looking at the boy's stuff, I would head over to the girl's section. Some said that the "bump" on her tummy was pointing outwards and so "you'll be having a boy..."; either way it didn't matter what we were having; I just had to make sure I was tight lipped.

As the weeks slowly passed by, I often found myself wondering about our day trip to Round Island and the Brisbane TV crew that were there; would we be on TV? Would they decide our 5 minutes of fame would never actually happen? Back in Australia, Raj was at someone else's house where the TV was switched on but not being paid attention to. As he became immersed in conversation, he casually looked towards the TV and thought he saw himself. Mesmerised by it all, he stayed glued and realised that he was watching the footage recorded at Round Island. He then called us to say he'd just seen it but I was gutted that they didn't know when it was going to be aired as I wanted them to record it. Undeterred, I soon started my Google searches, found the main contacts at channel 9 TV and bombarded them with emails requesting that they provide me with the video link.

Most of the emails I sent resulted in automatic replies that basically said "thanks for the email, we will get in contact shortly". Unfortunately, it did get quite disheartening because nobody got back to me until I had a little breakthrough. I managed to find the on line profile of the actual presenter who was with us that day and through her profile managed to get the email address of the director of the TV station. In my email to the head honcho, I stated that considering I took part in the recording and the fact that we don't get channel 9 TV in the UK, the least they could do is post the video on line for us all to see.

I never heard back from this guy and just as I was about to unleash another stroppy email, I got the result I was looking for. They had posted the video on Australia's You Tube and with one click on the link, we finally got to see what was aired on Brisbane TV. Between myself, Raj, Sunita, Sarita, Monique and Rishi, we were in the video several times and although my part was cut down heavily I had a small but starring role. Unfortunately for Sunita, they decided her presenting skills just weren't up to the mark (probably because she kept laughing!). I must say it was quite strange seeing the finished product and it painted a good picture for the Round Island trips and Hervey Bay in general.

The nights were closing in as we ventured yet again into autumn. One of the most obvious signs for me was my 5.30am wake up call. In order to work my 4 day week, I cram 5 days' work into 4 days which means an early start, leave the house @ 6am and at my desk ready for work at 6.15am. In the summer i'd wake to pure daylight but now it was getting darker and darker by the day. The big next event in our lives was our second child that was now only months away. Sunita was still ok, healthy as ever but getting tired as the countdown began to the big day. Never one to sit still, she kept herself busy regardless of being pregnant or not which I think is a good thing; far better than lazing around feeling sorry for yourself.

Names; baby names that is, was a hot topic which was made even more difficult because I was the only one who knew we were having a boy. Sunita and her legendary "lists" were out in force; all the things she/we needed to do before, during and after the baby arrived was neatly written down. One of the lists contained baby names; both boys and girls and to honest we agreed on more girls' names than boys. I played along - I didn't have a choice but despite many of these chats we were no closer to agreeing on boy names. I think Sunita would agree that since this was to be our 2nd child, we were both a little more chilled out than the first time. We knew what to expect and although there could be surprises, we were ready for the arrival. As with her first pregnancy, Sunita decided to work close to the due date and if I remember correctly, she finished work during the last week of December 2008.

48

The Rishi experience
& kids, kids, kids

As you'd expect from a young kid, they often ask questions, sometimes at awkward times and our Rishi was no different. Questions are good, but some of them were quite deep and interesting. The one I liked best was the one he hit me with whilst we were watching Top Gear one evening. *"Dad..."* he said as his voice slowly picked up pitch (I knew from that moment that a question was on its way...), *"How was the first person born?"* Hmmm, good question but how on earth was I meant to even begin to answer that?

The reality is I couldn't answer it; the possible answers depend on whether you choose to follow science or religion. Religion would say *"god created the first person"*, science would go on about evolution and how the first human started off as a living cell or something. Then again, *how did the cells get here?* Ok, cells are made up of chemicals and molecular structures... how did they get here? You get the picture right and hopefully can now see it's a question that I don't think anyone will ever answer let alone trying to explain it to a 7 year old! My answer went something like *"I don't know"* but I clearly remember Rishi's response; *"search on Google dad"*!

Other interesting questions included *"**Is the future real?**"*

*"**Dad, when we were in Australia... why didn't we fall off?**"* - he had noticed that Australia is "much lower" geographically than the UK when viewed on the world map and I thought it was very much a thought provoking question.

*"**Dad, are bananas made of milk?**"*

Aside from the questions, he often had days where he'd make you laugh one minute then drive you mad the other. Whilst out walking with Sunita one day, he had to stop as he had "a rock in his shoe" whilst on another occasion and totally out of character he wasn't happy about something and during a trip to Asda refused to shut our front door despite asking him repeatedly. Sunita, who is usually one of the "calmest" people I know remained calm and simply got out if the car and shut the door. By the time they got to Asda, Rishi still wasn't playing ball and this time refused to get out of the car. In the end Sunita didn't have time to waste and simply locked the car with Rishi inside it. It didn't take long before Rishi snapped out of this uncharacteristic behaviour and it hasn't happened since. I just found the whole thing quite funny simply because it was so unlike him to do such stuff!

In our immediate family, it had been several years since we heard the cries of a baby. For my brother Vip and my sister in law Heena who were expecting their first baby, things were about to change. They came around to see us one evening and with Sunita pregnant too, most of the talk was baby related. It seemed to me anyway that Heena just wanted to have the baby as soon as possible; I guess carrying a small child for so long was taking its toll and I clearly recall discussions on how there was still a few weeks to go. Little did we know that later that night the baby had other ideas - the labour pains started and Vip rushed her into hospital.

At work the next morning, Sunita sent me a text message with news that they'd had a baby boy - fantastic news; it was such a shock after our discussions the night before! Later that evening the only plans we had was to go and see them all at the hospital. Heena looked exhausted which was to be expected after such an ordeal but both Heena and my brother were happy. The little baby or Kaylen as he was named didn't look like either of them and it was amazing holding such a tiny thing once again. On a personal note, I was extremely happy for them both but especially for my brother who I felt really turned his life around - good on you bro!

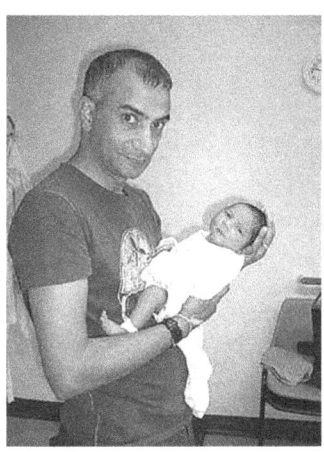
VIP holding a "VIP".

Kaylen is the youngest of my 3 nephews and I also have 2 nieces. The age range is remarkable; one is coming up to a year old (likely to be well over a year old by the time I finish this) whilst another is 18 already! Rahul is a cheeky young boy full of beans who puts up with my brother (Kiran's) sense of humour. His sister (Priyanka - my niece), is a typical teenager of today. Rarely seen without her Sony Walkman mobile and headphones, my *homie'* loves the latest trends, loves music and loves to party. She's a great kid, you can have a real laugh with her and above all she shows the utmost respect to those around her.

For a short spell she used to pop round on Fridays so I could teach her to mix vinyl on my turntables. Priyanka ("Yankee" - you get me?") is incredible at sending text messages. Whilst most of us are starting to put a few words together, she can write whole sentences without even looking at the keys. In the evenings we'd often chat over MSN Messenger; she'd be there updating her Facebook profile whilst I would try to keep up with her speed of messaging.

My other niece "Preeya" is quite different from Priyanka. I would describe her as young, a real queen of music and full of drama! She has a fantastic singing voice which I heard for myself during a school concert she performed in. She might play it down but such was her performance that evening that many parents could be heard asking *"who's that kid who just sang?"* and one parent even tapped her on the shoulder to compliment her. I think she could have a wonderful career in acting/drama/singing or perhaps all 3 but deep down I think her talents, rare amongst the Asian community (or should I say not exactly encouraged) will probably not be used. She also seems to know all the words to almost any song that is transmitted over the radio airwaves; it must be the tunes that my sister plays in the car that got her started on this!

Onto Ashish now; the first born and oldest of all the nephews and nieces, I can only describe him as "a favourite with the girls!" Now 18, he's made easy work of GCSE's, A Levels and is now studying a degree in Chartered Surveying at Nottingham University. Whilst other kids or young adults I should say at university are living it up and running up huge debts, he has his head screwed on right and manages to find the right balance between work and play. A big fan of music, he too loves to party and just like Priyanka and Preeya he has a Facebook account full of pictures of what he's been up to. Talking to Ashish is like talking to your best mate which is great because I can chat to him about anything and everything...I have great aspirations for him, I know he'll make something of himself because he seems to have the determination to make it happen.

49

When Santa got stuck ~~up the chimney...~~ in the kitchen window

The build up to Christmas was the same each year; cold winter days with star filled frosty winter nights, our Christmas tree was brought down from its resting place in our garage and put up to the side of the TV, Rishi and Sunita decorated it with our lights, tinsel, baubles and finally the fairy and in about 30 minutes our lounge was transformed into a winter wonderland (well close enough anyway!). The final touch was to kick start off Rishi's advent calendar - "can I eat the chocolate dad?" he'd ask as he tore off each tiny piece of paper that hid the day. One of the funniest moments is Rishi's letter to Santa. It would start off quite normal; he'd inform the man from the North Pole that he's been good throughout the year and that he hopes to get a visit from him on the big day.

Having explained to Rishi that Santa needs to share the presents with the children all over the world and that he's only likely to get one present, Rishi was fine about it but decided to give Santa a helping hand. Just in case the big man couldn't think of what to get, our Argos catalogue came to the rescue. At the bottom of the letter, Rishi had written down about 12 different toys complete with page number, order number and price. It was hilarious watching him as he turned straight to the toy section and started ticking off the things he wanted. I guess it did show initiative and he was being helpful so well done son!

Whilst kids are young I think it's brilliant that they have something that they believe in. When I was his age, we genuinely had no presents at all. If the truth be known, having a roof over our heads and food to eat was all we wanted but above all I would have swapped anything to put all the arguments to bed. Sadly, that never happened during my early years; I guess that may be one of the reasons that I have certainly tried to make Christmas extra special. I'm not saying Sunita didn't try; far from it; it's just that she had more of a "normal" upbringing than I did and perhaps couldn't relate to things as much. Anyhow one Christmas I was determined to make it a special one...

It was about 10pm on Christmas eve; Rishi knew Santa only came to those houses where the children were fast asleep so as soon as we said it's time to go to bed, he never questioned it and was ready to dart up the stairs. There was, however, one thing he had to do first; leave a mince pie, a carrot and some milk for Santa and his reindeers. He took the pies out of the fridge and poured out some milk, placing it next to the carrot that Sunita had already taken out. Our house was all set for Santa - the question was, would he come to visit? Just before we kissed him goodnight we reminded him that he mustn't get up in the night as if Santa hears any noise, he'll jump straight onto his sleigh and you won't see him again - trust me, there was a reason we said this...

Around 30 minutes later, I checked on Rishi who was fast asleep - it was time for the fun to begin! We got a pair of red Santa trousers and wedged them into our kitchen window so that part of the trousers were inside the house and the rest was dangling outside. I then put on my trainers, went into our back garden and trod in as much mud as I could. Once muddy, I carefully made dirty foot prints from just below our kitchen window to our lounge and around the Christmas tree. I did the same with my hands; made them very dirty and then pressed hard against doors so that the prints were clear to see.

The master plan was complete once we'd put the present from Santa under our tree. We couldn't help but smile at our handiwork and we knew that Rishi would love it.

Just before we went to sleep ourselves, Sunita drank some of the milk and took a chunk out of mince pie whilst I broke the carrot piece into several smaller pieces. The setting was great, roll on Christmas day! Right on cue, Rishi got up early as usual and was eager to come downstairs but wanted someone to go with him. In the end I think we all went down together and Rishi knew something had happened when he saw that the door to the kitchen was wide open (in our house all the doors are always shut tight before we go to sleep so he knew something wasn't quite right...). He began to walk even slower down the stairs but as we reached the bottom, he looked to his left and he looked stunned. I don't know what he saw first - was it Santa's trousers hanging out of the window or the fact that some of the milk, carrot and mince pie had vanished? He couldn't comprehend what he was looking at; I think it was the trousers that he was more shocked at but there was no time to waste - what was in our lounge?

I pointed out the dirty hand prints and then Rishi saw the dirty foot prints too. The door to the lounge was ajar (open that is, not a circular, glass thing ok?) so he carefully pushed it open. Once again, his expression changed totally; he was amazed at what he could see. "Dad! Santa's been", "Mum, look at the present" were just some of the things he came out with in his excitement. The look on his excited face was priceless and I cannot put into words how it felt to give him such as surprise; he was overjoyed, over the moon and straight over to the presents quick time. Santa had decided to bring him a radio controlled Range Rover car; something Rishi had written down from the Argos catalogue! From that point onwards, he knew Santa was real and it felt even better when Sunita read out the letter he'd left for Rishi (written by Sunita several days before).

Within 30 minutes the lounge was filled with bits of paper, torn cardboard and empty boxes as all the presents were opened. That was the big Christmas morning over and done with; just the Christmas dinner to go. We'd either go to my sisters for dinner or around to Sunita's parents. The whole day was just spent eating far too much and then suffering in the evening. Most understand what Christmas is all about but what about boxing day? What's the story behind it? From what I understand it's officially the first day *after* Christmas but i've read in many places that it's meant to be the first weekday after Christmas because it's a public holiday. The so called "box" was opened on this day to share gifts with the poor hence the name boxing day evolved. Traditionally, boxing day is also a day when fox hunters gather, send out their dogs in the hope of seeking out, tiring them out and then killing foxes. So, there you go, on Boxing day you can relax, sort your box out or go out killing foxes - nice!

The next big event was New Year's Eve; a time when Sunita was usually out "up town" with her friends and cousins. There would be none of that this year; she was days from giving birth so our new year's celebrations were strictly confined to watching revellers all over the world via tv. Footage of countries such as New Zealand and Australia who were already into 2009 flooded in whilst our phones started beeping like mad as the SMS messages came in thick and fast. Soon it was all over, Big Ben hit midnight signalling the end of 2008; an important year for us but a more important one was just about to start...

January 1st, 2009 meant there was only 11 days till our 2nd child would be born. Well that was the date we'd been given anyway and I wasn't confident it wouldn't happen on that day. A few weeks earlier, our friends had kindly arranged a baby shower for Sunita and we received many useful gifts which certainly helped. In short, all we could do was wait for the day to arrive. As suspected there was no sign of the baby on the original due date which meant that there was a high chance of Sunita having a caesarean section again. The days passed and still no sign but eventually we were given a date that she'd be induced if "nothing happened".

Well, "nothing happened" so we both (Sunita more so than me), prepared herself mentally for going into hospital the next day - the wait was finally over! Sadly, this wasn't the case; an urgent, higher priority case meant that Sunita's date was postponed a few days. Now throughout this pregnancy *and* whilst she was carrying Rishi, nothing bothered Sunita at all. She was strong and never let the pregnancy get in the way of much and just got on with it. The news that she had been "bumped", pardon the pun, was devastating to her. I've never seen her so upset and I was quite worried at that stage - the news that she wasn't going into hospital that day played havoc with her emotions and it was a pretty tough time. Thankfully the tears didn't last long and my (fat !!) Sunita was back to her cheerful self....

We were now into the 3rd week of January; 22nd to be exact and this was the date we'd been given to go back into hospital; would this be *the* day? Arriving at the hospital quite early, we were shoved into a waiting room and trust me we waited a long time in there. Eventually we were made our way to the beds where those there to be induced were told to change into a gown and "get themselves comfortable." The obstetrician came around, asked a few questions, checked the medical notes, and got the nurse to check the basics like blood pressure. "Everything is ok" we were told, "just relax and someone will be with you soon." It wasn't long before we heard "Sunita Patel..." from outside of the curtains; our time, or Sunita's I should say, had arrived. We followed the nurse across the corridor and into another section of the hospital where Sunita went one way and I was told to go and get dressed in another. Just to be clear, I *was* dressed; just not in the attire required for the delivery of a baby!

I knew the drill; she was off to have the epidural whilst I did a Mr.Ben special and transformed myself by putting on the blue coloured shoes and gown of the hospital. I must admit, I *really* did look like one of the baby delivery team and was waiting (hoping even!) that someone would call out "Dr.Patel..." - sadly they didn't. Anyway, I must have been in that waiting room for about 30 minutes before I was finally called for. I was led into the delivery theatre where the first thing that crossed my mind was the number of people in there. I'm sure I counted 11; they were certainly prepared but it kind of made me more nervous; were all these people needed? Was there some kind of complication which made them draft more people in? I just didn't know but all I did know was that I didn't want anything to alarm Sunita. She was lying down looking quite chilled, machines were hooked up to her and a separating sheet was put up so that she couldn't see what the doctors were doing...

Meanwhile I could see exactly what they were doing. The bulky theatre lights that were directly above the bed had a massive reflective surround which was just like a mirror and offered a ring side view of the proceedings. The staff did all the last minute checks and then it was time for the show to begin. The cut was made with extraordinary precision; by now my eyes were fixed to the surgery taking place before me. Periodically I would look towards Sunita and say "you ok?" - she was fine but I guess it must have been quite frustrating for her as she couldn't see anything. With only a few minutes passed, there was masses of blood everywhere... "suction" bellowed out from the operating staff and a few seconds later the sucking noise of the pipes drew out the blood. There was no panic, no commotion and to be honest little emotion from the staff; it was just routine and just another day in the office...

Several minutes later and there was lots of pulling taking place; the medical staff seemed to get to their "stations" in preparation of the baby's arrival and then I could see one of them grab something - it was our baby. They give him (I knew it was a boy) a quick check over, cleaned him up a little and then came over to us. Meanwhile Sunita knew the baby was out but kept asking if it was a boy or girl. I stalled as much as I could opting not to tell her but let her see for herself. Within seconds Sunita got a glimpse of baby and it was then that she finally saw for herself that we had our 2nd boy! It's hard to describe the emotions you go through; the process is simply amazing but the culmination of going through the whole 9 months is something else. I can't speak for Sunita but I was just pleased that both mother and child were ok.

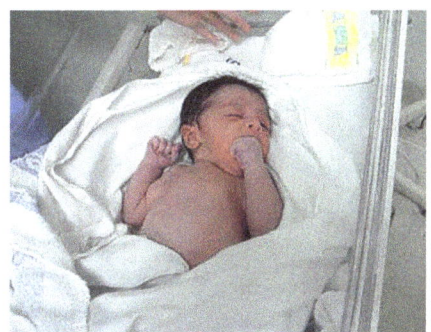
Little baby was here.

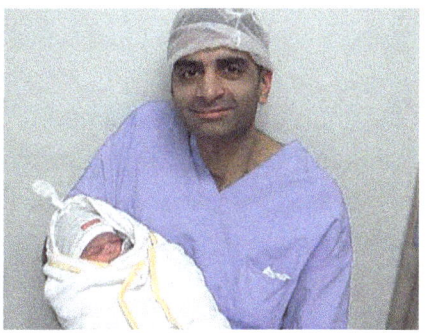
Dr. Patel.

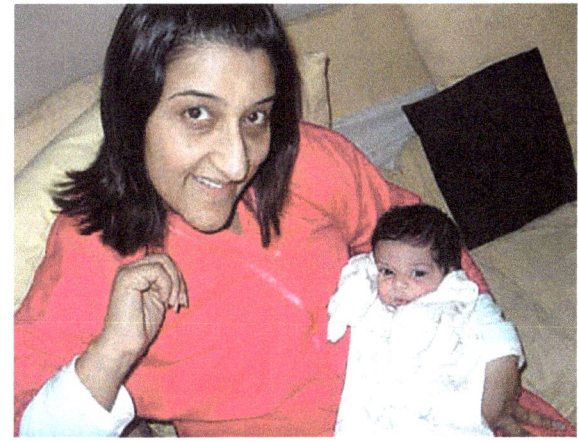
Sunita & baby united!

The one thing I do remember clearly is how small he was. He looked incredibly tiny and I actually thought he must be under weight. He looked like he had fat lips but the long eye lashes and big round eyes were his most striking features - he looked just perfect! For the medical staff there was still lots of work to do; they had to make sure there was no post-operative issues and started to stitch Sunita up as soon as possible. Our baby was handed back to the staff who wrapped him again to keep him warm and then I tagged along whilst they weighed him. Once on the scales, it was hard to believe he actually weighed 7lbs (or 7 "lubs" as Rishi once tried to pronounce!) and 10 oz. but I was assured the scales were correct!

I wasted no time in taking loads of photos; I was adamant that i'd capture as many pictures as I could literally minutes after being born because I just knew he'd look different soon after. Our baby (no name as yet!) was wide awake, very alert and was checking out the surroundings. Meanwhile in a theatre not so far, far away, the staff were almost done and Sunita was about to be moved into a room where she could be monitored closely. Her blood pressure was high and although it wasn't too much cause for concern, it was decided to monitor her very closely - we were told that they'd expect the pressure to lower itself to "normal" levels pretty soon. Unfortunately this didn't happen and as a result the doctors weren't happy to let her go back to the maternity ward just yet.

I took the opportunity to tell everyone about the arrival as we knew they'd be many anxious people waiting for that all important phone call. There was no question who I was going to tell first; it *had* to be Rishi. It was around midday when I called his school to ask if I could speak to him. I thought he might be in class or something so they'd go and grab him but I think they said he was having his lunch. There wasn't much I could do about it so I asked the office staff to pass on the message that "he had a baby brother..." Little did I know that the headmistress was in the office when I called and once she heard of the news she wasn't happy with them telling Rishi so she called me back and said they'd get him into the office in about 30 minutes so that I could call back and give him the news myself. The news was, in her own words, "too important" to leave to someone else!

I could have told countless other people our news whilst I was waiting but I still decided to hold on until i'd told Rishi. 30 minutes seem to drag on but it was worth it; when I called back I was told to "hold on" whilst they gave the phone to Rishi. He must have been scared stiff when the call went out that the headmistress wanted to see him and I could tell he was little worried on the phone. I told him that he "has a little baby brother" and I knew he was so happy but he just couldn't express it sat in the office surrounded by countless office staff and the headmistress. Unsurprisingly most of his replies were single words: "yes", "ok", "oh" ... and with that I said he might be able to see his mum and brother later; I didn't promise because unless Sunita's blood pressure returned to "normal", nobody would be coming to see them and I knew Rishi would be gutted and hence I refused to make a promise I couldn't keep!

I then made countless phone calls and sent just as many SMS messages to friends and family telling them about the good news. Within a few minutes my phone wouldn't stop ringing and continually 'beeped' as the text message replies came back in thick and fast. I called my sister, expecting her to pick up straight away but damn it... voicemail. I must have tried 3 or 4 times after that but I just couldn't get through. Don't know why but I just wanted my sister to know first but all I could do was leave messages to those that didn't pick up; 20 or so minutes later and everyone that needed to know knew so I headed back into the hospital to see how Sunita was doing.

Unfortunately her blood pressure showed no signs of dropping and she looked even more exhausted than she did before. I guess the pounding her body had taken was slowly taking its toll and she really needed to rest. Still nil by mouth, I remember her being very thirsty but luckily she was allowed to drink water and in fact was encouraged to drink lots of it! Meanwhile our little bundle was having a bit of a crying fit so I was pacing around the room trying to calm him down. I still couldn't believe it and i've heard many people say it before but you really do forget what it's like to hold a new born baby; it's an amazing experience and more so if you're holding your own child. As the daylight started to fade, winter darkness swept in but despite a slight improvement in Sunita's condition, she was still being monitored closely and it was unlikely that she'd be moving onto the maternity ward before I left.

As the clock struck 8pm, visitor time was over and I had to go albeit unwillingly. Although I never mentioned it to Sunita, I was very worried about her condition and hoped her recovery picked up soon because until that happened I knew there could be complications. Before I went home I passed by Sunita's mums; Rishi was there as they had picked him up from school that day but sadly none of them were allowed to see Sunita and the baby due to her condition. Sunita's mum ("mum") asked if i'd eaten and not wanting to put her out said "i'm not that hungry..." She wouldn't have it and within 10 minutes brought out a whole load of food that she'd cooked specially; she even made my favourite daal bless her....

Shattered is an understatement; it felt like a very long day and I was incredibly tired. The unrelenting questions from an excited 7 year old who now had a brother didn't help but it wasn't Rishi's fault - he was just excited and above all just being himself. Most of us yawn at various times during the day and it doesn't necessarily mean you're tired. Rishi on the other hand *only* yawned when he was tired and he was yawning big time now. It was time for some fruit, a glass of milk, time to clean his teeth and then straight to bed. For me there was still no time to rest - I decided to power up the laptop and email out some of the pictures i'd taken earlier that day but finally after going through one of the most memorable days of my life I could finally go to sleep with the awesome feeling of being a dad to our second child...

The next day I dropped Rishi off to school and headed straight back to the general hospital. Sunita looked better, her blood pressure had returned to normal and she was back on the main maternity ward. Her first night alone with the baby was a mixed affair; he was awake for some of it and kept Sunita up in the process but the staff, knowing full well that she had to sleep, took care of him when he started to cry later on in the night. After just a couple of days in hospital, Sunita and the baby came home. The new arrival, yup - still unnamed, changed our lives; whilst Sunita and I had to adjust quickly to a constant cycle of making baby feeds, feeding, changing nappies and a few sleepless nights, Rishi was getting used to having a brother around the place and he was loving every minute of it.

We'd talked baby names on and off for a while but never came closer to agreeing on names at all. One day I just said "what if we call him Jai?". I liked that name and ironically Sunita had written down the name in her diary along with the list of other possible names. Despite neither of us ever talking about that name, we both seemed to like it and the decision was made - his name would officially be "*Jai Kumar Patel*". Rishi pointed out that Jai's nickname would be "J" so in essence he wouldn't have a nickname as the nickname would be his name - get it? Eager to get his name registered so that we could get hold of his birth certificate, I arranged an interview with the 'births' department based inside Leicester Town Hall.

On the day of my appointment, I arrived to a packed waiting room so I was glad when my name was called out. To prove my identity I had to answer several questions and one of them; "what was your wife's maiden name?", seemed to trigger a strange response when I told her it was "Dhunna". I watched as the lady stopped writing and looked out of the window - she seemed to be in deep thought. Thinking there was something wrong, I said "Is there a problem?". "No, not at all", "when you and your wife got married, did she arrive in a horse and carriage?" Quite taken aback by her question, I said "yes, why?" and she revealed that she was the one who witnessed our marriage almost 12 years ago. In her own words she said "she cannot remember anyone else arriving at the Pocklington's Walk registry office in a horse and carriage" and "there's not many Dhunnas around". So there you go, she seems to have 'Dhunna', 'horse' and 'carriage' lodged in her brain and I don't think anything will actually dislodge it!

Paperwork complete and with Jai's birth certificate in my hand, we could now apply for his passport. We needed the passport pretty urgently because the visa application for Australia required all our passport numbers as well as photocopies of the bio data page. As weeks turned into months, our home life wasn't exactly "routine" but more "settled". We adjusted to a new member of the family, sleepless nights were virtually a thing of the past and life as we knew it continued at a steady pace. One thing that was absolutely clear was that Rishi loved, truly loved his brother. It was impressive watching as he wanted to hold him, could always make Jai laugh, loved to push him in his pushchair and proudly showed him off to all his friends at school.

Super picture; looks like Rishi has taken a selfie here! Just look at Jai's smile!

Sunita with her boys!

By the time June came round, all paperwork for our Australian visa application was finally ready and emailed over to our agent in Brisbane. The next time I logged into my Hotmail account I received a confirmation email telling me that our application 'had been lodged' with the DIAC (Australia's Department of Immigration and Citizenship). Now began the long waiting process; we'd been told that the immigration department had tightened up the rules and it was much harder to be granted a visa. It didn't matter though; both of us had received a positive assessment from the regulating body who assesses our skills so it was really just a matter of waiting until our application had been picked by a case officer and once this happened, we were told that our application would proceed pretty quickly after that! Although there was nothing we could do about it, it was quite frustrating because it felt as if our lives were put on hold. Still, the summer was here and if we were going to emigrate we had to make the most of the time we had here...

One thing both Sunita and I were eager to read was Rishi's end of term year 3 school report. I wouldn't say Rishi loved school but he wasn't one of those kids that "didn't want to go" so that's a good thing right? His previous mid-term or end of term reports were average and we both got the feeling that there were far too many kids for them to give accurate results per child. Perhaps we were being too harsh or negative about the schooling but that's how we felt and was probably the reason we thought this would be another "average year" with the standard "must try harder" or "could do better" comments. How wrong we were... the report was awesome, full of top marks and some fine comments about how well he was doing. As parents I don't think we've ever tried to push Rishi too much; of course you need to nurture and encourage your kids to do well but all we've ever asked him to do is to try his best and that's it.

There's no question about it - he certainly did is best and I made sure he read some of the comments himself so he knew and understood that the hard work he put in really paid off. I'm certain we treated him that weekend although I can't remember exactly what we did but it was a fine end to the school term and we hoped it could continue into year 4... The summer holidays, all 7 weeks of them, were pretty daunting for Sunita. Having a baby was hard work anyway let alone having a very active 8 year old in the house too. I hoped we had a decent summer but it just wasn't to be - it was fairly warmish but simply not the summers of the years gone by where you would almost be guaranteed week after week of warm and often hot sunshine. Regardless of whether it was warm or not Rishi made the most of the summer. On some days his friends would come and "knock" for him whilst Rishi was still in his pyjamas or midway through his breakfast. A few minutes later and the breakfast was gone, he'd get dressed and he was out the door!

At the height of our UK summer, it was sunrise at around 3.30am and sunset at around 10pm so the kids had plenty of time to climb up trees, run around, cycle around on their bikes and kick footballs around. When we were lucky enough to get some warm weather out came the water pistols and water bombs which was great fun - except for the victims! Sometimes when I went into our bedroom i'd hear Rishi and his mates chatting to each to each other (they'd often just sit on the pavement just outside our house...). I know I shouldn't have but I often listened in on their conversations - it's fascinating what 7/8/9 year olds talk about and the games they muster up but anyway, it was the summer and it was *their* time to have some fun. The kids super sensitive "ice cream ears" were fully operational and whilst the adults couldn't hear the music blaring from the ice cream man's van, the kids could hear it when it was several streets away! As the van turned into our road I could count to 20 seconds and I knew Rishi would come tearing into the house... "can I get an ice cream dad" or "ice cream man's here mum..."

We never managed to jet off during the summer but instead went out on many day trips. Jai, getting bigger all the time, was starting to get a real personality and was a real joy to watch getting older. Well, I say getting older but by the time Rishi started year 4, Jai was close to being 8 months old so was still a baby! Whilst Rishi made a good start to the new school term, Sunita was back at work for some meetings to discuss her return to work! In fact, she went to work asking for some revised hours so she could work around the kids but she had no idea how well that request would go down. What if they turned her down? What if they said she had to come back full time? These were just some of the questions which turned the next few weeks into a nerve wracking ordeal for her. It's very rare that Sunita actually worries about stuff but this really got to her and although we discussed it many times there wasn't much I could say to make any kind of difference.

During the summer, we had some visitors from down under - both Ravi and Ruby were back in town. It wasn't a social visit, quite the opposite really and if the truth be told, it was Raj that suggested they take a break from the shop and Australia. Since they got married and moved out of the UK, Ravi settled down pretty well but Ruby didn't. Tensions started to rise in the household, things were said in the heat of the moment and there was a clear personality clash between Raj and Ruby. Ravi, felt stuck in the middle, torn between his brother on one side and his wife on the other. To his credit, Ravi stuck with it and tried to keep the peace but it was inevitable that tensions would soon explode big time. I wasn't there so I can't say what really happened but what I do know is that their visit back to the UK was meant to give them both - I say both but I mean Ruby really, time to reflect, consider their options and then return to Australia where hopefully the clashes, disputes, arguments, and general bad feelings could be put to bed permanently.

Having arrived in July, they were only meant to stay until September because the huge extension that was underway at their shop in Hervey Bay was scheduled for completion at that time and Raj would need Ravi back to help with the refit of the shop. Unfortunately, constant delays meant the extension completion date got pushed further and further back. Raj now had a dilemma - does he call them back or let them stay in the UK until the work is done? In the end he told Ravi to "chill" in the UK so a 6 week break was turning into a 6 month mega holiday! Chilling at home was ok for a few weeks but food, clothes and going out all costs money. Both of them needed to find work and quickly and luckily got themselves jobs quick time. Neither of them enjoyed the work but it was only for a few months anyway so it didn't matter.

With the summer over, Rishi was back at Launde Primary School and started year 4 whilst Sunita, after several phone discussions with her boss, finally arranged a meeting to discuss her return to work. Sunita was very well respected at her work and was a real 'people's champion' amongst the several hundred staff that worked there. In fact recognition definitely came her way several years earlier when she won the prestigious "Employee of the year" award - a real achievement in my eyes even though she plays it down as nothing special. Anyway the pre-meeting nerves and concerns over her return to work were all resolved - the company agreed to reduce her hours to 4 per day - result! This was excellent news, it meant she could drop Jai off, drop Rishi off, start work, finish work, get Jai and then pick up Rishi.

Jai settled into nursery ok which was a huge relief to us both. There's nothing worse than leaving your child at childcare only for them to cry uncontrollably at the thought of you leaving them there. Mind you, Rishi was ok too so we've been pretty lucky although I believe that kids that have lots of interaction with others tend to settle better anyway. With Jai at nursery and Sunita back at work, the week was hectic. On Mondays Jai would be looked after by Sunita's mum - "mum". On Tuesdays and Wednesdays, he went to nursery whilst on Thursday he went to my mums. On Fridays I had Jai all to myself for a big chunk of the day as I don't work on Fridays. Trust me, although looking after him can be quite exhausting, the fact that I could spend so much 1-2-1 time with him was awesome.

50

Life begins the day after your 40th!

I did have plans to finish this book *before* I was forty - well that didn't quite work out did it? Hitting 40, the big '4' '0' was something I never really thought about but was something that many others reminded me about constantly. *"You having a big party?"*, *"you're forty soon"*, *"what's happening on your 40th?"*. The answer was quite simply: No party, no celebration, and no big deal. I've never liked birthdays or anyone making a fuss. I put this down to the fact that as a toddler we never celebrated birthdays at home which is a really sad thing. I just got used to the fact that it was just another day and nothing special happened. Sunita knows full well that I can't stand any kind of celebrations in my honour; i'd rather skip my birthday and just move on...

Well, October 2009 approached quick time and it was getting closer to the big day. Thankfully we were heading north to Manchester for a weekend break where Sunita had booked a tour of the Manchester United Football ground - that was a proper birthday present! The tour was great, seeing the inside of the ground finally was a great experience as well as walking close to the pitch, the dugout, the changing rooms whilst the trophy room was incredible. After the tour it was shopping at the Trafford Centre - I clearly remember Ravi ringing me and saying "Happy birthday old man" - yeah, nice one Ravi - that made my day! Once back at home I thought it was all over and secretly hoping that everyone would just forget the 40th.

On 18th October 2009 (which happened to be our 12th wedding anniversary), we were invited to my sisters for a Diwali dinner. A short while after we'd finished eating, in came the entourage, "happy birthday to you" echoed around the house and in came the birthday cake they'd sneaked in. Mid-way through the English "happy birthday...", Sunita switched and started her trademark Indian version to rapturous applause. Thankfully there were no calls for "speech" - good job really because all they would have heard was a silent version! Cake eaten and 48 pictures later, it was time to head home - phew it was over! At work our "intranet" has a section on "employee information" that has details of when they started work, when their birthday is and so on.

Inside Old Trafford, Manchester.

Rishi loved it!

Patel footballer!

Rishi outside the ground.

Hoping nobody would look at it that day, I made sure I kept my mouth firmly shut but unfortunately our "birthday alert" system came back to haunt me. On an employee's birthday, an email is automatically sent to the employee's manager so unbeknown to me, my manager knew it was my birthday and it wasn't hard to work out it was my 40th too. Thinking I was safe I continued working at my desk but at around 11am I could see several people gathering behind me. As I turned to see who it was, my eyes soon focused on the 10 or so colleagues standing there. Some were holding balloons with "happy 40th" on them, some of them burst into song whilst the others proceeded to hand me a small bag which contained a "1969" mug - full of facts and figures about this special year. It was quite embarrassing but finally, I thought it was all over. It was now!

 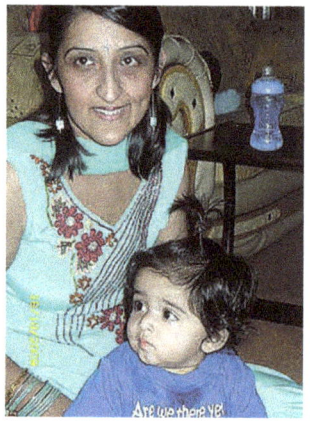

40 and with my family.   A dribbly Jai.

Celebrating my 40th @ my sisters on our wedding anniversary!

As we rolled into November 2009, the situation between Ravi and Ruby got worse and worse. Ruby made it perfectly clear that she didn't want to go back to Australia whilst Ravi made it clear he *would* be going back. It was an awful situation and at the big house things were very tense. Meanwhile many 1000's of miles away in Australia, the shop extension still wasn't near completion so it looked as though Ravi and Ruby would be here for Christmas and new year too. One evening everything changed; Ruby and her family had planned an 'exit' from the house. She came home as usual and acted as if everything was ok. Her father arrived and the arguments started. Poor Ravi got a torrent of abuse from her dad who basically accused him of not looking after his daughter.

Worse still, Ruby added to the abuse even though her dad should have put a stop to it the moment she started to speak. Ruby went upstairs then minutes later was at the front door with her dad - they left! It was very bizarre; no-one really knew what had happened. Mum, Sunita's mum that is, came home from swimming to a very quiet house, unaware of what had just happened. Once everyone realised that she'd gone they were all shocked. Though things were said in the heat of the moment, it was clear in Ravi's mind that there was no going back and their short marriage was well and truly over.

51

Is Santa real?

The winter of 2009 / 2010 was one many people would remember for a long time to come. Unlike winters of the past where we'd have some cold spells, this one was different. Helped along by strong southerly winds, bitter cold Arctic weather was being blown towards the UK - well that's what the weather forecasters told us anyway. Secretly I was hoping they were right; a mild December would be no good for the Christmas atmosphere but even worse would be the lack of snow. We wished for snow and we got it - big time. Overnight in the middle of December, the snow, which had covered the Northern part of the UK, headed South and covered the rest of it.

Most of us were disappointed when the snow stopped falling but a few days later we got even more - this time it lasted for 2 weeks so you can imagine how much fell. In an instant the great outdoors turned into a magical place; everything was white, kids were outside throwing snowballs and I was out testing out the ABS system on the car and doing hand brake turns much to Rishi's delight. Rishi who up until now had always believed in Santa, was asking whether Santa was actually real or not. Curious as to why he was asking us that question, it turned out that several of his friends at school said he wasn't real. Real or not, one thing Rishi longed for was the presents but he wouldn't know if Santa was real or not until Christmas day...

On Christmas morning, Rishi was itching to get downstairs as quick as he could whilst it was just another morning for our Jai. For us it was a little bit more special than that - it was Jai's first

Christmas! All the neatly wrapped presents were soon turned into a bag of recycling material as Rishi tore his way into them. We had to stop him though; if he had it his way he would have opened all of them! We let Jai attempt to open his own presents - he was just happy playing with the boxes and mess that Rishi had left behind! Whilst Rishi flicked through the Sky channels and picked out what he wanted to watch, little Jai played happily with his toy cars.

Meanwhile I tried in vain to read through the Christmas TV guide because I was constantly interrupted by a toy car flying in my direction or Rishi's relentless barrage of questions - trust me, 2 kids are tiring! Sunita on the other hand was in "Come dine with me"

The boys enjoying Christmas. Jai's hair had to be tied back...

Jai mesmerised here!

Family photo.

Sunita with one of her many hair styles!

mode and deep inside her comfort zone. Christmas dinner was at our house this year so mum, dad and Ravi would be heading to the Patel's @ number 12. Sunita loves dinner parties; mind you she loves parties full stop so whilst the boys were inside she was a busy bee in the kitchen. The food smelt and looked great whilst everything on the dining table was organised to perfection.

By the time everyone had arrived it was around 2pm; I was well hungry whilst Ravi looked remarkably fresh considering he was out the night before. Whilst Sunita and "mum" were in the kitchen making the final preparations for our Christmas lunch, the rest of us watched Christmas programs on the TV. Our family Christmas was great fun, lots to eat, lots to drink, lots of awful jokes and as always happens over Christmas, I ate too much and vowed not to eat for several days! After a perfect lunch (thanks Sunita!), we just lounged around for the next few hours and in the evening drove the short distance to my sister's house.

We never stayed there long, my sister tried to persuade us to eat some more but we were still stuffed from our lunch! Sunita may have said no to food but there was no way she was saying no to drink. Last Christmas she was pregnant with Jai so had to give the festive drink a miss but this year there were no excuses. Rishi excited as ever was busy telling everyone about the Christmas presents he received and asking everyone else what they got. After a few hours we decided to head back home so we could get changed, sort out the kids and then chill in front of the TV.

For the first time in many years, Sunita didn't have to go into work that much during the Christmas holidays which was good and bad. Good because she could relax but bad because much like Rishi, she never stopped talking! Seriously though, it was good that we were all off because we had time to do whatever we wanted and for once not be constrained by work commitments. In the week leading up to New Year's Eve we discussed the new year celebrations over and over again but still couldn't decide what, if anything, we'd be doing as 2009 ended and 2010 rolled in. In the end my sister decided to have a little get together at her house so the plans were all made. I wasn't DJ'ing this time, but instead put together a load of CD's that we would just shove into the cd player!

The last day of 2009 had arrived and we all piled into my sister's house. All my immediate family were there as well as some of my sister's friends too. There were kids everywhere so it was a noisy affair. The time soon flew past and by the time we'd eaten and played party games, it was time to switch on the TV. We watched as the countries around the world celebrated 2010. Midnight approached and as the countdown started, I asked myself the question that I always ask on New Year's Eve - "why didn't we go to London and join in with the celebrations?" It didn't matter now, "10,9,8,7,6,5,4,3,2,1 happy new year 2010" - London's night sky erupted in light and sound as thousands of fireworks were let off; out with 2009 and in with 2010.

Priyanka celebrates with a
drink – what was in it?

Crazy girls...

2010 started as cold as 2009 had ended and we had more heavy snowfalls. As most of the working population returned to work, i'd be starting my 11th year at Magnetic North Software

Jai – clearly not bothered.   Lovely picture of the snow falling!

Very natural!   Couldn't resist.   Nor could Sunita...

D Jai.

- somewhat of an achievement even if I say so myself! The kids returned to school and Christmas seemed a long way away! It was hard to imagine that Jai was almost a year old - where had the preceding 12 months gone? Something else that was hard to imagine was the fact that Ravi had been in the UK for 6 months now and was actually planning to fly back to Australia - minus his wife. The marriage was well and truly over so Ravi quite rightly had to get on with this life. On 19th January 2010, he left the UK as "Ravi" and got back to Hervey Bay as "Ralph". He wasn't the only person travelling either; mum or dad flew to India a few days later - a real jet setting family you know!

We never made a big deal of Rishi's 1st birthday; probably because we were in Malta at the time, but Sunita really wanted to do something for Jai and in the end we decided to have a small family gathering at home. Out came the "to do" list and before long each item on the list was ticked off. On the big day, Jai wasn't fussed at all; he was too young to know what was going on; he just crawled around and played with the countless balloons and banners that had transformed the house. We sung happy birthday, (Sunita tried and failed to sing the Indian version), we ate, drank, joked around and just had a great evening with our family. Jai had a great time, not because of his birthday, but because there were probably more people in our house than he's ever seen and he loved all the attention he got.

Jai's cake!   The boys played under the table.

Jai & Preeya.

Jai with his Bha.

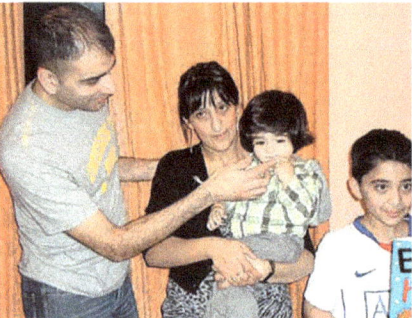

My sister making sure the sister in laws are kept in check...

Time for cake.

All together!

52

Cheeky boys, champions & planes

As one of our kids turned one, it was hard to imagine that in a few months, our other baby (they're always your babies right?) would be turning 9 - goodness me! Watching our kids playing and growing up together, despite the age gap, was something that I find difficult to put into words. The joy of seeing the most important things in your life changing daily, doing funny things, asking relentless questions (Rishi....) and just knowing that they're always smiling is incredible. When Rishi was younger I often looked at him as he was tucked up into bed and thought "I'm going to miss you being young." As strange as that may sound, it's true - Rishi was always such a fun boy that I always worried in case he changed as he grew up.

One thing I will say about Rishi is that he *really* loves and looks after Jai. Often when either myself or Sunita are in the middle of something and need Rishi to look after Jai, you can count on him to take care of him and you know that he'll do a proper "big brother" job. Before Rishi goes to bed he'll always make sure says goodnight to his little brother whilst when Jai wakes up in the morning, his first words are usually "ishi", "ishi!" - he can't say "Rishi" at the moment! At school, Rishi was now half way through year 4 and was the current Mathematics champion in his class. They have this thing where the teacher asks quick fire questions and the person who answers the quickest is the champion. I'm glad to say that Rishi has held onto the crown for a few months now and nobody can see to knock him off the top - well done son!

As for Jai, well he was out of crawling and onto his feet now but still couldn't walk unaided. He'd pull himself up using one of the sofas and then hang onto it as he made his way around the room - a step in the right direction. He was a real character now and as he got older our evenings at home were kept real busy with these 2 crazy kids of ours. When either Sunita or myself were out in the evening, you'd be lucky if you got 5 minutes to yourself. By the time we've played, fed them, bathed and showered them, helped with homework, changed nappies and answered questions, you'd be shattered but this was just a normal day in the Patel household.

Papá, ¿podemos ir a Madrid? ("Dad, can we go to Madrid?)

Having watched many programmes about it on the Discovery channel, Rishi loved the revolutionary Airbus A380. He loved everything about it, the sheer size, the fact that it was a 'double decker', the sheer luxury of the first class cabin and the fact that it could carry many more hundreds of people than its nearest rival the Boing 777. I was asked many, many times if we "could go on one" and when I explained that yes, we could go, but it may not be for a few years, you could see the disappointment on his face. One weekend when we were visiting friends in London, we stayed at a hotel close to Heathrow airport.

As we got closer to the hotel, you could see the planes in the distance as they queued behind each other as they prepared to land. Rishi loved it; when we finally got into the car park, the planes were so low you could read the airplane number on the under carriage, the landing gear was down and the engine noise was immense - our hotel was literally overlooking the airport runways! Whilst Rishi and I stood and watched as the airplanes landed, Sunita wasn't too pleased and just wanted to get inside! Sadly, all the rooms that overlooked the airport were taken so Rishi and I headed back downstairs to continue watching them land.

The next day, on route to our friend's house, I decided to drive around the airport so that Rishi could see the planes. As we passed the British Airways hanger, he saw massive 747's and several Concorde's too. Just as we were making our way out of the airport, we saw a Singapore Airlines Airbus A380 taxiing but we couldn't tell if it had just landed or was about to take off. Seeing the A380 made Rishi's day and as we drove around the outer ring road that surrounds Heathrow airport, he just couldn't control his excitement! At one set of traffic lights we could hear what sounded like thunder in the distance. The lights changed from red to red and amber and then green and as I started to drive on, the thunder like noise was getting closer and closer.

In an instant Rishi wound down the window and shoved his head outside - to his amazement, the same Airbus A380 that we'd seen just a few minutes ago roared above us. It looked awesome in the sky, a real engineering marvel and I was so glad that Rishi got to see it for rather than in some documentary. A few days after that, I searched the internet for "A380 factories" and was pleasantly surprised when the Airbus Toulouse Factory web site came up. After quickly switching the language from French to English, I read all about it and it felt as if i'd struck gold. The Airbus factory allowed visitors to tour the entire site and you could see real A380's being built - Rishi would love this!

Having read many reviews of the site, one thing that was apparent was its popularity. Many people commented that "you need to book early" - they weren't wrong. I checked for available bookings over several weeks and all of them returned as "no booking available". This wasn't good news, especially as Rishi's birthday was coming up and this *was* the ideal present! Not wanting to give in, I phoned the factory instead and made up a story that the web site keeps crashing and it keeps telling me there are available dates. Whilst on the phone, the lady I spoke to kept trying the web site and informed me that it was working correctly. Amazingly, she managed to find a free booking and our visit was confirmed...

I hadn't even thought about how to get there, I mean; how difficult can it be to get to Toulouse? Big mistake that was; although the southern French city had direct trains from Paris and direct flights from the UK, the timing was awful. Getting there by train would be ok but you had to alight from Paris and you'd arrive in Toulouse minutes before the start of the tour. Flying was an option but all flights arrived after the tour would be finished so that was useless too. Worst of all was that i'd already told Rishi about the tour and he was really excited about going. After several days of trying route after route I gave up - there was no way we could there on time especially since we were constrained by time - we only had a day in which to make the trip. It was no good, I had to accept defeat and I told Rishi. The look on his face was horrible but once I explained the reason behind it, he was ok...

Though Rishi forgot all about it, I was still planning to take him somewhere to make up for the disappointment of not seeing his beloved Airbus A380 being built. On several occasions he mentioned his Spanish pen friend and how they had exchanged several letters and he often mentioned the things that his friend did in Spain and how it differed to what Rishi did in the UK. Sunita and I gave him a birthday choice; we'd either take him to Madrid or he could have a birthday party. Thankfully he chose Madrid and with that I started to search for flights again. I booked the flights at work and came home that evening and handed the Easy Jet booking confirmation into Rishi's hand. His eyes lit up, we were flying to Madrid for the day. Yes, it would be a long day but who cares - the only downside was that we swapped an Airbus A380 for a Boeing 737!

We flew out on 24th April 2010, 2 days before his 9th birthday. It was an early flight - 6.45am to be exact and before long we were en route to Madrid, home to one of the most famous football teams in the world. About an hour after we saw the Pyrenees mountains from 36,000 feet, we touched down in Madrid, got our underground tickets and were ready to explore the city. Our first port of call was to the Real Madrid football ground, known locally as "Santiago Bernabeu". It was well busy there; 1000's of people, mainly football fans, were standing outside this great venue, taking photos and getting tickets for the infamous stadium tour. We were just happy to see the outside of the football ground - we'd been to Manchester United already and a pitch is a pitch right?

It was then a long train ride to the other side of the city where we hopped on board the cable car that offers phenomenal 360 views of the city. The cable car takes you quite far out of the city where you then get out and can explore the area. By now it was very warm and the sun was beating down. Rishi and I sat down on one of the benches for a rest but soon got up once we saw massive ants crawling all over them. As we looked closely, the whole area was covered with huge ant's nests and huge ants - we've never seen them so big. We then jumped back onto the cable car and headed back - it was lunch time!

Plaza Mayor, one of the most popular tourist areas of Madrid, was where the locals hung out so we decided to have a well earnt rest there, get some food and just chill out. By the time we got there it was close to 1pm and it was well busy. People were taking in the hot sun whilst sipping cool drinks and having a bite to eat. The water fountains were particularly busy, probably because the wind that was blowing would send water into the sky and then crash down on those longing to get cooler! The place was full of entertainers, artists and there was a strong police presence which was actually good to see. Lunch over and done with, it was time to head south of the city to a famous park called "El Retiro" or if you're local, the "El Parque de Retiro" - home to sculptures, monuments and a boating lake.

The early start to the day and relentless heat was slowing us both down now. We were tired and our bodies were telling us to rest. We pressed on and as we walked through the huge gates, we realised how popular this park was. The waiting time to hire a boat on the lake was around 2 hours - there was no way we were waiting that long! After strolling around the park we found some

Rishi on his travels...again!

All aboard.

On the cable car.

Chillin'.

Home bwoy!

@ Madrid airport.

shade and chilled out for a while before our time was up and we needed to make our way back to the airport. This park really is one of the focal areas of Madrid, locals and tourists all seem to flock there and it's just a nice place to be. We dragged ourselves out of the park, down onto the Metro and back to the airport where we caught our flight back to Luton. I loved our day out and i'm pretty certain that Rishi did too. For me, it was a real father son day, a real adventure and hopefully something he'll remember for a long, long time.

A few weeks after our Spanish trip, we all ventured South-West to Cornwall where we were meeting up with Paresh and the kids. We stayed in a place called Hayle, right by the sea and in fact we had sea views from our static caravan. Though we had lots of rain during our short break, it thankfully rained during the night when we were all asleep. It was great to catch up with everyone and the kids had a fab time. During our stay we visited the beautiful town of St. Ives, headed to Land's End, visited the St. Michael's Mount (home of the legendary giant!) and passed through the surfing town of Newquay on our way home. I must admit that I was sceptical about the Cornish pasties and the hype about how good they were. I was proved wrong; they tasted great and although I managed to shove a few down, Paresh managed a lot more - he even took one back with him in case he got hungry.

53

Jai walking

In case some of you are wondering... no pun intended ok? I'm not referring to the American commonly known "Jay walking" offence where pedestrians cross busy road junctions in a dangerous manner but actually that our Jai finally took his first steps. For many weeks now he was taking what appeared to be a few steps but as soon as he got to his feet he had to grab hold of something as he knew he'd fall. I think Sunita mentioned that he took a few steps at her mums and then one evening I saw it for myself. I'd just come home from work, Jai was sitting on the floor; Rishi was doing his homework whilst Sunita was in the kitchen. No sooner had I sat down, I saw Jai haul himself up and then take a few steps towards me - he was walking! He didn't walk for long though - about 3 steps before he crashed to the floor but he'd finally done it.

For me it was quite weird because I clearly remember Rishi walking for the first time and they both seemed to take their first solo steps at exactly the same spot! Jai was quite lazy though - it was as if those few steps had worn him out; there was no way he'd get back onto his feet straight away - he only walked when he was ready! His confidence grew over the next few days and he was able to walk further and without the need to hold onto something. Over the next few weeks Jai was everywhere, trying to squeeze behind the tv, grabbing the curtains, trying to get behind the sofas and so on. In the kitchen we'd already re-fitted the cupboard locks to prevent him from opening them but he found a way of opening the fridge, playing with the washing machine controls and also playing with the oven. Thankfully though, we knew all this would happen and the first thing we started to do was to switch the oven off from the plug so even if he did switch it on, nothing would happen!

As Jai approached 18 months, he'd turned into a super active little boy with a cheeky character to match. He was loads of fun, smiled most of the time, did lots of funny things and alongside his older brother Rishi, kept both Sunita and myself very busy indeed. Though still very young, he knew what he could and couldn't get away with. Often, he'd start to cry uncontrollably if he didn't get something he wanted. With Sunita he'd just cry relentlessly but I wouldn't have it. If he wanted to cry then fine but i'd put him in the middle of the room and leave him to it. Not in a nasty way of course but once he knew he wasn't getting any attention from me he'd soon stop.

Both Sunita and I found that half the battle with kids is that they love getting attention and they play on it. As soon as attention is removed from them, the odds are stacked in your favour. This may sound weird to someone but trust me, unless you've got kids, you have no idea how a simple thing such as putting them to sleep can be - hard work man! Anyway, i'm very proud of what both Sunita and I have achieved as parents and I think it's the "use common sense" approach that we've used that has helped. I mean, we never ever used a dummy for Rishi and the same applies for Jai. Babies simply get used to having a dummy in their mouth and it can be a real struggle to get them out of the habit. Our solution is simple, don't give it to them in the first place, clearly you *can* bring your kids up without them...

With work and kids filling up our time, the days, weeks and month continued to pass by at an alarming rate. It only seemed a few months since we applied for our Australian visa and here were over a year later still waiting for it. In financial terms at least, 2009 was the start of a worldwide recession. The economy was hit hard, big companies were shedding jobs and it was doom and gloom worldwide. Australia was no exception and they cut down the number of available visas and also slowed down the speed of applications. For us it was just a waiting game, no news and no updates meant there was little we could do so basically we just had to put it in the back of our minds. From time to time I contacted our visa agent in Brisbane but they had no news so that was that.

Time check, it's now the beginning of August 2010 and Rishi has just finished year 4. His 7 weeks of summer holiday have started and at the end of them he'll be starting year 5 and more importantly, the last year at Launde Primary. He had an excellent end of year report, full of very good grades and i'd say he probably enjoyed this year more than any other. Around the world, Aussie Rita, Jasmin, Surita and Max are still living the Aussie life some 5 years later and are just getting on with it. It's been a while since Rita jammed up the mobile networks but you can guarantee that wherever she is in the world, her mobile phone isn't too far away.

The good guy and good girl combination that is Raj & Sarita are working as hard as ever in their shop; Foodworks to be exact and are in the middle of renovating their newly purchased house that will become the family home for all of them. Little Monique, the girl who would cry as soon as she saw my face is not so little now, has a real character and loads to say! Last but by no means least, the one they call Ravi is working hard in the business too and helping to build the Dhunna empire.

On the UK family front, everyone is just getting on with things. Mum and dad (Sunita's mum and dad that is) are taking each day as it comes and slowly but surely planning to move to Australia as soon as they tie up their loose ends over here. My mum continues to do what she does best; being a great mum. She looks after the grandkids a few times per week and makes a huge fuss of all of us whenever we visit her. Preeya is acting and dancing her way through life and studying for her GCSE's.

Priyanka, the crazy party animal niece of mine has finished her GCSE's and awaiting the results after which she'll be moving onto college. Ashish, still a firm favourite with the girls, has finished 2 years at university and trying to find a placement job. Rahul is slowly becoming a karate expert and being the one to watch at Brookside school whilst little Kaylen has no worries and is just enjoying life! As for my brothers and sisters, well what can I say? They just get on with it, work, kids and then some - it never ends.

54

Australia 2010

I'm one of those "spur of the moment" people so when I started to think about Australia I started to get the infamous 'itchy feet'. Soon I was checking out the flight prices and before long the flight was booked. I say singular flight because i'd be travelling alone. I had holidays to use up, the kids had school and someone (Sunita!) had to stay behind. To be honest she didn't mind anyway and I needed the break so I was all set – game on! The route was pretty standard – overnight flight from Birmingham to Dubai and then a mammoth non stop flight from Dubai to Brisbane. Having touched down in Brisbane I was picked up @ the airport in style. I was met by Raj and the salesperson from the local Mercedes Benz dealership who was going to whisk us both back there for a spot of breakfast! This was a special morning you see; this morning Raj was going to pick up his new car....

After a hearty breakfast, we picked up the car and headed back to Hervey Bay. I was battered from the drive and ready for a good night's sleep! Raj & Ravi had **excel**led at their office skills and had organised a jam packed 2 weeks; everything from movie nights, delivery nights, karting and fishing had been sorted - it was going to be fun. Meanwhile aussie Rita was just a few streets away (I knew that because my mobile phone struggled to get signal!)

With a fun filled 2 weeks behind me I was soon jetting back to the UK. A few days after I landed the wintry weather came and the temperatures plummeted. For the kids (Rishi at least) it was great but Jai wasn't so keen and neither was Sunita but one

Nice ride!   Rollin' with Raj...

Family time @ the beach.   Good girl / good guy.

Yours truly with the kids (Max sorting   Up in the air with Ravi heading towards
the food in the background!)   the Great Barrier Reef...

Night out in Brisbane.

What a catch!

thing she was looking forward to was Christmas and all the nice things she could plan for – after all, she loved all that stuff! To be honest I liked Christmas too, it was a good time of the year but the weather had to be right. It *had* to be cold – a mild Christmas day just didn't feel right. Kids opening presents on Christmas day is a special thing – even if they don't understand why – does it really matter?

At school Rishi was busy rehearsing "no room @ the inn" as well as rehearsing for his role in the school Christmas play.

As 2010 came and went another year was upon us. As usual I had no plans to make any new year's resolutions – all a big waste of time as far as I was concerned. 2011 started off pretty much as it ended – cold; very cold in fact and it lasted several months. Still, no time to waste and as the weather got better I was keen to get out and about – you had to make the most out of the weather when you had it right?

Jai, nice and warm.

It snowed! For Sunita there was no time to get changed...

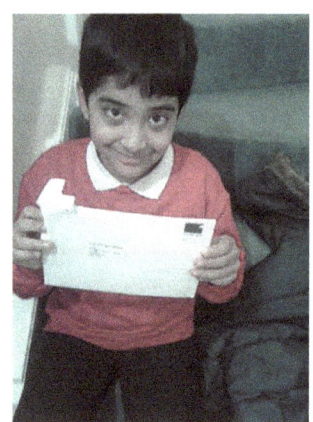

Letter from Santa...

Christmas play.

It was cold outside but warm in here.

Christmas day = presents!

Forget the present; the box
was lots of fun.

The hat was out and the reindeer
had been drinking.

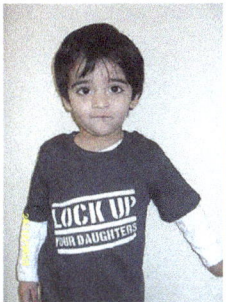

Where's our dinner?

Present from Raj
& Sarita.

Jai had been inside
the cupboards again.

The boys were cheeky as ever, kept us busy and life seemed to be moving at an ever increasing pace – was it ever going to slow down? In April, my uncle and aunt visited from India so they did their "rounds" so to speak and travelled up from London to Leicester for a few days. For them it was a chance to see the kids. They'd seen Rishi before but not Jai so it was good for a good old catch up. My culinary skills have often been challenged in the past but I surprised Sunita on Mother's Day by making a special "Mother's Day" cake for her on behalf of the kids – to this day she still doesn't believe me that I actually made it – I wonder why...

Mother's Day celebrations at home.

Time to hit the slide.

Priyanka and I ready for some fun fair action!

Mama & mami, my sister and I at Abbey Park, Leicester.

Sunita in hood control!

Outside 12 Whitebeam Road.

Back on the swing again.

Time for a spot of lunch.

Time to chill; this time at my sister's.

At my mum's – looks more
like a prison line up!

At Paresh's house in High Wycombe.
Jai chilling with Laxmi...

At home the music scene was very much alive. When I got as little as 20 minutes to myself I would still try to lock myself into the "music room", power up the turntables, shut the door, close the blinds and "turn it up". Music was still an addiction but the moments to myself were very rare but actually those 'moments' were drawing the kids in too. Whenever the music was filling the air, the kids were slowly getting drawn in. The drum and bass beats, the hip hop snares, the house 4 to the floor – it didn't matter...the kids were getting hooked to the sound and it was great!

On some days, it took just a few minutes of getting into the mix before Rishi would come running into the room only to be followed by Jai. Sometimes Sunita would follow and before you knew it i'd be on the decks and the others would be dancing around the room – a real family affair! Soon the requests would fly in, the music would sometimes stop dead (it would be Jai flipping the cross fader!).

Talking of Jai I had a started to make hats out of his clothes and then tie them around his head - endless fun (for me, not him!) – check him out: -

 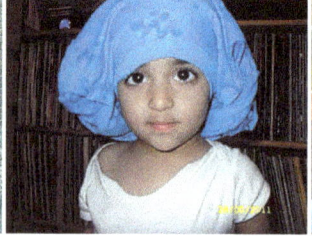 

Garden hat Jai.   Record room hat Jai.   Cheeky hat Jai.

From one little boy to another little boy who had grown up into a young man! Yes, i'm talking about our Ashish who was about to hit the milestone age of 21. As the first of the nieces/nephews it was kind of special. I remember everything about the day he was born; the day his mum (my sister) came to his grandmothers (my mum's) to stay for a few weeks (you keeping up?). I should remember...I had to sleep on the sofa – thanks Ashish – you were a matter of a few days old and you were already calling the shots; ha ha – just kidding mate!

Rather than have a party at a venue somewhere they decided to hold the party at their house; the place which had seen many good parties over the years so the tradition would live on. There was no question over who would be supplying the music; it would be the Grandmaster P (aresh) and myself of course so both of us would be on turntable duty. Sunita loves all the organisation side of it so she helped with the theme and we all looked forward to what was going to be a great night.

DJ Set up...

Marquee all done...

Only missing = Jai & Pravin!

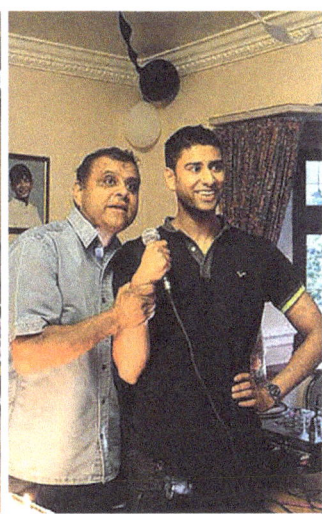

Pravin and another great speech.

Time for cake.

Happy!

In contrast to the freezing winter of 2010, the summer of 2011 was a hot one. In between weddings we ventured out to the beach, country parks and made the most of the summer.

Work commitments never stopped and in August of 2011 I was back in the air – this time I was heading to the Cisco labs in Richardson, Texas, USA to get our software verified for "compatibility". It would be a highly pressured trip, no time to mess around; the job had to be done right. Lab time was very costly and there were always plenty of things that could wrong so I had to be on the ball so to speak. Anyhow I was in the USA so I figured I may as well get the job done and take a break at the same time....

582

Rahul & Rishi ready for the beach.   Jai not overly keen on the beach...

Happy with bucket & spade.

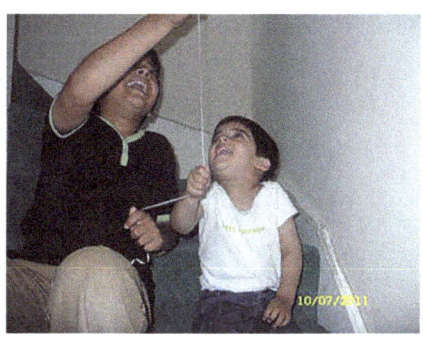

Time to cool off.   Boys having fun.

Smart boys, especially
the guy on the right.

The women could have
made more of an effort!

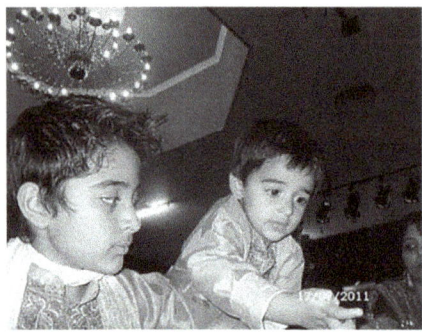

The kids looked cute.

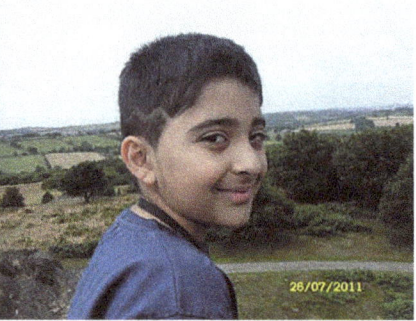

Beacon Hill, Leicestershire.

In the background is Dealy Plaza –
the site of the assassination of the
USA president – John F Kennedy
in Dallas, USA.

'X' marks the spot where the
assassination took place.

So, after work was done I thought I would fly onwards to San Francisco to meet up with my cousins who had emigrated out there – it would be a great end to the trip! After landing in Texas, the first thing that hit home was the heat – it was boiling! Mind you at least I had a day to myself before I got stuck into work so I ventured into downtown Dallas to see the infamous tourist attractions surrounding the JFK incident.

Tourist attractions over I got stuck into work and trust me it was hard. I was in the lab at least 2 hours before the rest of them turned up. For some reason the Americans tend to start later (well in this lab they did anyway...) so if I ran into an issue that needed their assistance I was always delayed as I had to wait for them to get in – trust me, I wasn't happy!). Whilst I was keen to get all the tests executed and passed as quickly as possible, these guys weren't in any rush at all. This was all very frustrating and soon they could tell by the changes in the tone of my voice.

One person that I was unfortunate to be "paired" with was really taking the piss. He had no idea what he was doing and there was a very real risk that his lack of focus and drive could fail lead to an overall failure of the entire test project. I wasn't going to let this happen and I approached his manager armed with facts. Within 15 minutes of our discussion, the fool I was paired with had been called into the office and around 10 minutes after that he came out a different person. Admittedly he hardly spoke to me after that but when he did what he did say made total sense and we made real progress. Listen – I don't care if you're my friend or not. When it comes to work, I need to get the job done and done right – end of story. After 5 very long and frustrating days it was now 3.30pm on Friday afternoon and I sitting in Starbucks which was literally a few minutes' walk from the lab and I slowly made my way back to the labs to pick up the final test result from the lab manager.

The testing had been very close to the wire but our products had passed which was a fantastic result. I knew they would pass anyway but coming to the labs is extremely difficult because you're working with people who do not understand your products, who do not understand their own labs and in my case people who can't be bothered to do their own job properly. To succeed you must be one of those people who knows when something isn't going right and be prepared to identify it and do something about it – I just happen to be one of those who is prepared to do that...

The hard work had paid off and I called my manager back in the UK to say that we'd passed and with that I could head back to my hotel; get my things and head for the airport to catch my flight to San Francisco... It was great meeting with my Chandresh, Lina and Avnish after so many years – just like the old days as they say. I was only with them for a couple of days but it was great catching up on what had been happening over the last few years. We had a great laugh, went out for meals and generally just picked up where we left off. Lina made some great food – she's such a great cook! The view from Twin Peaks is amazing (Sunita and I never made it here when we visited San Francisco on our first visit) but it was lovely to see you all!)

Twin peaks.   Golden Gate bridge.

55

Bar Bar Din Ye Aaye... (Sunita finally hits ~~38~~ 40)

People are funny; whilst some age well, some unfortunate ones also age quite badly too. Sunita was one of those who didn't look her age. For around 10 years she maintained she was still 38 years old and she even managed to persuade the kids she was 38 as well. As the birthdays rolled on, *this* was the year that she would reach that infamous milestone that is the age of 40. I have no idea what the big deal is – it's just a number. Anyway, opinions aside, Sunita is always up for a good party no matter what day of the week it is and so having a 40th birthday was not going to be a quiet affair.

In true Sunita style the party would be organised meticulously, nothing would be left to chance, the food would have to be right, the decor, the venue, the people and most importantly the music of course! It can be hard to find a set of DJs to play the kind of music that will get the party going. DJ's that know what they're doing, know how to read the crowd and how to create a real vibe for the party people. Luckily for her she had yours truly and the mix master P (aka Paresh)!

Before you can say put the needle on the record, the party night was here. Friends and family were all set for a great night, the speciality cake was ordered so it was time to party! Birthdays, Sunita and a certain Hindi track have a special relationship. You see whenever it's someone's birthday, Sunita **always** sings "Bar Bar Din Ye Aaye...." to them and over the years it's become traditional that she does this. On her 40th it would be simply unacceptable not for this to be played to her irrespective of whether she liked it or not...

Check out the cake –
awesome or what?

I was on turntable duty.

Sunita was in good voice!

The boys were in town!

Pramilla - is Alpa there?

Aarti & Vina joined the party.

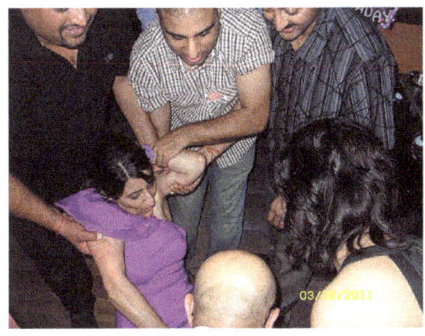

There was no escaping the bumps!

Rumit lifted me up with ease;
Sunita was out of control...

5th September 2011 –
40 today!

Sunita had *exactly* 40 birthday cards on
her 40th birthday!

Her 40th was a great night, friends from school, college, and university as well as family all got together and partied the night away – there was some sore heads the next day!

Summer 2011 soon disappeared into winter 2011 and Christmas talk was soon upon us. Adverts, bill boards, magazines – everywhere you looked the UK were engulfed in the annual event that is Christmas. At work things never slowed down no matter what time of year it was. In fact, in all the years I have worked there I cannot ever remember a "slow week" – it just doesn't exist. One thing about Magnetic North Software is that they like to keep you guessing when it comes to Christmas events. Whilst other companies probably decide what they're doing in June, we sometimes have no idea in December. Don't get me wrong, as frustrating as it sounds it makes Magnetic North what it is – different! I was pleasantly surprised when I spoke to Selina, Mel & Kim (no jokes please!) about Christmas and the so called plans. When the company sent out the email telling everyone about the Christmas event was it was something different. Our own private cubicle on the London Eye, ice skating @ Canary Wharf via a cruise on the Thames followed by a slap up meal – this was great. It's quite difficult arranging a date that everybody in the company can make so as usual not everybody in the company was free to make the trip down to London but I was free and looking forward to it. The usual suspects would be there including Anita, Selina & of course the boss himself, our very own Dominic Gray. Sadam did the usual of taking ages to decide if he was going to come or not but I eventually persuaded him so we were all set for a great day!

There was nothing out of the ordinary on the Midland mainline train from Leicester to London and it wasn't long after getting into London before the drinks started to flow. After passing the massive queues @ the London Eye and getting onto our own cabin, the Champagne bottles were opened. The girls in the finance office soon polished off a few of them whilst those not drinking (Sadam and I were amongst them) enjoyed a glass or 2 of orange juice whilst we looked out at London in the glorious winter sun.

Christmas 2011 came and went and before we knew it 2012 had rolled in and it was *very* cold. So cold in fact that the timing was perfect when my Emirates Air Miles statement dropped into my inbox. 2 trips to India and a trip to Australia had boosted my air miles sky high and I had enough points for a free return flight to Dubai (all I had to pay for was a small amount of airport tax). A few weeks later the miles were exchanged and I was all set for my first trip to Dubai (it was warmer there. I would be travelling by myself – nobody else could spare the time or travel at such

Sadam – he doesn't like photos!

The main man Dominic – always a laugh!

Mel & Kim skated away.

Nick & I opted out of the skating and opted in for a coffee - cheers!

Kim & Sadam chilling out

Something funny going on here...

short notice and to be honest I didn't mind going by myself anyway – sometimes you just must roll with it).

On 7th February 2012 I arrived at work with a twist; I had a small rucksack with me. After a full day, I drove to Birmingham airport; left the car in the car park and boarded the Boeing 777 which arrived in Dubai at around 7am the next day. No time to sleep, I jumped on a tourist hop on, hop off bus and had a good tour around the city. The sun was shining, it was warm and I had left the cold UK behind. It was a long day which ended with a calm cruise along the Dubai Creek. By the time I got to my hotel I was shattered; it had been almost 48 hours since i'd slept so the bed was welcome! The next day it was time to head for the Burj Khalifa – the world's tallest building. After that I had to make a quick exit and head for the airport to get my flight back to the UK. It had been a short but memorable trip. When I tell people about it now some still don't believe that I did it and some still can't believe I went by myself – I don't see what the fuss is all about!

2012 was an incredibly important year for the UK as they would be hosting the Olympics! For many years' millions of pounds have been invested into new sports centre, training grounds and facilities to accommodate athletes from around the world but little did we know that on a rainy day the Olympic torch which started its journey in Greece would be coming to Oadby and we would be there to see it!

The streets were packed, there were flags everywhere, people were in good spirits (Sunita had been drinking earlier!) and we were all eagerly waiting for our first glimpse of the torch. It was like a carnival atmosphere but without the sun but nobody cared...

Oadby was packed – the Olympic torch was on its way...

It's here...

With the eyes of the world focused on the UK, we had our eyes deeply focused on holiday brochures! We needed a break and fast and this year we had company because my sister and Preeya were coming along too – yippee! Our destination was Turkey; hot weather was guaranteed and it would be an adventure for Jai who'd never been on a plane before; it would either go well or very bad. The holiday in fact was great – Jai was fine on the plane. An added bonus was that we left for Turkey on the closing day of the Olympics and the pilot flew over the Olympic park in London and we were sitting on the left hand side of the plane so we saw all the dazzling lights of the closing ceremony – a once in a life time show!

Turkey was crazy; from our "Kremlin" themed (several thousand room) hotel, the countless different food options (we went all inclusive for the first time), to the beach that was literally minutes away to the local bus that was a mad push and shove affair to get on let alone getting off we had a great time as these pictures show.

Pool side.

Local shop; Jai made a friend.

The girls needed a drink – clearly a large one!

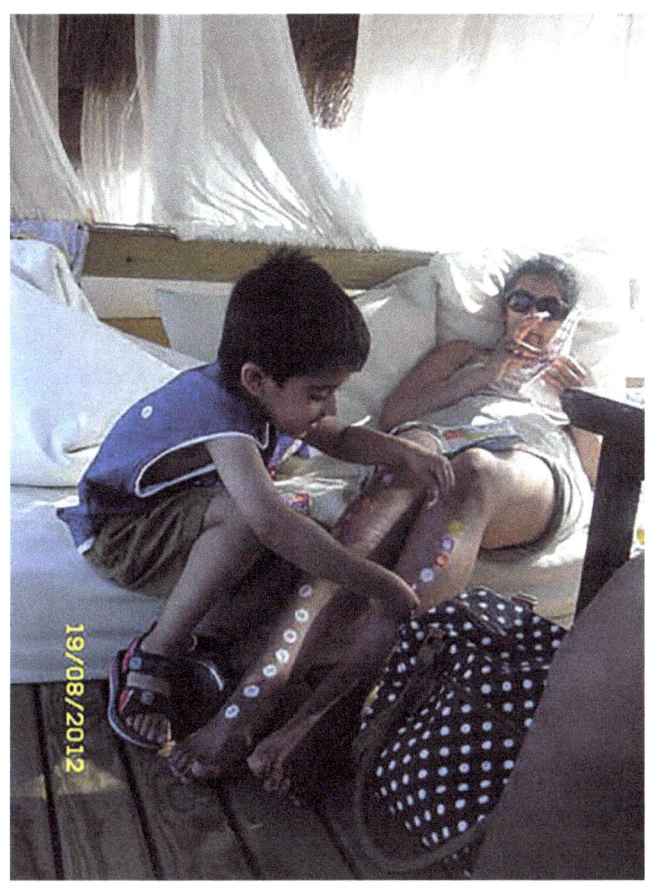

Jai loves stickers and doesn't care where he sticks them!

56

Mum's the word...

"A mum knows what a child does not say..."

I have no idea who said that but i read it in a book of sayings and I firmly believe it is very true. Mind you I would also like to think that dads have a fair idea as well! Anyhow mums are special and whether dads agree or not, they are usually the first port of call when kids fall ill or just need a cuddle. If on the other hand the WI-FI decides to stop working, then the dad is suddenly *very* important!

2012 was another important year because mum was turning 70 and we decided to do something a little different – we'd go away for the weekend. This was going to be something out of my mum's comfort zone and as a result we couldn't mention it to her otherwise she would have refused point blank and would have made dinner and told us all to come around. The plan was to book a weekend retreat, hope the weather holds and basically have a nice family weekend. A fictitious wedding was made up as well so my mum could be fooled into being picked up and taken to it – my mum is very suspicious so we figured she may figure out something was being planned....

Dinner time – full of jokes

On the train towards Minehead

At the beach, Minehead.

Jai was excited at going on the train.

Hot tub was lovely!
Ashish, Rahul, Sunita, me,
Priyanka, Rishi.

The house was tucked away
in the hills with huge trees...

The weekend away *really* was long overdue. With all of us busy in our own lives you forget how little time we spend together and it's usually at "special occasions" where you really make the effort to get together or in this case get away. For me, this was the first time we had all gone away as a family and when you think about it that's quite strange really. I understand that work and home commitments make things difficult but if you want to, I mean *really* want to then you can plan and get away. Anyway, enough of that and back to our weekend. We spent our days venturing out, enjoyed the wonderful surroundings of the wonderful house we rented, took the train to the beach, tucked into home cooked food in the evenings with the banter that came with it, watched shooting stars whilst sitting in the hot tub and then played games together to round of the evenings and to top it off the British weather didn't let us down; it was warm and sunny – perfect!

On mum's birthday, we went out for a walk whilst on the way back some went ahead to put up some decorations. When mum walked through the door to "surprise" she had the shock of her life and was moved to tears. It was a lovely moment; surrounded by her family at which point we gave her a framed photo of all of us – perfect! We'd all had one of the best weekends of the year...

Back home Jai & Sunita were spaced out; not literally of course although I sometimes wonder about Sunita! What I meant was that we were out growing our 3 bed house and Sunita was on my case big time. In my mind, I had never planned on moving; the thought had never crossed my mind but the reality was somewhat different. My turntables and thousands of 12" vinyl records were stored in Jai's bedroom which hardly left any space left and Jai was a growing boy.

We considered an extension but that would eat up valuable garden space so we quickly forgot about that idea so the only option available was to move. However, there was one caveat – I wasn't going to sell our house. It was our *first* house, the house that we had put all our extra money into and paid off so we weren't going to sell it – no way! So, the house search began and trust me buying a house is a full on, crazy affair. We saw bungalows that were beautiful but too small right through to homes where the sellers couldn't be arsed to clean them and were so disgusting inside it makes you wonder how these types of people will ever sell them. One home we saw was a sort of 'upside down' home where the kitchen was upstairs and a couple of the rooms were downstairs. It had a stream running through it as well to add to its charm but sadly when we read the results of the home buyer's report, the results weren't good. The main structural walls had 'movement' which could have been caused by the stream. The seller was adamant there were no structural issue but then again, she would; after all, she was trying to sell it. The house was just too risky so we pulled out of the sale and the search was back on. A few months later Sunita noticed a small advert in the local newspaper for a 4 bedroom house in Wigston that was for sale that ticked all the right boxes.

She called up and made an appointment quick time – you can't hang about you know and we went to see it. The house was just what we were after; a huge lounge; it has an extension downstairs, a modern kitchen, a small but manageable garden and 4 bedrooms and it was in a quiet location. The kitchen / diner was the key selling point and the current owners had clearly spent good money on detailing and the finish and quality was excellent. It was clear that a house like this was going to sell quickly and the owners knew it.

With no time to mess about we offered the asking price on the basis that they took the house off the market – thankfully they agreed and the house was ours! All I can say is Sunita did a good job spotting the house in the newspaper that day!

The next few months were crazy; we'd already decided that we would not be selling our house so we started considering what we needed to do to rent the place out. Alongside that, the purchase of our new house was going on as well so overall it was a very busy time. Solicitors, letting agent – it was all systems go but exciting, nevertheless. Renting our house was not going to an issue; we lived in a prime area of Leicester where the schools were brilliant and homes, both for purchase and rental, were always in demand. Within days of our house going up for rental the agency had found a couple who were interested and after the standard security and background checks had been completed they had signed up!

After what seemed like an age and filling in many piles of paperwork we had the keys to our house. We also had a date that the tenants were moving into our current house. So, we had to get packed and get moving but before that could happen our "new house" had to get blessed in the traditional Indian way which meant having a ceremony at the house.

The weeks prior to moving into the new house were *hard* work I can tell you. I honestly don't think that the previous owners bothered cleaning their house properly – two of the radiators were so disgusting in fact that we didn't even attempt to clean them and simply replaced both! Worse still was the tedious, monotonous job of wall paper stripping? I have no idea how anybody can enjoy this job but the lounge took several days of hard, manual work to get the old wallpaper off. To make matters worse it was summer and as if using the wallpaper steamer didn't make it hot already

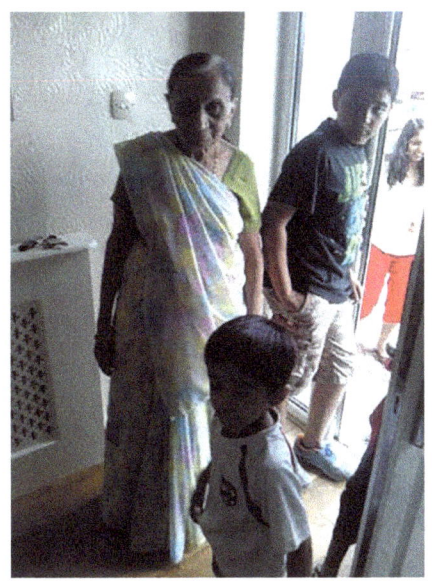

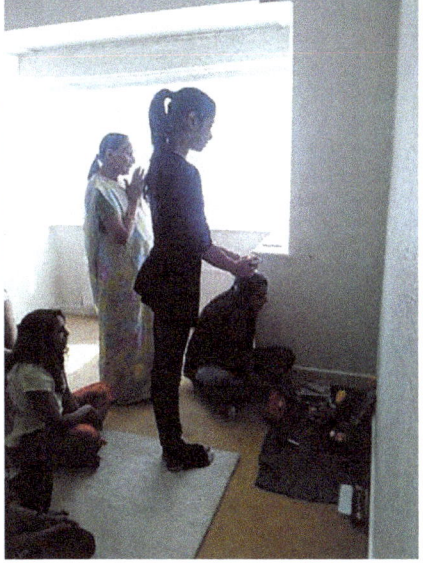

The new house – everyone involved started to arrive...

Prayers were said...

The kids drew all over the walls before they were stripped.

Rishi knew where the TV was going!

the outside temperature didn't help! Anyhow Sunita and I managed to get remove all the old paper whilst Rishi and Jai managed to draw all over the old paper just as quick! Once the paper was off i removed the old carpet and the room was ready for decoration. Thankfully we would not be decorating (painting is ok; hanging wallpaper is simply torture!)

Over the next few weeks the lounge had a mini transformation as the new radiators went in, the wallpaper was hung, the paint went on and the new wooden floor was laid. Elsewhere rooms were painted and the "music room" was sorted. The kids had their own room and the work had been done – phew!

Now that things have settled on the house front, things on the 'work' side of things were still busy as ever. Every few years I was often asked for fly to the USA to 'test' our software in the Cisco labs in Dallas as part of something called 'Interoperability' verification and in the first quarter of 2014 I had to jet over there again. As I had done previously I made plans for work and play; I would spend the whole week working and then fly to San Francisco at the weekend to meet my cousin Chandresh and Lina who lived out there for some chill time. The work part of the trip was standard; those on site were pretty clueless – I had to sort lots of stuff out and make sure I was in control to stand a fighting chance that we got the 'Pass' we needed. There was no way I was coming back with a failure and after a hectic week on site we got the pass and the certification I flew out there to get so that was a great but expected result.

I was the first to arrive at the labs…lazy Americans!

Our software was installed and ready to go…

Evening arrival in San Francisco.

Cruising around the Bay with Chunk & Lina!

The weekend trip to San Francisco was amazing and before I knew it I was back on the Virgin 747 heading back to Heathrow. However a few weeks later and I would be heading back to America again for a different reason. You see our Rishi was 12 years old and in a few weeks would be turning into a teenager. Through TV (Top Gear!) and media in general he was fascinated by the USA and was keen to see the country that invested the 'muscle car'. I had hitched a plan to give him a shock of his life in the same manner that I had done with Sunita many times in years gone by. The plan was so secret that I didn't even tell Sunita. The thing is, she *really* cannot keep a secret so I couldn't risk my master plan failing so one Friday on my day off I headed to our local Co-op travel and told them I wanted to book a long weekend to New York. The trip *had* to coincide with his 13th birthday – doing it a style of my own and all that. As I sat there with the travel agent trying different departure times and airlines we finally got a set of dates and times that worked out perfectly.

With everything booked, I had to tell Sunita; she was pleasantly surprised and between us we decided that we would have a 'USA' themed dinner one evening and then give him the present. That evening came and as he read one of his birthday cards another fell out. Looking inquisitively as the one that fell out, Rishi then started the read that one whilst I continued to record it all. Suddenly he realised what was going on; the penny dropped; the needle hit the record (ok, ok – you get the message...) – Rishi burst into tears as the emotion of it all got too much. Rishi was going to New York City and I guess for a 12 year old it was quite a lot to take in. Jai didn't know what all the fuss was about. It was a lovely moment and although the trip was far from priceless it was a priceless moment.

Teary Rishi gets a nice surprise!

Rishi enters the USA.

Freedom!

Brooklyn Bridge.

Central Park.

Rishi turns 13 – New York City.

Face time with
J: Leicester /
New York City.

Rishi on the streets of New York City.

Having just landed back in the UK, Rishi would be soon jetting off again because in July 2014 Sunita, Rishi & Jai all spent 6 weeks in Australia. The kids had 6 weeks of summer holidays whilst Sunita wasn't working at the time so it was the perfect time to head off into the sun. It had been almost 8 years since their last trip to Australia whilst for Jai it was his first. I wouldn't be travelling but my summer would be quite busy nevertheless; odd jobs around the house, the garden needed an overhaul and a trip to Ibiza would keep me busy - the whole family were jetting around the world!

However before that Dudley Rita was busy organising Rumit's 40th surprise birthday party. Rumit, like me, doesn't like surprises so the surprise might not go down too well. However Rita wanted to get all friends and family together and have a party. The date and venue were set and as the date got closer Rumit obviously knew that something was going on; he just didn't know *what* was going on.

The afternoon of the party was crazy and it was a last crazy push to get the food set up, set up the turn tables whilst Rita was wondering if it all would all go to plan. A few hours later and we were all set – the guests were inside whilst Rita and Rumit were about to enter...within a few minutes there was a rapturous "surprise" and all the hard work that Rita had put in had definitely paid off. I don't think Rumit was that surprised but seeing all his friends and family around him put that familiar Rumit smile to his face – the party could begin! First of all he knocked back a few drinks just to steady the nerves because, as is customary, I *had* to get him on the microphone to say a few words...

The party was a great laugh; it always is when you're surrounded by your best mates and as usual when man like Rumit is on a level the jokes just keep on coming. It was a shame that Sunita had to leave early though; we had no-one to look after the kids so she came for a short while and then left – she was definitely missed!

Talking of the wife she was very busy @ home preparing for 6 weeks in Australia. She won't admit it but she *loves* all the pre-holiday arranging, sorting out all the clothes along with the hassle and chaos that most people don't like – she thrives on it! With 3 of

606

The main man enters...   Time for some words please Rumit!

Bob said a few words – we hoped he kept it clean!   Well done Rita!

My man Rumit – touching down!

them going she sorted 6 weeks of stuff out for all of them and before you could say Castlemaine XXXX they were all packed and ready for their trip.

You'd think that 6 weeks alone with no kids and no wife would be bliss but to be honest the time went *really* quickly. I worked throughout the time they were in Australia and due to massive time difference keeping in touch was difficult during the week but with my new smart phone (yes technology had caught up with me!) WhatsApp (thanks Android) & FaceTime (thanks Apple) made it easier to stay in touch). After my standard long shift @ work my evenings were spent in the garden digging and spreading bark to try and keep the weeds under control as well as planting roses to add some colour too.

Who's holding onto who?   Strange kids!

Sarita – she has lyrics you know. Ravi – always in control (!?) The girlies full of smiles.

There was, however, some fun time to be had as well; on 14th August I flew to Ibiza with my man Rumit and met up with the man from the FBI (aka Snoop, aka Grandmaster P, aka Paresh) who was already partying there...). Rumit, wanted to extend his 40th celebrations a little longer so Ibiza seemed the perfect place.

During the day we chilled around the resort, sat on the beach and enjoyed the Balearic sun beating down on us. When we were thirsty all we had to do was take a short stroll across the road and order us a cool drink and if we were hungry there were countless bars and restaurants where we could order food and eat as we chilled and watched the world go by (Sunita would have loved it!). To cool off we headed off into the sea which was awesome. On one of the evenings we ventured to one of the most famous places in Ibiza; the infamous 'Ushuaia Tower' which was right on the

Early flight out...

Ashish heard there was a party going on and turned up....

My man Paresh!

Time to chill @ a beach party
The world famous Ushuaia Tower...

beach and on this night Pete Tong was DJ'ing. The sun was beating down, the tunes were rolling and the atmosphere was phenomenal; this really was Ibiza at its best. No need to be in a super club at all and at that very moment you could tell by the look in Rumit's face that he understood what Ibiza meant to people and what the real attraction was!

The atmosphere may have been electric but the drink prices were shocking (get it? Shocking?) (£15 for a soft drink); oh well Ibiza and all that – just roll with it! When Tong left the stage another house music legend DJ Sneak took over the turntables. Well, let me make something crystal clear right now; they were *not* turntables – they were CDJ's.

Anyway I wasn't overly fussed about the superstar DJ's; to me they were DJ's playing other people's music; it was the tunes and the people that made the atmosphere and that day/night was awesome. We were only in Ibiza for a long weekend and our last night was how can I put it "a mad one" – let's leave it at that!

Fast forward a few years and many things have happened; I still meet regularly with my dear friends, most of whom I've known since nursery. Incredibly by the time this book gets released we will even have a friend's wedding! Yes, my friend Nila is now a mother in law as her daughter got married – what a journey. My friends are still pretty much the same as they have always been and I am grateful for their friendship...

Shanti, Nalini, Nila, Bindy & me – most of us have kept in touch since we were 3 years old!

The summer of 2017 was going to be a busy one because Ashish was getting **married**. This was a *big* deal; he was the first of the nieces / nephews to be getting married in the family so it was really special. Though the date had been set a long time ago the weeks and months were creeping upon us really quickly. A common talking point is how couples "met" and to be fair it is a good question. Some people meet at a club, some through mutual friends, some er, swipe right (or is it left?) whilst others let the Indian network do its thing and go down the introduction method. Whatever method you go for, it's all good. Casting my mind back to my first date (well I say date but it was more of a meeting!), we often met at the University library where the 'no talking' policy suited me fine but absolutely finished her off... have you tried to shut Sunita up?

Libraries are a funny thing; on one hand they are meant to be a place of quiet study but nowadays they tend to be a place of social gathering where the youth of today spend their time trying to show each other Insta' pictures without using too much of their data. A true source of information, you can probably find information about anything inside one – that's pretty cool. But hey, don't just take my word for it, here are some famous quotes about the word many people don't often speak highly enough of: -

"The only thing that you absolutely have to know is the location of the library." (**Albert Einstein**)

"Libraries will get you through times of no money better than money will get you through times of no libraries." (**Anne Herbert**)

There you go, some thoughts to make you think eh. You might wonder what the hell I keep going on about libraries for. Well you see our Ashish and his bride to be Nisha didn't meet at a bar over drinks. They met at a table over an ISBN number so things were a little different. Both were working somewhere in Birmingham (it may have been somewhere else but let's go with it for now) and basically the damsel in distress (that's Nisha by the way) needed to grab a book but couldn't reach it. From nowhere Ashish popped up – some may argue that he was stalking her but that's a different story. Anyway this tall, dark, handsome stranger (did I say dark?), sorry I meant brown) person reached out and grabbed for the magazine from the top shelf. Now, look – I've told Ashish about the "top shelf" many times but he just doesn't listen. Anyway, seriously I don't really know exactly what happened except that he grabbed the book for her, their eyes met, he thought "she's a bit of an alright" and that was that.

In the months that followed the formalities were done (apart from formally telling the close family), there was the engagement in December 2016 and then the civil followed by the reception. Nisha is great fun, a real laugh to be around and one of the people you definitely need with you if you are going away or having a party! Extremely close to her family she also likes the odd drink (often in the quiet!) but if she ever gives you a lift don't ask her to turn right!

Speaking to Ashish in the build up to the engagement, this was the one he was most worried about. Meeting many new family members for the first time, the formalities and most importantly the dance! It all went brilliantly as the pictures show...

In 2016 I had around 3 weeks of holiday still to take and was thinking about going back to Australia – I must have changed my mind many times but in the end decided to book and go so around mid-December I headed away from the cold UK and touched down in the warmth of the Australian summer where as usual I had a blast. This trip was more of a chilled one but Raj planned some trips, we dug the garden, the boys got drunk, we had a laugh, I chilled with the kids and had a great time – what more do you need!

Having arrived in Australia, I chilled for a few days but Raj had already planned a trip to the 'Twin Waters' resort at the Novotel, Sunshine Coast – nice one mate. This picture was taken the morning after the night before. Sarita was hungry and thirsty!

Simon (AKA Amar) being his cheeky self, Monique being her crazy self and Raj chilling! As for Sarita, well she had too many glassee the night before...

Christmas day in Australia and it was hot! A really strange experience but we had a great day. Ravi came over and more presents were opened and we all went out for a meal – thanks Raj (again!)

Sarita and Raj planned another lovely afternoon out.
Here we had a nice lunch and chilled on the beach...

Back in the UK, the next "big" event would be the Ashish / Nisha wedding in the summer – we were all looking forward to that. It was now July 2017 and *that* time had arrived. For the women in the house weddings involved lots of planning (hair, makeup, outfits). For us men it was quite simple: get up, put a suit on and job done. Why then did I find myself up at 3.30am on the morning of the wedding I have no idea. Yes, it's true – when the 'hairdresser' came at a crazy hour to start doing the hair I just couldn't sleep and just sat and watched. Then Jai decided he wanted to come downstairs but we managed to force him into bed!

I think Ashish managed to get into bed at a reasonable time but Nisha probably got hardly any sleep at – this was no doubt going to be the most nerve racking day of her life – or maybe not! By the time we got to my sister's house, friends and family had started to arrive and for Ashish it was more photos and soon after that it was time to head to the wedding venue.

Ashish was looking *very* smart indeed and there was no trace of yellow on his face at all from the cleansing ceremony – that would have been a *pithi*. Thankfully he was dressed up and had somewhere to go so it was off to the wedding. Whilst he chilled in the calm environment of a Rolls Royce, I was left to go on the coach with the crazy woman who decided not to sit but instead dance up and down the aisle (it was a good laugh really and the coach is the best place to be!).

Chilling at the back of the coach with Rishi & Rahul.

Around 90 minutes later and the baraat (friends and family) were outside the venue. Traditionally the baraat makes a loud entrance and are greeted by the bride's family. Little they know they know we had Sunita with us. Forget the dhol player, Sunita pulled out the whistles and in a matter of seconds the place was more like a bhangra gig!

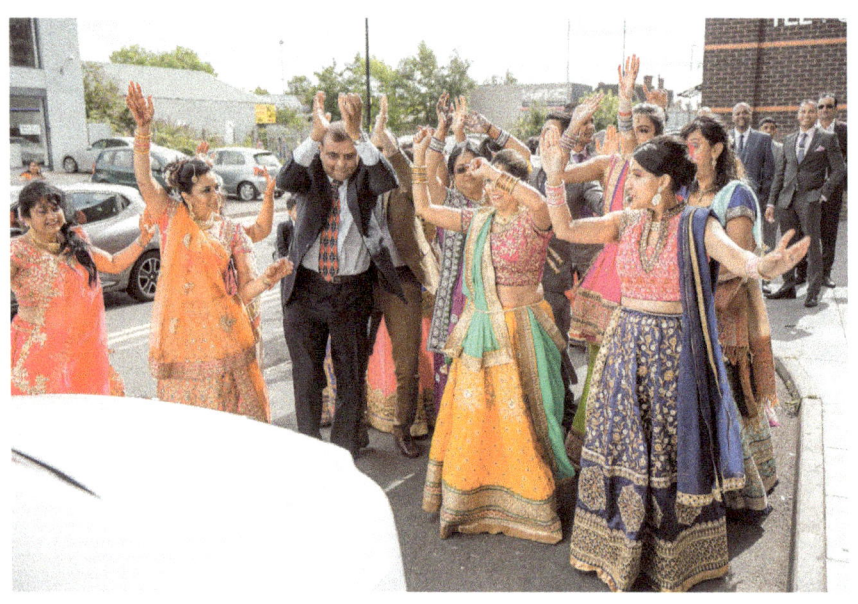

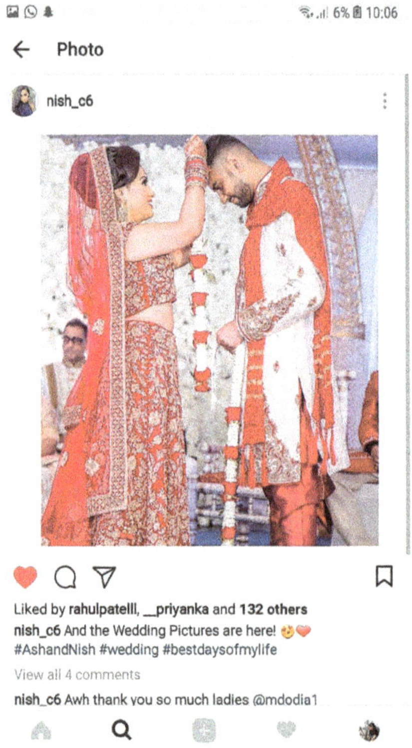
6% 10:06
Photo
nish_c6
Liked by rahulpatelll, __priyanka and 132 others
nish_c6 And the Wedding Pictures are here!
#AshandNish #wedding #bestdaysofmylife
View all 4 comments
nish_c6 Awh thank you so much ladies @mdodia1

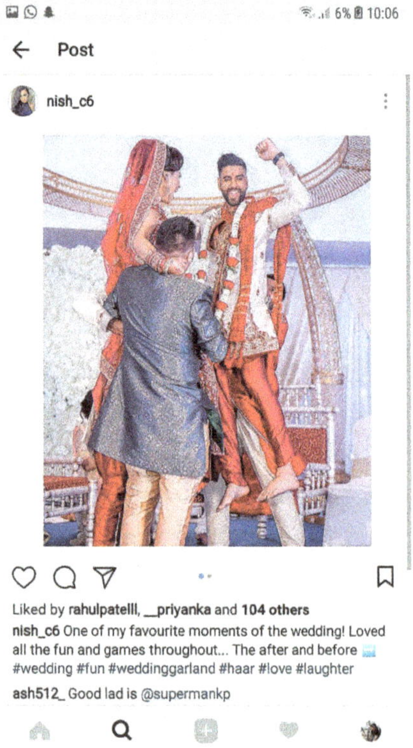
6% 10:06
Post
nish_c6
Liked by rahulpatelll, __priyanka and 104 others
nish_c6 One of my favourite moments of the wedding! Loved all the fun and games throughout... The after and before
#wedding #fun #weddinggarland #haar #love #laughter
ash512_ Good lad is @supermankp

First up was Nisha...

As soon as Ashish stepped up to put the flowers on Nisha, she suddenly gained height! Ashish was not done yet and superman came to his rescue - classic!

After the formalities of the Indian wedding, the next events were on the same day; the formal civil ceremony followed by the reception in the evening...

He said yes, she said yes!
Congratulations Mr & Mrs Patel!

With the couple now married it was time to hit the dance floor but they had their own special entrance planned first. Ashish planned to **come dancing** but he didn't know how it would go down. Meanwhile Nisha was definitely going to be the **dancing queen**. On the night it all worked out well and Ashish could relax – well done mate!

Pravin delivered a faultless roast on Ashish which went down a storm.

620

Party people!

← Post

nish_c6
Leicester Marriott Hotel   ⋮

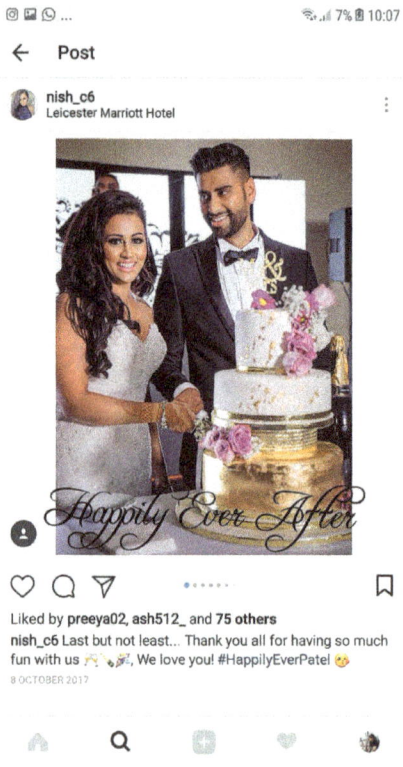

♡ ○ ◁   • • • • •   🔖

Liked by **preeya02, ash512_** and **75 others**

nish_c6 Last but not least... Thank you all for having so much fun with us 🙆‍♀️💕🎉, We love you! #HappilyEverPatel 🥺

8 OCTOBER 2017

⌂   Q   ⊞   ♡   🌑

622

The pictures say it all; it was an awesome night and a perfect end to weeks, months and even years of planning. "*HappilyEverPatel*" – can't get better than that.

2017 was a very busy year at my work and with the wedding celebrations over and done with, Sunita, Rishi, Jai and I were looking forward to our holiday to the USA. Jai had never been before so was super excited. Our plan was to spend a few days in New York, then fly to Orlando where we'd meet up with Paresh, Miyura, Laxmi and Shivani, spend time with them and then pick up our Mustang Convertible and drive to Miami where we'd be meeting Rumit, Rita and the kids – we had serious holidaying to get started on....

At the top of the Empire State Building.

The famous Statue of Liberty.

You've got to have it!

The park to be...

Donuts? Dunkin' of course!

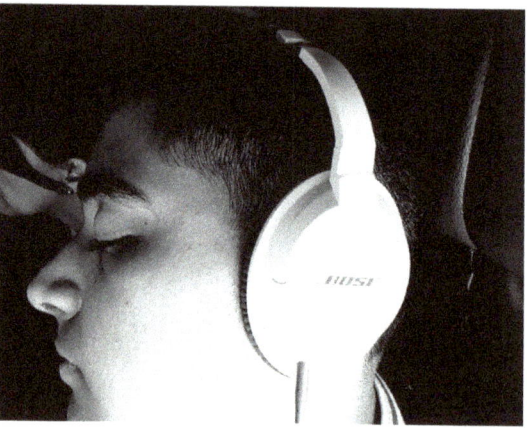

On the flight to Orlando, someone was tired!

In New York it was warm but in Orlando it was hot and humid. We checked into our hotel and met up with Paresh. Jai had his eyes on the swimming pool – we spent many hours in there!

Day 1 @ Universal Studios! It was a hot, sunny and adrenaline fuelled crazy day. We went faster and got wetter than at any other theme park.

Snoop & Laxmi in the house...

Back at the hotel,
Jai was loving the pool.

Time to venture out one evening...

Close to our hotel was a shopping outlet so we popped in. As usual we lost Paresh on the way but we bumped into Rita & Rumit who invited us back to their house in the evening. After a full day's shopping we had a crazy evening at their massive house they had rented (complete with swimming pool!) and then headed back to our hotel – we would meet Rita and the gang next in Miami!

The drive to Miami was a long, hot one and although we started with the roof down on our Mustang, we had to raise it.

Time for a break – Jai enjoying the sun by the Mustang!

Jai - Miami South Beach.

Double trouble.

Mum and son! Sunita in high spirits!
Perhaps Rishi was too....

Can't remember what was in this
bowl but it was big and it was
finished in no time!

Walking around the streets of Miami South Beach –
it was warm and sunny...perfect.

On a hot afternoon I drove the boys across
town to a Lamborghini dealership that Rishi had
somehow found. It was a packed with supercars
(not just Lambos') – the kids loved it!

Rita collared Rishi – there was
no escape!

A chillin' evening – Miami style!

It was time to venture South – Rumit got hold of a
Mustang and we headed for the Florida Keys.
The drive was spectacular – something you
really need to see for yourself. You can see
one of the bridges in the background and we
just chilled when we got there...

Look at the sea –
crystal clear!

It was our last day in Miami and of our holiday. Our bags were packed and we were ready for the airport...

Our flight back coincided with the solar eclipse that rolled across the USA in July 2017; here's Sunita taking a look...

In September 2017, my mum had her 75th birthday and as we had done 5 years ago on her 70th, we decided to all go away for the weekend. This time we were heading to Woodpecker Cottage, which was in the Forest of Bowland, Lancashire and although there were 17 of us in total we didn't need to worry about space – this had 6 bedrooms and was huge. Once we had all arrived the fun, games and jokes started and this continued throughout the weekend! From card games to drinking games – it all went off. There was even a mini bar in the kitchen (well an impromptu one anyway!)

Time to venture out and check out the local area.

Nisha and Sunita wanted to keep something quiet here — wonder what it was!

Happy 75th mum!

Happy 75th bha!

It was nice to get away and to spend quality time as a family. Often you don't get to do that even if you live in the same town and for mum it must have been super special being surrounded by her family in one place!

As the summer drew to an end and the daylight shortened, we had the unfortunate UK winter to look forward to. On the drive to work at 6am I often relived the days when I had hopes of relocating to Australia. I said "I" because I think it was really only myself that was really bothered about moving. The thing is you see that after being in the Australian visa system for 7 years and hoping and wishing that we would get approved the news came that our visa "group" was being cancelled. In short it meant that the visa we applied for was being cancelled and that the dreams of a move to Australia were shattered.

For Sunita it didn't really make any difference as she wasn't too fussed about moving in the first place. For me, it was a real blow, the reality was that my dream of emigrating for the second time had been shattered – clearly things are just not meant to be. I never really spoke to Sunita about how devastated I was – didn't see the point really but if I'm honest then I was gutted beyond words.

The end of 2017 saw incredibly cold weather even for UK standards and if 2017 was bad when 2018 rolled in, the infamous "Beast from the East" brought utter chaos with it. The temperature dropped even lower, we had huge snowfalls and Britain literally ground to a halt. Jai was ok as he was used to being taken to school and back in the car but on the odd day Rishi would have to walk so he was *really* pleased when he turned 17 because it meant he could get behind the wheel and **start driving!** Yes on April 26th, 2018, he could officially start his practical driving and being a car fanatic he couldn't wait. His mum had secretly found and booked a driving instructor on recommendation and Rishi had no idea about his first lesson until around 15 minutes beforehand…

The first lesson was pretty much standard; talk for around 20 minutes and then start to drive but having discussed the lesson with the instructor afterwards, it was clear that our Rishi had driving skills. He appeared to have a natural talent for driving according to Adam (his instructor) – a good thing and even better was the fact that he was very confident too.

The rest of 2018 kept us busy with University Open days – yes, Rishi was not only learning to drive but was also in his final year of 'A' levels and off to University which meant open days, filling in forms, UCAS etc. In addition to that we had the hottest summer on record – following a record winter, we literally boiled as day after day we had hours of hot sunshine and the rain was nowhere to be seen.

His driving was improving by the week which was excellent and by the time we had reached winter we had travelled up and down the country visiting many Universities. In October Rishi got over one major hurdle to getting onto the road – he passed his theory test!

First lesson – April 2018.   October 2018.

When I was learning to drive I remember paying £5.50 an hour but we were now paying £24! We had been telling Rishi for a long time to get himself a job so he could save some money for himself! To his credit he managed to land himself a job at Wickes and although it was only a temporary one, it would help him to develop his skills and to understand what it takes to earn £££

Although he was apprehensive at starting his first job, he needn't have worried. In a matter of days he was working the till (the one thing he was dreading) and everything else was pretty easy to him. He actually enjoyed it so that was a really positive thing he did – well done mate! As the dark winter nights drew in, I knew he had booked his driving test but didn't know the date. On the day of the test Sunita was actually a little strange, nothing strange in that given that she is a little strange but she was stranger than the usual strange. Anyway enough of that – I had a suspicion he *was* having his test and Sunita, who simply cannot keep anything to herself, told me he was having his test. We both sat watching TV, eagerly waiting for him to pull up outside.

Eventually the little Audi pulled up and neither Rishi nor Adam got out; they just sat inside and we were trying to look at their faces, their expression, trying to get any kind of idea as to whether he passed or not. After what seemed an age Rishi looked towards the house and he had a massive grin on his face but it wasn't until we went outside that we knew for sure – he PASSED – wicked!

I remember the sheer joy of passing my test; the feeling is immense and one that is really hard to describe and he was just as excited and relieved but above everything Rishi had one main question: "when can I get a car then?"

A happy Rishi and a happy Adam!

Rishi's first drive in his Polo – the look on my face!

The new edition on the drive! The **"P"** plate didn't last too long!

Passing your test is a major achievement but the real test is having the confidence to really get into the driving seat and just get on with it. To his credit, Rishi had all the confidence in the world. He was raring to go and within a few days was taking the car to college, driving himself around the city and within weeks his confidence had grown massively. There were occasions where I had to tell him to slow down but if I think back to myself I was just the same. For Jai this was great; he was already a front seat regular and now both of them were at the front which meant one thing – parents at the back!

Rishi driving, Jai chilling...   Sunita and I at the back...
are we there yet?

Rishi's new whip looking good!

In our house one thing is for sure – there is *always* laughter. Add into that a sizeable chunk of sarcasm and everyone either turns into a joker or goes bonkers. Our Jai is all of those rolled into one, turned 10 in January 2019 and is as crazy as he has always been – wonder where he gets that from...

Not a day goes by without him doing something or saying something "out there". He never tires, still says what's on his mind and is a never ending ball of energy that can eat continuously! At school he is simply the kid that cannot do anything wrong so well done son; what on earth happens to him when he gets home?

2019 was certainly going to be a busy year; Rishi was in preparation for his final year A level exams and would be heading off to Leeds University after the summer – a big thing! Before that though he would be turning 18 and we had been talking about having a party for many months now. Initially Rishi only wanted a "small" gathering but it soon got bigger and bigger. Sunita decided that it would now be a full on 18th birthday bash but it's all good. If anyone is familiar with the way Sunita organises anything then she leaves nothing to chance. She has to oversee *everything* which is a good thing. You just have to get one thing clear – it's her way or no way (!) Anyway the overall plan was sorted – venue, food, DJ's (myself, DJ Paresh, aka Snoop, aka Mix Master P) and my boy, DJ Rishi would also be touching down as well – what a memorable night that would be for him and all of us!

The invite was sorted – nice one Simran!

The guest list was put together, final tweaks made to the food menu, Rishi got his play list sorted and before you knew it, the day of the party was here! Jai *really* wanted to be at the party. It was similar to when Sunita had her 40th and Rishi wanted to come to that! Jai came during the day to help us set up so was involved at least! My only concern on the night of the party was that the needles on the legendary turntables may jump. It's very unusual to see turntables in clubs but the good old Technics are still going strong – now in their 28th year!

We came armed with special rubber mats and good old MDF board which did the job on the night and thankfully none of the tracks jumped! The right turntable did give us a little trouble with the earth strap but let's not get too technical – we sorted it in the end! During the day we came to the venue to put all the DJ equipment together, sound check, put up all the decorations and the collages (made up of hundreds of individual pictures that Sunita and Rishi collected). The collages were a real winner that night – the photos spanned close to 20 years so everyone was very much taken down memory lane!

After the balloons were filled and last minute checks were signed off by Sunita, we all headed back to get changed – the venue was finally ready and the countdown to the party had begun...

Jai – there are no words!   Name not down? Not getting in!   My DJ – all set!

By 9pm it was pretty quiet inside Sumo but then a mass of friends and family rolled into the venue – a sudden rush of party people meant everyone was frantically saying "hellos". It was quite surreal because as the night wore on we realised that so many of our friends and family knew other friends and family so we were all connected through others. It was a really intimate party; a real *family* affair so time to touch down and party on. The sound system was pretty loud and the venue perfect. A good mix of space, places to sit, dance and generally room to just chill. The DJ set up was, as you would expect, nothing short of excellent – Paresh and I deepened the bass, sharpened the treble and adjusted the mid – the sound was awesome.

As the drinks flowed and the food arrived, Rishi's friends finally turned up – it turned out they had been pre-occupied with pre-drinking. There was no time to waste – the night was young and there was an after party (apparently!)....

You can see Rishi through the years stuck to the wall!

It was only a matter of time before someone grabbed the MIC – that person *had* to be Anita (of course it did!). With her confident voice filling up the dance, nobody could say no. The bhangra muffins were separated from the dancing queens and the battle was on. With yours truly on the turntables, everything from Bhangra classics like Tera yaar bolda met 'Once Dance' by Drake – the dance off went down a storm. Alpa went off on one as usual – the night wasn't complete until Mantronix was played. 16 people wanted different types of music, there were people pissed, My man Munsha was there – hoorray, and after the dance off we kicked the party into life. A short while after that it was time for the speech – Rita K (there are several Rita's) was so good and came armed with her own slide show as well!

Sarj grabbed Rishi from the crowd so he could be seen by everyone and so began the speech. It was a beautiful moment as one of our dear friends rolled out a perfectly tuned reflection of Rishi as he reached 18. It just goes to show you how much people care and how something simple as a few words can mean so much. She ended to a rapturous applause and ironically pictures of Rishi and his Rita kaki appeared on the slide show as she spoke – thank you Rita K!

Rishi soon buttoned up as Sunita told the story.

Rita's speech.

After the speech it was time to get round 1 of the party started. MC Rav on the M.I.C busting out the lyrics to the crowd who were loving the old skool vibe as Arrested Development mixed into Dr.Dre. No sooner had the mix dropped when shouts for the "rewind' came from the crowd - we were having a real party! As the tunes touched down I felt in my element: I was with my friends and family, my selector was to my left – Paresh – the one from the FBI, I was dropping tune after tune, the crowd were going mad and the vibe was crazy...

The party people were partying hard. Every time I looked for Sunita she was at the bar and slowly but surely the alcohol was starting to take its toll on some people! As mix master P touched down I tried to catch up with people I had not seen for a long time but it was so difficult. I was dragged all over the place and the crowd loved their bhangra so that meant I had to get onto the turntables and touch down.

Rishi wasn't too bothered about DJ'ing in the end but I *was* – this was *his* party and *his* night so I persuaded him into playing to the crowd – I knew he would love it...

643

As Rishi stepped up the turntables, MC Rav started to prepare the crowd for what about was about to drop. I had to give Rishi some last minute technical data and he was all set! Rahul was on Insta' duty!

Whilst Rishi was busy behind the decks, his friends were busy putting on the "Rishi" masks. He had no idea what was going on until he looked into the crowd and suddenly spotted a crowd of Rishi's looking at him – the look on his face was priceless!

Rishi played an excellent DJ set – no nerves or anything –
a sign of a true DJ – very proud of you son!

My partner in crime – a party well organised – good girl!

57

You have reached your destination

It's Friday 3rd November 2023 and I have, unbelievably, come to the end of my story. It's been a long journey and looking back I cannot believe i've actually finished! The truth is I actually finished several years ago and I spent lots of time trying to format the content and inserting pictures and so on. However, life got busy as it does and I found I had less and less time to spend on the book so the finishing line got further and further away...

I finally realised that a book about your own life never really ends and that you have to decide when to stop. The final push is therefore the epilogue so you can see what's been happening, what's the low down, what's the real deal, what's the word on the street, what's going on innit' so here goes....

The whole world went through the Covid pandemic and thankfully we managed to get through it. It just goes to show how fragile life is. In July 2020 we sadly lost my father in law; Mr. Mohanlal Dhunna, Dad, Nana, Brother, Husband but affectionately known as "Mr.Leta". Larger than life, Mohanlal Dhunna was a kind, considerate and incredibly humble family man who definitely lived life to the full.

Me – well I've now hit the age of 54 and yes, I agree, I do look very good for my age. Happily married to Sunita who still talks too much and have 2.2 children (national average!). The kids are ok; thankfully they're boys (hopefully they'll want to stay as boys!). In case you're wondering why I say that - have you ANY idea how much Indian weddings cost if you have daughters?

I'm still working for the same company, now in my 23rd year! Still haven't managed to fulfil my ambition of travelling the world but one day Sunita *will* surprise me with a round the world ticket (won't you?). Failing that I will just have to have to keep on travelling and cross off them countries one by one – there's still a few to go! I'm not quite sure that I will be able to get into space though – just a hunch but I think that time has gone!

I'd like to think I haven't changed as a husband although Sunita is the only one who can answer that but before you ask her make sure you have plenty of time. I mean she *loves* to talk as I keep saying. As a dad I don't think I've done too badly. I'd like to think the kids would say I'm a fun, jokey type of dad but they know that if they cross the line then *'somebody gonna' get hurt....real bad'.*

Sunita – (still 38 years old) Idiot, mum or Sunita, take your pick; she answers to all of them in our house, but one thing is for certain, the house does not run smoothly without her. I am surprised though given that she's hardly at home so the one thing that has definitely been maintained throughout the years that I've known her is the party animal inside her. Even to this day she can party harder than most people I know and generally speaking doesn't really suffer the morning after the night before. Back at work now she's in her element, goes to work for a few hours; coffee, has a chat, lunch, has a chat, comes home and does stuff in the kitchen.

I spent many, many minutes thinking about what to write and then finding I deleted what I'd just written only to start again. It's not that I couldn't think what I wanted to write, it was just that I couldn't find the *right* way to say them. Well to me, Sunita is my best friend. We can talk about anything and everything even when we don't agree on things. To date we've never had a full blown argument which is down to her diffusing the situation and she is without doubt one of the most genuine and caring people and I love her to bits...just stop drinking Vodka neat and we'll be fine!

Rishi – our first child is 22 years old and it's crazy to think where the time has gone. He has now graduated from Leeds University with a Music Technology degree and is currently in Australia on a one year working visa. Both Sunita and I encouraged him to take time out and not worry too much about getting that first job. Sometimes you just have to live a little and let life's experiences help you to make decisions about which direction you want to take in life.

As you can see from the pictures below, he has grown into a smart, responsible, young man and I hope he has listened to the life lesson stories from his parents and uses them to his advantage (Rishi – some things are *not* to be shared ok!). I am sure with hard work and effort he will fulfil his dreams of making it into the music world...if that's the path he wishes to take.

Jai – our hyperactive youngest of the family is now 14 years old and has started his GCSEs. He loves football, his iPhone and his favourite thing in the world is his mum (thanks mate!). This boy keeps us busy and has a super appetite to match. King Jai as he known in our household (he is known for shouting "mum" about 300 times a day to ask for food, water, etc) knows what he wants and knows how to get it! In school he is a super clever young boy and in top set for everything. He has a real passion for flags and can identify them just by the colours, the way the stripes are arranged, its distinguishing features and the tiniest of detail. He really is a flag superstar so well done mate!

Writing this has been a truly inspiring thing to do and something i've wanted to do for many, many years. In the time it took to write this, i've been on many journeys, both personal and as a family, we've been through good times and bad, laughed and cried. People often say that behind every man is a great woman but that's just rubbish. Sunita has always been a tower of strength, my soul mate, my wife and my best mate all in one so in this case I have a truly super woman behind me.

Before I go, a final message for Sunita, Rishi & Jai. I love you. In your own special ways you all brighten up our house, usually by leaving the lights on.

S

www.ingramcontent.com/pod-product-compliance
Ingram Content Group UK Ltd.
Pitfield, Milton Keynes, MK11 3LW, UK
UKHW020308160325
456296UK00003B/23